THE PIANO BOOK

THE PIANO BOOK

Buying & Owning a New or Used Piano

Second Edition

Larry Fine

Illustrated by Douglas R. Gilbert

Foreword by Keith Jarrett

BROOKSIDE PRESS • BOSTON, MASSACHUSETTS

Brookside Press
P.O. Box 178, Jamaica Plain, Massachusetts 02130
(617) 522-7182
(800) 545-2022 (orders)

Printed in the United States of America

Cover design by Laurie Dolphin

Library of Congress Catalog Card Number 89-81394

ISBN 0-9617512-3-1
ISBN 0-9617512-2-3 (pbk.)

To three whose generosity and devotion during my youth enriched my musical life:

Beatrice Fine, my mother
Lucille (Boyd) Spreen, my piano teacher
Anna Lenti, my friend

Contents

Foreword

Pianos are complicated instruments. Some have deep, dark secrets, some have sunny dispositions, some have no secrets at all. There are pianos with a grey, metallic "European" sound; some with a stringier but brilliant "American" sound; some with a laser-sharp "straight," "Japanese" sound. There are pianos with a wealth of overtones, and some with very few; some thick-sounding instruments, some thin and weak but interesting. But if a dozen people were asked to draw pianos, they would almost all look the same.

There have been some extraordinary shapes of pianos in the past (square, left-handed, "giraffe"), but the important thing about a piano is what's inside the case. If we drew a portrait of a piano, we would have to deal with its moods, not just its clothes. So, obviously, the piano is not its case. But is this really so obvious? Certainly not to the people (too numerous to conceal themselves) who have their piano in a sunburnt area of their house with the top perpetually open (in case unexpected guests arrive? or so they can feel "artistic"?). To them a piano has to look the part, not demand proper treatment. These people don't need a piano, they just need something that looks like one.

I grew up with pianos; I've literally spent my life with them. I don't remember ever thinking, "Oh, this is a neat-looking piano. I bet it's really good." If I played it and it told me something, it was an interesting instrument. If I played it and it said little (although it might be noisy), I hoped I would never have to meet it under more crucial circumstances. In fact (and this is fortunate) there is no perfect piano. How good a piano is depends on what its use is to be. It could be the "perfect" piano for playing Debussy and a disaster for Stravinsky. But I think the best pianos can handle both with great success. Out of the hundreds or thousands of instruments I've played, I can recall perhaps five or six that could play almost any music equally well under a large variety of circumstances (different halls, for example).

I personally feel the piano to be far in advance of any of the more recent keyboard instruments in that it still demands that you use your whole body and all your muscles, whereas everything since has been de-

nying that need. Artificially adding piano-like touch control to a synthesizer is about as much of an improvement as electrifying a pepper mill. So what?

The piano was a historic achievement in that it both incorporated the true innovations before it and answered the artists' need to be more involved, *not* to get more done with less effort. The "artistic need" that has generated instruments since the piano, on the other hand, is the need to find something that could be successfully played at Yankee Stadium or played by typists on a lunch break. One is a media need (although "need" isn't the right word); the other is the desire to be creative in one's "spare time." To me, leisure and creativity are as far apart as the *Reader's Digest* and the *Well-Tempered Clavier*.

Piano music is a kind of medium between our "progressive" age and the feelings that existed before this age. The piano may be relatively sophisticated, but it is by no means always civilized. In my opinion, a good piano can produce more variations in tone color than any other acoustic keyboard instrument, and more than *any* keyboard instrument can without flipping a switch or turning a knob.

When I consider, now, what I know about pianos, it's still not very much, but probably much more than most professional pianists. Since most pianists don't carry their instrument with them, they tend to let piano technicians take care of the instruments they encounter. By contrast, a clarinet player doesn't have a clarinet tuner backstage in case something goes wrong. After a while, ignorance becomes apathy. So pianos begin to get the reputation of being these amazingly stable pieces of furniture with strings and some mysterious workings inside that just last and last and are good investments and are always ready just in case some talented friend comes over to tickle the ivories.

It's all a bit more serious (and quite a bit more intriguing) than that. Pianos respond to care with amazing lifelikeness. I used to have to have my piano tuned several times a month if I was working on something, but after I decided to control the humidity and temperature year-round, magically, the piano didn't really need tuning more than twice or three times a year. In contrast, I played a beautiful German Steinway in San Francisco, and after it spent a few months as a rental in Jamaica, it came back a disaster. Oh, it *looked* the same, but when my technician asked me to play it and tell him what I thought, I not only didn't recognize anything about its sound, but immediately knew it was a terrible instrument. Only a few months before, it had been one of the pianos I might have purchased at almost any price. So pianos can die as suddenly as humans.

Speaking of technicians, there is a commonly held belief that, just as all pianos are shaped the same and go "bong . . . bong," all technicians are the same. Please do not make this mistake! Find the one good local technician you *might* have in your area, and if there isn't one, don't be afraid to spend a little more to get one from farther away. I once had a "legendary" technician (the few legendary technicians I've met should have stayed legends) come out to find a mysterious little buzzing noise in the second D above middle C. He came out month after month looking for that little devil. He even brought a second legend with him and they crawled around on the floor, inspected the windows for rattles, voiced (tone-regulated) and re-voiced the instrument until I'm sure it felt eighty years old in some places; but they did not remove the buzz. About six months later, I decided to ask my traveling technician to come down from Boston and check out this sound. He came, had dinner, went upstairs, and it took him about three minutes to adjust the string around its pin and eliminate the buzz . . . forever!

A young technician who used to work for me was very excited to be hired to tune the piano at a music festival in the Northeast. Just before a favorite pianist of his was to go on stage, the technician walked on to check the piano, which, he knew, was badly in need of tuning. The pianist asked him what he was doing, and the technician explained that he heard how badly the piano was holding pitch and that he was going out to tune it. But the pianist said, "No, it's okay. It doesn't matter." I think perhaps one could take this attitude to its logical conclusion by saying that, then, the music doesn't matter either.

I have been in countless situations where I've asserted myself regarding the poor condition of an instrument and it's been considered bad mannered. "But, Monsieur Jarrett, Mr. _____ and Mr. _____ played on this piano only a matter of months ago." (Months! A piano doesn't need more than a matter of days to be destroyed.) Or: "Mr. Jarrett, so-and-so played on this piano last week and he didn't complain." Or: "Oh, Mr. Jarrett, everyone complains about this piano. . . . I don't know what to do." "Have

it voiced," I said to one club owner. "Really. What is voicing?" "Something not enough pianists know anything about." (The club owner said okay, not a word he used often.) In fact, numerous pianists had been playing on his instrument and complaining, but offering no insight as to whether there was anything that could be done. "These artists, they're so moody and temperamental." Well, pianos can get that way too, and we have to work together.

Actually, I have gotten a reputation for being a prima donna or a perfectionist based on only one thing: I know what I need to make the music I will be making. If I don't know this, only the music can suffer. If the music suffers, then what am I doing here halfway around the world from home? Jet lag doesn't help either, so why have more things wrong than just the unpredictable?

I could tell a lot more stories about my piano experiences, but what I'm getting at is this: We are not well enough informed about the nature of the piano to either know what we are missing or appreciate what we have. We can complain or we can hope for a chance love affair, but if we don't *know* something about our own instrument, our limits are the limits of our luck.

This certainly applies to purchasing a piano as well, and Larry Fine's book will make it harder to ignore many things about the piano that can either contribute to a successful purchase or lead to a rip-off. Don't think someone else will make the right choice for you. Not even pianists can choose pianos for other pianists. Attempts to do so have failed many times. Of course, if you end up after all this with an instrument you love or an instrument that satisfactorily fills your needs, you may not have to ever go piano shopping again. Pianos can easily outlive people.

As good as this book is, it has its limits. It cannot tell you how to hear or what sound to like (though it can tell you some things to listen for). It can't be responsible for the care of your instrument (but it provides lots of pointers). And it can't help you at all if you want a piano just to put a silk throw over it and some antique vases on it. But you already know that, or you probably would have spent your money on *The Silk-Throw Book* instead. (I wouldn't be surprised if that book has a chapter about just which pianos look better under the silk!)

So we're back in the solarium with a sunburnt, cracking finish on the wood (although this part faces the wall—and the heat ducts, of course—but *not* incoming guests), a soundboard that, every sunny morning, knows the real meaning of stress, not to mention a cast-iron frame that could fry an egg once a day. I have absolutely no tolerance for humans behaving in this way toward pianos because, as I said before, I've lived with pianos all my life and have learned to respect their needs. To me, they are often much more alive than the people I see every day.

However, for those of you who are truly interested in buying a piano to make music on it (or in learning about the piano you already have), *The Piano Book* is the most comprehensive and helpful guide to the mysteries of the piano, and how to buy one, yet published. It ought to be on your bookshelf.

KEITH JARRETT

Preface

For well over a century, the piano has been a mainstay of home entertainment, and of Western musical culture in general. It has been estimated that there are at least ten million pianos in the United States; each year about 150 thousand new ones are sold and, in addition, hundreds of thousands of older ones change hands. More than twenty million people in this country play the piano. Yet despite the piano's popularity, most people—piano owners included—know virtually nothing about how a piano works or how to go about buying one, and countless numbers of people continue to make blunders in purchasing a piano that only the most naïve would make in buying a car or appliance.

Why is this? To at least some degree, the fault lies in the nearly complete absence of consumer information about the piano. The crying need for such information becomes immediately obvious to almost anyone who attempts to buy a piano. The large variety of brands, models, and styles, strange terminology, competing claims by manufacturers and dealers, the relatively small number of piano experts and technicians, and the lack of criteria by which to evaluate pianos—all these factors and more make purchasing a piano like navigating through a foreign land without a map. This fact faces me almost daily as I field telephone calls from anxious customers begging for a few scraps of information to guide them in a bewildering endeavor.

But if all I intended to do was to tell you which brands are worth buying or how to find a used piano, a book of this size and scope would hardly be necessary. Indeed, I have two other motives for writing. One of the by-products of the scarcity of consumer information is a climate in which shoddy merchandise, unethical selling practices, and poor service can flourish. I'm sure that the vast majority of piano dealers, salespeople, and manufacturing personnel are honest people doing their best to make an honest living. Very few, if any, are consciously trying to defraud the public, and those few who from time to time do are pretty quickly put out of business. But as in any competitive business where the difference between competing products and services is often subtle or nonexistent, or even where the difference is large but the public is uninformed, small acts of dishonesty gradually creep into the business in the form of distorted or outright false technical claims, phony sales, and less-than-satisfactory service. Because these practices evolve slowly and are so widespread, they are passed off as "business as usual," rather than the deception and disservice that they really are. The same phenomenon occurs in countless other fields of business, and I'm sure that the piano industry is no worse than any other. Ironically, when a person in one industry encounters these tactics in another industry, he or she complains loudly (for example when a piano dealer buys a car), without ever noticing the similarity—such is the capacity of the human mind to ignore what it doesn't want to see. Throughout this book I give examples of such products and behavior, which I can assure you are not just isolated or bizarre occurrences.

But, as I said, business people do not usually mean to be deceptive. Most businesses are simply doing what they perceive to be necessary for their survival in a highly competitive environment. Though I won't deny that each person in business must take ethical responsibility for the way he or she responds to business pressures, in truth, most businesses offer just about what the consuming public wants, which are usually the products advertised as having the most "features" and sold at the biggest "discount." To ask them to do otherwise would be to ask them to go out of business! All the moralizing in the world will not improve products and services as much as will changing consumers' desires and demands through education. This book is a modest attempt at such education.

My other motive for writing is simply to share with you my thirty-year love for this incredible instrument. The piano is, I believe, unique in our culture in the way it weaves music, craft, history, business, science, and engineering—both low-tech and high-tech—into a remarkable tale worth telling. One very practical way to tell this tale is through a consumer guide such as this.

There has been no better time in the past twenty-five years to buy a piano than the present. The large influx of foreign imports and the growth of computerized manufacturing technologies have caused the prices of new pianos to plummet and the quality to rise. Also, the renewed interest in piano technology as a profession over the past fifteen years means that many competent piano technicians stand ready to sell you a used or restored instrument and to service it in the years ahead. I offer this volume with the hope that it will inspire you to take advantage of this opportunity to invest in a good piano and—whatever piano you buy—to appreciate what went into making it.

I would like to give special thanks to:

Kathleen Cushman, editorial and publishing consultant, of Harvard, Massachusetts, for so generously contributing her time, skills, and resources to this project, and whose enthusiasm, encouragement, and assistance were chiefly responsible for publication of *The Piano Book*;

Doug Gilbert, illustrator, whose quick grasp of the subject and insightful questions taught me to look at the piano in new ways, and whose friendship, support, and skillful, dependable work were indispensable parts of this project;

Linda Ziedrich, for meticulous copyediting and expert book design that made an otherwise complicated book easy and enjoyable to read and use;

Keith Jarrett, for writing the Foreword;

Fifty piano technicians who must remain anonymous, for examining pianos and making themselves available for consultation, and many piano dealers and manufacturers, for providing information and assistance;

My family and friends, for their patience and support during the long period of time in which this book was written and produced;

The staff of *Keyboard Magazine*, for giving me the opportunity to write a monthly column, in which parts of Chapters 3 and 7 first appeared in slightly different form, and to William McDonald, some of whose illustrations for those columns have been adapted for use in this book;

The following music industry publications, which were especially useful to me in my research: *The Music Trades, The Purchaser's Guide to the Music Industries, Musical Merchandise Review,* and Ancott Associates' *Music Product Directory.*

Thanks also to the following people who read portions of the manuscript, offered constructive criticism and suggestions, and in other ways made significant contributions to this book: Donald Bancroft, Alan Bern, Del Fandrich, Alan Frank, Harriet Goldberg, Frank Hanson, Sally Jameson, Donald Jaynes, Roy Kehl, Jack Krefting, Robert Lane, Richard Lehnert, Robert Loomis, Christine Lovgren, Joseph Meehan, Robert Meyers, Robert Moog, Paul Murphy, Joseph Pagano, Anthony and Joseph Paratore, Arthur Reblitz, Robert Sparling, John von Rohr. It should not be assumed, however, that each of these people necessarily agrees with everything written herein; I, alone, am responsible for any errors.

Preface to the Second Edition

This second edition of *The Piano Book* comes to you with a bit more difficulty than did the first edition. When the first edition was being compiled I was, for the most part, politely ignored by manufacturers and industry executives. I continued to gather information anyway, and successfully published the first edition in September, 1987. In the years that followed a transformation took place: As consumers became aware of the book, its impact on piano sales was felt, and I found myself and my work very much noticed in the industry.

As I compiled this second edition, as before, I've attempted through various sources and personal research to cut through much of the hype that permeates the business of selling pianos. This time, though, I was not ignored. Given the opportunity to preview and comment on their own reviews, a few manufacturers (and their attorneys) attempted to rewrite the reviews from an "industry" point of view, or to dissuade me from publishing at all. As a result, some reviews have been "softened" a little to keep the peace and avoid expensive litigation. Although I don't think any reader will be misled, you may wish to "read between the lines" as you read the brand reviews, paying special attention to my personal suggestions, and be sure to read the "Overview" beginning on page 73.

In addition to new brand reviews, there are other important changes from the first edition. After consultation with piano engineers, some revisions have been made to the explanations of piano features and marketing gimmicks in Chapter 3 (Buying a New Piano) to bring them in line with current research and opinion in the field. The special chapter on Steinway pianos has been eliminated and most of the subject matter divided between Chapter 4 (A Consumer Guide To New and Recently Made Pianos) and Chapter 5 (Buying a Used Piano). A new section, "Other

Items of Interest," discussing digital pianos, electronic player pianos, and recent advances in piano technology that might be of interest to consumers, has been added following the brand reviews in Chapter 4. A depreciation schedule to aid in determining the value of a used piano has been added to Chapter 5. Finally, the very popular but troublesome numerical ratings of piano quality have been removed because of overuse and abuse, and prices have been omitted because they go out-of-date too fast.

How to Use This Book

Readers will undoubtedly come to this book from many different backgrounds and with many different questions. Some will have had considerable experience with pianos; others will be buying their first piano just so that their child can begin taking lessons. Some will want to buy a new piano, some a used piano, and still others won't be sure. Some will have only a few hundred dollars to spend; for others, money will be no object. In designing this book, I've done my best to make sure that these interests are addressed to some extent. But not all interests can be equally well served in the same volume. If your interest is in buying the least expensive instrument possible, exclusive of all other considerations, you probably don't need this book. Just look at the piano ads in the Sunday paper. Conversely, if your needs and resources are such that only the finest concert grands will do, you may find this book interesting, but of little practical help, as you are traveling in the rarefied air where the differences between pianos are more a matter of personal taste than quality, and by now you probably know your taste quite well. It is to the broad middle range of buyers—those who are interested in both quality and price, are relatively inexperienced with pianos, and are curious about them—that this book is largely directed.

It's tempting, when writing a consumer book on a technical subject, to aim it at the lowest technical level possible so it can be understood by everyone. I've avoided doing this, partly because it would render this project terribly boring and unsatisfying for me, and partly because the piano is an unavoidably complex instrument, and to pretend that it's not is to rob it of a great deal of its beauty and mystery. Nevertheless, like many complicated pieces of machinery the piano can be broken down into some rather simple parts and concepts, and in describing these things, I've assumed no previous piano-related knowledge or technical expertise on the part of the reader. For those readers who have an aversion to anything more technical than a pencil, there is also plenty of completely nontechnical material here from which you can glean a great deal of useful information.

The following summary will help you locate the kind of information and level of complexity you seek. Chapter 1, "How the Piano Works," describes the piano's workings in the simplest possible terms. It also names and illustrates the most important parts. Everyone should read at least the first part of this chapter.

Chapter 2, "Buying a Piano: An Orientation," is a completely nontechnical introduction to the subject of buying a new or used piano. Every potential buyer should read this whole chapter.

Chapter 3, "Buying a New Piano," begins and ends with nontechnical information on the piano market and how to shop for a new piano. The large center section of this chapter consists of a mildly technical discussion of how pianos differ from one another in quality and features. It includes many "Buying Tips"—what to look or listen for or ask about. This section will also be useful in evaluating the quality and features of a used piano, especially one that is relatively young, to the degree that they have not yet been obscured by age and wear.

Chapter 4, "A Consumer Guide to New and Recently Made Pianos," is a reference section that lists and, where possible, describes and evaluates virtually every brand of piano made or sold in the United States during the last ten years. Be sure and read first the nontechnical "Overview" beginning on page 73—it will help you decide which brands to look up.

Chapter 5, "Buying a Used Piano," begins and ends with nontechnical information on how to find a used piano and how much you can expect to pay for it. The middle of the chapter is mildly technical; it gives instructions on how to take off the outer cabinet parts to look inside and how to tentatively evaluate the piano's condition—how it has been affected by age and wear—pending a final inspection by a piano technician before purchase. This chapter also contains a brief history of the piano. An addendum to this chapter gives special information that may be useful to those considering the purchase of a used Steinway.

Chapter 6, "Moving and Storage," and Chapter 7, "A Brief Guide to Piano Servicing," are mostly nontechnical.

CHAPTER ONE
How the Piano Works

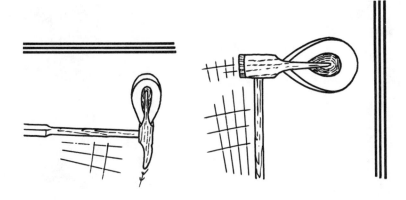

FIGURE 1-1.

STRIPPED DOWN TO ITS BAREST ESSENTIALS, A PIANO CONSISTS OF TAUT METAL WIRES, called **strings**, that vibrate when struck by felt-covered wooden mallets, called **hammers**. A **grand** piano is one whose strings are stretched horizontally, parallel to the floor. A **vertical** piano, not surprisingly, is one whose strings are stretched on a vertical plane, perpendicular to the floor. The construction of a vertical piano is described below, in Figures 1-2 through 1-9. Note that the parts are presented in the order in which they are most easily understood, not necessarily the order in which the piano is constructed.

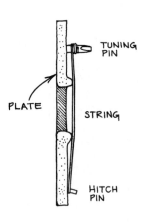

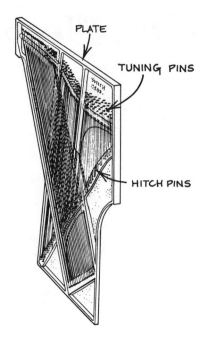

FIGURE 1-2.

The more than two hundred strings in a piano are stretched across a cast-iron frame called the **plate**. One end of each string is attached to a **hitch pin** on the plate; the other end is coiled around a **tuning pin**. Turning the tuning pin adjusts the tension at which the string is stretched.

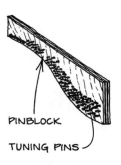

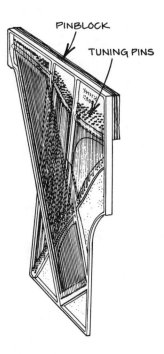

FIGURE 1-3.

The tuning pins pass through holes in the plate and are embedded in a laminated hardwood plank called the **pinblock**. The pinblock holds the tuning pins so as to prevent the stretched strings from unwinding, but the tuning pins can still be turned with a special wrench known as a "tuning hammer."

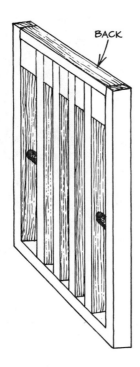

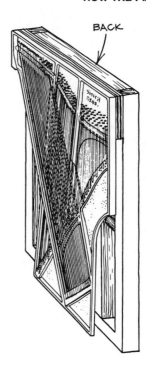

FIGURE 1-4.

The plate is bolted, and the pinblock glued and screwed, to a wooden structure called the **back**. The plate, pinblock, and back together form the structural framework of the vertical piano.

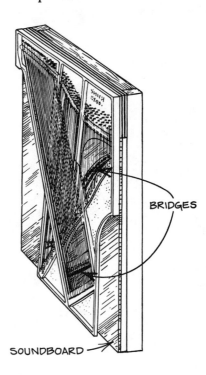

FIGURE 1-5

The sound of a piano string vibrating is rather feeble and must be amplified. This is done by a large, thin wooden diaphragm called the **soundboard**, glued around its perimeter to the back. The vibrations are transferred to the soundboard by wooden **bridges**, against which the strings press. The large vibrating area of the soundboard amplifies the sound of the strings.

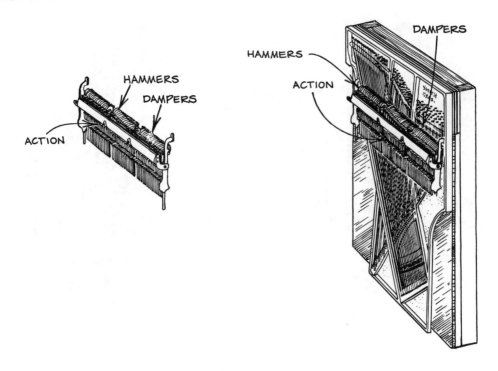

FIGURE 1-6.

The hammers, which strike the strings to make them vibrate, are part of a complicated contraption of levers and springs called the **action**. Another set of felt-covered action parts called **dampers**, located behind the hammers, stops the strings from vibrating.

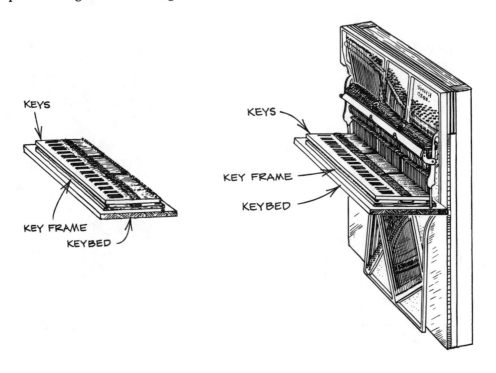

FIGURE 1-7

The action parts are activated by eighty-eight wooden levers called **keys** (collectively known as the **keyboard**), covered with plastic, wood, or ivory at their playing end, which pivot like seesaws on a **key frame**. The keys, key frame, and action are supported by a structural member called the **keybed**.

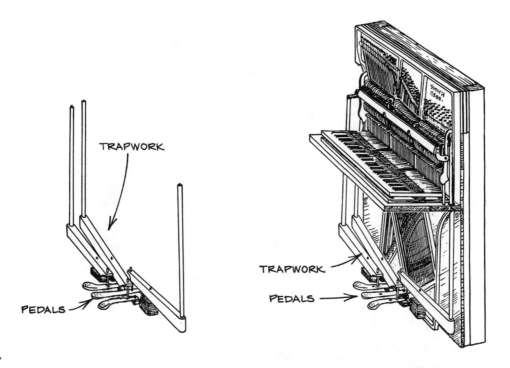

FIGURE 1-8.

The **pedals**, usually three of them, perform special operations like sustaining or softening the sound of the piano. They are connected to the action by a series of levers, dowels, and springs called the **trapwork**.

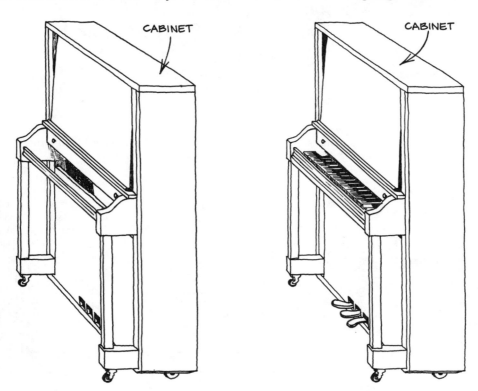

FIGURE 1-9.

The piano **cabinet** covers the internal parts, adds aesthetic beauty, and provides some additional structural support.

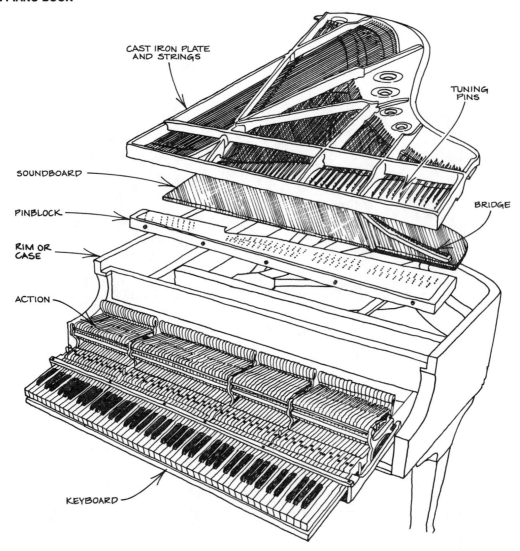

FIGURE 1-10. Exploded view of a grand piano. (Adapted from "The Coupled Motions of Piano Strings" by Gabriel Weinreich. Copyright © 1979 by Scientific American, Inc. All rights reserved.)

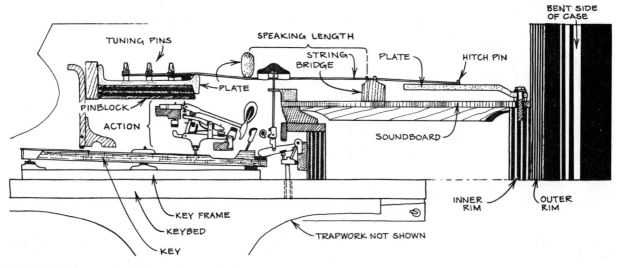

FIGURE 1-11. Cross-sectional view of a grand piano.

As shown in the exploded and cross-sectional views opposite, the grand piano resembles a vertical piano laid on its back and raised up on legs, except that the vertical's back is replaced by the grand's curved wooden **rim** or **case**, and the action, pedals, and trapwork are redesigned to accommodate the horizontal layout of the instrument. Otherwise, the basic principles of construction are similar.

Note, by the way, that only part of each string actually vibrates. This part, called the **speaking length**, is delineated by two *bearing points* that the string contacts. The "lower" bearing point is the point of first contact with the bridge; the "upper" bearing point is a portion of the plate, or hardware attached to the plate, that contacts the string near the tuning pins. ("Lower" and "upper" refer to the relative positions in a vertical piano; in a grand, "lower" translates as the end of the piano opposite the keyboard.) The portions of the string other than the speaking length—one near the hitch pin and the other near the tuning pins—are either muted with cloth or vibrate only sympathetically.

Here are a few other details to answer some questions that may have come to mind:

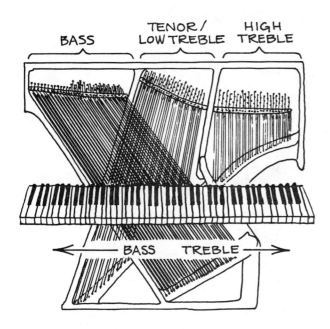

FIGURE 1-12. Bass and treble.

Q: What is meant by the terms *bass* and *treble*?

A: Bass refers to the lower-pitched notes, which are sounded by the keys toward the left end of the keyboard. *Treble* refers to the higher-pitched notes, sounded by the keys toward the right. Technically, the structure of the plate divides the strings into sections

(Figure 1-12). The section that is arranged above and diagonally across the other sections is the bass. The remaining strings make up the treble, which may be further subdivided as shown in the drawing, or in other ways depending on the particular piano.

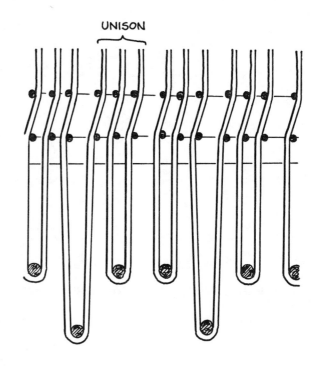

FIGURE 1-13. Loop stringing.

Q: If there are only eighty-eight keys, why are there more than two hundred strings?

A: With a few exceptions and variations, there are three strings for each treble note, two strings for each upper bass note, and one string for each lower bass note. This is because higher notes are made by thinner strings. If solitary, the thin treble strings would be overpowered by the thick bass strings. Each set of one, two, or three strings is called a *unison* because all the strings in a set must be tuned at exactly the same pitch (i.e., in unison) to sound as one note when struck by a hammer.

An interesting twist to this, however, is that in the treble section of most pianos, each length of wire serves as *two* strings, first passing over the bridge and around the hitch pin and then passing over the bridge again as a neighboring string, as shown in Figure 1-13. Because of the wire's tension, and its stiffness where it bends around the hitch pin, each string can retain its own pitch without affecting its neighbor. This scheme is known as *loop stringing*. Bass strings, and occasional odd treble strings, each have a hitch pin to themselves and serve as one string only.

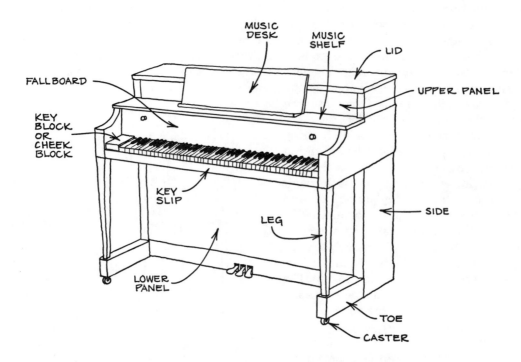

FIGURE 1-14. The cabinet parts of a vertical piano. Depending on the size and style, some parts may be omitted or may look slightly different.

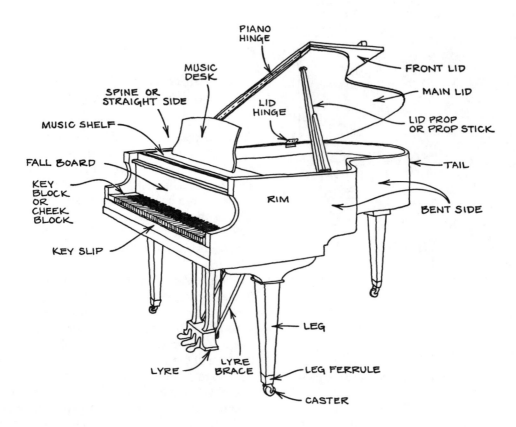

FIGURE 1-15. The case or cabinet parts, and accessories, of a grand piano.

THE ACTION

The piano action, with its five to ten thousand parts (depending on how you count them), is easily the most complicated part of the piano. An intimate knowledge of how it works is not really necessary in buying a piano, but certainly can't hurt, especially when trying to track down the reason why a note doesn't work on a used piano. Those readers who love Rube Goldberg–style mechanical contraptions will find a piano action absolutely captivating.

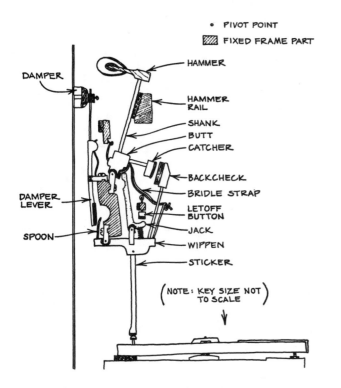
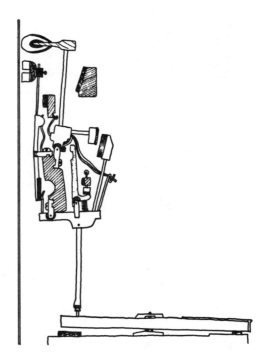

FIGURE 1-16. The vertical piano action (left) at rest and (right) at *letoff* (step 3).

How the Action Works in a Vertical Piano

1. When the key is pressed down at the front, the back end rises and pushes up (sometimes via a **sticker**) on the escapement mechanism, consisting of the **wippen**, and hinged to it, the **jack**. The jack pushes against the hammer **butt**, causing it to pivot and move the hammer toward the string.

2. When the hammer is about halfway toward the string, the small metal **spoon** on the back of the wippen contacts the bottom of the **damper lever**, making the damper lever pivot and lift the damper off the string. This allows the string to vibrate freely when struck.

3. When the hammer is about ⅛ inch from the string, the "toe" of the jack (if you look at the jack as a boot) contacts the **letoff button**, causing the top of the jack to pivot out from under the hammer butt.

This is called *escapement* or *letoff*. Without letoff, the hammer would jam against the string, causing parts to break and preventing the string from vibrating (Figure 1-16 right).

4. With the jack disengaged, the hammer goes the remaining small distance to the string on its own momentum, strikes the string, and rebounds. On rebound, the **catcher** on the hammer butt is caught by the **backcheck**.

5. When the key is released, everything begins to fall to its rest position. The spoon releases the damper lever, allowing the damper spring to push the damper back onto the string, stopping its vibration. The hammer **shank** returns to its rest position on the **hammer rail**. The coil spring under the toe of the jack causes the top of the jack to pivot back under the hammer butt, where it will be ready for the next stroke.

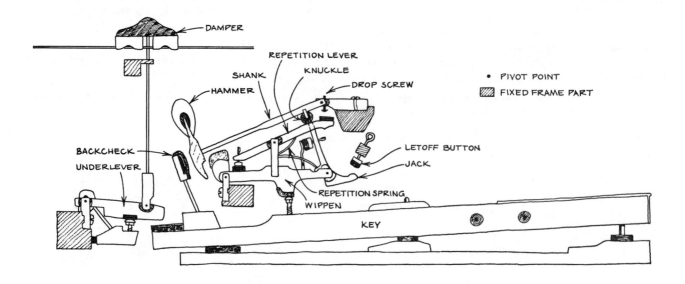

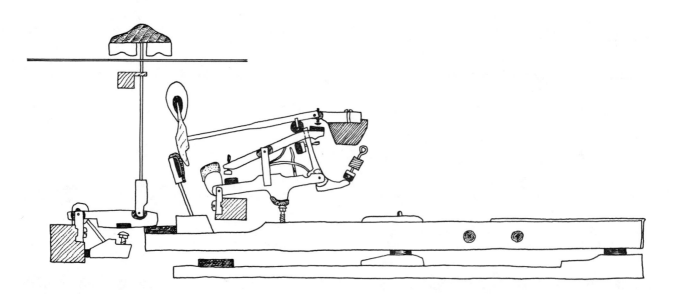

FIGURE 1-17. The grand piano action (top) at rest and (bottom) after the hammer has hit the string, rebounded, and been caught by the backcheck (step 4).

How the Action Works in a Grand Piano

1. When the key is pressed down at the front, the back end rises and pushes up on the escapement mechanism, consisting of the **wippen**, the **jack**, and the **repetition lever**. (Notice that the jack sticks up through a slot in the repetition lever.) The repetition lever and the jack jointly push up on the **knuckle** attached to the hammer **shank**, sending the hammer toward the string.

2. When the hammer is a third to half of the way toward the string, the back end of the key contacts the damper **underlever**, causing the damper to rise off the

string. This allows the string to vibrate freely when struck.

3. When the hammer is about ⅛ inch from the string, the "toe" of the jack (if you look at the jack as a boot) contacts the **letoff button**, causing the top of the jack to pivot out from under the knuckle. Simultaneously, the end of the repetition lever contacts the **drop screw**, preventing the repetition lever from rising any further. These two actions constitute an event called *escapement* or *letoff*. Without letoff, the hammer would jam against the string, causing parts to break and preventing the string from vibrating.

4. With both the jack and the repetition lever disengaged, the hammer goes the remaining small distance to the string on its own momentum, strikes the string, and rebounds. On the rebound, the hammer knuckle lands on the repetition lever, causing it to pivot and compress the **repetition spring**. At the same time, the tail of the hammer head is caught by the **backcheck**, which prevents the compressed repetition spring from pushing the hammer away (Figure 1-17 bottom).

5. When the key is released even a little bit, the backcheck releases the hammer tail just enough so that the compressed repetition spring can now push the hammer (via the repetition lever and knuckle) toward the string again. The hammer doesn't actually strike the string a second time, however, because the drop screw is still limiting the upward movement of the repetition lever. But the upward movement of the hammer gives the jack, pulled by its spring, enough room to pivot back underneath the knuckle, ready for another stroke, even though the key has not yet returned to its rest position.

6. When the key is fully released, everything falls back to its rest position. The back end of the key releases the damper underlever, allowing the damper to drop back onto the string and stop its vibration. The hammer shank falls back to its rest position, just a little above the hammer rail or rest cushion.

The operation of the pedals in both grand and vertical pianos is described on page 53.

CHAPTER TWO

Buying A Piano: An Orientation

THE PURPOSE OF THIS CHAPTER IS TO PROVIDE a basic orientation toward the piano market for those people who have little or no experience in this field. We'll be considering some of the general factors that will influence your choice of a piano, and we'll be developing an attitude that will make shopping for a piano more enjoyable. This chapter gives only very general advice; more specific information on quality, price, warranty, condition, and so on, is presented in later chapters.

It's useful to have some knowledge of piano terminology and of how a piano works when looking to buy one. For this reason, I suggest that, if you haven't done so already, you should read through Chapter 1, "How The Piano Works."

INITIAL CONSIDERATIONS

There are a few basic points you need to consider before beginning that search for the right instrument. These considerations will assist you in determining your needs and in taking stock of what resources you have available to meet those needs.

Proficiency Level

If you (or whoever will be the primary user) are a beginner, you may not want to invest a lot of money in your first piano. But resist the temptation to pick up an old "klunker." It's difficult enough to learn to play an instrument without having to deal with problems within the instrument itself, such as squeaks, rattles, and keys that stick or otherwise don't work properly. Children, especially, get discouraged easily by such annoyances and will be quick to comment on how different their piano at home is from their teacher's piano. In addition to sapping your motivation, this kind of piano may also sap your bank account with the necessity for extra tunings and frequent repairs. In my experience, in fact, some of the pianos that have been the most expensive in the long run were initially obtained for free or "just for the moving" because nobody would pay anything for them. Little did the recipients of these "gifts" know what they were in for!

In general, it's a good idea to buy a piano of slightly higher quality than you think you deserve and then grow into it. If there are several pianists in the family, aim your purchase toward the most advanced. You'll be more motivated to learn because the piano will be more fun to play and also because you will have made more of an investment. Pianos tend to be excellent investments. If your attempts to learn to play don't work out, chances are good that you can sell the piano for close to what you paid for it, provided that you chose wisely to begin with and maintained it properly.

Space

A vertical piano is about 5 feet wide and about 2 to 2½ feet deep. Add to this about 2 more feet for the piano bench and room to sit at it. That makes a total of 5 feet wide by about 4½ feet deep that should be allowed for a vertical piano, not including any space on the sides that you may want to leave. *The height of a vertical piano makes no difference in the floor area needed.*

The width of a grand piano is also about 5 feet. The length will vary from 4½ to 9½ feet, depending on which you choose to buy (5 to 7 feet is best for most homes), and again, add 2 feet for pianist and bench. These dimensions indicate the least amount of floor space allowable. Grand pianos, especially, may need more space for aesthetic reasons; verticals can more easily be tucked into corners.

When planning the layout of your room, don't forget to take into account sources of heat and cold. Since they respond very readily to temperature and humidity changes and extremes, pianos should be placed well away from radiators, heating vents, direct sunlight, drafty windows and doors, woodstoves, fireplaces, and so on. Failure to heed this warning will, at the very least, make it difficult to keep the piano in tune. At worst, it could lead to premature structural damage to the instrument.

Money

Money is the biggest factor preventing people from getting the piano they want, and is the one about which potential buyers are the most naïve. Piano prices vary widely according to size, brand, condition, location, and so on, but very generally speaking, a used old upright in half decent shape purchased from a private owner might cost from $300 to $800, while a used grand in similar condition could run from $1,500 to $3,000. Used verticals of more recent origin, or older verticals that have had significant repairs, could be priced at $1,000 to $2,000, younger or better-quality grands from $2,500 to $5,000 (much more for a Steinway and certain other fine makes). New verticals of reasonably good quality begin at about $3,000, new grands at about $7,000 (and soar upward to astronomical figures). The days when a good old upright could be had just for moving it are largely gone.

While it's true that people still do sometimes find spectacular bargains, it's also true that for every person who pays $200 for a Steinway grand, at least a dozen others pay $2,000 for a piece of junk.

I strongly suggest that if you can't afford to buy a reasonably good-quality piano now and can't arrange a loan or credit plan, then save up for the piano you want rather than temporarily settling for a poor one. A poor-quality piano will cost you more in the long run for maintenance and repairs and will rob you of your enthusiasm, as mentioned before. While you're saving, see if you can arrange to use the piano at a friend's, a school, or a church, or rent a practice studio. You might also consider renting a piano on a plan that permits you to apply some of the rental payments toward purchase later on.

Don't forget to set aside money for moving, tuning, and other maintenance. Generally a budget of about $150 to $250 a year will suffice for tuning and maintaining a piano in good condition in the home. Pianos in schools and other institutions may require two or three times this amount (though they rarely get it), depending on the extent of their use and abuse. If you buy a used piano, it may initially require a larger expenditure to bring it into normal operating condition before this budget can apply. *If you can't afford to maintain your piano, you really can't afford to buy one.*

Furniture

There's nothing wrong with wanting a good-quality instrument to look nice too, but if your major reason for buying a piano is for its value as furniture, let's be honest about it. There's definitely a portion of the piano industry that thrives on selling worthless instruments inside of beautiful cases. You'll be an easy mark for them if your primary interest is in a piece of furniture. Of course, there are some legitimate questions to ask about the piano's cabinet; for instance, how solid is its construction? how durable is its finish? But some of the pianos that come in the cutest decorator styles score very low on these points, and you may find yourself having to decide just how important it really is to you that a piano fit in with your present furnishings.

These four general considerations will lead naturally to three specific questions:

Should I Buy a Grand or a Vertical Piano?

The answer to this question will depend on the space and money you have available and on your playing requirements. The action of a grand piano generally allows for faster repetition of notes and for better, more subtle control of expression and tone than does a vertical action. Also, the horizontal construction of a grand allows the tone to develop in a more pleasing manner. In a vertical, the sound tends to bounce right back into the performer's face, or else remains boxed in. For these reasons, the grand is always the choice of concert artists. But for many other uses and levels of proficiency, a vertical piano may be more appropriate.

Space is an obvious consideration. A grand may need more space for aesthetic reasons than a mere measuring of the instrument would indicate.

Grands usually cost from three to six times as much as verticals of similar quality and condition. The imposing quality of a grand piano can bring prestige to your home, but be forewarned: To buy a cheap grand or one in poor condition just for prestige is to make a terrible investment. Your expectations will be higher, and therefore the pianos's faults will be more noticeable. The results will be disappointing and expensive. If your playing truly requires a grand piano, save up and buy one of sufficient quality to be worth your while. If your playing doesn't justify a grand, or if you're not willing to spend the money for a good one, you'll probably be making a better investment, both musically and financially, if you buy a high-quality vertical piano.

What Size Piano Should I Buy?

Both grands and verticals come in a number of sizes. The height of a vertical piano is measured from the floor to the top of the piano. The length of a grand is measured from the very front of the keyboard end of the piano to the very back of the piano, with the lid closed (Figure 2-1).

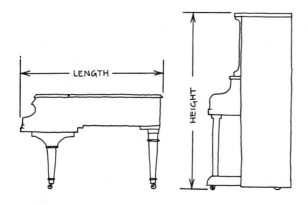

FIGURE 2-1. How a grand piano (left) and a vertical piano (right) are measured.

Vertical Pianos

Full-size Upright	48–60"
Studio	43–47"
Console	40–43"
Spinet	36–39"

Grand Pianos

Concert Grand	7½–9½'
Medium Grand	5½–7½'
Small (Baby) Grand	4½–5½'

The names and sizes listed above are quite general and there is some overlapping between them. Vertical piano types are defined not only by their height, as shown above, but also by the kinds of action they have (which tend to vary with the size). This is important—please read about different kinds of action in detail on page 44. Note that old pianos labeled "upright grand" or "cabinet grand" are really just uprights.

The size of a piano is probably the single most important factor influencing its tonal quality. The longer strings, particularly in the bass section, and the greater soundboard area of the larger sizes of grands and verticals result in greater volume and resonance of tone and in a harmonic content that is most pleasing to the listener. The smaller the piano, the worse the tonal quality, especially in the lower bass, and also in the tenor, just above the bass.

An additional factor, though, makes the question of size even more important: because the tonal quality of small pianos tends to be poor, the people who buy these pianos are usually more interested in the styling and looks of the case than in the quality of the instrument inside the case. Therefore, the manufacturers invest more of their money in the appearance of the instrument than in its quality. The result is that, quite apart from any effects of acoustical laws, smaller pianos are often more poorly built than larger ones.

If space and money were no obstacle, I would place the different types and sizes of piano in the following order of preference:

1. Concert Grand
2. Medium Grand
3. Full-size Upright
4. Studio   } Small Grand
5. Console
6. Spinet

The placement of a particular small grand in this list would depend on its size and quality. While most grands have longer strings and larger soundboards than most verticals, some larger verticals may surpass some smaller grands in these respects and for this and other reasons may be better instruments.

Unless your ceilings are only four feet high, "lack of space" is not a valid reason for getting a small vertical, since the only difference in size between small and large verticals is their height, not the floor space they occupy.

Spinets have been placed at the bottom of the list, not only because of their small size and generally poor quality, but also because their action is inaccessible and hard to service. Please read page 45 for the many reasons to not buy a spinet.

If you can, buy a grand piano at least 6 feet long or a vertical at least 48 inches tall, but in no case should you buy a grand less than 5 feet or a vertical under 40 inches.

Should I Buy a New or a Used Piano?

Many people, when thinking of a "used" piano, conjure up images of a piano on its last legs, in terrible need of repair. This image is based in part on the incredibly large numbers of such pianos that actually exist. But "used" can also refer to several other classes of piano:

- The older piano that still has many years of life ahead;
- The piano that needs only minor repair to be in good shape;
- The piano that is only a couple of years old and practically like new that is being sold because the owner is moving or wants to buy a better instrument;
- The piano that has been reconditioned or rebuilt by a competent piano technician and is in excellent condition. Some pianos like this are actually better than new ones, carry a similar guarantee, and cost almost as much.

I find that people spend large sums of money on new pianos that are smaller or of lower quality than they would have liked, or that really don't suit their needs, because they aren't aware of the used-piano option. It's especially sad when someone buys one of those new, pitifully small grands when they could have spent no more on a used grand of decent size.

There are other good reasons to buy a used piano. Since the average life of a piano is around fifty years, and with proper restoration at least fifty more, it's silly to waste our resources buying new pianos when old ones can be so effectively recycled. Some used pianos have exquisite veneers, leg styles, carved cases, and ivory keys unavailable today on new pianos at reasonable prices. Many of the companies that produce new pianos today are huge conglomerates that turn out pianos by the thousands in far-away cities. How much more satisfying to contribute to your local small-scale economy by buying a used piano that has been restored to usefulness by local craftspeople.

Of course, there's a trade-off when buying a used piano—you may have to look harder to find what you want, you'll take a greater risk, and you may give up a warranty and some number of years of a piano's life in return for paying less money. This means that it's especially important to have a competent piano technician inspect the piano before you buy it. He or she can advise and teach you about pianos during your search, as well as inspect and maintain your piano after the search is over. There will be few others who will be able to help you, for while professional pianists and piano teachers may have opinions about the tone and touch of a piano, they usually know next to nothing about the technical aspects of their instrument.

LOOKING FOR A PIANO
(Or Zen and the Art of Piano Buying)

"Looking for a piano" is a process of developing a "piano awareness," and this begins by doing your homework—asking yourself some basic questions about your needs and resources and learning all you can about pianos before you start to look for one. The process continues as you shop for a piano and find out what's available, become more aware of the differences between pianos, and discover what it is that you like. It's been my experience that the attitude with which you approach the piano market may be just as important as any technical information or expertise you possess.

Two common pitfalls tend to trap prospective piano buyers. Those who have had some previous experience with pianos have often accumulated notions about them that may not be accurate—notions based on misconceptions, incomplete information, and isolated experiences with particular brands and models. "Brand X pianos are always too loud," they say, or "Grand pianos always have a hard touch," or "No used piano would ever look good in my living room." It's helpful to have some idea of what you want before starting to look, but unless your needs are very specific—say, you're a concert artist looking for a concert grand—it's best to remain as flexible and open as possible at the beginning of your search. Then if you discover that some of your original ideas were faulty, it will be easier to change your course of action.

Buyers with little or no experience with pianos, particularly people who tend to feel intimidated by mechanical devices, fall into the opposite category:

they often feel swamped by the sea of options available to them, feel bewildered about how to begin looking, and resign themselves to getting less than they deserve. These people often settle for one of the first pianos to come along.

Know that it *is* possible to make a successful purchase without being a piano expert yourself. Actually, shopping for a piano is an important part of the process of learning about pianos. I would suggest that you begin your search by setting aside a certain amount of time (for instance, an hour or two a week for two months)—during which you forbid yourself to buy a piano—for examining the entire new and used piano markets. Bring along a trusted friend (preferably one who plays the piano, if you don't) and try out as many pianos as you can in the allotted time. Visit piano dealers and rebuilders; look in the want ads and make some inquiries; even try out pianos that aren't for sale, as in friends' homes or community buildings. Include in your sampling a few pianos you know you could never buy, such as a concert grand (or a spinet!). This approach will take the pressure off while you're developing piano awareness and discovering where your pianistic needs fit into the scheme of things. It will also be a lot of fun. Later, when you feel more confident, you can narrow your field with an intent to buy.

Trust your feelings about the pianos you meet—don't be intimidated by other people's opinions—but *analyze* your reactions. "I don't like the tone of this piano" is not a very useful statement. However, "The bass notes don't sound clear, and the treble is brilliant but lacks depth" gives you a basis for comparison with other pianos by turning a blanket judgment into a useful observation. The ability to analyze the tone,

touch, and looks of a piano this way will come to you gradually as you meet more of them and learn to be specific about your feelings. Pianos that before had all seemed alike will then begin to assume personalities of their own, and you in turn will discover that you prefer some over others.

At some point you'll want to stop looking. Some people don't stop until they find a piano that is obviously the one they've been looking for, one that practically shouts "Take ME!" Others set a time limit, after which they make a choice from the pianos they've seen. Caution: Beware of the "buy of a lifetime"—the offer that can't be refused—when the major attraction is the price tag. Be sure you are completely satisfied with the instrument in *all* respects. After the money has been spent, the price will no longer be of interest to you and you'll have to live with what you bought.

How much time you spend looking for a piano will depend on your priorities, but be sure to allow enough time for things to happen in your life—for the feelers you've put out to produce some results—and for your piano awareness to develop. And again, when you find a piano you like, don't forget to have a professional piano technician inspect it before you buy it. The small fee you pay for this service (usually forty to sixty dollars)* may save you much grief later, for pianos can have expensive problems that are not obvious.

---

*When inspecting a piano, some technicians prefer to tune it as well, at an additional charge, because some piano problems that might not otherwise be apparent may show up during a tuning, and because it is impossible to accurately judge the tone of a piano unless it is in tune.

CHAPTER THREE
Buying a New Piano

IF YOU'VE EVER STOPPED BY A PIANO STORE with the thought of buying a new piano, you may well have been overwhelmed by the number of choices you would have to make to do so. It's not enough that there are a variety of brands, models, sizes, styles, and finishes to choose from. You also have to choose between particle-board and real wood case construction, laminated and solid spruce soundboard, and copper-plated and solid copper bass strings, just to name a few. Then a perusal of the sales literature reveals such ponderous space-age terms as "Mezzo-Thermoneal Stabilizer," "Duraphonic Multi-Radial Soundboard™," and "Vacuum Shield Mold Process." About this time, you begin to wonder if it might not be simpler to take up the kazoo!

My purpose in this chapter is to guide you through this maze of choices and technical terms and to identify the real differences between brands and models, as opposed to those that are just advertising hype. This may aid you in your defense against fast-talking salespeople and slick ad copy that make every piano, no matter how poor, sound like God's gift to humanity. Tips are also given on checking out a piano prior to purchase, negotiating the price, and other matters you should know about to conclude the deal successfully. Information in this chapter is of a general nature; specific brands are covered in Chapter 4.

MARKETING

When I first began to research the piano market, I was struck by the fact that some manufacturers produced several versions of the same size and type of piano. These versions differed in the sophistication of their cabinet styling, of course, and were priced hundreds of dollars apart. But the higher-priced models also contained different technical features which, I came to realize, were sometimes of minor importance and often involved little extra in production cost. What's more, the manufacturers were changing these technical features in a seemingly random manner every year or two.

For example, this year "Smith Bros." (a fictitious name) might produce a cheap console with blued tuning pins and "10-pound" hammers and a more expensive version with nickel-plated tuning pins and "12-pound" hammers—not much of a difference, I can assure you. Then next year might see the retirement of the bottom-of-the-line model and its replacement with a "deluxe" model which, in addition to the "better" hammers and tuning pins, has a solid spruce soundboard instead of a laminated one. Why (I thought naïvely), if the production cost is about the same, doesn't the manufacturer simply put all the best technical features into all the models and just build different cabinets around them? It wasn't long before I discovered the reason for this craziness: marketing.

Marketing is the process by which the need or desire for a product is measured and the manufactured product is advertised and sold. It includes everything except the actual design and manufacturing of the product. Marketing is a vital part of any business, for the best product in the world will come to naught if the buying public is unaware of its existence or does not sense a need for it. In the hands of many companies and their marketing experts, though, marketing takes on an additional dimension and challenge—how to trick the public into desiring and buying whatever the company finds most profitable to produce.

In the world of pianos, this latter kind of marketing works something like this: A company produces a limited number of absolutely bottom-of-the-line pianos, often spinets, but sometimes consoles or even grands, that are so terrible that the company hopes nobody will buy one. Why? Because these pianos are to be used only as advertising bait to get you into the store. When you see an ad in the paper that says, "Sale—Pianos from $995," the $995 piano is the bait. The manufacturer makes a smaller profit on this piano; the dealer, if he or she sells the piano, may take a loss; and the salesperson will probably make little or no commission. Once you're in the store, therefore, the salesperson will do everything possible to try to get you to buy a more expensive piano.

This kind of product is known as a "promotional piano," "loss leader," or just "leader." It performs the same function as the fifty-nine-cent can of tuna that the supermarket hopes will induce you to buy fifty dollars worth of groceries. If everyone walks out with nothing but two cans of tuna, the grocers lose their shirt. Although it is illegal to advertise something one has no intention of selling, you may find the leader "nailed to the floor" if you try to buy it. For instance, the dealer may say that you'll have to wait three or four months for the shipment to arrive. After all, if you buy the bait, the dealer will have to lose money on another one in order to continue the scheme.

In a typical scenario, Mr. Jones, the father of an eight-year-old girl who is about to start taking piano lessons, walks into our piano store and asks about the $995 wonder he has just seen advertised. Somewhat reluctantly, the salesperson guides him to it (it's probably in a dark corner at the back of the store), remarking that it hasn't been tuned since it arrived from the factory. Predictably, it sounds wretched.

"You know, Mr. Jones," says the salesperson, "for only a few more dollars a month, you could own our Deluxe Spinet, with its rust-resistant, nickel-plated tuning pins and its heavy-duty, reinforced, 12-pound hammers, and of course its more attractive custom styling." As our shopper fingers a few keys on the Deluxe Spinet, the salesperson, trying to sound sincere, asks, "Mr. Jones, have you ever considered a console?" Without waiting for a response, the salesman continues his pitch: "Our Custom Console features the more responsive direct-blow action, and with its diagonally-grained laminated spruce soundboard, guaranteed not to crack for sixty years, and its price hardly any higher than that of the Deluxe Spinet, it's a terrific bargain." And on and on this goes, each higher-priced model offering some wonderful new feature, until the bewildered father calls a halt when the prices being asked begin to exceed his budget.

Each of these technical characteristics is called a "step-up feature" and is designed to persuade you to buy a higher-priced piano. I'm not saying that these features don't have any technical value; some do and some don't. But often they aren't installed for their actual technical value, only for their perceived value. By organizing the piano market in this fashion (and incidentally, many other consumer goods markets operate similarly), a manufacturer is able to offer a piano with specific features and perceived advantages at each of many different price levels, *and thus to sell you something regardless of how much money you have to spend*. If the dealer didn't have a model whose price matched the amount of money in your pocket, he or she would have to suggest you buy a different brand of piano, or, worse yet, direct you to a competitor down the street.

Each of these price levels, usually spaced a few hundred dollars apart, is called a "price point," and at each price point a manufacturer tries to provide a feature that no other manufacturer offers in a piano at the same price. ("Mr. Jones, did you know that this Deluxe Console is the only console at this price that offers a genuine, solid spruce soundboard?") To match changes made by the competitors, as well as to respond to other market factors, this game requires a periodic reshuffling of models, features, and styles, which accounts for the seemingly random changes in manufacturers' offerings.

Obviously, I've exaggerated this sales pitch to make a point. Although I *have* heard conversations like this, lest you be too concerned I should say that most salespeople have good manners and will give you the kind of personal service you deserve. But this brief example illustrates the way the piano market has traditionally been structured, and that structure determines to some extent what products you will find in the store and how they will be sold to you.

Not all manufacturers use this sort of marketing scheme to the extent I've described, and in recent years its use has declined slightly. Some have relatively few models, with features that remain unchanged for many years at a stretch. A few companies build all their pianos to a single technical standard, varying them only in size and cabinet style. These firms are more interested in building a high-quality instrument than in trying to sell something to everybody. The difference between the two types of companies is not quite so apparent in retail advertising, where all try to look their best, as it is on the wholesale level, where much of the pretense is discarded. A glance at one of the trade magazines, for instance, shows that some manufacturers use quality as their sales pitch to dealers, while others unabashedly shout "Profits, profits!" in large letters, their ads complete with dollar signs and pictures of gold bars. Of course, all businesses want to make a profit; it's a matter of emphasis I'm talking about, and a number of manufacturers fall between the two extremes. And to be sure, the "quality-oriented" makers also have marketing departments, which are only too happy to take advantage of whatever myths you've absorbed about certain technical features when those features are present in their pianos.

As you might expect, the quality-oriented companies are often small; many make a limited number of rather high-priced pianos using a great deal of human, rather than machine, labor. But this is by no means the whole story. Every piano manufacturer today uses a mixture of hand and machine labor, and the Japanese are known for turning out vast numbers of pianos in unbelievably automated factories while maintaining high levels of quality. The terms "handcrafted" and "precision machine-made" are popular in piano advertising literature, but the truth is that both human labor and machines can be used for good or ill, depending on the philosophy and orientation of management and their relations with labor. Expensive machines can turn out sloppy parts by the thousands if designed only for speed and misused by their human operators. On the other hand, humans can do very careful work if well trained and well treated and if high standards are set, or they can turn out junk if treated like the machines just mentioned.

Another buzzword to be wary of is "tradition." This word is sometimes used in relation to the number of years a firm has been in business, a figure that might be thought to indicate a company's ability to produce good products. Rarely so in the piano world. Most companies that claim they date back to 1830 (or whenever) do so only through numerous sales, mergers, acquisitions, and changes in management and ownership, and have about as much relation to the original company as you and I do to Adam and Eve. In many cases, seeing the pianos now made in his name would make the old master roll over in his grave.

"Tradition" is also used with respect to materials and methods of manufacture. In some cases, the traditional methods and materials *are* better, or you may have an aesthetic or philosophical preference for them. Sometimes, though, the original reason for using a particular material or method has been forgotten, or a better one has become available. Yet some companies continue to follow the old way because their marketing departments are afraid the public won't accept a departure from tradition. This fear causes a certain amount of tension between the marketing and engineering ends of most companies; marketing, needless to say, almost always has the final say. So when companies resist the use of plastics, particle board, and other synthetics in piano manufacturing, it's often because they feel their image may be damaged by using these materials, rather than because the materials are inferior. You can bet that when the use of synthetics becomes widely accepted, the resisting companies will jump on the bandwagon and begin using the ones that have been proven superior.

Ironically, a marketing department sometimes boxes itself into a corner with its concerns. One company, for instance, after years of touting their scale design (tonal design) as a great one (which it wasn't) and using it as a major selling feature, decided to replace it with a better one. Because they feared that people would ask, "If that one was really so great, why are they replacing it?" they phased the new design in very slowly, one model at a time and didn't advertise it. Frankly, I sometimes think these marketing people take themselves a little too seriously: how many people do you imagine would really lie awake at night wondering why a mediocre piano company decided to change its scale design?

HOW PIANOS DIFFER IN QUALITY AND FEATURES

To the uninitiated, chances are that one piano in a piano store looks pretty much like another, except for the price tag and cabinet styling. And if the piano is being bought just so Junior can begin taking lessons, why pay more money than absolutely necessary? This is the question technicians and dealers hear every day. Sometimes, no doubt, these buyers simply can't afford a more expensive piano. But just as often they are moderately well-to-do people who have just spent fifteen thousand dollars on an automobile, which will last less than one-tenth as long as the piano before being replaced. Why, then, the resistance to investing in a good instrument? Probably a large part of the reason is that a fancy car confers much more prestige upon the owner than a high-quality piano does. But I think that at least some of the reason is simply that most piano buyers don't understand what they are getting for their money. Technical information and brand comparisons abound for cars, but little or nothing of the kind exists for pianos. People therefore have very little incentive to purchase something whose value is not clear.

It's largely, though not entirely, true that the price of a piano is a fairly good indication of its quality. Just what makes a well-made piano more expensive? Briefly, good pianos require better raw materials, which are prepared to more exacting tolerances and subjected to stricter standards of quality than materials in lesser pianos. Sometimes a great deal of expensive material (such as wood, felt, or leather) that does not conform to these standards is rejected or discarded. In both design and workmanship, much more time and attention is paid to details that might otherwise plague the owner or technician later. In the best factories, workers are more apt to be treated as craftspeople and given considerable responsibility, while in lesser factories most jobs are broken down into tiny, easily learned tasks, rendering workers replaceable cogs in a machine. Workers on the high-quality pianos are therefore better trained, stay with the company longer, and receive higher pay and benefits. Where machinery is used, it is at least as much in the interest of quality as efficiency, which may entail greater expense in its design. The result is pianos that are more uniform from one to the next, perform better, last longer, and require less remedial maintenance than lesser instruments.

Of course, cost is not always related to product quality. The lower cost of foreign labor, or of non-union labor in this country; differences in rent and taxes in various locations; savings due to larger production runs and greater manufacturing efficiencies; and the fanciness of the furniture all play an important part in the price of the instrument.

In the following pages, I'd like to discuss selected technical aspects of pianos and elaborate a bit on the ways pianos differ in quality and construction. Some of these differences can actually be seen, heard, and felt, whereas others, nonetheless important, can't be observed as separate entities in the final product. Though I could cite hundreds of such details, I include here only those most important for the consumer to know, or most widely advertised but actually least important, or easiest for the purchaser to inspect.*

"Buying Tips" scattered throughout identify those features that you can and should inspect yourself or ask about.

Several themes run through these descriptions: Which features are really just marketing gimmicks? (I'll detail some more marketing nonsense to entertain you.) What will I gain (or give up) if I buy a more (or less) expensive piano? How important is it to me to buy a piano with "traditional" as opposed to synthetic or nontraditional materials? How important is it to me to buy a piano that will last a lifetime (or longer)?

Before I begin, though, several cautions are in order. First of all, much about pianos is simply unknown or cannot be judged good or bad. This is because little basic research has been done, as piano manufacture has evolved along empirical, rather than experimental, lines, or because the choice among some features is simply a matter of taste. My intent here is to present a consensus of informed opinion where such a consensus exists, and to be honest about where it doesn't. Even knowing what *isn't* known can be useful when confronted with unwarranted claims.

Second, no piano is perfect. Every piano, no matter how expensive or well made, has limitations inherent in the physical laws governing the various aspects of design and construction, in which conflicting needs may necessitate compromise. Most piano designs require compromises simply to make the product affordable to the average person. And, too, some otherwise wonderful instruments may have a thing or two about them that is just plain faulty. Therefore it would be a mistake to categorically dismiss a piano just because it contains some feature that I have labeled here as "incorrect." Each piano must be seen in its entirety and evaluated in terms of its intended use, longevity, and price.

Third, this book is written from the point of view of a consumer advocate and therefore necessarily focuses attention on the negative aspects of the piano industry—false technical claims, shoddy products, and poor service. After all, as a piano shopper you will soon enough hear from the dealers how wonderful their products and services are. Presumably you have bought this book to find out those things that the dealers won't tell you. The problem with this approach is that you may get the erroneous idea that all piano dealers, salespeople, and manufacturers are crooks. In fact, many conduct their businesses with

---

*For a more complete and detailed account of how a high-quality piano is manufactured, I highly recommend *The Wonders of the Piano: The Anatomy of the Instrument* by Catherine C. Bielefeldt (Belwin-Mills, 1984).

great integrity and admirably support and service their products. You need fear being ripped off no more than with any other comparable consumer purchase.

Pianos have improved a lot during the last few years. Some of the grosser defects in piano design outlined in the following pages are rarely found in pianos being made today. However, they will be found in abundance in pianos made from about 1960 to the early 1980s, a period in the history of the American piano when a particularly large amount of junk was produced. So although this chapter is written mainly for those buying new pianos, most of it will also be useful in evaluating the quality of a relatively young used piano. Besides, some pianos made in the early 1980s are still languishing on showroom floors, especially those made by companies that have since gone out of business.

Nontechnical information about shopping for a new piano continues on page 60.

Case and Cabinet Construction, Styling, and Finish

I know that many of you reading this are concerned at least as much with the furniture aspect of the piano as with its musical aspects, so we'll begin there. A piano's furniture value is reflected in two ways: how it looks now and how it will hold up over the years. For a piano, "over the years" is a long time, for you should expect a well-made piano to last long enough to be enjoyed by your children and their children, too, and it takes very careful craftsmanship to accomplish that. Making a piano look good now, at least to the untrained eye, is a lot easier to do; every company allocates a large portion of its budget to this end, often at the expense of both the piano's musical value and its long-range furniture value. When you buy a cheap piano, not only might you be getting a poor instrument, but its beauty may be only as deep as three coats of lacquer, its imitation Mediterranean styling notwithstanding.

Panel construction. A discussion of furniture begins with the subject of wood. Contrary to popular thought, most fine furniture is not made with planks or pieces of solid wood just as they are cut from the tree. For one thing, most trees that are cut down for furniture wood these days are too thin to provide large planks. Panels more than a few inches wide are usually made by gluing thinner strips of wood together edge to edge. For another thing, large panels of solid wood are not dimensionally stable; they tend to warp and change size from season to season. Thus, they are not suitable for furniture in most cases. Solid woods are used, though, for such parts as legs and moldings, which are not likely to be much affected by warping.

Most furniture these days is made of some kind of plywood, though not the cheap grade you use to board up windows or walk on over ditches. The word *plywood* refers to any wood product made of several layers glued together in a sandwich. Five-ply "lumber-core" plywood (Figure 3-1 top) is the most common type used in piano cabinetry. It consists of a core of "solid" wood (that is, thin pieces glued edge to edge), usually poplar or birch, covered on each side by two layers of veneer with grain running at right angles to each other. Wood expands and contracts more across the grain than along it, so this cross-banded veneer construction lessens warping and changes in size. Another kind of plywood used less often in pianos is "veneer-core" plywood, basically a sandwich of cross-banded veneers.

Plywood has many advantages over solid wood. In addition to minimizing warpage, plywood is equally strong in all dimensions and can be manufactured in a wide variety of sizes and thicknesses to suit specific purposes. Whereas solid wood made from edge-glued strips might have a chaotic grain pattern, the visual characteristics of a plywood panel can be controlled by the manufacturer through the choice of face veneer (the outer veneer layer). Most well-constructed furniture today is made from a combination of solid wood and plywood, each used to its best advantage.

Particle board. As the wood supply dwindles and wood prices increase, greater and greater use is being made of *particle board*, a material made of compressed chips, flakes, particles, or fibers of wood or sawdust held together by glue. Although much of the public doesn't realize it, a lot of so-called fine furniture today is made of particle board, usually as a substitute for the solid lumber in lumber-core plywood. Its use in piano cabinets, somewhat controversial, is mostly limited to verticals, but at least one maker uses it even for grand piano lids. While no piano maker advertises that it uses particle board, many advertise that they *don't* use it. Its use, though, is easily disguised.

GIMMICK: "Mr. Jones, Smith Bros. pianos contain no particle board, unlike lesser pianos. As you can see from the edge of this panel, we use only real plywood construction."

TRUTH: When the subject of particle board came up on one of my factory visits, the factory technician beckoned me to follow him and ushered me into a room whose walls were lined with his competitors' pianos. Approaching one well-known Japanese make, he pulled off the lower panel, a large piece measuring about two feet by four feet, and pointed to its edge. The familiar stripes of cross-grain layers indicated that the panel was made of seven-ply veneer-core plywood construction. Then he pointed to the center of the panel, where a large gouge had been made through the black finish and into the wood. Looking closely at the intentionally damaged spot, it was clear from the texture and appearance that the panel was actually made of particle board. Why was the edge different from the rest of the board?

Particle board is frequently "lumber-banded" along its perimeter with solid lumber or plywood (Figure 3-1 bottom) to increase the overall strength of the panel and to allow the edge to be shaped or contoured, an operation which is difficult to do successfully with most types of particle board. It also camouflages the particle board, allowing it to be used even by those who would rather not be known for it. The giveaway,

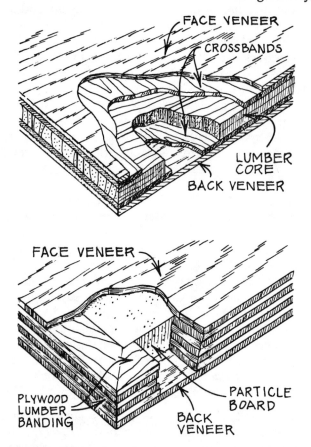

FIGURE 3-1. Most large furniture panels are made of some form of plywood. Top: Traditional five-ply lumber-core plywood. Bottom: Particle board–core plywood with plywood lumber-banding to strengthen and camouflage the particle board. Not all particle board–core plywood is lumber-banded.

by the way, is the weight of the case part. Particle board is very dense. If the part seems to weigh more than any wood you know, you can bet it's particle board.

Particle board has a number of advantages over wood. Having no grain or knots, it doesn't warp, can be easily cut and machined, and is very easily veneered. It uses materials that used to be considered waste and discarded, and thus makes good ecological and economic sense. By varying the density, type of "particle," and method of manufacture, it can be made to suit many construction needs, and the technology for this industry is rapidly expanding. It's even possible now to print a simulated wood grain on the faces and edges of particle board that looks so realistic it can't be told from the real thing. (Though I use the term *particle board* generically throughout this book, the material in fact comes in many different forms, which vary in their strength and suitability for piano construction.)

Particle board also has some drawbacks. Its screw-holding power is limited; each time a screw is removed it brings with it a trickle of sawdust, and within a short time the screw hole becomes stripped. This can be gotten around either by lumber-banding the piece and screwing into the wood, or by redesigning the cabinet so that removable screws are unnecessary. Particle board also tends toward brittleness, and when broken, is pretty much unrepairable. Breakage of this sort is not common in piano cabinetry, but sometimes occurs during shipment, and could result from vandalism or rough play. If you expect rough treatment, I'd recommend "the real thing," — that is, plywood — not particle board.

There is also some indication that, because of its density, particle board may muffle the sound of a vertical piano somewhat. But the proof is in the sound: if a particle board piano sounds good, this argument becomes academic.

Particle board has a bad name in piano cabinetry mostly because of the poor quality of its early days and the inappropriate uses to which it was put. Today the production of particle board is more sophisticated. When it is used appropriately, particle board has huge technical advantages to the mass producer and only slight technical drawbacks, if any, to the consumer. The chief objection to it at this point seems to be a psychological one: it lacks aesthetic appeal. After all, part of the lure of the piano has always been its fine wooden cabinetry and all that that symbolizes: a connection with nature, with old-world craftsmanship, and with the skill it takes to make something out of wood that will weather the seasons and endure. But much of this, today, is pure fantasy, since plywood, with all its glue, is already halfway toward particle board, and, in most large piano factories, "old-world" craftsmanship is hard to find. Craftsmanship these days is often of the high-tech and impersonal kind, of which particle board is a natural extension.

It suffices to say, then, that when you shop for a piano, your choice of particle board–core or lumber-core plywood will be largely based on aesthetic and economic, rather than technical, considerations. Most of the large piano manufacturers are making increasing use of particle board, while the makers of more expensive pianos use it only sparingly or not at all.

Quality in woodworking. While the debate about particle board rages on, the more important differences between quality and mediocrity, as might be expected, are subtler. Regardless of whether a piano contains real wood or particle board in its large panels, it still uses real wood elsewhere—in structural and acoustical parts, veneers, action parts, and in smaller cabinet parts. Some manufacturers are fussier than others in the quality of wood they purchase, insisting on greater uniformity of grain pattern and absence of knots, voids (empty spaces), discoloration, or other imperfections, even in parts that don't show. They pay a premium for the highest-quality woods available. Where certain critical parts—soundboard, pinblock, bridges—are involved, the better piano makers use large amounts of quarter-sawn lumber, whose grain orientation ensures maximum dimensional stability (Figure 3-2a). But quarter-sawn lumber is many times more expensive than plain-sawn, so lesser makers use the cheaper material or let planks of plain-sawn lumber slip in when expedient. In the long run, this can have disastrous consequences.

Many kinds of wood are used in a piano. In deciding which kind to use for a particular purpose, piano designers have to take into account such factors as moisture content, strength, weight, stiffness, and how well the wood seasons, as well as its availability and cost. For makers of lower-quality pianos, availability and cost figure more prominently. Spruce is often used for structural parts like vertical back posts and grand braces because its long, uniform, close grain gives it stiffness with less weight. Other woods are also used. Spruce is used for soundboards because of its excellent acoustical properties. Where hardness is required, such as in pinblocks and action parts, maple or beech is used. Wood for grand piano cases, which are made of many thin layers bent and glued around a form, is best chosen for its acoustical, as well as its structural, properties (in verticals the structure affects the sound only minimally). The better makers of grand pianos usually choose the denser and more expensive maple (or beech) over the

cheaper but less satisfactory mahogany or poplar. (Note: the outer veneer, being decorative, may be different).

Wood must go through an extensive drying process before it is usable for construction of any kind. First it must be air-dried for from six months to two years, and then the moisture content is usually further reduced by drying in automatic kilns. Attempts to hasten this process, or not drying the wood to a sufficiently low moisture content, can result in warped, cracked, or binding case or structural parts. Even after this dried wood is made into parts, some manufacturers are fastidious enough that they will cure these parts for long periods of time before using them. For instance, after gluing up a grand piano rim, most makers of fine pianos let it sit in a conditioning room for months before using it. Foreign manufacturers newly importing to North America have the most severe problems with improperly dried wood; they often underestimate the effect that our extremes of dryness and dampness will have on their pianos.

After the wood is selected and dried, there are literally dozens of examples of proper woodworking procedure in which a manufacturer can show its true colors. Most of these you will never see any sign of—if the job is done right (Figure 3-2). The manufacturer must take into account the species of the wood, the direction of the grain, the stress that will be applied, the type of wood joint to be used, the tolerances to which the wood will be machined, the kind of glue to be used, and many other factors.

In each case, the manufacturer must decide whether the piano will be built to last a lifetime or if portions of it will begin to disintegrate about the time the warranty runs out. And even if nothing disastrous occurs, there will be many problems to plague the person who owns or has to service a poorly made piano: a fallboard that binds in sticky weather and won't slide or fold down over the keys without scratching the finish, parts that warp and prevent the free movement of the keys, legs that are very unstable and come loose or break too easily, screw and knob holes that strip out, grand piano lids or other case parts that split where the hinges are attached, and music desks that split and come unhinged (these are a few of my fa-vor-ite things).

If you are not experienced in cabinetmaking, judging the quality of woodworking in a piano cabinet is not an easy thing to do. But by inspecting and comparing pianos you know to be of widely differing quality, you can begin to develop an eye for such things. The thickness (though not necessarily the weight) of cabinet sides, rims, panels, music desks, lids, and lyres; the extent to which particle board is used (though not necessarily important per se); the

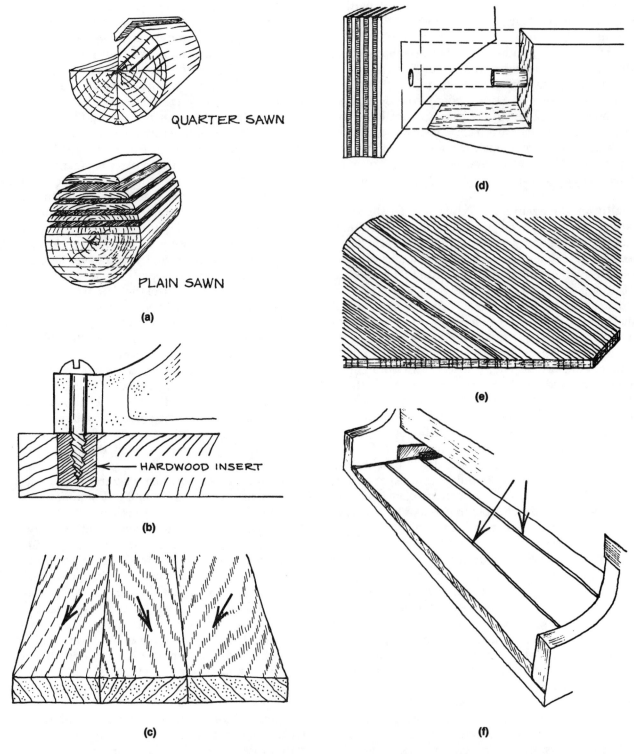

QUARTER SAWN

PLAIN SAWN

(a)

HARDWOOD INSERT

(b)

(c)

(d)

(e)

(f)

FIGURE 3-2. All piano manufacturers must pay close attention to proper woodworking principles to ensure that their instruments will perform well and hold up over time. Some manufacturers are more conscientious than others. Shown here in generalized form are several examples of steps some makers take in building a durable product: (a) quarter-sawn lumber for maximum dimensional stability versus the cheaper, but less satisfactory, plain-sawn lumber; (b) the use of hardwood or hardwood inserts where screws or other metal hardware would otherwise wear away the wood; (c) careful attention to grain direction where pieces are joined (to prevent warping), or where acoustical properties are involved (the latter not shown); (d) tight, carefully fitted doweled joints for structural integrity; (e) close-grained wood with uniform grain pattern for acoustical, structural, and aesthetic reasons; (f) expansion joints to prevent warping and consequent mechanical problems.

ease with which panels lift off for service; how well adjacent parts seem to fit together; the appearance of the finish (discussed later)—all these taken together give a good idea of the intentions of the manufacturer with respect to the model.

Sophistication in cabinetry. There are a number of differences in piano cabinetry that indicate not so much the quality of woodworking as its level of sophistication. That is, the absence of certain features would not make a piano potentially defective, it would just make the piano plainer. Some of the items shown in Figure 3-3 differ between manufacturers; others differ between the various offerings of a single manufacturer. Some companies make dozens of models and styles, all with more or less the same instrument inside of them, but they may be priced many hundreds of dollars apart because of these cabinetry differences. You pay through the nose for sophisticated cabinetry, not only because of the extra material cost, but also because of the additional costs of design, inventory, handling, cutting, scrap, fitting, and finishing involved, and the profit margin added on.

Furniture styles. Period furniture or decorator styling is very popular in the vertical piano market, and to a lesser extent in the grand market. With most brands, the styling differences are found only in the shape of the music desk and the legs. That is, a Smith Bros. Deluxe Console in Mediterranean style could be changed to French Provincial by just switching the music desk and the two front legs. Some manufacturers, in some models, may alter other features or occasionally even completely redesign the cabinet from style to style. This is obviously much more expensive to do. In addition to period styling, there is also the "continental" style, popular in European and Asian vertical pianos and distinguished by its plain, nondescript lines and the absence of front legs; and the "professional" or "institutional" style with legs supported by "toe construction" (Figure 3-5).

Finish. Most piano companies put their cabinets through a very elaborate finishing process—much more elaborate than the process that the musical portion of the instrument goes through—for they know this is what will sell the piano. The finishing process, with sometimes twenty or more steps, consists of staining, sanding, filling, shading, sealing, more sanding, lacquer, more sanding, more lacquer, hand rubbing, and polishing. Staining is done to make wood with a large natural variation in color look more

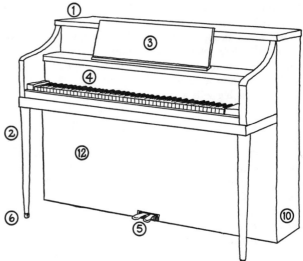

FIGURE 3-3. Pianos can differ in the sophistication of their cabinet design, which is not necessarily related to the quality of construction. Shown here are some of these differences: (1) grand-style lid with beveled edges versus regular lid with square edges; (2) fancy, curved legs doweled into case sides versus plain legs screwed into keybed; (3) fancy, carved music desk with metal grillwork hinged to music shelf versus plain, stationary music desk; (4) folding fallboard with brass appointments versus sliding fallboard or no fallboard at all; (5) three solid cast brass pedals with horns versus two simple stamped brass or brass-plated pedals; (6) casters on front legs versus no casters; (7) brass kick plate around pedals; (8) "tone louvers" and other special features; (9) carved features on legs and moldings; (10) angled sides versus straight sides; (11) relief features on panels; (12) well-matched or even book-matched veneers versus bland veneer patterns (detail not shown).

Buying Tips: Piano Cabinetry and Finish

The average piano purchaser pays an inordinate amount of attention to the way a piano looks, while often not seeing the real differences in cabinet construction at all, not to mention the musical differences. The serious musician is usually less concerned about appearances, but both groups miss a number of very mundane, yet highly practical, cabinet-related considerations.

Here are some buying tips relating to the cabinetry and accessory parts of pianos. Some of them are minor and shouldn't prevent you from buying an otherwise high-quality instrument, but they may prove useful to you in avoiding future problems.

Legs. Manufacturers say that broken spinet and console legs are among the most common warranty problems reported to them. Take a look at these legs yourself and you'll have to agree they look rather weak and unstable. They get broken in shipment or even just from repeated moving away from a wall for service or cleaning. There are two types of legs—those that are glued and doweled into the case sides and those that are screwed into the keybed at the front (see Figure 3-3). I'm not convinced that one is inherently better than the other, though the former is considered fancier. The best way to avoid the problem of broken legs is either to buy a studio or full-size upright piano with toe construction that supports the legs, or to buy a piano with continental styling that has no legs at all (see Figure 3-5). If you buy one without legs, be sure it's properly balanced. Some have a slight tendency to tip, especially when standing on thick carpeting (try giving it a gentle push).

One more thing about legs: If you buy a spinet or console with legs, make sure the legs reach the floor. You heard right! Sometimes, because of inaccurate case construction or maybe even twisting of the whole piano structure, one leg will not touch the floor.

Casters. If you do buy a piano with unsupported legs, make sure the legs have casters, which may help slightly to prevent breakage. If you plan to move a piano like this around a lot, you should have it permanently mounted on a "piano truck" made for this purpose (see Chapter 6). Some continental-style pianos have no casters—don't plan on moving them much. A few cheap pianos have fake casters with wheels that neither turn nor touch the floor.

Finish. In my opinion, high-gloss finishes are too ostentatious for most homes and are difficult to keep looking good, since they glaringly reveal every scratch, fingerprint, and speck of dust. Note that most high-gloss finishes are polyester, but a few expensive pianos have high-gloss *lacquer* finishes—very time-consuming to produce but much less artificial-looking.

Some points to consider when evaluating the quality of the finish are:

- If the piano has a natural wood finish, do the legs and other cabinet parts match one another in coloration?
- Have the edges been sanded through and then touched up with stain, or have the surfaces been so carefully sanded that no touch-up is necessary?
- Have the back sides of panels been thoroughly sanded and finished, or have they been left rough? Failure to finish both sides with the same amount and type of finish can cause warpage of even the sturdiest panels and trim parts.
- Has the finish been hand-rubbed, and, if so, have all exposed surfaces been rubbed, or just the ones that are most obvious?
- Does the natural wood finish look completely transparent, or does it appear like a cloudy protective guard?
- Are there any ripples or unevenness to the finish? This can be caused by slight movement of the veneer underneath if the woodworking was faulty. (I once saw a foreign-made piano with a high-gloss finish that looked like it was covered in crumpled plastic wrap. The veneer was buckling due to moisture problems.)

Fallboard. Technically, a fallboard (keyboard cover) isn't really necessary, but all good pianos have one. Only some of the cheapest promotional pianos have no fallboard at all. Vertical piano fallboards come in two varieties—one slides down over the keys, the other folds down. The folding kind is definitely superior. The sliding fallboard is a nuisance to remove for servicing the keys, and can even make tuning more difficult. Be sure that the fallboard, when fully open, doesn't stick out over the keys so your fingers would hit it as you played. Grand pianos always have a folding fallboard. Be sure it isn't prone to shutting on your fingers at the slightest opportunity.

Lid. Many vertical pianos now come with a "grand-style lid;" that is, a lid that hinges on the left side rather than at the back (see Figure 3-3). On the right side, inside the piano, is a propstick that props the lid open, just like on a grand. On first thought, this seems like a good idea—it looks elegant and gives an outlet for the sound in a direction other than right into the performer's face. But upon further reflection the advantages fade. For one thing, what will you do with your music, lamp, metronome, and knickknacks if you keep the lid up? They would all slide off onto the floor. I've serviced many of these pianos and I have yet to find a single one in which the lid was kept propped open.

That buyers fail to use this feature may be of no consequence, but these lids may also be very hard to remove to tune the piano. On some of them the hinge pin is practically nonremovable, and keeping them propped open far enough for servicing becomes an exercise in resourcefulness. If your ceilings are low, a fully open lid can even hit the ceiling, and because of its unsupported length, this kind of lid is prone to warpage. Think about whether you really need this feature. (Nowadays, it might be hard to find a good console piano without it.) If you do buy a vertical with this feature, please make sure the lid hinge pins can be easily removed. Your technician will thank you for it.

Grand piano lids are in two parts, usually connected by a long "piano hinge." On the cheapest grands, the hinge is missing, and the front part of the lid must be removed entirely. When it's removed, however, the music desk comes with it. It's probably best to avoid this kind of piano. Some grands also have only one propstick for the lid. You will probably find it most convenient if the lid comes with both a long and a short propstick. One more thing: make sure the lid isn't too heavy to lift!

Music desk. Most spinets and consoles employ a music desk that's hinged on its thin edges by two wood screws, which act as hinge pins (Figure 3-4). Imagine—using wood screws as hinge pins! This must be one of the stupidest designs ever used in piano construction. It makes about as much sense as polishing your high-gloss piano with sandpaper. Here's what's likely to happen: In order to stop the desk from rattling, the screws will be overtightened. After a short time, one of the screws will strip out its hole and fall out, and the desk will collapse. If this doesn't happen, someone will lean on or tug on the desk, splitting out its fragile thin edge, and then it will collapse, requiring woodworking repair or replacement. These are both very common occurrences, and I'm constantly amazed that no one has blown the whistle all these years. Only if the desk is especially thick or reinforced with metal brackets should this design even be considered.

In fairness, I should say that it's next to impossible to find a really secure music desk hinge system, one that's reasonably immune to destruction. Music desks that employ regular desk hinges attached to the back will probably last a little longer, but some technicians report having to repair as many of one kind as of the other (as well as

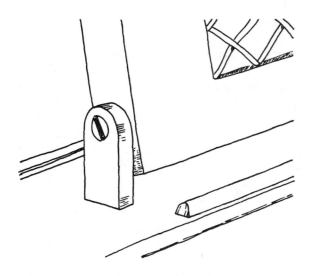

FIGURE 3-4. A music desk hinged on its thin edge with screws serving as hinge pins is likely to come apart or break unless it is especially thick or reinforced with metal brackets.

bent-beyond-recognition brass folding hinge supports, the operation of which was beyond the intelligence of a user).

Be sure that the music desk is capable of holding the amount and type of music you plan to use. Some desks may have trouble holding single sheets of paper upright, or large books, or may be too small for the large amounts of music used in teaching. The music desks I like best run the full width of the piano, and the horizontal portion is covered with cloth or a leather-like material that grips the bottom edge of the sheet music so it doesn't slip down.

One more minor note about music desks: There are reports that buzzing sounds occasionally emanate from the wire grillwork in some fancy music desks.

Lyre. The grand piano pedal lyre should be attached to the underside of the piano with a metal lyre plate or with bolts that screw into threaded metal holes. Even though it's partially reinforced by the diagonal braces behind it, the lyre takes an incredible beating by the feet over the years. Although it isn't done today, in the recent past some cheaper pianos used only wood screws to attach the lyre, and invariably these screws stripped out their holes (a familiar story?) and the lyre fell off. A permanent repair usually involves installing lyre plates anyway, so you might as well have them from the beginning. (If you're buying a used grand piano, a technician can check this for you.)

If you compare lyres of pianos of widely differing quality, you can see how much more substantially and solidly constructed the better one is. Make sure that the lyre doesn't move or twist when the pedals are pressed.

Keybed. When you sit on the bench that usually comes with the piano, be sure that the keybed is at the right height for you. It should allow adequate room for your legs, and the keyboard should be at a comfortable level. This height is fairly standard, but there is some variation. Check to be sure that the bottom of the keybed isn't rough; there have been a number of reports of clothing being filled with splinters.

Bench. Some bench tops are made of particle board, some of wood. Since benches get a lot of use and stress, I recommend a wood-top bench. Benches vary considerably in the quality of woodworking, especially in how well the legs are jointed to the frame. Many benches have legs that are bolted on, allowing you to tighten them as they loosen over time. This is preferable to a bench that is glued together "permanently" but poorly. Benches finished in high-gloss polyester often squeak, no matter what you do. A few pianos come with benches that are adjustable in height, which is great if you are fussy about this or are of an unusual size. Lastly, some benches open up to store music; some don't. You may not have much choice in the matter of what bench you get with a particular piano, but most dealers will allow you to trade up to a better bench for an additional fee.

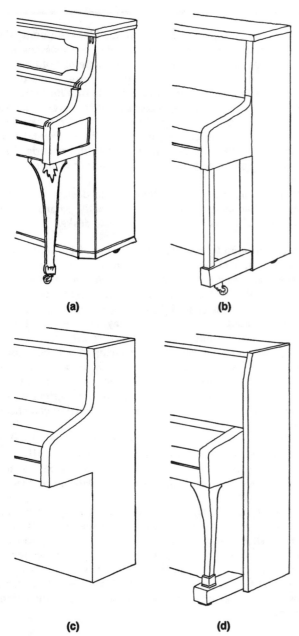

(a)   **(b)**

(c)   **(d)**

FIGURE 3-5. Four common vertical piano styles: (a) period or decorator style with free-standing front legs; (b) institutional or professional style with legs supported by toe construction; (c) continental style without legs; (d) hybrid style combining (a) and (b).

left unfilled to let their open grain show. Hand rubbing and polishing with very fine sandpaper and pumice give the utmost in smoothness and elegance to the surface.

The top finish coat is either lacquer or polyester, lacquer being the favored finish among North American firms and polyester predominating among the imports. Polyester is usually applied in one or two thick coats and so is suitable primarily for pianos whose cabinets have little surface detail, which would otherwise get buried, such as the continental-style pianos. Lacquer is applied in many thin coats and so is used for period-style pianos with their sometimes elaborate ornamentation. Polyester is more durable, but harder to repair when scratched or damaged because it has no known solvent. Lacquer has been the traditional preference for many years and is usually quite satisfactory.

Most finishes are either "satin," which reflects light but not images, or "high gloss" (also known as "polish"), which is mirror-like. Though all are applied in a similar fashion, finishes do differ in the number of steps involved (the number of sandings, the number of coats of lacquer) and, certainly, in the care with which the process is carried out.

A black finish is known as an "ebonized" finish, an imitation of ebony wood. Generally a lower-quality veneer is used for this finish since it won't be seen. The veneer is stained black and covered with a topcoat of lacquer or polyester containing a black pigment. Some manufacturers also make pianos with a white, off-white, or colored finish (I've even seen red and blue finishes!).

uniform, or to change the color of the wood entirely, or to make a cheaper wood look like a more expensive variety. For instance, we usually think of mahogany as being dark reddish brown, but much mahogany actually starts out a honey-colored brown. Through staining, a cheaper wood like gum can be made to look like mahogany. Filling closes or fills the pores of open-grained woods to make them smoother and less porous. It also adds color. Some woods are intentionally

Structural and Tuning Stability

Wooden structure. A piano has more than two hundred strings, and when they're all stretched to vibrate at their assigned pitches, they exert a combined pull of sixteen to twenty-three tons, depending on the size of the piano. To handle this kind of stress, the strings are stretched across a cast-iron frame called the **plate**. The plate, in turn, is usually bolted to a wooden framework. In a vertical piano, this wooden piano **back** generally consists of several vertical posts with connecting horizontal pieces (Figure 3-6); in a grand, the familiar curved **rim** and its connecting braces do the job (Figure 3-7).

GIMMICK: "Mr. Jones, this Smith Bros. Deluxe Console features six strong oak posts permanently attached with bolts that go all the way through the piano, while some lesser pianos have only five posts, and no bolts. This piano will stay in tune longer than others will."

TRUTH: Actually, there is no agreement among engineers on the amount of wooden framework needed in a piano, and anyway this amount undoubtedly varies from piano to piano depending on the design of the plate and the distribution of the string tension across it. Many foreign manufacturers make pianos with an extra-thick plate and sell them with only three posts, or sometimes with no posts, in their own countries, but market them here with five or six in order to satisfy customers who come into the store counting back posts. In many cases, close inspection will reveal that these posts are useless appendages tacked on for show. Some U.S. companies market their six-post pianos abroad with only three posts. Resulting changes in tuning stability have not been documented.

Almost certainly, pianos with regular, thin plates need some kind of wooden back assembly to keep the plates from warping. Just how much is not clear. But to whatever degree the posts *are* necessary, it's their total size, not their number, that's important. Witness that the five back posts of some verticals may have nearly twice the total cross-sectional area of the six posts on some other pianos. Pianos go out of tune primarily because the seasonal swelling and shrinking of the soundboard alters the tension on the strings, and this happens regardless of how strong the structure is. A stronger *total* structure (plate and wooden framework) will accept these seasonal changes more gracefully than a weaker one and therefore will go out of tune less chaotically, if no less often. But counting and measuring wooden posts will not tell you how strong the piano is or how well it will hold its tune; only examining the piano's performance and service record over time will.

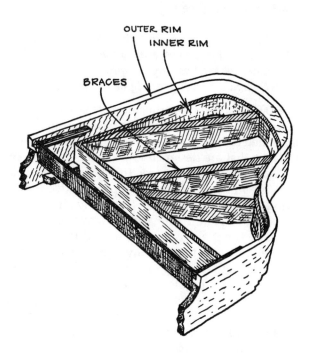

FIGURE 3-7. The rim of a grand piano is the wooden framework to which the cast-iron plate is bolted and the soundboard is glued. Notice that the rim is in two parts, an inner rim and an outer rim. The plate and soundboard are actually attached to the inner rim. On some of the best pianos, the inner and outer rim are made as one piece to provide a firmer foundation, both structurally and acoustically. On others, the outer rim is added later, and is mostly decorative.

As far as back post material is concerned, spruce is often considered the optimum wood because of its high strength-to-weight ratio and stiffness. But commenting on the five woods most often used—spruce, maple, oak, beech, and poplar—one factory technician said that for most companies the choice is a matter of appearance, cost, weight, availability, and what the competition is using. Strength is taken for granted.

In grand pianos, the wooden structure is thought to have an additional function—to reflect sound back into the soundboard for a more resonant, singing tone. As mentioned before, better pianos usually have denser woods in their rims. They may also have thicker, sturdier rims and substantial amounts of wooden bracing underneath the piano, connecting parts of the rim. As with the verticals, however, the amount of wooden bracing needed depends on the particular piano design and the strength of the plate. Some grands, especially small ones, may have wooden braces for only marketing, not engineering, reasons. Although additional research needs to be done in this area, it is speculated that a grand piano will sound better, and sound better longer, if its wooden structural parts fit together perfectly.

FIGURE 3-6. The vertical piano back is the wooden framework to which the cast-iron plate is bolted and the soundboard is glued. Left: Traditional back. Right: The "X" back is an attempt to cope with the complex torsional stresses present in a vertical piano.

Cast-Iron Plate.   (See Figure 3-8.)

GIMMICK: "Mr. Jones, this piano has a full-perimeter plate. Many other pianos employ the traditional harp-style plate, which has large empty spaces around its perimeter and couldn't possibly be as strong."

TRUTH: A true full-perimeter plate is massive, with a very thick ridge of iron all the way around it. As mentioned before, this extra-thick plate is used mostly in pianos that are designed to do without a supporting wooden back structure (though not all thick plates are full-perimeter). Many pianos advertised as having a full-perimeter plate have only an imitation. Independent plate manufacturers have assured me that there is not enough metal around the perimeter of these imitations to make any substantial difference in their strength (although it may possibly make some flimsy pianos slightly less so), and that any claims to the contrary are phony. The traditional harp-style plate employs metal where it's needed to counteract the pull of the strings, which is not necessarily around the perimeter of the piano.

Perhaps the more important difference among plates is not so much their strength as it is the accuracy of the casting and the drilling of the holes for the tuning pins and other hardware. These are critical because a piano is virtually built around its plate. Irregularities in the casting or drilling can cause structural and cabinet parts to fit improperly, tuning pins and strings to be unevenly spaced, and strings to bear irregularly against the plate and bridges, creating tonal problems. Sometimes these imperfections can be great enough to create a really defective piano. The better companies put more time and care into the preparation of the plate, sometimes doing it themselves in their own facilities, rather than having the plate manufacturers do it for them.

The plates for most U.S. pianos are made by The O.S. Kelly Co., an independent plate foundry in Springfield, Ohio. The traditional casting method involves pouring molten iron into a mold of moist green sand. This process, though fraught with difficulty, has been pretty well mastered over the last hundred years. If manufacturers properly maintain their plate patterns (which they often do not), this process usually produces plates that are very acceptable, though perhaps not perfectly consistent from one to the next. A new vacuum system of plate casting ("V-process") is now being used by some Japanese and Korean makers, producing smoother, more uniform plates with finer decorative detail. These plates may be slightly faster and less expensive to produce because they require less finishing work, but other than the finer decorative detail, they are functionally about equivalent

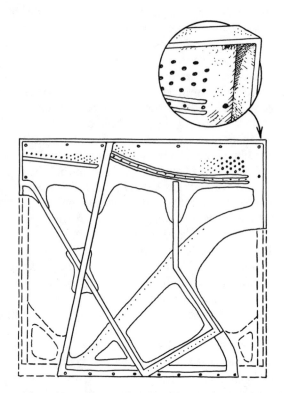

FIGURE 3-8. The cast-iron plate is the primary structural framework of the piano, withstanding the sixteen or more tons of tension exerted by the strings. The dotted lines show the additional metal pieces added around the perimeter of some vertical plates to imitate a "full-perimeter plate." The inset shows that a real full-perimeter plate (or any other plate intended for use in pianos with no wooden back posts), is very thick and massive. Compare this to the plate in Figure 3-9.

to well-made traditional castings. (Some say the two types of casting have different effects on the piano's tone, but the jury is still out on this.) In general, grand piano plates, being more visible, are given the royal treatment in sanding and finishing. Vertical piano plates are left in a rougher condition, except that "deluxe" models may have their upper halves finished smooth.

Pinblock and tuning pins.   Also part of the piano structure is the **pinblock** (Figure 3-9), sometimes called the **wrestplank**, a laminated hardwood plank running the width of the piano and attached to the plate, the wooden framework, or both. Embedded in holes in the pinblock are steel **tuning pins**, around each of which is coiled one end of a piano string. The pinblock has to hold the tuning pins tightly enough, by friction alone, so that all the strings are maintained at the right tension without unwinding. The piano is tuned by turning the tuning pins slightly with a "tuning hammer," thereby increasing or decreasing the tension on the strings, as needed, to make them sound in harmony with one another. Alternate layers of the pinblock run cross-grain to each other to prevent warping and cracking and to aid in even gripping of the fine threads on the tuning pins.

GIMMICK: "Mr. Jones, this Deluxe Console has a two-inch-thick, sixteen-ply pinblock, thicker and with more laminations than even some of the biggest-name pianos on the market. The tuning pins will never get loose, I guarantee."

TRUTH: There is no particular advantage to having a large number of pinblock laminations per se, so don't bother counting them. Pinblocks come in several varieties, which differ in the number of laminations they contain (from three to forty-one), the thickness of each layer, and their density. The denser pinblocks may perform better and last longer when subjected to extreme dryness and dampness, but all types are capable of good service under normal conditions. Pinblock failure resulting in loose tuning pins in poorly made pianos, when not due to abusive treatment, is caused by inferior wood that hasn't been seasoned long enough, or by inaccurate fitting of the pinblock to the plate (Figure 3-10), or by sloppy drilling of the holes for the tuning pins. In any case, this failure is unlikely to have anything to do with the number of laminations in the pinblock. Furthermore, the maximum penetration of a tuning pin in the wood is only about 1¼ inches, so some pinblocks are endowed with

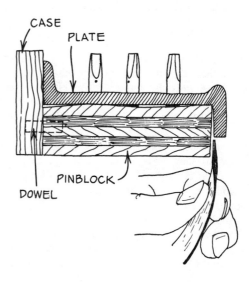

FIGURE 3-10. The pinblock must be perfectly fitted to the plate at the surfaces they share in common. Otherwise, when tension is applied to the strings, the pinblock may move (even though it's screwed to the plate), creating tremendous tuning and structural problems. One of the hidden differences between pianos of differing quality is in the care with which this fitting process is done. The fitting of the pinblock shown here is abysmal, both at the top and at the flange. (Sometimes technicians will test the fit at the flange by attempting to stuff a piece of paper between the pinblock and the plate. If they can, the fit is not good enough.) Makers of the finest pianos not only screw the pinblock to the plate, but dowel or mortise it into the case as well.

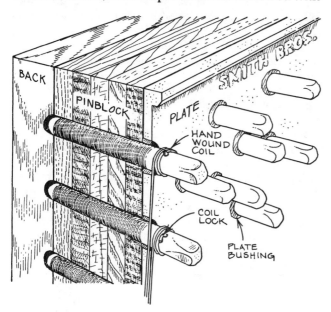

FIGURE 3-9. A laminated hardwood pinblock grips the tuning pins to keep the strings from slackening. On most pianos, a hardwood plate bushing surrounds each tuning pin where it passes through a hole in the plate. They are, however, not necessary, and not all pianos have them.

extra laminations only because they are thicker than they need to be to hold the tuning pins. In some cases the extra thickness may help make the structure a little more stable, but it's not the number of laminations per se that accomplishes this.

GIMMICK: "Unlike some other piano brands, all Smith Bros. vertical pianos have a strip of wood covering the top of the piano back structure, acting as a protective moisture barrier to assure the long life of the pinblock. Other pianos are exposed to the elements."

TRUTH: "Moisture barrier," my foot! It should be called a "sight barrier," as its real purpose is to keep you from seeing the rough workmanship underneath.

GIMMICK: "All Smith Bros. Deluxe pianos have tuning pins that are nickel-plated to resist rust, rather than blued."

TRUTH: All tuning pins undergo a "bluing" process—a controlled oxidation that makes them hold better in the wood. In addition, some tuning pins are nickel-plated. But most technicians I have spoken with feel that plated pins rust just about as fast as nonplated ones. The plating is just for show.

Pinblock Quality

The issue of quality is probably more critical with respect to the pinblock than it is with respect to any other single part of the piano. Repair or replacement of the pinblock is so expensive that, for vertical pianos and many cheap grands, when the pinblock is shot the piano is dead. A defective pinblock might compare with, say, a badly cracked engine block in a car. We're not talking about just a tune-up job here—we're talking about junking the instrument and buying a new one. As incredible as it may seem, many of the cheapest new pianos made in recent years have started out with pinblocks already on their last legs.

Most pinblocks fall into one of three categories (Figure 3-11). The type traditionally used in North American pianos consists of five or six laminations of hard rock maple, each layer about ¼-inch thick. Provided that the wood is of good quality, dried properly, and so forth, this material is entirely satisfactory under most normal conditions. Steinway has always used this kind of pinblock, as have many other makers.

A second type of pinblock material, known as a "multi-laminated," is made of about nineteen to forty-one highly compressed veneers of beech or maple. This extremely dense, hard material is used in most Baldwin pianos, as well as in many expensive European and other foreign pianos, often under the brand name Delignit. Critics of this material point out that veneers, being rotary-cut (peeled off a log like paper towels off a roll), don't have the best grain orientation for supporting the tuning pins, and that there is almost as much glue as there is wood in this type of pinblock, making it more subject to wearing away. So far, however, experience has not proven out these fears. Most technicians find this material to be so dense and stable that, provided it's installed properly, it's likely to perform well in almost any place or climate, from the dryness of the Sahara Desert to a ship on an ocean voyage. If you anticipate an unavoidably hostile climate for your piano, this is the kind of pinblock to get (but see Chapter 8 for information on climate-control systems for pianos.)

The third kind of material is also "multi-laminated" (sort of), with from nine to sixteen ⅛-inch plies, but is less dense than the second type. My sense is that this third type of pinblock material is used by those manufacturers who want to jump on the multi-laminate bandwagon, to satisfy customers who come into the store counting pinblock laminations, without actually using the denser material. As with the other types, the success of this one depends on the quality of wood used and the accuracy in drilling the tuning pin holes. (Besides probably costing more, the high-density material requires a level of accuracy in drilling that some companies may be unable or unwilling to meet.)

Drilling the tuning pin holes accurately is the most critical part of making a good pinblock. The tuning pins must be uniform in their angle and position in the holes and uniform in tightness, with a torque (resistance to turning) high enough to allow for some loosening with age, but not so high as to prevent fine tuning. One look at some of the cheaper vertical pianos made in recent years will reveal the sloppiness with which the holes were drilled—tuning pins at slight angles to each other and off center in their holes. And tuners can tell you how much the tightness of these pins varies—usually from too tight to too loose. Many of the pianos will be untunable before the warranty runs out. Their owners, if they have their pianos tuned at all, will probably blame the tuning problems on their tuners.

What accounts for the differences in pinblock quality from manufacturer to manufacturer? The more conscientious makers have used pinblock material that is more uniform in quality and density and a drilling apparatus that controls for angle, speed of rotation, and the speed with which the drill enters and leaves the wood, producing very uniform holes. In contrast, the sloppier makers have lacked many of these controls, counting on the fact that most people who buy their pianos will neglect them anyway or not notice the difference.

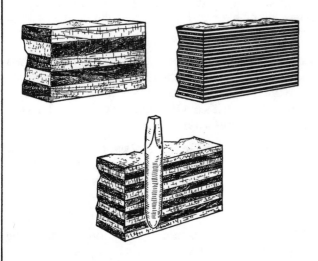

FIGURE 3-11. Three types of pinblock material: traditional five-ply, very dense multi-laminated, and a type in between.

GIMMICK: "Mr. Jones, let me demonstrate to you the superiority of the Japanese tuning pins that Smith Bros. uses in all their pianos. As you can see, when this tuning pin is twisted inside a hankerchief, it snags when turned counterclockwise, but moves smoothly when turned clockwise. This is because the process by which the threads are cut leaves microscopic teeth angled so that the pin can be easily turned in a direction of higher pitch, but encounters resistance when turned in a direction of lower pitch. This helps keep the piano in tune."

TRUTH: This is absurd. For one thing, it assumes that pianos go out of tune because the tuning pins turn. In fact, as I said before, pianos go out of tune mostly because the seasonal swelling and shrinking of the soundboard alters the tension on the strings. If a piano goes out of tune because the tuning pins turn by themselves, then the tuning pins are loose and the piano is defective. Second, this sales ploy implies that tuners only turn the tuning pins in the direction of higher pitch when tuning the piano. In fact, we turn the pins just as often in one direction as the other. (What Smith Bros. doesn't tell us is why the teeth don't grind out the holes and ruin the pinblock.) This is a good example of how marketing will take a simple, neutral fact concerning the manufacturing process and turn it into an "advantage."

Scale Design and Strings

Scale design. The musical design of a piano (as opposed to its cabinetry) is known as its *scale design*. In its everyday usage, this term usually refers just to the stringing scale—that is, the dimensions of the strings (length, thickness, tension) and their arrangement across the plate; but in formal usage, it also includes such factors as the point on the strings contacted by the hammers and dampers, the placement of the bridges, and the construction of the soundboard, to name a few. The scale design is like the "genetic code" of a piano. It is the principal determinant of piano tone, and it differs from one piano brand and model to another.

Since there is a practical limit to the height of a vertical piano or the length of a grand we can fit in our homes, strings are made thicker, instead of just longer, to create lower-sounding notes (Figure 3-12). The smaller the piano, the more thickness must be substituted for length in producing sounds of lower pitch. When the steel strings would otherwise become too thick and stiff to produce a good tone, they are wound with copper to give the requisite mass without sacrificing flexibility too much. These *wound* strings are principally used in the bass section, but they may also

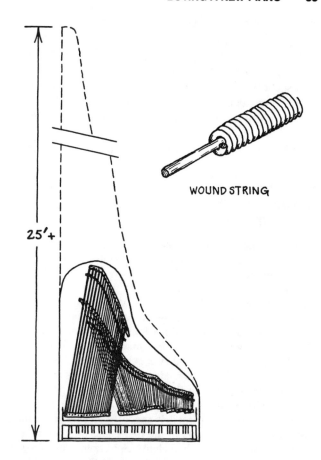

FIGURE 3-12. Foreshortening of the scale. If all piano strings were of the same thickness and tension, the piano would have to be more than twenty-five feet long to play all eighty-eight notes (the required string length doubles with each octave). Since this is impractical, the strings are made thicker as well as longer, and the tension varied as needed, to produce the lower notes. Where the steel strings would be too thick to vibrate well, the required mass is attained without reducing flexibility by instead winding copper onto thinner steel. These *wound strings* are used mostly in the bass section. The bass strings are also *overstrung* or *cross-strung* above the treble strings to achieve maximum length and optimum tonal quality in a case of a given size. The particular combination of all these factors varies from model to model and is known as the *stringing scale*, an important part of the *scale design*.

be used judiciously in the area of the treble section just above the bass (often called the *tenor* section), especially in small pianos, where plain strings would otherwise have a poor tone.

This method of using thicker strings instead of longer strings to produce lower-pitched notes has its limitations. The smaller the piano, the harder it becomes to get a good tone out of the strings in the tenor and lower bass sections, regardless of the use of copper windings. All piano strings give off slightly distorted harmonics, a property known as *inharmonicity*, which contributes to the characteristic sound of the piano. But the relatively short, thick tenor and bass strings of small pianos have an excessive amount of inharmonicity, producing a nasal or hollow sound and making it impossible to tune the piano so that the various sections blend together in harmony. The tuners of these instruments must harden their sensibilities much as one might grimace when taking an unpleasant medicine. For this reason, other factors being equal, you should always buy the largest piano that you can afford and have space for.

Buying Tip: Check for Inadequacies in Stringing Scale

1. On small pianos, it's common to find wound strings in the tenor section, but you should avoid pianos in which the wound strings extend farther up the scale than the note E_{32} (the E below middle C). This somewhat arbitrary limit is based on the fact that most tuners use a tuning procedure that begins on the note F_{33}; the procedure is complicated by the presence of wound strings from that point upward in the scale. More important, only a piano that is just plain too small would require wound strings higher than E_{32}.

2. Virtually all pianos made today have three strings per note throughout most of the treble, two strings per note in the upper bass, and one per note in the lower bass (see page 7). A few cheap models made in recent years have only two strings per note in the treble and one per note in the bass, and far fewer than eighty-eight notes total. Even if you are looking for a small piano, avoid the temptation to buy one of these. They are so poorly made in every respect that they would best be classified as junk.

GIMMICK: "Mr. Jones, all Smith Bros. consoles are a full 42 inches tall. Most other consoles are only 40 or 41 inches."

TRUTH: No single factor is more important to the scale design and tone of a piano than its size (meaning the height of a vertical piano or the length of a grand). But don't be fooled by the difference of an inch or two in height or length. For example, 40-, 41-, and 42-inch pianos may all have only a 40-inch scale design. In a vertical, the difference in height can easily be created by an extra-thick lid, larger casters, or a redesigned cabinet—in a grand, by a slightly longer case—and may not contribute one iota to the tone quality.

GIMMICK: "Because the Smith Bros. console is taller, its longest bass string is a full two inches longer than that of its nearest competitor. This means that the tone will be superior."

TRUTH: Because string length is so important and this idea is easily communicated to consumers, some manufacturers make a very big deal about the length of

their longest strings. Usually they advertise the length of the string for A_1, the lowest note on the piano.

But scale design is too complex to characterize an entire piano by the length of one string. Under certain circumstances, a slightly shorter speaking length with a different combination of thickness and tension or a longer tail length might produce a better tone, and some pianos may be scaled well in one section and not in another. The maxim that longer strings make for a better tone, while essentially correct, is most useful when comparing pianos whose scale designs are substantially different in size—at least three to six inches—not for making nitpicking comparisons between similarly sized pianos.

Furthermore, there are trade-offs in scale designing; an insistence on the longest strings possible may create problems elsewhere in the piano. For instance, you'll notice that bass strings are always positioned above and diagonally across the treble strings, partly to achieve greater string length in a given size case. The bass hammers are mounted on their shanks to match, as closely as possible, the angle of the bass strings. But the maximum angle at which the hammers can be mounted is very limited, and when the bass strings are at too great an angle to the treble strings, it's impossible to align the hammers to match. Bass hammers in such pianos, mounted at the maximum possible angle, have a tendency to collide with each other during playing or to graze adjacent strings, causing discordant sounds. Therefore, excellence in scale design cannot be communicated through marketing gimmickry because such excellence depends on the masterful coordination of all tone-related factors, rather than on the single-minded pursuit of any particular factor.

Figure 3-13 shows some of the more common physical and service-related problems caused by sloppy workmanship and poor scale design in many pianos made during the past two decades.

GIMMICK: "The scales of Smith Bros. pianos were all designed by the famous scale designer Frederick Klein with the help of the Tasmania State University computer. They are the best scales possible."

TRUTH: With the advent of the computer age, some piano makers are now claiming that their scales are designed by computer. Since scales derived from formula always need to be corrected, to some extent, by trial and error, computers can be an aid, but by no means do they assure success. Some companies also boast that their scales were designed by some famous scale designer earlier in the century. Pay no attention to this—it means nothing to you. Even if the original design was brilliant, the scale now in use is the product of many changes over the years—possibly for the worse.

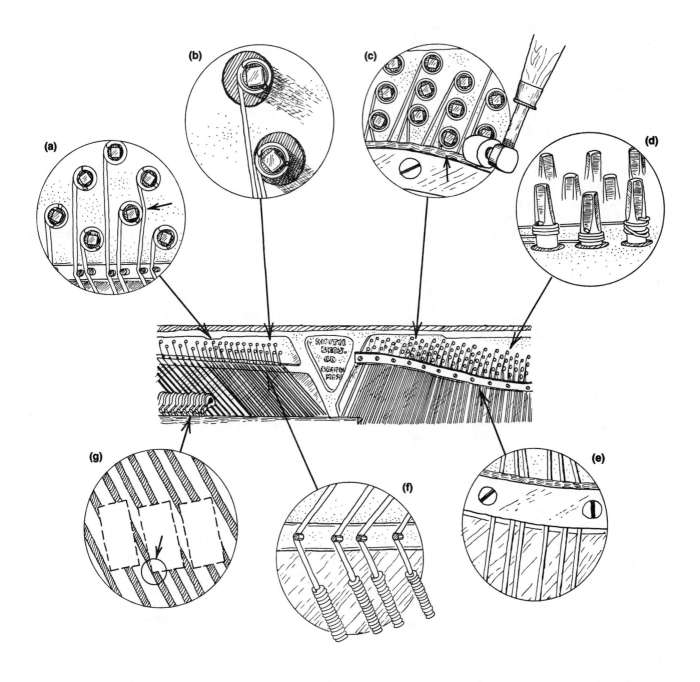

FIGURE 3-13. Some examples of sloppy workmanship and poor scale design. Only a few of these are found in pianos being made today, but most are common in cheaper pianos made from about 1960 to the early 1980s. Clockwise from top left: (a) strings bend around neighboring tuning pins, causing tuning problems; (b) tuning pin holes drilled off-center; (c) tuning pins too closely spaced or placed too close to the pressure bar so the tuning hammer won't fit over them; (d) sloppy string coils around tuning pins, or coils at uneven heights above plate, the latter indicating possible pinblock problems; (e) treble strings poorly spaced or shifting position, resulting in uneven wear to hammers and dampers; (f) bass strings haphazardly spaced and strung at too great an angle around the upper bearing point (the latter may result in premature breakage); (g) bass hammers at an angle to bass strings such that the hammers strike the strings of neighboring notes, producing discordant sounds.

Buying Tip: Check for Discordant Sounds

As mentioned above and shown in Figure 3-13g, the scale design of some pianos is such that the bass hammers tend to graze strings belonging to neighboring notes. If the dampers are sitting on those neighboring strings, you may not hear them. But if you are using the sustain pedal (the right-hand pedal)—which lifts all the dampers to allow the tone to sustain—this misalignment of hammers and strings will show up as an ugly dissonance. If this problem is inherent in the design of the piano, there is literally nothing you can do about it (except chop off part of the offending hammers). The smaller the piano, the more likely this problem will occur, although it happens even on some otherwise well-designed studio pianos.

When inspecting a piano you're thinking of buying, you can check aurally for this problem; a visual check alone may be misleading. First, look inside the piano to see on what note the overstrung section (angled bass strings) begins (on a vertical piano, have the salesperson remove the upper panel for you). On small and medium-size pianos the overstrung section usually begins about an octave or less below middle C. With the right-hand pedal depressed, play the note loudly and listen carefully. You will hear a general sympathetic reverberation of all the strings, but this is not what you're listening for. Listen for a dissonance—a sound as if you had also played the next lower note at the same time. (If you're unsure of what that would sound like, try actually playing both notes at the same time.) Next, release the pedal to stop the sound. Now, press the pedal again and play the next lower note loudly, listening again for the dissonance of two neighboring notes sounding simultaneously. Continue in this manner down the keyboard through most of the bass section. Where the hammers begin striking only one string per note (the lowest portion of the bass section), you can stop, as the problem won't exist there. If you have found only one or two dissonance problems, you can inquire as to whether they might be corrected by adjusting the spacing of the hammers. If you have found many such problems, think twice about buying that model.

GIMMICK: *"The Smith Bros. grand contains a duplex scale for added tonal color, just like the world's best pianos."*

TRUTH: Usually the back end of each string, between the bridge and the hitch pin, and the front end, near the tuning pin, are muted with cloth so they don't vibrate sympathetically. On some grands and a few verticals, though, the back end of the string is further subdivided with a small metal bar or plate called an **aliquot**, and the section of string between the aliquot and the bridge is allowed to vibrate sympathetically at some higher frequency (Figure 3-14). The

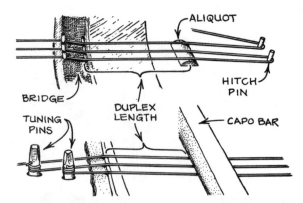

FIGURE 3-14. Duplex scale. The length of string between the bridge and the aliquot, and the length near the tuning pin, instead of being muted with cloth, vibrate sympathetically and add color to the tone.

waste end of the string near the tuning pin may also be left unmuted for the same purpose. This *duplex scale* can add tonal color, brilliance, and sustain to the treble, and is usually an advantage. Sometimes, however, a duplex scale adds objectionable overtones and buzzes to the sound, or makes no difference at all. Because it's so visible, duplex scaling is frequently used as a selling feature, regardless of whether it actually improves the sound of the piano. Interestingly, although the portion of the duplex scale at the back end of the string is the most featured and celebrated, the portion near the tuning pin is often the most effective, or the most troublesome, as the case may be.

Strings.

GIMMICK: *"Our regular console has copper-plated bass strings, but the Deluxe console uses pure, solid copper for better tone."*

TRUTH: Bass strings are made with steel wire weighted down with a winding of solid copper to slow their vibration without impairing their flexibility. Really, they could be wound with any material that produced the required mass—iron windings were used in the old days—but copper has been found to produce a nice tone, and it doesn't rust like iron. Some of the very cheapest pianos use iron that has been plated with copper. Their tone tends to be poorer, at least in part because the plating is uneven and so the vibration is faulty. Pieces of plating may also chip off over time. Though copper-plated bass strings decrease manufacturing cost slightly, they are used mainly so the salesperson can point out the advantages of buying the fancier and more expensive model piano with the solid-copper strings. (Note: On some pianos, a few of the thinnest bass strings may be copper-plated for legitimate technical reasons.)

Buying Tip: Check for Rattling Bass Strings and Buzzing Treble Strings

Play each bass note loudly and listen for a rattling or buzzing sound indicating a faulty bass string. This is a very common defect and dealers are accustomed to correcting it—you need only point it out to them. Also check for any buzzing treble strings, often caused by manufacturing debris lodged against a string at the bridge, or by poor contact between the string and its bearing points.

GIMMICK: "The string coils around Smith Bros. tuning pins contain a patented coil lock that prevents the coils from ever slipping off the tuning pins."

TRUTH: A coil properly made by a piano technician will never in a hundred years slip off a tuning pin. Some factories, however, have automated their stringing process, the strings being wound around the tuning pins by machine in one department and much later installed in the piano by hand in another department. If not for the coil lock—which is just a bent piece of the wire (see Figure 3-9)—the string might indeed slip out of its hole in the tuning pin while waiting to be installed, making the installer's job more difficult. Many companies still perform the entire stringing process by hand in one operation, in which case the coil lock is not needed. The presence of the coil lock makes tuning pin and string repairs more difficult for the service technician.

Buying Tip: Check String Spacing

Strings should be perfectly and uniformly spaced in relation to each other, as in Figure 3-15. Poorly made pianos will frequently have strings spaced incorrectly (see Figure 3-13e). The spacing can be temporarily corrected by a technician, but the strings may gradually creep back as they are played. Defective design or construction can actually make correct alignment of the tuning pin, plate, string, and bridge impossible. Over time, the hammers hitting incorrectly spaced strings will wear unevenly, the dampers won't be able to seat properly to stop the sound, and, in extreme cases, tuning may be more difficult. Badly spaced strings are one of the most obvious signs of a badly constructed instrument.

One way the string spacing problem is solved on some pianos is with the use of small brass fittings called *agraffes* (pronounced *AY-grafs*), which are screwed into the plate. The agraffes have holes through which the strings pass, keeping them perfectly spaced regardless of whatever forces may be inducing them to shift. Generally considered an indication of good quality, agraffes seem to be most useful in the tenor and bass sections of the piano, where the string spacing is especially critical for the operation of the dampers. Some pianos have "full agraffes"—eighty-eight of them—but this is not necessarily good, even though it looks pretty. Some technicians feel that agraffes above the middle treble tend to diminish the tonal palette to a rather "woody," thin sound, and they consider full agraffes to be a disadvantage tonally in many pianos.

Also check that the coils around the tuning pins are neat and reasonably uniform in their distance from the plate.

When a piano is new, the tuning pins are installed so that the coils are ³⁄₁₆ inch (give or take a little) from the plate. This allows some room for tapping the tuning pins further into the pinblock if they should get loose with age. If the coils are uneven in height, or if many are already down against the plate, this may indicate that the tuning pins have already gotten loose and the pinblock may be faulty (see Figure 3-13d).

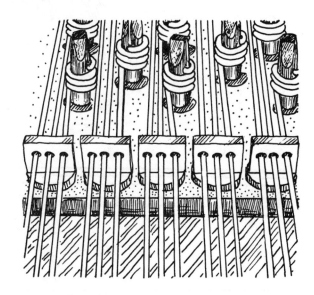

FIGURE 3-15. Agraffes keep strings perfectly spaced and provide a good upper bearing point for the speaking length (vibrating portion of the string).

Bridges and Soundboard

Bridges. The strings pass over wooden **bridges**—a long, curved one for the treble and a shorter one for the bass strings—which transmit the vibrations of the strings to the soundboard. The transmission of energy is aided by the slight *downbearing* of the strings against the bridge and by the *sidebearing* of the strings against pairs of staggered metal **bridge pins** driven into the bridge. The bridge pins also delineate the end of the vibrating part of the string, just as a violinist's or guitarist's fingers "stop" a string by pressing it against the finger board or frets. So the strings don't touch the bridge before contacting the bridge pins, the bridge is *notched*—cut away—at its edges (Figure 3-16).

Bridges must be well constructed, both to transmit vibration properly and to avoid splitting under the pressure of the strings. Most bridges are made of maple or beech, either solid or vertically laminated, sometimes with a top layer or **cap**. Some are horizontally laminated (Figure 3-17). This last type is easiest to manufacture and often used on cheaper pianos. Because these pianos at times don't sound very good, it

has long been thought that this type of bridge construction was faulty due to the horizontal grain orientation and glue lines. Some experts now believe that this type of construction can be as satisfactory as the others if good materials and design are utilized.

The accuracy of bridge notching is extremely important (see Figure 3-16). Inaccurate notching can result in "wild strings" (which produce permanently out-of-tune sounds known as *false beats*), buzzing sounds, and tinny tone. The traditional method of notching—still used on many of the finest brands of piano—is by hand; that is, by a woodworker with a chisel, working by eye. Other methods include using hand-held routing machines guided by a metal template or a beam of light, and using computer-controlled routing machines. Any of these methods, either by hand or by machine, can produce good or poor work depending on the standards set by company management. For instance, at one factory I visited I observed that a metal template set up to guide a router was moving every time the router hit it. This particular "machine" produced an inaccurate cut.

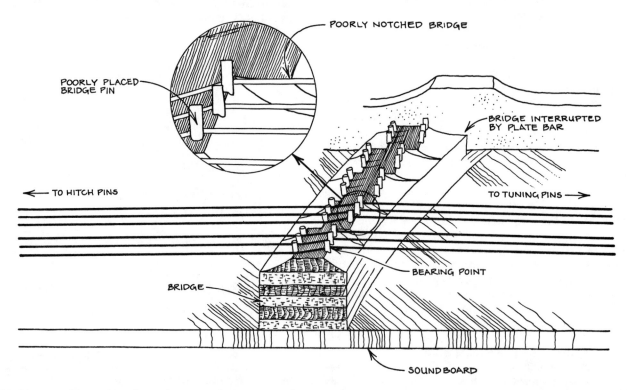

FIGURE 3-16. The point where the string first contacts the bridge is one of the string's bearing points (the ends of its speaking length). To avoid poor tone and wild strings, each string must contact the wooden bridge at the exact same point it contacts its bridge pin. That is, the beginning of the notch in the bridge must bisect the row of bridge pins. The inset in the drawing shows a poorly spaced bridge pin. The string that contacts it will be "confused" as to whether its bearing point is the edge of the notch or the pin, resulting in a "confused" sound. The inset also shows a notch that is not wide enough; the string may touch the side of the notch and cause a buzz. The main drawing shows a bridge interrupted by a part of the cast-iron plate. Often the tone of the notes immediately on either side of this interruption will be deficient. Better pianos avoid this kind of arrangement.

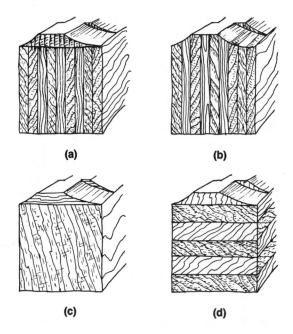

FIGURE 3-17. Four types of bridge construction commonly used: (a) vertical laminations with cap, used by Steinway; (b) vertical laminations without cap, used by Baldwin; (c) solid bridge with cap, used by many makers; (d) horizontal laminations, sometimes used on cheaper pianos.

Traditionally, both the front and rear of the bridge are notched, even though the rear ends of the strings are usually muted with cloth. In theory, this is so the strings will contact only a minimal area of the bridge, allowing the bridge to vibrate more freely. On some of the cheaper verticals, to save money, only the front of the bridge is notched. The result of this shortcut may be a greater chance of problems with buzzing strings, hardly worth the miniscule savings realized on each piano. In any case, you can take the lack of rear notching as a signal that corners are being cut slightly on that model. (At one time there were also cheap pianos whose bridges were unnotched throughout, front *and* rear. The tone was so bad that they were virtually untunable.)

Soundboard. The bridges are glued to the **soundboard**, which changes the strings' vibrating energy into sound waves that we can hear. The soundboard has a slight curvature, or *crown*, built into it to help it resist the downpressure of the strings on the bridges; also, wood under tension transmits sound better. As mentioned before, the downbearing of the strings against the bridges is necessary for good transmission of tone, but the sum total of all this downbearing can be as much as a thousand pounds, and without the upward crown of the soundboard, the strings would simply push the bridges away until contact was negligible.

Soundboards are traditionally made of a solid sheet of quarter-sawn spruce, ¼- to ⅜-inch thick, made by gluing narrower boards together edge to edge. Spruce is used because it has a fine, straight grain, is strong and resilient, and reproduces the sound of the strings better than any other material. It is also used in violins and other fine stringed instruments. The best-quality spruce has from eight to twenty annular rings (growth lines) per inch (the more the better), a very uniform grain, and is quite light in color. Coarser and darker spruce is sometimes used in cheaper pianos, but not as successfully. However, top-quality spruce is getting more scarce and expensive all the time.

Over the past few decades, an increasing number of pianos have been made with laminated soundboards consisting of three layers of spruce or other woods, or spruce combined with other woods. Usually a thick layer in the middle is surrounded by two layers of veneer (Figure 3-18). Sometimes the three layers are of equal thickness. The advantage of a laminated soundboard is that it is virtually immune to cracking and loss of crown. Most laminated soundboards are in fact warranted against these problems for from fifty to eighty years!

FIGURE 3-18. Top: Solid spruce soundboard. Bottom: Laminated soundboard. Right: It is usually difficult to tell whether the soundboard is solid or laminated by looking at the front or back since the outer veneers may be chosen to resemble a solid spruce board. If the wood is clearly not spruce or the grain runs horizontally, you can be sure the soundboard is laminated, because all non-spruce boards are laminated and all solid spruce boards are installed with the grain running diagonally for best tone. If there is a hole in the soundboard through which a plate bolt passes to a vertical back post or grand rim brace, careful inspection of the exposed edge may reveal the soundboard's true nature. But sometimes the veneers are too thin to be seen or the exposed edges are actually doctored to deceive the customer. Note: Turn the drawing on the right clockwise 90 degrees to picture a grand piano's soundboard.

GIMMICK: "Many of our Smith Bros. pianos contain laminated soundboards, guaranteed not to crack or lose their crown for sixty years."

TRUTH: Solid spruce soundboards are highly affected by changes in humidity, and if special care isn't taken in their manufacture and installation, or if they are subjected to extreme conditions, they can quickly develop cracks or lose their crown. Even the best solid spruce soundboards under normal conditions may develop cracks after a few decades in certain climates. Laminated boards, on the other hand, are virtually immune to these problems because the outer layers run cross-grain to the inner layer. Manufacturers can take less care with these boards and still guarantee them almost indefinitely.

The problem with most laminated soundboards made during the last thirty years is that either they were installed in horrible promotional pianos or they were simply substituted for solid spruce soundboards without any regard for the special design requirements of laminated boards (such as for ribbing and downbearing) due to their different stiffness and weight characteristics. It comes as no surprise, then, that most pianos with laminated soundboards have been judged to have a poor tone. The tone has often been described as being "muddy," "thumpy," or weak in the bass and tenor, and uniformly bright in the treble in a way that initially sounds interesting but eventually wears poorly on the ears. Sometimes the sound dies away too quickly, too, particularly in the middle area of the keyboard. The worst ones have been made of basswood or mahogany, not spruce. Makers of these pianos have been concerned only with keeping down cost, or inducing you to buy their next more expensive model with a better soundboard. Proponents of laminated soundboards have also claimed that pianos containing them go out of tune less from season to season because plywood is resistant to humidity-induced warping. This may potentially be true, but my experience has usually been exactly the opposite, possibly because these soundboards have been installed in pianos that were structurally inferior.

During the last few years, though, laminated soundboards have greatly improved in both tone and stability as they have graduated from the "lower class" to the "middle class" of pianos. As market acceptance increases, so will research into the best ways of designing this type of soundboard. Even if laminated soundboards never replace solid ones in the highest quality pianos, we can still expect to see them more often in the years ahead in pianos of average and good quality.

My advice, however, is to pay attention only to how the piano sounds and not to buy a piano just because of claims that its laminated soundboard won't crack. These claims, though true, are only capitalizing on the great fear of the Cracked Soundboard. Contrary to popular myth, a cracked soundboard does not mean the death of the piano. It's true that cracks indicate that drying has occurred, with a possible loss of some crown and attendant tonal changes. But, in practice, most cracking does not seem to adversely affect the tone unless the cracking is extensive (and sometimes not even then), and many wonderful-sounding pianos have cracked soundboards. Anyway, if you buy a good piano and don't subject it to abusive conditions, it will be a long time before cracks appear. Laminated soundboards were invented as a way to cut costs in the manufacturing process and reduce warranty problems, and their sixty-year warranties are a way to promote them. If a piano with a laminated soundboard sounds good, fine; in the long run this soundboard may have some slight benefits. Otherwise avoid it.

GIMMICK: "All Smith Bros. pianos have full-length ribs to better support the crown of the soundboard."

TRUTH: The **ribs** on the back of a soundboard help to maintain its crown (curvature), transmit vibration across the grain of the soundboard, and generally "tie" the soundboard together. On most pianos, the ribs extend all the way to the edge of the soundboard and fit into notches cut into the liner to which the soundboard is glued (Figure 3-19). These ribs are said to be "let in" or "full length." This construction practice was developed for the purely practical reason that the animal hide glues used during the first few decades of piano development were not always very reliable, and the ribs sometimes came loose if not tightly fit into these notches. In some of today's factories this practice may still be advisable, but if modern glues are used and the gluing process carefully monitored, it is no longer necessary. No test evidence I am aware of indicates that having the ribs set into notches helps to maintain crown. This practice seems to continue primarily for reasons of marketing and tradition. One way some companies save money is by cutting off the ribs just short of the liner. Usually this is an indication that the piano is cheaply made, but it's entirely possible that this type of construction could be called for as part of a well-thought-out scale design.

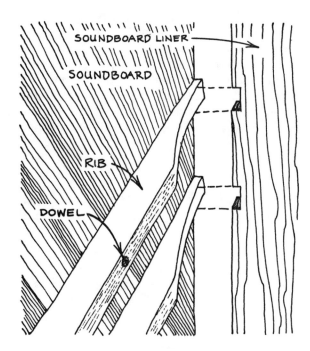

SOUNDBOARD LINER

SOUNDBOARD

RIB

DOWEL

FIGURE 3-19. In a vertical piano, the soundboard is glued to a "liner," a simple frame attached to the wooden back. In a grand, the soundboard is glued directly to the inner rim, under the plate. In most pianos, the ribs extend all the way to the edge of the soundboard and are recessed into notches cut in the rim or liner. In some pianos, the ribs are cut short, usually to avoid the expense of cutting the notches, but possibly for other reasons. Also shown: On some of the finest pianos, the bridges are doweled to the soundboard—for extra holding power—in addition to being glued, and the dowels extend through to the ribs. Note: To picture a grand, turn this drawing clockwise 90 degrees and substitute "inner rim" for "soundboard liner."

Buying Tip: Check for Crown

As already mentioned, a soundboard must have crown to ensure good tone. Some pianos—even some expensive, top-quality pianos—are reportedly coming out of the factory with no measurable crown, or with so little crown that it disappears entirely when the soundboard shrinks during the dry season. In theory, a piano with no measurable crown shouldn't sound good—at least not for very long. But in reality, plenty of fine pianos, both old and new, have no crown and sound great. Small, cheap pianos have so many other tonal limitations that I'm not sure you should fuss too much about soundboard crown. But if you are buying a top-quality instrument, you owe it to yourself to check for crown (or have your technician check for it), and to at least place a question mark next to any new piano with no measurable crown. See page 134 to learn how to check for crown.

Buying Tip: Look for a Strike-Point Adjuster

To a very large extent, the tone of each note is determined by the exact point along the length of the string at which the hammer strikes. The *strike point* is especially critical in the high treble section, where a variation of barely ¹⁄₁₆ inch can make the difference between a dull thud and a clear, ringing tone. The strike point is set in the factory, but sometimes needs to be changed later by a technician when servicing the hammers or when the factory setting appears to be wrong. For this reason most grand pianos have a "strike-point adjuster" mechanism, which can reposition the whole action relative to the strings. The mechanism is located inside of or near the treble keyblock (see Figure 1-15 for the location of the keyblocks). Some less expensive grands—the ones most likely to need this feature—don't have it. A grand piano is a long-term investment, and at some point in the life of your piano you are likely to need this adjustment. Verticals don't have a strike-point adjuster per se, but adjustment can usually be made by other means, and often needs to be. Some verticals, however, are mounted so as to make strike-point adjustment virtually impossible. A technician may be able to identify these models for you.

Listening to Tone

This is certainly no place to pay any attention to the promotional literature, as all the manufacturers will tell you how marvelous their piano's tone is. The only way to judge is to listen, take a lot of time, and make numerous comparisons between instruments. Compare pianos of the same brand and model and pianos of different models. (Nothing beats having two pianos sitting right next to each other for comparison.) Frankly, though, when shopping among today's pianos, especially consoles, it's easy to get lost in a sea of mediocrity and forget just what a good piano sounds like. When you do, the cure is always to go back and play some of the finest pianos money can buy—even if you have no intention of buying one—just to refresh your memory of what a great piano sounds like so you can place other pianos in comparison. (Warning: This advice may be hazardous to your bank account.)

As your ear tries to make comparisons, however, two obstacles will stand in the way: (1) In order for you to judge its tone, a piano must be in very good tune. As I will explain later in this chapter, it may be hard to find many pianos that are in tune on the showroom floor. There's not much I can do to help you about this. (2) If you are inexperienced with pianos, you may not know just what to listen for. Writing about how to listen to tone is something like writing about how to look at art—only worse. Nevertheless, here's some information that may help.

What we call *tone* consists of several components (Figure 3-20): *volume* of sound—how loud or soft it is;

harmonic content, which manifests itself as "bright," "mellow," "nasal," and so on; *attack*—the initial sound of the hammer striking the string, lasting only milliseconds; and *sustain time* or *decay*—how long the tone sustains when you hold a key down, and how it fades away. These should be fairly uniform from note to note and from one section of the piano to another, and different sections should blend in pleasing harmony with each other when played together. To accomplish this requires very careful design and coordination of scale design, strings, soundboard, bridges, and hammers.

When smaller pianos were first introduced, they suffered from the problem that their smaller soundboards produced a smaller sound. To compensate for this, their scales were redesigned to stretch their strings at a higher tension, which produced a louder, brighter tone. But this also made the strings stiffer and reduced the quality of tone even while increasing the

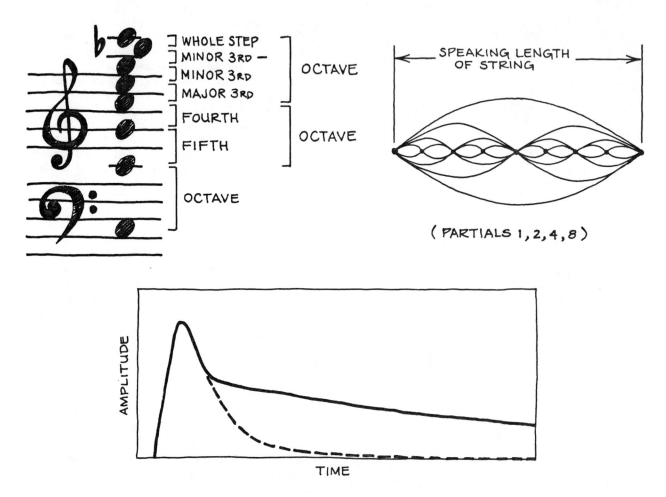

FIGURE 3-20. Two major components of tone. Right: Harmonic content. When a string vibrates, it subdivides into many smaller vibrating segments that simultaneously give off fainter, higher pitched tones called *partials* or *overtones*. These partials bear a definite harmonic relationship to one another called the *harmonic series*. Left: The first eight tones of the harmonic series for low C are shown here in their approximate relationship on the musical staff. The note actually played (in this case, low C) is called the *fundamental*, or first partial. Theoretically, there are an infinite number of partials. We can actually hear dozens of them, usually without knowing it. The relative strength of each of these partials and the degree to which they deviate from their theoretical frequency (this deviation is known as *inharmonicity*) make up what we interpret as *tonal quali-* ty. For example, a tone said to be "bright" contains many loud higher partials; a "mellow" tone has fewer high partials. Bottom: Attack and decay. When we play a note on the piano, we first hear an initial burst of sound, called the *attack*, lasting milliseconds, followed by a rapid but incomplete *decay* lasting a fraction of a second, followed by a slower, more lingering decay, until the sound dies out completely. When the slow portion of the decay is relatively loud and long-lasting (as in the drawing), the tone could be said to be "singing." When the sound dies out quickly (shown by the dotted line), the tone might be called "dead" or "short." This is actually a gross simplification, as each individual partial has its own attack and decay rate. The possible varieties of tone are therefore virtually infinite.

Buying Tip: Put the Lid Down

Some dealers make a point of displaying all their grand pianos in cavernous rooms with hardwood floors, and with the lids up, because they know that in such a "live" acoustical environment *any* piano will sound "grand." A buyer of one of these pianos may be in for a rude awakening when the instrument is delivered to his or her home. You may not be able to change the dealer's showroom acoustics, but you can at least put the lid down, which will probably more closely simulate the way the piano will be played in your home.

volume. It's tempting for beginners to confuse loudness and brightness of tone with quality. Therefore, many of these pianos have done quite well in the marketplace even though they sound horrible to experts. (There are, however, many pianos today with well-designed high-tension scales.)

The volume of sound and the harmonic content are often difficult to differentiate from each other; in fact, they are very closely related. They can also be changed to some extent through a process known as *voicing*; a loud or bright piano can be made softer or mellower, or vice versa. But keep in mind two things when listening to these aspects of tone: (1) room acoustics strongly affect the loudness or brightness you hear, and (2) pianos become brighter over time as the hammer felt packs down. If your home has carpeting, draperies, and upholstered furniture, then the piano will probably sound more subdued there than it will in the dealer's showroom because all these objects absorb sound, particularly high frequencies. However, the piano will get louder with time, so choose one that sounds now just about the way you'd like it to eventually. If your room acoustics are about the same as the dealer's, then choose a piano that is softer than you'd ultimately like; otherwise, it will become intolerably bright over time (though this can be adjusted—at some expense—when the time comes). It's usually better to err on the mellow side. Also check to see that the piano has an adequate dynamic range—that it can be played both soft and loud and many shades in between. Many pianos today can be played only loud and louder.

Play notes in different areas of the keyboard and observe how long the tone sustains. Consider only that portion of the tone loud enough to be useful in playing. The sustain time will naturally be shorter in the treble. Sustain time can be difficult to judge note by note. Try playing a piece of music in which a melody must be sustained against the background of an accompaniment. Does the melody "sing"? Or do the notes seem to disappear under your fingers, so to speak?

Listen to make sure that the tone is fairly uniform from section to section. There are a number of special problem areas to which you should pay particular attention. The transition from treble strings to bass strings is hard to scale smoothly on small and medium-size pianos. This transition usually occurs somewhere within the octave between middle C and the C below it. Often the bottom few notes in the treble string section will sound peculiar and the sustain will be deficient. Listen also to the highest notes in the treble. Do they sound clear like the other treble notes, or do they sound like wood hitting metal? Now listen to the bottom bass notes. Do they sound musical, or do they just go "thud"? How definite is their pitch? (This is largely a function of the piano's size.) The quality of sound from the little-used notes on either end may or may not be important to you.

Finally, listen for how the piano blends in harmony with itself. This is largely a function of the piano's size and the length of its bass strings, as well as the skill with which it has been designed. Play a chord in the middle of the piano and, while holding it, play a corresponding note in the low bass. Do they blend smoothly in harmony, or do they sound jarring, as if two different intruments were being played, one bass and one treble? (This can be partially remedied by clever tuning, but not entirely.)

I want to repeat that all of these listening tests depend on the piano being in very good tune. Out-of-tuneness, from slight to gross, can make a piano sound either better (occasionally) or worse (usually) than it really is.

Buying Tip: Listen to Differences in Tone and Form Your Own Opinion

Whether by cultural accident, successful marketing, or its inherent qualities, the kind of tone that has been most sought after in North America for the last hundred years is the "Steinway sound," best described as having a strong, singing treble and a powerful bass, rich in high harmonics. But the Steinway sound is not the only tone in town. Other manufacturers, by preference, tradition, or an inability to match the Steinway sound, offer other models of tone for you to choose from. Some European pianos, for instance, emphasize the fundamental tone rather than the harmonics, and probably because of their style of construction, have a shorter sustain time. This results in a much less powerful sound that Steinway enthusiasts would likely find dull, but one which has been traditional in Europe since before Steinway was founded. Many Japanese pianos have a bright, brittle tone, also short on sustain, which is often preferred by jazz pianists for its crispness. Listen for these differences and form your own opinion and tastes.

The Action

Defining vertical piano types. Defining the different types of vertical piano may seem like a straightforward and objective task, but there is actually much confusion over it. Vertical pianos come in four basic types, depending partly on their height, and partly on the size of the **action**—the mechanical playing mechanism—and its position in the piano, which in turn depend mostly on the piano's height. However, the popular definitions of these types take into account their height and furniture styling only, ignoring the action. These definitions are often reinforced by salespeople, who are instructed not to get "too technical" with their prospects. So there are pianos on the market which are of a size and style usually reserved for consoles, and which the dealers will call consoles, but which have spinet or studio actions in them. This is because the console market has been the hottest part of the piano market in recent years and every company has wanted a piece of it even if they weren't producing a real console. Whereas it may be useful for interior decorators to look at a piano in terms of its styling, musicians will find it more instructive to see these different types of piano in terms of their action.

As shown in Figure 3-21, vertical piano actions come in two different sizes—full-size and compressed (sometimes called "compact")—which can be connected to the keyboard in three different ways—direct blow, extended direct blow, and indirect blow—depending on the action's location in the piano. While the hammers must be positioned to strike the strings at a certain point along their length for good tone (and this position is obviously higher the taller the piano), the keys, in contrast, must always be at about the same height regardless of the size of the piano so that they can be comfortably played by the average person. Because the action must span this distance between the keyboard and the hammer striking point, its size and position depend on the height of the piano.

When most vertical pianos were *full-size uprights* (before about 1930), their actions were full-size and of the extended direct blow–type. The action, located toward the upper end of the strings, was connected to the keyboard with stilt-like extensions called **stickers**, which were attached either to the action or to the back of the keys. With extended *direct-blow* action, when a key was depressed at the front, the back end would rise and push up on the action parts via the sticker, sending the hammer to strike the strings. In the first round of size-cutting, the *studio* piano was created by simply eliminating the extensions and placing the action right on the back end of the keys. With further reduction in the size of the piano, the full-size action wouldn't fit, so it was "compressed" by reducing the size of some of its parts, and the *console* piano was born. When the piano was made so small that no action would fit in the usual manner at all, the keys were shortened and a full-size, but *indirect-blow* or *drop*, action was installed behind and beneath them. This action gets its name because it is connected to the keys with metal or wooden stickers that extend *downward* and *pull* up on the action parts instead of extending upward and pushing up on the action as with

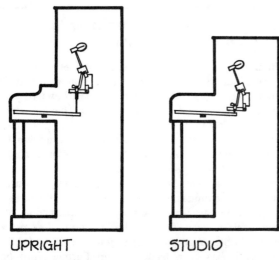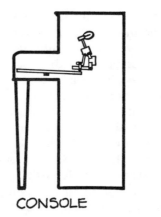

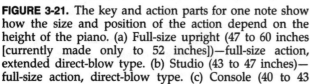

FIGURE 3-21. The key and action parts for one note show how the size and position of the action depend on the height of the piano. (a) Full-size upright (47 to 60 inches [currently made only to 52 inches])—full-size action, extended direct-blow type. (b) Studio (43 to 47 inches)—full-size action, direct-blow type. (c) Console (40 to 43 inches)—compressed action (notice the smaller action parts), direct-blow type. (d) Spinet (36 to 39 inches)—full-size action, *indirect*-blow type. Nearly all vertical piano actions made in the past hundred years fall into these general categories, but occasional hybrid or unusual actions may defy classification.

Buying Tip: Look For a Full-Size, Direct-Blow Action

When buying a vertical piano, choose one with a full-size, direct-blow (or extended direct-blow) action. This means either a studio or a full-size upright. Traditionally, these pianos have been 45 inches tall or taller and sometimes rather imposing. Some manufacturers, however, have been able to fit a full-size studio action into a piano as small as 42½ or 43 inches tall, styled as a console. This satisfies the need for both a more responsive action and, for those that require it, attractive low-profile styling. You may find these small studios variously called consoles, studios, and studio consoles, among other names. Only by inquiring as to both the size of the piano *and* the type of action can you determine just what kind of vertical piano you are really getting.

the other types. Pianos with indirect blow actions are called *spinets*.

The advantages and disadvantages of the various sizes of piano have already been discussed in terms of their string length and tone—basically, the larger the piano, the better the tone. This is generally the case with the action as well: all other things being equal, the compressed actions found in consoles do not perform as well as the full-size actions found in studio or upright pianos. The smaller parts of the compressed action meet at greater angles, resulting in more friction and wear, poorer leverage, and lowered ability to repeat notes quickly.

Spinets, although they employ a full-size action, are very difficult to service because even the smallest repair requiring the removal of the action becomes a major ordeal. Each of the connecting stickers has to be disconnected and tied up to the action and all the keys have to be removed from the piano before the action can be lifted out. Then the process has to be reversed when the repair is completed. What would be a five minute job on a piano with a direct-blow action could take a half hour or an hour on an indirect-blow spinet action. Because of the location of the action, even minor adjustments not requiring action removal can be hard to perform, and the connections between the keys and the stickers are often noisy and troublesome. The shortened keys offer very poor leverage. Add to this the short strings and resulting poor tone, and do you need any more reasons not to buy a spinet?

Action design and manufacturing. Actions are made in several different designs by a number of manufacturers. Some firms, such as Wurlitzer, Baldwin, and the large Japanese companies, make some or all of their own keys and actions. Some U.S. companies buy keys and actions from Pratt-Win (formerly Pratt-Read), now owned by Baldwin.

(There have been many complaints about the quality of Pratt-Win actions during the past decade, causing a number of manufacturers to go elsewhere. A few small manufacturers who still use Pratt-Win actions report having to correct many assembly defects to bring these actions up to their quality standards. It is hoped that under Baldwin's aegis, the quality will eventually improve.)

Other action suppliers include Herrburger Brooks, a Kimball affiliate in England that makes the "Schwander" and "Langer" actions, and Renner, a West German company reputed to make the finest actions in the world. Sometimes an action made by one company will be of a *type* originally designed by another. For instance, many actions are of a "Schwander-type," although not actually made by Herrburger Brooks.

Both vertical and grand actions come in a number of different designs. Most of these designs differ in the location and type of various springs, the leverage between parts, and other engineering specifications. These variations translate into differences in the "feel" of the action, the speed with which notes can be repeated ("repetition"), and the accuracy and ease of adjustment. For most average pianists, some of these differences are probably academic. (After all, does it really matter whether an action is capable of repeating

Buying Tip: Check for Buckskin

Traditionally, buckskin has been used for minimum friction and maximum durability on certain action parts that get a great deal of wear, such as the hammer butts in a vertical piano. At one time, when buckskin was scarce, cloth was substituted in some of the cheaper verticals. Those early cloth actions quickly led to disaster when the cloth compressed and wore right through, but the cloth has since been substantially improved and may now be preferred to some of the rough buckskin, cowhide, and other mediocre substitutes sometimes used. For pianos that get regular or strenuous use, though, fine-textured buckskin is still suggested. In addition to wearing away faster, inferior materials may add unwanted noise and friction to the action. The dealer or technician may be able to provide you with information about the material used for a particular piano.

Buying Tip: Testing the Action

If you are an advanced pianist, test an action with your most technically demanding passages, especially those with trills and repeating notes. Also test to make sure you can play very soft passages without the action "missing." If you have problems, of course, the fault could lie in the "regulation," or adjustment, of the action. The dealer's technician may be able to cure the problem, but don't rely on a promise; make sure the action is fully capable of performing to your satisfaction before agreeing to buy the piano.

On vertical pianos, all pianists should make sure they can play lightly without the hammers double-striking (hitting the string several times on a single stroke of the key). This is especially a problem for people who have a naturally light touch, such as children, and occurs primarily in the center area of the keyboard of pianos with a Schwander-type action, most of which are of Asian or European origin. Sometimes this problem can be corrected, sometimes not. These Schwander-type vertical actions are very well designed and well made in many respects, but tend to be more sensitive to slight changes in adjustment that cause malfunction than the standard American action (Figure 3-22).

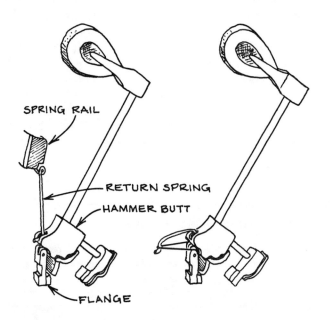

FIGURE 3-22. Left: An American-style vertical hammer assembly. The hammer return spring is attached to a separate rail and bears against a groove in the hammer butt. Right: A Schwander-type hammer assembly. The return spring for each hammer is part of the hammer butt itself and bears against a silk or nylon cord attached to the hammer flange (hinge). This kind of spring may be a little weaker and lead to the phenomenon of "double-striking" on some pianos.

fourteen or sixteen times a second when most pianists can barely play at half those speeds?) However, for the more advanced pianist, and in some special situations, the design differences may be significant.

For instance, Pratt-Win actions, both vertical and grand, and American-style vertical actions in general, are more "crudely" designed than most of the foreign types. That is, they will usually not repeat as fast and will not respond as well to nuances of touch, making it more difficult to play at different dynamic levels. The other side of the coin, though, is that the American-style actions will tolerate going far out of adjustment before they will begin to malfunction, whereas the Schwander-type, for example, may fail to work properly if the adjustment is off by even a little bit. The American-style actions, when properly assembled, are usually also more rugged, and will outlast most foreign ones under heavy use and adverse climatic conditions, as in schools.

Actions also differ in the accuracy with which they're made. Cheaper actions have rougher, less uniform-looking parts, use lower-quality cloth and other material that will compress and wear away faster, are liable to be more sloppily assembled, and may not be capable of fine adjustment or regulation. Parts are more likely to get stuck, rub against one another, and otherwise make life miserable for the pianist (and for the technician). Actions in some of the cheapest promotional pianos actually omit some parts that have traditionally been considered essential, such as bridle straps and key buttons. Companies can generally be expected to use an action whose quality is consistent with that of the rest of the piano, sometimes employing one style for their cheaper or smaller pianos and a better style for the larger, more expensive ones.

Many people expect a vertical piano action to perform as well as a grand. Actually, the two differ significantly. The grand action employs a special "repetition mechanism" (Figure 3-23; also see page 10) that allows it to reset itself for the next stroke of the key much sooner than a vertical action. Thus a grand action will usually repeat notes faster than a vertical. The grand action uses gravity, rather than springs, to return the hammer to rest position after a note is played. Thus a grand action is likely to feel more even from note to note than a vertical. In general, a grand action can be played with greater control and expressiveness than a vertical.* However, a well-made and properly adjusted vertical action may actually perform better than that of a mediocre grand.

---

*However, see page 115 for information on the Fandrich vertical action, which functions almost like a grand action.

GIMMICK: "Mr. Jones, unlike some other brands, all the action parts in Smith Bros. pianos are made of solid maple—no plastic parts in our *pianos!"*

TRUTH: Some manufacturers are now using a high grade of plastic for certain action parts, mostly in their vertical pianos. Tooling up to produce these parts is too expensive for all but the largest firms, but in the long run saves money over the expensive hardwoods normally used in actions. Those companies that are *not* using plastic use *that* fact as a marketing weapon against those that do, telling customers that plastic action parts used in pianos during the 1940s and 1950s crumbled into a sticky mess after a few decades. This is true, but the plastic being used today bears no resemblance to the stuff used back then. As you are probably aware, the plastics industry has come a long way since 1940. Considering that, and how embarrassed the piano industry is about what happened to the old plastic, you can be sure the new material has undergone very extensive testing before being put on the market. Several plastics engineers I consulted assured me that modern plastic deteriorates only when regularly exposed to ultraviolet light, and that types of plastic similar to those in piano actions are now used in many kinds of industrial machinery.

Plastic parts actually have a number of advantages over wooden ones. They can be made more uniform in shape and weight, are indifferent to temperature and humidity changes, and have no glue joints to come apart. One potential problem with them is that they are harder to service and repair should they become damaged. The main disadvantage, though, as with many other synthetic materials, is aesthetic. Plastic is a sterile material, whereas the charm and spirit of a wooden mechanism is what draws many piano owners and craftspeople to the instrument in the first place. (But, as one technician quipped, "The spiritual quality of the run-of-the-mill upright is minimal anyway and the use of plastic would seem to have little effect on that. Why waste good wood?")

Although plastic action parts have some advantages, the important advantages are really for the mass producer, who can make more parts at lower cost, using less labor, skill, care, and craft, without sacrificing the technical quality of the instrument. Except for the fact that the cost savings may be passed on, the advantages of plastic to the consumer are only very slight. Well-made wooden parts are quite uniform and relatively trouble-free, and have worked well for many, many years.

Keys

There is no part of the piano with which you will become more intimate than the keyboard. Keys are very innocent-looking sticks of wood, but their design is actually rather complex. What is boils down to, though, is this: If keys are too short, too angled, or not weighted properly, the action will feel uneven (requiring different pressure on the keys from note to note) and unresponsive (making it difficult to express yourself musically), parts of the keys will wear away quickly, and keys will get stuck easily. It will be impossible to develop any kind of decent playing technique.

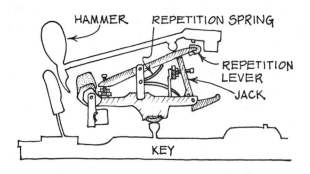

FIGURE 3-23. The repetition mechanism from one note of a grand piano, surrounded by its key and hammer. This complicated mechanism has an extra spring and lever that hold the hammer up in the air, after it rebounds from the string, so that the jack can reset itself for another stroke without the necessity of bringing the key all the way back to its starting position first. This allows notes to be repeated much faster on grands than on most verticals. See Chapter 1 for details of this mechanism's operation.

Key length. A key is like a seesaw: it pivots on a fulcrum, or *balance point*, located behind the fallboard. And as with a seesaw, the closer you are to the balance point the more force (known as *down weight*) you have to apply to get the key to go down, and the shorter the distance (known as *key dip*) the key will travel downward. The shorter the overall length of the key (including the part behind the fallboard that you can't see), the shorter the distance will be between the pianist's fingers and the balance point of the key. And the shorter this distance, the greater variation there will be in down weight and key dip between the front and the rear of the playing portion of the key (Figure 3-24).

To see why all this matters, try the following exercise on a piano (Figure 3-25): Using either hand, place your thumb on a B-flat and your little finger on the B-flat an octave higher or lower (depending on which hand you use). Now play the D and F in between with your index and middle fingers. Notice that you were forced to play the white keys way back near the

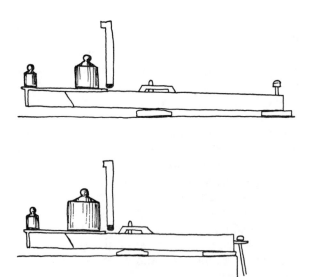

FIGURE 3-24. On short keys there is a greater variation in down weight between the front and back of the playing surface than on long keys. This makes it more difficult to develop control and good playing technique. Also see Figure 3-25.

FIGURE 3-25. A very common hand position shows why the touch at the rear of the playing surface is as important as at the front (from Figure 3-24).

fallboard instead of at the front in order to play the black keys. This is a very common hand position.

Some variation in touch between the front and back of the key is inevitable, but the less variation the better if a pianist is to have proper control of his or her playing. When every movement of the fingers on the keys requires a different amount of force, there is no way of accurately controlling how loud or soft the sound produced will be. This can foul up the playing

of beginners and advanced alike. Short keys are typically found in a spinet, where the key length must be reduced to accommodate the indirect-blow action, and in any vertical piano where the designers and marketing people have decided that the piano must be as slim as possible to attract buyers. Because the decision about key length tends to be made on the basis of cabinet styling, unfortunately, there may be little correlation between the length of the keys and the quality of the rest of the piano.

Buying Tip: Measure the Overall Key Length

The overall key length in a vertical piano should ideally be 14 to 16 inches or more. On some spinets or ultra-thin pianos, the keys may be as short as 11½ inches. If the total depth of the piano is less than about 23 inches, check the length of the keys to see if they're short. Key length is not generally a problem in grand pianos.

Buying Tip: Measure the Length of the Key Covering

In addition to varying in the overall length of their keys, pianos can also vary in the length of the *covered* portion of the keys—the part you can see and play. Some verticals feature "grand-length" or "international-length" keys; the exposed portion of the key is slightly longer than usual. This may be an advantage for players with long fingers or those who for various reasons (like flamboyant playing) would otherwise hit their fingers against the fallboard. To check the length of the key coverings, measure the *sharps*, or black keys (see Figure 3-27). Regular length is 3½ inches; grand length is 3¾ inches. The length of the *naturals*, or white keys, varies correspondingly. When testing out pianos in the showroom, be sure to pay attention to this very small, but surprisingly important, difference.

Key angle. Another problem with short keys is that they often have too great a bend in them (Figure 3-26). Notice that behind the fallboard the keys fan out slightly to line up with their respective action parts. The shorter the key, the greater the bending angle necessary. On angled keys, most of the weight of the action parts is borne by the side of the key toward the inside of the bend, causing the metal guide pin at the balance point to wear away the cloth key bushing on the opposite side. Premature wearing away of the key bushing on one side causes the key to become lopsided and greatly increases its chance of becoming sluggish and failing to return properly. This is a major problem in pianos with highly angled keys, especially spinets.

Key weighting. The forces required to maintain key movement, collectively called *touch weight*, include *down weight*, the force required to make a key go down, and *up weight*, the force with which the returning key pushes up against the finger after being played. Down weight usually measures between 45 and 55 grams (with the damper system disengaged). Much more than this and the piano will be too tiring to play; much less and the pianist will not be able to maintain adequate control of his or her playing and the keys may be sluggish in returning. Don't make the mistake of choosing a piano with too light a touch.

An element of touch weight important to pianists but rarely addressed is *inertia*, a measure of which is the force required to accelerate a key in actual playing, which is a function of the total amount of mass in the key and action parts of each note. An action with too much inertia may be difficult and tiring to play even though the specifications for down weight and up weight are correct.*

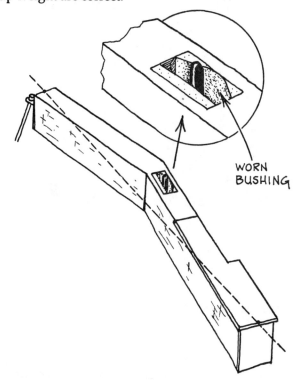

WORN BUSHING

FIGURE 3-26. In theory, a straight line from the front to the back of the key should pass through the balance point. If the key is highly angled in such a way that this condition is not met, then it will lean slightly in one direction and prematurely wear away the cloth key bushing on the opposite side, resulting in sluggishness and noise. The possibility of this happening is much greater when the bend in the key begins behind the balance point instead of right behind the key covering material, and when the key has no key button for added support (see Figure 3-27). Angled keys may also have a greater chance of breaking because the grain of the wood may not always be oriented in the direction of maximum strength.

To attain the proper touch weight and balance the weight of the action, most keys have lead weights called **key leads** imbedded in them (see Figure 3-27). In grands, these are essential; the required touch weight couldn't be attained without them. Because of the different leverage of vertical piano keys, though, cost-conscious manufacturers of these pianos may be able to get away without using key leads. Most of their pianos will still be quite playable; some will tend toward a very light touch and will be prone to sticking.

GIMMICK: "The keys on Smith Bros. pianos are individually weighted for a more uniform touch."

TRUTH: There are two kinds of key weighting used. "Engineered weights" are installed according to an average—the same in every piano of that model regardless of slight variations in wood density, friction, and so on, that may exist from piano to piano or key to key. On most grands and some higher-quality verticals, to even out these differences, the touch weight of each key is individually measured and the key fitted with the appropriate key leads. Keys that undergo the latter process are said to be "individually weighed-off" or "individually weighted and balanced."

In theory, weighing off keys individually sounds like a good idea, and perhaps it works well in some factories. But most factories weigh off their keys before the final regulation, with key bushings of varying tightness, hammers not yet shaped, and many action adjustments not yet made. Once these are done, the weigh-off will no longer be accurate. Sometimes key leading is even used to compensate for gross errors in manufacturing. If quality control is reasonably good, it is not that difficult to predict the right amount of lead to use, and a well-engineered set of key weights will work quite well.

One particularly aggravating and pathetic problem sometimes occurs with unweighted or poorly weighted keys: under certain circumstances the weight of the action will actually be insufficient to hold the back end of the keys down. The pianist's complaint will be that some notes get "hung up;" that is, they don't repeat. When the technician makes the adjustment that normally cures that problem, the result is that the front of the offending key droops below the level of the surrounding keys—and the note still doesn't repeat. Short of adding extra weights, nothing can be done to remedy this condition. Notes will never repeat well, and the level of the keyboard will always be uneven.

---

*See page 115 for information on the Stanwood grand action, a low-inertia, variable touch weight action recently developed.

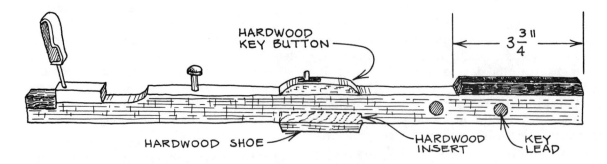

FIGURE 3-27. Some features in a high-quality key: It is long, thick, and straight-grained with a hardwood key button and a hardwood "shoe" or insert to protect against wear by the balance rail guide pin. Also shown are key leads and the measurement of the length of a sharp. Sugar pine and spruce are preferred for key making over the cheaper basswood.

Buying Tip: Avoid Key Weighting Problems

You can avoid key weighting problems by, first of all, staying away from spinets and other verticals that have very short, unweighted keys. Second, when "test driving" a new piano, play for a while with the sustain (right-hand) pedal depressed. Although this will create quite a din and annoy the salesperson, it will quickly show up keys that are sluggish in returning, because the weight of the dampers will be disconnected from the keys. Often this sluggishness is caused by excess friction, in turn caused by tight key bushings, and can be eliminated by some simple adjustments. When that fails, however, poorly weighted and balanced keys are likely the culprit.

Buying Tip: Check for Warped Keys

Sometimes keys will warp if the wood has not been properly seasoned prior to making the keyboard. This is especially likely on pianos made in foreign countries with a humid climate, but is certainly not unknown on American-made pianos as well.

Kneel down so the keys are at eye-level. Notice whether any keys are unevenly spaced between their neighbors, or tilted (Figure 3-28). These may just need some minor adjustments—or they may have been purposely misadjusted in the factory or in the store. Why? If keys are warped, the easy (read *lazy*) way to keep them from rubbing against each other at the rear is to "fudge" them at the front. This is less work than sanding them down—or sending the piano back for a new keyboard.

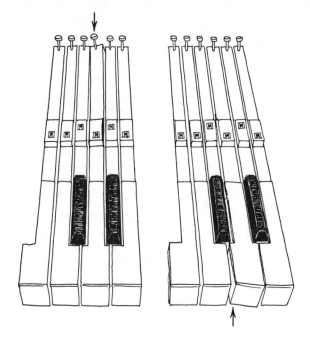

FIGURE 3-28. When a key is warped enough to be interfering with a neighboring one, the technician can correct the problem by slightly bending the guide pin at the balance point to tilt the key in the other direction. This is only permissible, though, if it does not cause the front of the key to be noticeably lopsided. If any keys appear to be tilted at the front, you should find out why. This is a common trick to avoid the more extensive woodworking that may be necessary to correct warpage.

Key quality. Believe it or not, keys actually flex slightly when played hard, robbing the hammer of some power, and can even break. Making keys as rigid and durable as possible is a high priority for makers of top-quality instruments. Measures taken include: using well-seasoned, straight-grained wood with the grain oriented in the direction of maximum resistance to breaking (which is hard to do if the key has a sharp angle bend in it); making the keys as thick as reasonably possible; and using hardwood key buttons and "shoes" at the balance point of the key, where it's weakest (Figure 3-27).

Buying Tip: Choosing Keytops

Practically all pianos made today have plastic key coverings for both the naturals and the sharps. Formerly the naturals were of ivory, whose importation is now prohibited because it requires the killing of elephants for their tusks. Ivory is usually preferred by pianists because it absorbs sweat from the fingers and so doesn't get slippery like plastic does. It is also said to have a "warmer" or "softer" feel to it. Several piano manufacturers are now developing synthetic materials that mimic the properties of ivory.

Sharps used to be made of ebony wood; the plastic sharps used today may be shiny or of a slightly dulled appearance. Personally, I would recommend the dulled sharps, which are often standard on the better pianos. Whether it's an illusion or not, I'm not sure, but my fingers seem to slip off the shiny ones more easily, and the reflection from them annoys me. See if you agree.

Also run your finger under the overhanging lip of plastic naturals to check for sharp edges or burrs that should be filed down.

Key frame. The keys pivot on a **key frame** and the key frame rests on the **keybed**. If either of these parts warps or changes dimension it will throw the action out of adjustment, so conscientious manufacturers take extra pains to use the best seasoned lumber and appropriate methods of joinery to prevent these occurrences. On a vertical piano, the key frame is permanently screwed to the keybed. Better verticals have a key frame with three horizontal rails; on cheaper verticals the back rail is omitted and the key frame cloth is glued directly to the keybed. On a grand, the key frame can be pulled out like a drawer for servicing, so measures have to be taken to ensure that it fits the keybed like a glove or it will slap against it under hard playing, making an unpleasant noise. The better companies also provide special hardwood inserts in those parts of the keys, key frame, and keybed where extra strength and durability are called for.

Hammers

Piano **hammers** are felt-covered wooden mallets that must be at once finely engineered, ruggedly constructed, and delicately balanced; capable of producing barely audible pianissimos and thundering fortissimos with equal ease; and able to endure literally millions of collisions with steel strings, with minimal wear. A tall order!

A **hammer head** consists of a wooden **molding** surrounded by dense **hammer felt** (Figure 3-30). The felt is

Buying Tip: Check for Slapping Key Frame

On a grand piano, play each note several times with a hard blow, and listen for tapping or slapping sounds indicating that the key frame is not properly fitted to the keybed. Listen especially to the keys near the ends of the keyboard. This problem can be fixed by the technician, so bring it to the attention of the salesperson (Figure 3-29).

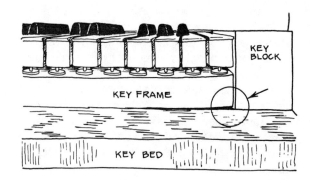

FIGURE 3-29.

applied to the molding under pressure in such a way that the outer layers are under great tension and the inner layers under great compression. The balance between these two forces makes the hammer resilient so that it can strike the strings and immediately rebound, leaving the strings free to vibrate. Each hammer head is mounted on a thin dowel called a **hammer shank**. Some manufacturers make their own hammers; others buy from companies that specialize in hammer making.

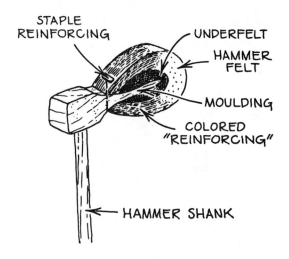

FIGURE 3-30. Parts of a typical hammer. Not all hammers have a staple or colored reinforcing or underfelt. Notice the dotted line under the staple. The best staples go all the way through the hammer in a specially drilled hole and are twisted or bent over on the other side.

Generally, one can't tell much about the quality of a hammer by simply looking at it. One has to listen to the tone produced and have experience servicing the hammers to make any judgment about them. Even then, a judgment must be qualified, as many other factors can also influence the tone. The better hammers use felt of higher-quality wool (such as with finer fibers) and more strictly controlled density and uniformity. They are more neatly trimmed and finished, and have fine wood moldings. One thing you *can* look at is how much felt is present at the striking point of the hammer. The felt packs down and wears away with repeated striking of the strings, and some treble hammers have too little felt at the striking point to enjoy a long life.

The felt in many foreign-made hammers is artificially hardened by being doped with chemicals or overly compressed during the manufacturing process. Pianos with these hammers often sound quite good in the showroom, but become harsh after a couple of years of playing. The traditional style of tone regulating depends on the balance of tension and compression inside the hammer. Thus these hammers may be more difficult and unpredictable to service.

Buying Tip: Check for Shaping of Hammers

Hammers develop a concave surface during the manufacturing process. To "finish" them, the felt is sanded flat and smooth so the striking surface is parallel to the strings (Figure 3-31) . On some of the cheapest pianos, this operation is omitted, and the hammers actually miss nearly one-third of the strings. With the front panel off a vertical piano, push some hammers toward the strings with your hand and check to see whether their striking surface is parallel to the line of the strings.

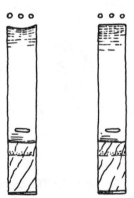

FIGURE 3-31. Two piano hammers seen from above. Because the one on the left remains in the concave shape formed in the manufacturing process, it will probably miss the center string of its unison (set of three strings). The one on the right has been sanded so its striking surface is parallel to the line of strings.

GIMMICK: "This Deluxe Console is the only one on the market to use 14-pound hammers; all the others use 12-pound hammers."

TRUTH: Hammers are the subject of several marketing gimmicks. One of them is the "weight" of the hammer. Usually ranging from "10 pounds" up to "18 pounds" or higher, this number expresses the weight of an entire sheet of felt, from which many sets of hammers are made. (The actual weight of the felt on an individual hammer head is only the barest fraction of an ounce.) Unfortunately, no industry standard specifies how many sets of hammers can be made from a sheet of felt, so this expression of "weight" is left without much meaning or usefulness. It is true that larger pianos require heavier hammers to set into motion the longer, heavier strings. But it is not necessarily true, as the marketing people would have you believe, that a console with "14-pound" hammers is always noticeably better than one with "12-pound" hammers. What is important is that the weight, shape, and density of the hammer be properly matched to the rest of the scale design, which you and I can tell only by listening (if then). Some pianos have hammers that are simply too small and light to elicit a strong sound from the strings, especially in the bass.

GIMMICK: "The hammers are also chemically reinforced (see this colored portion of the hammer?) and stapled so they'll never come apart."

TRUTH: Chemical reinforcing is one of the biggest jokes in the industry. Long ago, when weaker animal hide glues were used to attach the hammer felt to the molding, the felt was chemically treated to make it less absorbent so it would make a better glue bond with the moulding. With modern glues, it is no longer necessary to treat the felt. Although in a few cases an actual stiffening agent is still used on the felt in the belief that the stiffener helps the felt keep its shape longer, the vast majority of piano hammers contain only a colored dye, whose sole purpose is to fool you. Consumers are the only ones to be fooled; every manufacturer, technician, and salesperson knows that this is a hoax. The gimmick seems to have originated in an attempt to copy the looks of Steinway hammers, which do contain a real stiffening agent, colored grey. Other companies use yellow or green dye, and I expect a rainbow-colored hammer to appear on the market any day. Even when the reinforcing is real, there is no general agreement in the profession whether it's useful or desirable.

Stapled reinforcement is another gimmick. There are actually two kinds of staples, one worse than useless and the other probably useful, or at the very least harmless. The most common type of staple looks like the sort that comes out of an ordinary office stapler. During the manufacturing process, these staples are driven into the shoulder of the hammer. Often the staples never reach wood; they are imbedded in the felt only, where they perform no function whatsoever and can be easily picked out with your fingernail. Where they do reach the wooden hammer molding, they may occasionally split it. Better no staples should be used at all than this kind of staple! However, since stapled hammers are used as a selling feature, most hammers without staples are found in the cheapest pianos.

The other kind of staple is found in the better pianos. It is a long staple that goes all the way through the hammer in holes drilled especially for it, and is twisted or bent over on the other side. This kind of staple is thought to maintain the compression on the shoulder of the hammer so that the hammer will retain its resilience longer.

The maple hammer shanks on which the hammer heads are mounted are prone to warping and, eventually, to breaking. Manufacturers of premium-quality pianos take special care in curing their shanks, and then hand-select only those that are absolutely straight. Furthermore, these companies also install each and every shank with the grain of the wood oriented in the direction of maximum strength to protect against breakage. Few manufacturers indulge in such expensive precautions, especially for vertical pianos.

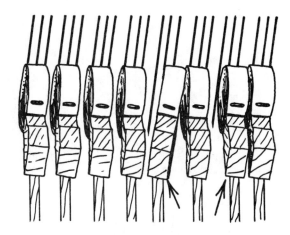

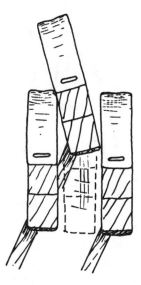

Buying Tip: Check Hammer Spacing

On a vertical piano, with the front panel removed, notice whether the hammers are all evenly spaced and aligned, with none warped or crooked (Figure 3-32). Push groups of four or five treble hammers at a time toward the strings with the back of your hand, and observe whether they line up perfectly with the strings, each hammer centered on its group of three strings. On a grand, this is harder to do. You'll have to observe how the hammers line up with the strings as you look down from above the strings while pressing several keys at a time.

The angled bass hammers move in a compound arc to strike the strings. The more angled the hammers are, the harder it is to space them so they won't collide with each other when in motion. Check visually to make sure that, when played, none of the hammers are rubbing against each other and getting stuck. Point out any problems to the salesperson or technician. On some of the smaller, cheaper verticals, getting the hammers properly aligned with the strings *and* spaced in relation to each other can be an almost impossible challenge, and the spacing may be so critical that the slightest change in humidity can cause a malfunction again.

FIGURE 3-32. Top: Arrows point to crooked and misspaced hammers, usually caused by warped hammer shanks and flanges. These kinds of problems can be corrected, but if there are many of them, the wood may not have been properly seasoned and the piano was probably not carefully prepared for sale. Bottom: Bass hammers (and some tenor hammers) move at a strange angle and are sometimes so tightly spaced that they will rub against each other and get "hung up" in transit. If this cannot be fixed by spacing and adjusting the hammers, it may be necessary to trim wood or felt off them (this is sometimes done at the factory anyway).

Pedals and Trapwork

With all the variables involved in buying a piano, at least the pedals operate the same on all of them, don't they? Sorry to say you're only about two-thirds right. See Figure 3-33.

The right-hand pedal, or **sustain pedal**, does the same thing on all pianos, grand and vertical: it lifts all the dampers off the strings simultaneously so that any notes played while the pedal is down will continue to

VERTICAL PEDALS

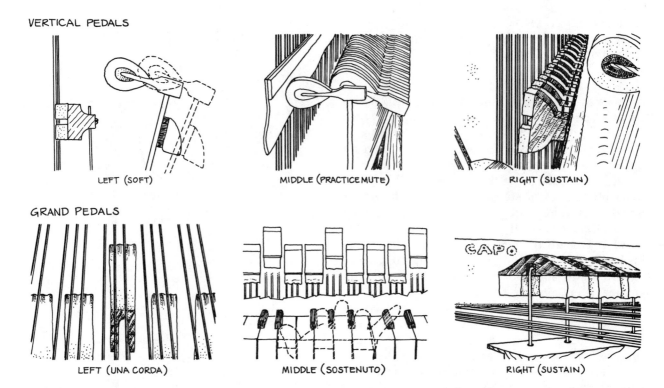

LEFT (SOFT)   MIDDLE (PRACTICE MUTE)   RIGHT (SUSTAIN)

GRAND PEDALS

LEFT (UNA CORDA)   MIDDLE (SOSTENUTO)   RIGHT (SUSTAIN)

FIGURE 3-33. How the pedals work. Left, vertical: **Soft pedal.** The hammers move closer to the strings, softening the sound. Left, grand: **Una corda pedal.** The entire keyboard and hammers shift slightly to one side so that the treble hammers strike only two of their three strings per note, softening the sound. Middle, vertical: Varies. Shown here is the **practice pedal.** A piece of felt drops between the hammers and strings, muffling the sound. Middle, grand: Usually a **sostenuto pedal.** Selectively sustains only those notes whose dampers are in the up position at the moment this pedal is pressed. Right, vertical and grand: **Sustain pedal.** Lifts all the dampers off the strings simultaneously, sustaining all notes played thereafter.

sound. When the pedal is released, the dampers fall back against the strings and stop the sound. This is the pedal we all use the most, and, for many pianists, the only one they will ever need.

The left-hand pedal, or **soft pedal,** always makes the sound softer, but operates entirely differently on verticals and grands. On verticals, depressing the soft pedal moves the hammer rail so that all the hammers move closer to the strings. With the shortened blow distance, the hammers can't develop as much speed before they strike the strings; therefore they produce a quieter sound. Unfortunately, this rather hokey system changes the relationship between the various action parts, puts the action grossly out of regulation, and makes the touch very strange every time the soft pedal is pressed. When the pedal is released, of course, everything falls back immediately into proper adjustment. On grands, the soft pedal, also known as the **una corda pedal,** shifts the entire action and keyboard slightly to one side so that the treble hammers strike only two of their three strings per note. This creates no action regulation problems.

It's really only with the middle pedal that you have some choice when shopping for a piano. On all good

grands and a few exceptional verticals, the middle pedal is a **sostenuto pedal.** Its use is a bit esoteric: Say you'd like to sustain a chord, but you need both hands to continue playing elsewhere on the keyboard. You know that if you simply pressed the sustain pedal, not only your chord would be sustained but also everything that followed, creating an unwanted blur. So how to do it? Play your chord, and, while holding it down, press the sostenuto pedal. With this pedal held down, you can now release your fingers and the chord will continue sounding. Keep holding that pedal down and you can now use both your hands to play elsewhere. Only those notes you played *prior* to depressing the sostenuto pedal will be affected by it; the new notes you play afterward will not be sustained unless you choose to sustain them with the sustain (right-hand) pedal. The sostenuto pedal is used almost exclusively in some nineteenth- and twentieth-century "classical" music. If you are an aspiring concert pianist, or even a serious student of the classical repertoire, you really should have this pedal. Others will not need it.

Cheap modern grands and most American-made verticals have a middle pedal that operates a **bass sustain.** When pressed, this pedal lifts the bass dampers only.

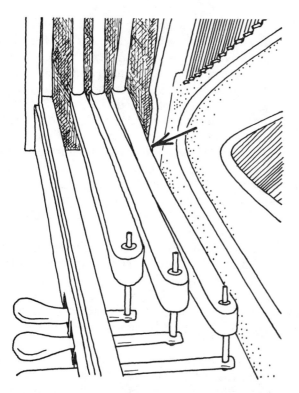

FIGURE 3-34. When the trap levers are made of wood and all three are on the same side of the piano, slight warpage or sloppy workmanship may cause them to rub against each other or against the cast-iron plate. Be sure this problem is corrected before the piano leaves the store.

This seems to be an attempt to mimic the sostenuto pedal, but it works only if all the notes you want to sustain are in the bass and all the notes you don't want to sustain are in the treble. Most people never use this pedal and don't even know what it does. When it appears on a modern grand, it is a sign that the grand is a cheap one indeed. (Note: Some good *old* grands also had this feature.)

A third kind of middle pedal, found only on verticals, and particularly foreign-made verticals, is the **practice pedal**. This is actually one of the better uses for the middle pedal. When it is pressed, a thin piece of felt is lowered between the hammers and the strings, muffling the sound to a whisper. The practice pedal is intended for those who live in apartment houses and want to practice at 3 A.M. (or in some similar situation). Sometimes the pedal can be locked into the "on" position, by sliding it to one side, so you don't have to hold it down. This may be a welcome feature if you've ever had to hold a pedal for hours.

The middle pedal on verticals can also be a duplicate soft pedal, a dummy pedal—just for show—or missing entirely. Interestingly, pianos with only two pedals include some of the very cheapest—the maker was apparently too cheap to bother—and some of the very best—perhaps the maker was too wise to bother.

The various levers and dowels, wooden or metal, that connect the pedals with the action are collectively known as the **trapwork**. The springs and pivot systrems used in the trapwork vary in quality. Some cheap verticals use crude "pelican" springs that can't provide precise control over the pedaling. The trap levers just kind of wobble around, eventually finding their way after bouncing off adjacent levers or nearby case parts. On inferior grands, the trapwork parts may not line up with each other perfectly, resulting in abnormal wear and squeaks and groans that become increasingly difficult to eliminate.

Buying Tips: Check the Operation of Pedals and Dampers

1. **Check for smooth and noiseless operation of the pedals and trapwork, and make sure that the pedals are not too stiff. (However, some pedals are intentionally made stiff for faster return, which may be an advantage to better pianists.) On cheaper verticals, there is sometimes insufficient clearance between the horizontal trap levers at the bottom of the piano. A little warpage results in their rubbing against each other or against the plate—a troublesome problem to correct (Figure 3-34).**

2. **Depress the sustain (right-hand) pedal very slowly while observing the dampers. The pedal should go down a fraction of an inch before the dampers start to lift. Then all the dampers should lift simultaneously, as if they were made of one single piece of wood and felt. Work the pedal up and down very slowly, watching for any early rising dampers or late stragglers.**

3. **On a grand, check the operation of the sostenuto pedal using the example given earlier. Another way to check the sostenuto pedal: First, press and hold the sustain pedal. Then press and hold the sostenuto pedal. Last, release the sustain pedal. All the dampers are now being held off the strings if the sostenuto pedal is working correctly.**

4. **On a grand, check the operation of the una corda (soft) pedal, making sure that when pressed, the treble hammers shift over just far enough to miss one string of each unison (set of three strings), but not so far as to hit the strings of the adjacent note.**

5. **On a piano with a well-engineered pedal system, the sustain pedal can be operated with a surprising amount of control to produce special effects such as "half pedaling," where the pedal is not quite "on" and not quite "off." For an accomplished pianist, this is a very important tool. Other pianos may require a player to "pump" the pedal up and down, producing a choppy, disconnected musical line. If you aspire to a high level of playing, be sure to check that the sustain pedal operates with the degree of musical control you need by playing a piece of music requiring a legato melodic line and complicated pedaling.**

6. **Play each note and make sure that upon release its damper cuts the sound off cleanly without buzzing or other stray sounds.**

Final Preparation

One of the very biggest and most visible differences between pianos of differing quality is in the final preparation they receive in the factory prior to being shipped to the dealer. I'm always amazed at how so many Japanese pianos can be shipped ten thousand miles and arrive at the dealer barely needing tuning, whereas many of their American counterparts require hours of remedial work by the dealer's technician after being shipped across town.

In the factory, final preparation of the piano includes such things as chipping and tuning, action regulating, voicing, and cleanup. The more of this done in the factory, the less will have to be done by the dealer. Since many dealers are notorious for doing very little prep work on their pianos (more about that later), conscientiousness in the factory will mean less initial servicing that you have to pay for or suffer without.

Tuning. New piano strings require many tunings before they stop stretching and will hold a tuning for a reasonable length of time. The first few tunings in the factory are done before the action is installed; the tuner plucks the strings with a wooden chip in a process called "chipping." Vertical pianos normally receive two chippings followed by one to four tunings, depending on the quality and price of the piano. Grands receive two chippings and from four to seven tunings. There may be a settling in period of days or weeks between successive tunings. Even with all this tuning, most pianos require at least four tunings in the home during the first year of ownership. A cheap piano that is not tuned enough in the factory, even if tuned by the dealer, may go disastrously out of tune in your home and need several remedial tunings (paid for by you) before it will even begin to hold its tune.

Buying Tip: Insist that the Piano Be Tuned

If a piano that you are seriously considering buying is wildly out of tune on the showroom floor, tell the salesperson that you are delaying your purchase decision until the piano has been tuned. This is entirely justifiable since it's impossible to tell what a piano really sounds like when it is out of tune. This in-store tuning should be *in addition* to the in-home tuning that customarily comes with the piano, not instead of it. In this way, you will make sure that the piano gets the extra tuning it probably didn't get at the factory or from the dealer, and that it will therefore need fewer remedial tunings at your expense. But don't abuse this request; save it for the one piano you really *are* thinking of buying. If the dealer refuses, shop elsewhere.

Action regulating. *Regulating* refers to the fine adjustment of the thousands of action parts so that they perform the way they were designed to. These adjustments may take the form of turning adjusting screws, making minute bends in wires, and placing small shims of paper and cardboard under keys. There are more than a dozen adjustments that have to be made to each note, some of them to tolerances of just a few thousandths of an inch, plus several adjustments for the action as a whole. The action must be regulated when the piano is new, of course, but it also requires regulating after an initial period of use has caused the cloth and felt parts to compact, and thereafter to compensate for wear.

Actions are regulated in the factory, at least enough to make them work, but sometimes not much better than that. Higher-quality pianos usually undergo a second, or even a third, regulation before being shipped off to the dealer. In a few factories, machines with eighty-eight rubber plungers pound on the keys thousands of times to simulate hours of playing, after which the pianos are regulated again (boy, do those machines make a racket!). This process of breaking in a piano is highly desirable, but it is time consuming and thus too expensive for most mass producers. Action regulating in the home is expensive too, so the more breaking in and regulating done in the factory, the longer it will be before you have to foot the bill.

Buying Tip: Check Action Regulation

Space doesn't permit fully describing here how to test the regulation of the action. A piano technician you hire to inspect the piano before purchase can test for that. However, instructions for checking certain aspects of the regulation, such as the hammer spacing and the pedal operation, have already been given. The alignment of the hammers and the adjustment of the dampers are two items that are frequently in disarray in lower-quality pianos unless a very conscientious dealer has corrected them. Two other problems to check for are hammers that bounce or hit the strings twice when you play softly up and down the keyboard and hammers that block against the strings.

Voicing. *Voicing,* or tone regulating, mostly involves adjusting the shape and density of the hammer felt to control the tonal quality of the piano. If the piano sounds too bright, the hammers are pricked with needles to soften them; if too mellow or dull, chemical hardeners are usually applied. If the shape of the hammer is wrong, too, the tonal quality will be affected; the hammer felt is sanded to restore the proper shape. There are also more sophisticated aspects of voicing, such as mating the hammers and strings so that the hammer contacts all three strings of a unison at the same time (see Figure 3-31).

As I mentioned under the subject of hammers, the cheapest pianos receive no hammer preparation at all and therefore start out with three strikes against them. Most vertical pianos have their hammers sanded to at least a reasonable shape, but aside from getting a few squirts of hammer hardener on the top six hammers to make them sound presentable, they receive no other voicing. Top-of-the-line verticals and most grands get more hammer voicing, though few get much attention paid to string and hammer mating. A knowledgeable technician you hire to inspect the piano should check for this.

Buying Tip: Voicing in the Home

Because room acoustics profoundly affect a piano's tonal quality, final voicing (tone regulating) should ideally be done after the piano is delivered to the home and tuned. Inquire of the dealer whether this is possible. Also, after the piano has been played for six months or a year, its sound will probably be much brighter, and it may need voicing again.

It's important to realize, however, that there is always some risk the piano will not sound just as you'd hoped it would, even after voicing in the home. Ignore promises from the dealer that the technician can coax any sort of tone you want from any piano in any acoustical environment. It's just not that simple.

Cleanup. During the manufacturing process, small chips of wood and sawdust collect in the piano, settling on the soundboard and bridges, against the strings, and in the bottom of verticals. Often chips of wood that have lodged against the strings on the bridges are responsible for buzzing sounds. Manufacturers are supposed to blow or vacuum this stuff out, but many cheap pianos arrive at the dealer full of junk. I've also seen new pianos in the home in which dripping glue from action assembly work had immobilized a hammer. Isn't it remarkable that neither the manufacturer nor the dealer noticed it?

Serviceability

Whether a piano is more or less serviceable depends mainly on how easily the case parts can be removed and how accessible the action is. Some examples of designs that hinder serviceability have already been

given: grand-style lids with nonremovable hinge pins on verticals, sliding fallboards, spinet actions, and so on. You may wonder what this has to do with you, however. After all, isn't poor serviceability the technician's headache? Maybe. But if your grand piano requires removing fourteen screws (instead of two) to pull out the action, don't expect your technician to conscientiously make those small adjustments to the action that he or she might otherwise do for free after tuning the piano. If you own a spinet, you may have trouble finding someone to service it at all. Most technicians balk at doing the finest level of work on an instrument that is difficult to service, particularly when it's a cheap piano and the results of their work are unsatisfying.

"Look on the bright side, Mr. Jones—the laminated soundboard is still under warranty for another 59 years!"

Warranty

RULE OF THUMB: The longer and more extravagant-sounding the warranty, the worse the piano.

Sound incredible? The reason is that the warranty, like most "features," is used as a selling gimmick. When the product has little in the way of quality or reputation to recommend it, the manufacturer hopes that a long warranty will provide the needed inducement to buy. Although this rule of thumb is obviously an exaggeration, witness that Steinway's warranty is for only five years, the shortest in the business. Several of the worst companies in recent years, however, have had a so-called lifetime warranty. Some others have a normal ten- to fifteen-year warranty on most of the piano, but boast a fifty- to seventy-five-year warranty on the laminated soundboard. A careful reading of the fine print, however, reveals that many of these extravagant-sounding warranties are practically worthless.

In 1975, the U.S. Congress enacted the Magnuson-Moss Warranty Act, which set federal standards for warranties on consumer products costing more than ten dollars. One requirement of the Act is that every warranty must be conspicuously labeled "full" or "limited." A full warranty is one that meets every one of the following five conditions. A limited warranty is one that does not meet one or more of these conditions. If a warranty is full for some parts of a product and limited for other parts, it is called a "multiple" warranty.

1. The manufacturer will provide warranty service to anyone who owns the product during the period covered by the warranty. (In other words, the warranty is transferable to future owners if you should sell the piano during the warranty period.)

2. The manufacturer will provide warranty service free of charge, including such costs as returning the product or removing and reinstalling the product when necessary. (In other words, you will not be charged for the labor necessary to replace a defective part, or for transporting the piano to the dealer or manufacturer, should this be necessary.)

3. The manufacturer will provide, at the consumer's choice, either a replacement or a full refund if it is unable, after a reasonable number of tries, to repair the product. (In other words, you will not be required to take a replacement if you prefer a refund.)

4. The manufacturer will provide warranty service without requiring that consumers return a warranty registration card. (Your warranty will not be invalidated just because you failed to mail in the registration card.)

5. The warranty will not limit the duration of implied warranties. (See Chapter 5, "Buying A Used Piano" for a discussion of implied warranties.)

A warranty must be clearly labeled on its face as full or limited. Beware of confusing phrases like "Full Ten-Year Limited Warranty," as one recent piano ad read. Please also note that the word *limited* does *not* refer to a limitation on the duration of the warranty; it simply means that at least one of the above federal standards for a full warranty has not been met.

Fine print in most warranties contains exclusions that may severely limit coverage. Some of these exclusions relate to the federal standards, and some don't. Some are reasonable and justified, and some, in my opinion, are not. For instance, accidental damage and normal changes in tuning, regulation, and voicing obviously should not be covered. Nor should damage to the piano caused by placing it next to a radiator. But why should warranty coverage cease when you sell the piano? Many piano warranties cover the original purchaser only, an unfair restriction.

One clause that renders some warranties particularly worthless stipulates that only the cost of replacement *parts* is covered, but not the labor to install them. If your piano had a defective pinblock and a new pinblock were delivered to your home, would you know what to do with it? The pinblock would be worth only a very small fraction of the thousand dollars or more it would cost to install it. Even with less severe defects, the cost of labor is almost always far greater than the cost of parts.

Some other possible exclusions you should know about are—

- Some warranties make you pay for transporting the piano back to the dealer or manufacturer if it can't be repaired at your home. Do you know how much it would cost to ship a piano across the country—or around the world?

- Some warranties become void if any rust appears on the strings or tuning pins, as this is considered evidence that the owner has not properly protected the piano from abnormally humid conditions. However, rust will sometimes appear for reasons unrelated to neglect, perhaps because of faulty manufacturing of the music wire. This leads to a "Catch-22" situation: the warranty becomes void the moment a defect is found.

- Some warranties do not cover the piano finish. I see no reason why a good finish should not be expected to last for at least ten years, subject to normal wear.

- Some warranties require that to collect on the warranty you furnish proof that you have had the piano regularly maintained by a qualified technician. This sounds reasonable, but, in fact, most piano defects are completely unrelated to whether or not the piano has ever been tuned. This is an easy out for the manufacturer, who knows that the vast majority of piano owners fail to maintain their pianos.

- Some warranties do not allow a refund, no matter what happens.

- Most piano warranties do not cover pianos used in commercial or institutional settings, such as in schools, hospitals, clubs, or restaurants.

Some so-called lifetime warranties are extremely vague: they fail to specify whether they are referring to the life of the purchaser or the life of the piano. If the latter, how does one determine when a piano has "died?" When a defect is discovered? Another Catch-22. Also note that a warranty said to last the purchaser's lifetime can never be a full warranty because if it were transferable to future owners (after the original owner died), the warranty would have to last forever.

As I mentioned earlier, extravagant fifty- to seventy-five-year warranties on laminated soundboards are marketing gimmicks. Since it's impossible for a laminated soundboard to crack or lose its crown, guaranteeing one will last is like guaranteeing that the sun will rise in the east tomorrow. If the tone is poor, you are also guaranteed it will remain so for fifty to seventy-five years.

Furthermore, all warranties cover only defects in material and workmanship. Most such defects show up in the first five to ten years of a piano's life. Any defects that appear later will probably be construed by the manufacturer as having been caused by wear and tear, dryness, and so on, and, therefore, will not be covered by the warranty. So, in practice, a very long warranty probably offers no more protection than one of normal duration.

Even if a long warranty covered every possible thing that might go wrong with a piano, the warranty has value only as long as the company offering it remains in business and cares about protecting its good name. Some piano companies these days do not actually manufacture pianos; they merely distribute and put their name on pianos made by other, mostly foreign, firms, and the warranty is issued in the name of the distributor, not the manufacturer. In fact, the consumer may not know who the manufacturer is. Of the three kinds of businesses—manufacturer, distributor, and dealer—the distributor, in my opinion, is the least likely to be around to honor the warranty in five, ten, or twenty years.

Cautions about fine print notwithstanding, the best manufacturers and dealers will go to considerable lengths to satisfy a customer when a bona fide defect is reported, even, at times, when they could conceivably avoid doing so. For instance, one customer of mine owns a vertical piano that had tuning pins made of an experimental material one company used very briefly in the mid-1950s. The experiment was apparently unsuccessful, as the tuning pins became extremely loose with time and the piano would not hold a tuning. The piano was not played or tuned for many years, and, following the death of the original owner, it was shipped to her daughter, at which time I was called to service it. Realizing that trying to tune the piano was a hopeless task and that there was something odd about the tuning pins, I contacted the maker's dealer in my area, who called the factory. Even though the warranty had been expired for *twenty years*, the factory authorized the dealer to install, at no charge to the customer, a completely new set of tuning pins and strings, which would otherwise have cost her more than five hundred dollars. No arm-twisting whatsoever was required on my part to get the dealer and factory to do this. It's interesting to note, however, that before authorizing this work the factory ascertained that the piano was still in the same family. Apparently companies with nontransferable warranties—even generous ones—balk at waiving that particular restriction.

Not all companies are so willing to cooperate. Naturally, the ones that produce the most lemons are the most difficult to deal with. One disreputable company, for example, initially refused to take back a piano whose strings had all rusted for no apparent reason within a few years of purchase. Then they agreed to

Buying Tips: Warranty Pointers

1. You are much less likely to have a serious warranty problem with a piano than you are with, say, a car. The exact terms of the warranty need not be an overriding concern if you buy a piano that comes otherwise well recommended.

2. Think twice about buying a piano that has a "parts only" warranty. Such warranties are next to worthless. If you must buy such a piano, ask the dealer to give you, in writing, a labor warranty that runs for as long as the parts warranty.

3. If you are buying a piano with the idea you might sell it if Junior decides to stop taking lessons, the resale value may be enhanced if the warranty is transferable to future owners.

4. Be sure you take a copy of the warranty home with you when you buy the piano, and take careful note of what servicing is required to comply with its terms.

5. Mail in the warranty registration card. It will make any warranty claim easier.

6. If you buy a piano from a dealer who is not authorized by that brand's manufacturer to sell its products, your warranty may be void. Beware of dealers who tell you they can get any brand of piano you want; they will buy those brands they are not authorized to sell from other dealers at prices slightly above wholesale—an unethical transaction called "transshipping"—and then resell to you. If in doubt, ask to see the dealer agreement, which authorizes the dealer to sell the brand in question.

7. The dealer shares in the responsibility for honoring the warranty, and can make things either easy or difficult for you. I can't emphasize this enough. In the example given earlier concerning the piano with loose tuning pins, it was as much the dealer's largess as the factory's that caused the warranty to be honored. The role of the dealer is especially important now that so many foreign-made pianos are being sold here through independent importers whose success so heavily depends on whimsical international currency fluctuations. Buy only from someone who seems likely to stay in business and will honor the warranty without hassles (more on choosing a dealer coming up).

take it back if the customer would foot the bill for shipping it to the factory (the dealer from whom it was bought had gone out of business). When the customer refused and her technician interceded on her behalf, the factory agreed to pay the technician to restring the piano, but at only one-third the commercial rate for the job.

The better companies produce very few really defective pianos. Most defects are extremely minor, such as rattling bass strings, and are taken care of by the dealer before the piano is sold or at the time of the first home tuning. If you or your technician should discover a defect you think may be covered by the warranty, the technician should contact the dealer from whom the piano was purchased (the technician can probably describe the problem more precisely than you can). The dealer will either send a technician to inspect the piano or will simply authorize your technician to make the repair and send a bill. If the defect is likely to be expensive to repair, or if a question arises about who is liable, the dealer will call the factory for instructions, since the factory will share the repair bill with the dealer.

If you are unable to get satisfaction from the dealer, or if either the dealer has gone out of business (which is a distinct possibility these days) or you have moved out of the dealer's area, your technician should call the Technical Services department of the manufacturer or importer. Someone there will refer you to a local dealer (if you have moved), authorize your technician to do the work, or turn your request down (at which point you can become an irate consumer.)

SHOPPING FOR A NEW PIANO

This section is about the actual mechanics of shopping for a new piano. Following a six-step basic guide is more detailed information on finding a dealer, prices and sales gimmicks, how to save money, servicing after delivery, and institutional pianos. Throughout this section, as in previous ones, I mention numerous potential problems and hazards to look out for. You may get the idea from this that buying a piano is likely to be a dreadful experience. Not so. In most cases, buying a new piano is pleasant and easy. The salespeople you meet will be helpful, and you will consider your purchase to be successful. But it is my job as a consumer advocate to warn you of the *worst* that can happen and the simple steps you can take to avoid problems.

Decide on your needs and resources. What type of piano, grand or vertical, do you require, and what size

piano is called for by your tastes, technical requirements, or the space available? How much money do you have to spend? What type of furniture styling seems preferable, and what types are clearly not appropriate? It's not necessary to stick to your preliminary choices under all circumstances, but it's useful to think about these things beforehand, just to get you started and to focus your efforts more efficiently. Chapter 2, "Buying A Piano: An Orientation" deals with these basic choices. Read it now if you have not already done so.

Do your homework. First, become acquainted with the basic technical features of the piano. You don't have to learn and memorize every detail; if you've read and understood the foregoing part of this chapter, you already know more than many of the salespeople you're going to meet. At the very least, you should know the basic features shown in Chapter 1.

Second, browse through the reviews in the next chapter and make a list of the brands that seem as if they might be appropriate for you. Now look in the Yellow Pages and at newspaper advertisements to see which dealers carry those brands. You might need to make some phone calls, since dealers may also sell brands other than those listed in the ads. If you live in a major metropolitan area, you may be able to find a dealer for practically every brand you're interested in. In other areas, though, the choice may be more limited.

Browse. As I mentioned in Chapter 2, you should spend plenty of time browsing. Make several trips, over a period of several weeks if necessary. Try to become attuned to the differences between pianos that have been pointed out in this chapter. Play as many pianos as possible, from the best to the worst. This is the fun part of buying a piano. Take written notes if you feel so inclined.

Narrow your choice. At some point you will begin to narrow your choice to a few instruments whose appearance, tone, touch, and features appeal to you. Naturally, you'll be looking at the price tags too, but a word of warning: Don't take the figures on the tags too literally; they are almost always inflated by at least 10 percent, sometimes 20 percent or much more, to allow for bargaining and "sales." So don't be afraid to include among your choices a few instruments at the very high end of your budget.

Have the piano inspected. You have narrowed your choice, consulted with the salesperson, and negotiated a price. While you were trying out pianos, you presumably pointed out to the salesperson any obvious defects or problems that needed correcting. (The Buying Tips throughout this chapter list trouble spots you can look for if you want to be extra conscientious or well informed.) Now it's time to have a professional piano technician check the piano over for those items that are beyond your ability to inspect, such as the regulation of the action and the tightness of the tuning pins. The dealer may need a few days to give the piano its final make-ready, if this has not already been done, and if you say your technician will be around later in the week to inspect the piano, you can be pretty sure it will be in good condition for you.

Be sure you choose a technician who is not connected with the store and owes it no favors. Hiring a technician to inspect a new piano can sometimes be awkward for all concerned, especially in areas where technicians depend on dealers for referrals. Some technicians, wishing to stay on good terms with local dealers, prefer not to enter a store to inspect a piano for a customer. If you are buying a brand with a reputation for arriving at the dealer in perfect condition, such as some of the Japanese pianos, and if you have superb confidence in the dealer, you may be able to omit this step. But it never hurts to get a second opinion.

If you have found, or your technician finds, any serious problems with the piano, you may want to make another trip to inspect it before agreeing to have it shipped. *Don't let the dealer tell you that the store's technician will fix everything after the piano is delivered to your home.* This promise is permissible for minor adjustments only. If the piano needs a lot of action regulating or if it is grossly out of tune or far from standard pitch, this should be corrected *before* the piano leaves the store. (The reasons for this are given on page 56 in relation to tuning and pitch and on page 66 in relation to regulating and other work.)

Before leaving the store, copy down the serial number of the piano, and then make sure the same piano is delivered to your home. Mistakes are rare, but possible. If a piano of the particular style or finish you desire is not in stock, don't accept the salesperson's offer to order one and have it sent directly to your home. Each piano is individual, even if of the same brand and model, and each must go through the same inspection and approval procedure outlined here before you accept it. It's true that some brands are so uniform in quality, tone, and action that you could probably get away with buying one sight unseen, but you're spending a lot of money here, so a little caution is advisable.

Take a copy of the warranty and service recommendations home with you.

Arrange for servicing after delivery. When the piano is delivered, make sure it is placed in a spot where the temperature and humidity will remain as constant as possible, and away from radiators, heating vents, and direct sunlight. See Chapter 7 for details on where, and where not, to put the piano. Within the first month or so, be sure to contact the dealer for your free home tuning. If possible, though, try to wait until near the end of the free-tuning period (usually about a month) before doing so. This will allow the piano the maximum amount of time to acclimate to its new environment and go out of tune and regulation.

Choosing a Piano Dealer

Most of the information on new pianos in this book concerns the differences between *manufacturers*. Almost as important to you—indeed, sometimes *more* important—is your choice of *dealer* from which to buy the piano. The principal reason for this is that most pianos, as we've seen, arrive from the factory needing a considerable amount of adjusting and tuning before they are ready for you to inspect, much less to buy. Dealers vary greatly in their willingness to provide this necessary pre-sale service, as well as in other ways.

Magazine articles on piano purchasing invariably advise the reader to find a "reputable" dealer. Just exactly what that means, or how to find such a business, the writers rarely say. (And do they think that without that advice you are going to look for a *disreputable* dealer?) Let's take a look at what you want from a dealer and how to find one to match your needs.

You want a dealer that maintains high service standards. As a technician from Colorado wrote me—

> I would expect, if I were buying a piano, that everything would be in order with it when new; that is, it would be completely regulated, up to pitch, and voiced to some degree of evenness of tone across the keyboard. Of course, most pianos are not. The best makes come in with keys badly out of square, unlevel, with too much lost motion, with uneven letoff, with too much lost motion in the pedals, and so on. Why don't they regulate them at the factory? Wouldn't the customers be more satisfied if they didn't have to pay a technician to regulate a brand new piano? "Dealer preps" are essentially nonexistent at our store. They want to pay technicians only for tuning— "Don't spend more than about an hour on a piano," the dealers instruct—and pretend that regulating is just sugar on top.

Most dealers realize they can get away without servicing their pianos at all, and hardly anybody will know the difference. Many take advantage of the cost savings, figuring that if you can't tell the difference, then you probably don't need—or deserve—the extra service. Some dealers, though, will service their pianos anyway, and to standards considerably higher than those of both the manufacturer and their unknowledgeable customers. They permit their technicians to do whatever is best for the pianos.

At the very least, a store that expects to service its pianos properly should have the facilities and personnel—either on staff or independent—to perform basic pre-sale service on the premises. Don't buy from dealers who don't service their pianos before they're sold, but who assure you the independent technician they hire will do all the servicing that's needed after the piano is moved to your home. Ask several independent technicians which stores have good service departments. If the salesperson has to take packing materials out of the piano before it can be played, you know it has not been serviced.

You can tell a good dealer by the company he or she keeps. You want a dealer whose offerings are mostly in the medium- to upper-quality range. Most dealers offer a variety of different brands, covering a broad range of price points, so they are equipped to cater to any needs. The particular brands they choose to sell depend on what franchises are available (since a franchise usually comes with a protected sales territory), the terms offered by the manufacturer, the popularity and reputation of the brand, and other considerations.

You can expect even very fine dealers to sell some brands or models that they can't honestly recommend. They may feel they need such pianos on hand for the customer who refuses to buy anything better, or they may be required by a manufacturer with whom they do business to stock its entire line, from cheap spinet to concert grand. But when a dealer sells *mostly* low-quality brands, you really have to question his or her knowledge and integrity, even if there are a few high-quality pianos on the sales floor.

Some insist this is nothing but wishful thinking on my part, but if someone is uncertain where to start, I suggest trying the Steinway dealer. The Steinway dealership is among the most coveted, and Steinway tries its best, though perhaps not always successfully, to choose only dealers who keep especially high service standards and have exceptional reputations. Don't worry—most Steinway dealers also sell less expensive brands. But the service standards they use on their Steinways are likely to rub off on their lesser brands. Conversely, the low standards with which dealers of mediocre pianos service those instruments are likely to carry over to the few higher-quality pianos they may keep around.

You want a dealer who keeps the pianos on the sales floor in tune. Nothing can be more frustrating than shopping for a piano when half of those you look at are out of tune. There's no way you can adequately judge the tone of a piano in this situation. Of course, it's unreasonable to expect that each of two hundred pianos in a store be in concert-perfect tune at all times, but most should be quite playable and musical. You can expect that some of the cheapest promotional pianos may be left untuned, at least partly to discourage anyone from buying them.

You want a dealer whose salespeople are knowledgeable, courteous, and helpful. Many salespeople know very little about pianos and could just as well be selling shoes or appliances. What little they do know has been fed them in special seminars sponsored by manufacturers' marketing departments, where they learn to promote the various gimmicks described throughout this chapter. But others have prior technical experience with pianos, are doubling as both technician and salesperson, or have taken the time and trouble to find out what this field is really all about. Even if they aren't technicians, they won't have to bluff their way through a sales presentation.

Even more than knowledge, courtesy is a trait you will appreciate in a salesperson. A good salesperson will be present when you have questions and scarce when you just want to browse. Many shoppers tell me the salespeople in certain piano stores in my area pester them and push them toward a sale until they are ready to scream and walk out. Some salespeople will also help you more than others in narrowing your choices to the piano that best meets your needs and resources. It helps to remember, though, that the primary job of salespeople is to sell you a piano they have in stock. You are responsible for looking out for your needs, just as they are responsible for looking out for theirs.

Many piano rebuilding shops carry new instruments as a sideline. Although I am, of course, biased, it seems to me that, all other things being equal, a dealership owned and run by piano technicians is likely to be more conscientious than one owned by businesspeople with little technical background. Technicians are more likely to be devoted to their craft, and so to carry better-quality instruments and service them more carefully than non-technicians. They are also perhaps more likely to be straightforward in their business dealings and rely less on deceptive sales techniques. But since there are always exceptions to generalizations such as this, this rule should not be followed religiously.

You want a dealer who seems likely to be in business for a long time and will be willing and able to provide you with warranty service should you need it. Of course, there's no way you can tell ahead of time which businesses are likely to fall prey to periodic recessions. My point here is to warn you against doing business with certain kinds of companies (not legitimate piano dealerships) who specialize in liquidating discontinued merchandise, or in certain shopping malls where businesses seem to start and fail with great regularity, with furniture stores that occasionally sell pianos, or with trucking companies that sell "repossessed" pianos out of the backs of their trucks. In the last case, you have no way of checking on the true status and condition of these pianos and too little time to make an informed decision. Also, contrary to these companies' sales pitches, identical pianos may be less expensive at regular piano stores. If the store from which you bought the piano does close down (or the truck drives away, never to be seen again), it may still be possible to receive warranty service (providing the manufacturer is still in business), but it will be more difficult.

Although no prescription can guarantee you'll find a "reputable" dealer, keeping these guidelines in mind and asking local independent piano technicians for their recommendations will most likely lead you to a dealer you can trust and enjoy doing business with.

Prices, Sales, and Merchandising

Most piano dealers aim for a gross profit margin on their pianos of about 40 percent. This means 40 percent of the retail price is profit above cost; the other 60 percent is the wholesale cost to the dealer (including freight, a significant expense). Depending on local economic conditions, competition, and the dealer's overhead, a slightly higher or lower profit margin may be desirable or acceptable, but 40 percent is considered about average. However, the price quoted to you or written on the price tag as the "list price" or "manufacturer's suggested retail price" is usually figured on a profit margin of 50 percent—that is, double the wholesale price—to allow for "negotiating" with you or for offering you a "discount." Indeed, sometimes the "list price" may reflect an even higher profit margin, as we shall see in a moment.

You might think that piano dealers must get rich on such a large profit margin on such a high-ticket item. After all, automobile dealers often make only a few hundred dollars on each sale. But, in fact, during the recent recession, hundreds of piano dealerships and other music stores went bankrupt. For one thing, pianos are very much a "luxury" item, the first to be crossed off the shopping list when times are hard.

Second, dealers usually have to borrow money to buy their instruments, often at outrageously high commercial interest rates. Since a piano may sit around on the sales floor for months (or even years) before being sold, much of the dealer's profit is eaten up by interest charges. In addition, a dealer often has to rent a rather large space in a busy downtown location, pay salespeople and technicians, keep hundreds of pianos tuned, maintain a repair and rebuilding shop, and pay for advertising. Unless business is quite brisk, there may be little profit left over for the owner. Though I'm a consumer advocate, I realize that a large gross profit margin (profit over the cost of goods) is absolutely necessary if a piano dealer is to pay for overhead, remain in business, and give good service.

In addition to the marketing gimmicks perpetrated by the manufacturer, which were described in the first part of this chapter, a number of sales gimmicks are also used by the dealer. I'm sure that piano dealers are no worse in this regard—and probably better—than other retailers; nevertheless, you should know about these ploys.

Not long ago, I received a call from a woman who had just visited a dealer who was having a spectacular "sale"—$1,000 off the "regular" price of their console. The sale was to end the next day, so she was soliciting my advice to help her make a decision in a hurry. I asked her what the sale price was for the model, and comparing it with the regular price from another dealer of the same brand, found them to be almost identical. The woman was taken aback by this news and was quite angry that the dealer had so brazenly lied about the "sale."

Unfortunately, this tactic is extremely common in the piano world, even among otherwise reputable dealers. The dealer will simply put an artificially high "list price" on each piano and then advertise a sale. Real sales of any consequence are rare. Even where prices are actually reduced by as much as 10 percent, most of the time the buyer could have achieved the same price simply through negotiation.

Some stores go so far as to use a similar tactic every day, without even advertising a sale. During my travels, I stopped at a store selling high-quality pianos in the Midwest. After playing a few, I examined some price tags and was surprised to find a price of $20,000 on a piano I knew to sell for about $14,000 back home. At first I thought that the tag must have gotten switched with that of the next larger model, but all the tags turned out to be too high by almost 50 percent. In response to my questioning, the salesman replied that any interested customers are immediately told that they will receive a 30 percent discount. He explained that all the piano stores in the area do this, and that his store would be at a competitive disadvantage if it didn't follow this practice. (And I had naïvely thought that dealers who sold the better pianos would be above such foolishness.)

A variation on this is the "piano warehouse." One famous piano store regularly takes out large advertisements in the local papers representing itself as a "piano warehouse" and "discount factory outlet." When customers enter the store, they actually have to pass through a warehouse piled high with piano crates with Japanese and Korean names on them before entering the showroom. Only very savvy customers can avoid the feeling that here they are *really* going to get a bargain. In reality, the "list prices" on the pianos at this store sometimes approach *two-and-a-half times* the wholesale prices, and even after striking a generous "bargain," the average customer will still pay more than twice the wholesale price. This "discount" store has a gross profit margin of over 50 percent! (This particular store has a reputation for giving excellent service and so probably earns its high profit, but I could do without the pretense.)

Other tricks are used to draw customers into the store. At the beginning of this chapter I mentioned "leaders," or "promotional" pianos—bottom-of-the-line pianos advertised at rock-bottom prices to serve as bait. Once you are in the store, the salesperson will attempt to sell you up to a higher-priced piano.

A variation on the "leader" is the "factory second." At another Midwestern dealership—this one selling low-quality pianos—a newspaper advertisement taped to the door announced that a limited number of "factory seconds"—pianos with slight cosmetic defects—were being sold at "half price." This piqued my curiosity, since it was my impression that most factories either touched up such defects and sold the pianos at full price or didn't sell them at all. A thorough inspection of several of these "seconds" failed to reveal anything that could be classified as a "defect" (except that the pianos were very sloppily made, but that was typical for the brand). After introducing myself as a technician, I asked the salesman to show me where the defects were. "Well . . . there really aren't any defects," he hesitantly replied. "That's just a way of getting people into the store." And as he turned to greet a customer walking in the door, he whispered, "It's what we call merchandising."

How To Save Money

Given that promotions are so often phony, how, then, can a buyer save money?

One school of thought suggests that, if you haven't yet chosen a brand, the best way to save in the very long run is to get the best, most durable piano money can buy, one that will last for generations and depreciate very slowly.

If you have decided on a brand of vertical piano, and are choosing a particular model, the best value will almost always be found with the school or institutional model. This will be ruggedly built, of adequate size, and much less expensive because of its plain furniture styling. The continental-style verticals are the next best value for the same reason, and the American decorator-style pianos offer you the least value for the money as far as the musical instrument is concerned.

Although dealers have protected franchise territories for most of the brands they sell, these territories are sometimes small. It's not unusual for several dealers to sell the same brand in a large metropolitan area. Even though sales and discounts are usually phony, prices are far from uniform, and it's worth your while to shop around and negotiate. In fact, it would be foolish not to negotiate, because most price tags are inflated in anticipation that you will. Sometimes it's possible to negotiate a very good deal, as the following example will illustrate:

Two friends of mine went shopping for a piano on which their young son was to begin taking lessons. After some looking around, they settled on a medium-quality console piano sold through an American manufacturer. The piano was actually manufactured by a Korean company (as indicated by a tag on the back of the piano), but was being marketed by the American company with its own name on the piano. The couple offered the dealer several hundred dollars less than the $2,600 price on the price tag, expecting him to negotiate. To their surprise, he refused to budge. "I think it's a fair price," he said, and that was that.

My friends next went to another dealer, where they saw a piano of the exact same model, style, and finish as the one described above, except that it had the *Korean* company's name on it instead of the American. It was selling for only $2,300, or $300 less than the identical piano with the American name on it. They were tempted to buy this piano, but decided that they would prefer a piano with an American name on it, even if not actually made here, so they continued looking.

Finally, my friends went to a store in another town, in which they found the same model with the American name, but, alas, not with the finish they liked. So they made the salesman an offer: If he could get them the piano with the finish they wanted and deliver it to their home with bench and tuning included, they would be willing to pay $2,100—and no sales tax. This might seem like an outrageous offer, but the salesman picked up the phone, called the first store the couple had visited to ascertain that they had the correct piano, and then accepted the offer. My friends now have in their home the same instrument they had refused to buy at $2,600—for 25 percent less.

Just what the relationship was between the first and last stores, and why the last store was willing to negotiate the low price, I don't know. Perhaps the dealer was tight for cash and was willing to forgo some profit to make a sale. My point is that opportunities for negotiating a lower price are there to be had. You may not be so brash as to ask for a specific price, but you can at least ask what the lowest price is at which the salesperson would be willing to sell you the piano. This is a more genteel and diplomatic way of asking for a discount.

My friends' experience also calls for a strong word of caution about doing business this way. When you buy from a store that habitually sells its merchandise at absurdly low prices, chances are the pianos are not being serviced properly and you may have trouble getting good warranty service should you need it. Many of a dealer's costs are fixed; there are a limited number of ways to reduce costs to lower prices, and service is the first to go. Dealers who price their pianos so low are often the first to go, too. This may not matter much if you are buying a piano that needs little preparation for sale, but if it does need work, you may end up sorry that you "saved money."

Even as I write this, though, I know that sometimes the concept of service is blown out of proportion to its real value. A very reliable piano may be sold unserviced at such a low price that even after you hire your own technician to service it completely, you still come out far ahead. In such a case, only the crazy or the very timid would pass up the chance to pocket the savings.

Here are some more points to consider when trying to reduce a piano's price:

- Sometimes a salesperson will offer to "throw in" a lamp or some piano lessons instead of dropping the inflated price on the tag. If these items don't interest you, say so and ask for a lower price instead.
- If you already own a piano, the dealer may offer you a substantial trade-in allowance on a new piano. But in this case, you are less likely to be given a discount off the "list price" of the new piano. You will usually come out ahead if you sell your present piano privately and use the money toward a negotiated price on the new piano. Actually, trade-ins are a nuisance for a piano dealer; most would be happy to give you a better price just to avoid having to deal with your old piano.

- Salespeople sometimes offer commissions to piano teachers and technicians for referring customers to them. But the salesperson cannot afford to both pay a big commission and offer you a big discount. If the salesperson must pay a commission, this may limit his or her ability to negotiate with you. Commissions make sense from a business point of view, but they present some ethical problems. How unbiased can such a referral be? If you are referred by a teacher or technician, you may want to ask that person whether he or she will be receiving a commission and, if the answer is yes, whether the commission could be waived or split with you.
- Sometimes piano technicians and rebuilders sell new pianos out of their home or shop. Their profit margin may be much less than that of a regular piano dealer because they may not be dependent on these sales as their principal source of income, they may be using extra space in their home or shop which would otherwise go unused, and they may not be located in a prime business location with a high overhead. The brands they sell may be less well known, because once a brand has achieved acceptance in the marketplace the manufacturer prefers to give a franchise to a large dealer in a good location who will sell many pianos. But some little-known brands are, in fact, excellent and worth your consideration. One drawback to shopping at a technician's home or shop is that the selection of models, styles, and finishes may be smaller because of limited space.
- The more expensive and little-known the piano and the longer it has been sitting around on the sales floor, the more irrelevant is the "suggested retail price" and the more room there is for bargaining. For this reason, it's not uncommon for discounts of 20 to 40 percent to be given on expensive European grand pianos.
- Spring and early summer are the slow times in the piano business, and therefore the times when you may be able to strike the best bargain. (Player piano sales are less likely to be seasonal, I'm told.)
- Whether you pay cash or buy on time is unlikely to affect the price you pay for the piano. Likewise, finance rates will probably be comparable whether you finance through the dealer or on the outside, though a bank will probably finance for a longer term. Still, you should shop around for financing. If you're buying a very expensive piano, you may save a bundle over the long run by borrowing at a lower rate on the equity in your home.
- Be sure, when negotiating, that a piano bench, moving, and tuning in your home are all included in the price. Almost every piano on the market comes with a bench (except some European pianos). It's not an "extra."

Servicing After Delivery

After your new piano has been in your home for a few weeks, be sure to get in touch with the dealer to arrange for your free in-home tuning. At this time, the technician will also take care of any minor problems not corrected at the store and any others you have noticed since the piano arrived at your home. If you had the piano inspected by an independent technician before it left the store, there should be little for the store technician to do now besides tuning, and everything should go smoothly.

If you failed to have the piano inspected, and if the dealer did little to prepare the piano for sale, you may now be faced with a problem. You see, the dealer and the store technician usually have an arrangement whereby the dealer pays the technician a flat fee for servicing a new piano in the home, regardless of how much work is involved. Furthermore, the fee is usually very, very low because there is an implicit understanding that the technician will be compensated by retaining the customer as a tuning client in the future. Unfortunately, this arrangement offers little incentive for the technician to do a conscientious job, and results in little more than a quick tuning and a brief attempt to correct whatever problems the customer actually notices, which may be far less than what the piano truly needs. Some dealers pay a higher fee and are willing to pay extra when more work is required, but many dealers, especially those who sell the cheaper pianos, do not. This is the cause of disharmony between many a technician and dealer, as the following letter from a California technician illustrates:

Dealer attitude is the worst offense in the piano business, at least here in the West. Dealers have no respect for piano tuners and pay the least wages possible. Always, the service technician is merely a "necessary evil" and nothing more.

Dealers refuse to put any money into the instrument prior to delivery, with the possible exception of a quick tuning for seven or eight dollars, or an in-home tuning at a very competitive price—from seven to seventeen dollars. (One dealer pays twenty-five dollars for in-home tunings, which is tops out here.) This fee includes everything, whether it takes thirty minutes or eight hours, which means that pianos get tuned and little else. In most cases, key level, action regulation, wire misalignment, etc., never get properly cared for.

For example, I was asked to do whatever necessary to satisfy a customer with a new_____ nine-foot concert grand. Several technicians had been to the house, leaving a dissatisfied customer behind. When I examined the piano, it was obvious that although new, it required a full action and damper regulation. There were wippens rubbing against each other, tight action flanges, hammers

badly aligned and not striking strings properly, jacks misaligned, letoff and general regulation totally unsuitable, dampers very badly in need of regulation, plus thoroughly wild strings. I proceeded to regulate everything and tune. I left a very happy customer who even called the store manager and thanked him for finally sending someone capable of correcting all the problems. Actually, some of the other tuners were equally capable, but how much could they be expected to do for a flat service fee of fifteen dollars? I thought I would get more than that after detailing what I had done and after the customer called the store. However, I received the same as the rest—fifteen dollars. I spent fifteen hours.

A second store and another grand of the same make with the same problems. I spent eleven hours plus travel time and sent the dealer a bill for fifty dollars. They paid, but cut me off—no more work since I dared charge the dealer so much.

And so the story goes. Customers are given all sorts of promises, but if they're not on paper—forget it!

Later on, the same technician writes:

Dealing with problems depends on both the dealer and the technician. Some dealers refuse to accept any responsibility and prefer to dish out lies or attempt to cover up with "It will go away in a while." Technicians (who are caught in between the dealer and the customer) deal with problems in many ways. For example, the problem of tight flanges [sluggishly moving action parts]:

• Spray with lubricant or anything else on hand and tell the customer that in a few days all the problems will go away. Then don't return when the customer calls to complain.
• Tell the customer you will look into the problem and let them know when you find out. Then walk away and forget about it.
• Go to the dealer, explain the problem, and get threatened with a lawsuit.
• Service the action on your own time and at your own expense.
• Contact the factory and see if they will assist. Often they will, but don't depend on it. Dealers are reluctant to deal with the factory, even though they can do so far easier than the technician can.

Many dealers would rather dump a conscientious technician and get one who just sprays [lubricant] and leaves.

If you failed to see that the piano was prepared and inspected in the store and are now faced with the sorry situation of not knowing what work the piano needs and how to get it done, you should speak to the store technician frankly about it when he or she arrives to tune your piano. Say you understand that the technician's fee doesn't come close to paying the true cost of doing the adjustments that may be needed, but that you would like a candid assessment of the piano and are willing to pay the difference between what the technician is paid by the dealer and what the job is worth. In fact, this is a good tack even if the piano needs only tuning. You will make a good friend and receive the most thorough job possible. Naturally, if the piano cost $1,500 and you are told that it will cost $300 to put it in the kind of condition it should have been in in the first place, you will be understandably upset. But before you complain to the dealer, remember that doing so will get the honest technician who gave you the bad news in trouble. (This advice assumes the technician is, in fact, honest. If he or she is not, you may get ripped off.)

I would also advise that even if you plan to use another technician in the future, you use the store technician for the initial tuning in your home. This technician has undoubtedly serviced scores of pianos of the same make and model and is acutely aware of all their idiosyncrasies and their remedies, where these exist. He or she also has easiest access to spare parts and advice from the factory when necessary. Another technician, even if extremely competent, may lack this specific experience and support and so may be less effective or efficient. You should be aware, however, that not all store technicians are equally qualified; many are beginners who stay with the store only until they build up a clientele sufficient to support themselves independently. If you don't have full confidence in the store technician, you may want to immediately follow up the free initial tuning with a service call by a technician of your choice.

Pianos often need more servicing during the first few years of their life than they need for many years afterward. Because the strings will be new and still stretching, you should have the piano tuned four times the first year. After that, the frequency of tuning will depend on humidity, usage, your ear, and your budget. See Chapter 7 for details on how often, and when, to have your piano tuned. During the first year or two, the cloth and felt parts in the action will compact, so you can expect to need some action and tone regulating during this time, too. Note that several manufacturers offer more than one free tuning and free action regulating during the first year of ownership, or a factory rebate on the cost of such service. Be sure to keep track of the warranty cards or other papers that allow you to cash in on these offers.

Player Pianos. One instance when it might be best *not* to use the store technician is when buying a player piano. Several manufacturers are still producing these relics of the past, which had their heyday in the 1920s and experienced a revival in the 1960s. A player piano is a regular vertical piano with a rather complicated pneumatic mechanism added. This mechanism en-

ables the piano to play by itself when a punched paper roll is inserted. The vast majority of piano technicians don't know anything about servicing the player mechanism and, frankly, don't care. In fact, because the player mechanism gets in their way, most technicians would rather not even tune a player piano. If you buy one of these pianos, therefore, you should immediately seek out a technician skilled in servicing them. In some parts of the country, this might not be easy. Writes one correspondent:

Player pianos should be serviced by qualified technicians only, but they would charge the dealer more. Dealers don't like that, so they have regular (cheap) tuners service players, quite often for a standard tuning fee. Some may pay as much as five dollars more, but not enough to perform much more than a quick, basic tuning. Therefore, the player mechanism goes unserviced and unregulated.

Player pianos in the home suffer the same consequences. Often owners, not knowing any better, continue to allow the store tuners to service their players. These store tuners are seldom qualified in player service. One manufacturer has training seminars in the technique of tuning player pianos. However, *tuning* a player is as far as it goes since few tuners actually understand the operation of the player mechanism, and most cannot service it or perform preventive maintenance on it. The manufacturer wants to make player piano service sound easy to convince the store owners that players are not troublesome and do not require anything more than the ability of a plain piano floor tuner, which in my opinion is not so.

If you are considering buying a player piano, please read the section "Players and Reproducers" in Chapter 5, "Buying A Used Piano."

Buying a School or Institutional Piano

Pianos in schools and other institutions take a terrible beating, and are usually appallingly neglected by the administrators charged with their care—even at some prestigious music schools and universities where one would expect people to know better. Sometimes one technician is supposed to maintain hundreds of pianos, but, due to the demand for service to recital and faculty instruments, can barely give the practice room pianos a quick tuning once or twice a year, though most of them are in dire need of regulating or even rebuilding. One might think that this neglect must be caused by a lack of funds, but at the same time, school administrators may budget tens of thousands of dollars for the purchase of new pianos, often citing the state of disrepair of the present crop as justification for buying new ones. "And if these don't hold up, we'll try a different brand next time," they all too often say.*

If you are an administrator charged with buying new pianos for your school or other institution, please stop for a moment and reconsider whether new instruments are really needed. Do you realize you could have *dozens* of pianos completely regulated, or at least several pianos completely restored or rebuilt, for the price of a single high-quality new piano? Or that by diverting some of the money budgeted for new instruments toward the hiring of another piano technician, you could save thousands of dollars each year that would otherwise have to be spent replacing neglected instruments? I realize that restrictions inherent in the budgetary process sometimes dictate how certain funds are to be used, particularly when the funds come from foundation grants or charitable donations. But you should make every effort to see that, wherever possible, the money is directed where it makes most sense. Seventy-five percent of the time, in my estimate, that means in piano maintenance and repair, not purchase.

Pianos in institutions suffer not only from lack of service, of course, but from overuse, occasional vandalism, and—perhaps more than anything else—lack of climate control. Throughout most of the country, overheating during the winter days, freezing at night and on weekends and holidays, and then unremitting humidity in the summer ages school pianos long before their time. Under these conditions, my contacts at schools and universities tell me, virtually all brands of piano hold up equally poorly. Spending some money on climate control would probably be of greater benefit than buying new pianos. But where this is not possible, purchasing pianos with plastic action parts, laminated soundboards, laminated bridges, multi-laminated pinblocks, and other indestructible features might actually be a good idea, especially for practice-room pianos, which are almost never in tune anyway and rarely expected to have a great tone.

In a slightly less cynical vein, as both a pianist and a piano technician I would recommend that you pay special attention to the quality of keys and action in practice pianos. Most of these instruments are being used by students to develop technical facility more than tone production, the latter being almost impossible given the weird acoustics of the cubicles in which the pianos are placed, not to mention the state of their tuning. Students can put up with a good deal of variance in tuning and tone, but are completely stymied when a key is stuck or the action is grossly uneven. Long, properly weighted keys and trouble-free actions that repeat well and are in good regulation will probably be appreciated more than most other features.

The bidding process for school pianos tends to be a rerun of the marketing gimmicks described earlier in this chapter. Typically, a school purchasing agent will decide what brand and model of piano he or she would like to purchase, but, because it's not considered proper to actually name the piano in the bidding specs, the agent will instead describe the piano in terms of its features—the number of back posts, the number of laminations in the pinblock, and so on. Of course, only one or two brands will actually fit the description. Dealers are allowed to enter alternate bids for slightly different pianos, and purchasing agents are usually given some latitude in awarding contracts for reasons other than a piano's fitting the exact description and bearing the lowest price; still, the agent usually ends up purchasing the piano that he or she had in mind at the start.

This bidding procedure is designed to protect the school district by setting minimum quality standards for its pianos, and probably to protect the purchasing agent from accusations of prejudice for or against certain brands or dealers. My guess is that this process was most useful in the sixties and seventies, when so many truly awful pianos were being built. But nowadays it simply adds red tape, requiring people to write, read, decipher, and match a list of specifications that may or may not be related to quality and that are simply a ruse anyway. One manufacturing executive told me his company could make a better school piano for less money if it didn't have to pattern its specifications after certain Japanese pianos that so many purchasing agents were using to write bids.

When buying a school piano, keep in mind a few additional considerations:

- Heavy-duty casters and locks for the fallboard and lid are standard features on many, but not all, institutional models. If any of these are not standard, you can specify that they should be added.
- You should specify exactly what pre-sale and post-sale service you expect to be included. A dealer's reputation for providing this service should be taken into account when awarding contracts.
- Be sure to check the manufacturer's warranty policy. Some consumer warranties do not extend to institutional or commercial use.

*Adapted from Jack Krefting, "The Technical Forum," *Piano Technicians Journal*, March 1983, p. 8.

CHAPTER FOUR

A Consumer Guide to New and Recently Made Pianos

THE NEW PIANO SURVEY

TO THE BEST OF MY KNOWLEDGE, A GOOD, detailed brand-by-brand review of new pianos has never before been written, even by consumer magazines that tackle everything from dog food to hair spray. There are some good reasons why this is so. For one thing, it's very hard to design "tests" for a piano. Sure, we could test how fast a note is able to repeat, or electronically analyze the scale design—and these tests could be useful to a degree—but, in the end, there are too few such tests that can be done, and they fail to tell us enough about the piano. Sometimes sketchy magazine articles substitute "features" for tests. If the piano has enough of the "right" features, it's recommended. But, as we've seen in the last chapter, many features are just marketing gimmicks with no real value, and despite having all the right features, some pianos still sound terrible.

There are other impediments to reviewing pianos. The number of different piano brands and models is probably comparable to that of automobiles, but the number of piano experts and technicians is much smaller. Furthermore, piano repair records are not generally kept in sufficient detail to provide long-term information on the incidence of repair. And, although given enough resources these obstacles could be overcome, the relatively small size of the piano market doesn't justify the expenditure of money that would be required to collect this data. Of course, that doesn't help *you*, one of those who need this information.

The Myth of Objectivity

One of the reasons often cited for not even attempting to review pianos is that the critique would be just a "bunch of opinions." It would certainly be hard to deny that evaluating a piano involves a lot of judgments; opinions about tone, touch, design, looks, and so on, are all central to such an evaluation. But a close look at many consumer product evaluations reveals that they, too, are much more subjective than the magazines in which they appear would care to admit. When a car is said to "handle well," "comfortably seat four," or "have a lot of engine noise," are these not matters of opinion? Subjectivity is present in more subtle ways as well: in simply deciding what information is desirable about a product and designing tests for it, one brand may be favored over another, even though the piece of information being sought may not be particularly useful to the buyer of the product. A good example of this is the amazingly complicated technical data that often accompanies reviews of stereos and speakers. "But does it sound good?" you ask. "Well, that's just somebody's opinion."

The fact is, though, we seek other people's opinions all the time in our daily lives, even on matters we know must be judged subjectively. One of the ways we determine whose opinion to trust is by the amount of experience they have with the subject and by the amount of detail they can offer to back up their opinion. We do this with the assumption that their experience has enabled them to develop more finely honed senses than ours (such as with music or art), and we do so at least as much for our peace of mind—to validate our own opinions—as to gather new information. Of course, sometimes we *do* receive new information, such as when an auto mechanic warns us of a problem common to a particular brand of automobile we are considering buying.

Thus, when someone calls and asks me for advice on buying a piano, it is precisely my *opinion* that they desire (as subjective as it might be), plus any facts that might support it or that might be useful or interesting to them. In designing a survey appropriate to the task of evaluating pianos, then, it was important not to shy away from subjective opinions, but also, to the extent possible, to survey as much useful objective information as possible.

The Survey and Its Limitations

To assist me in advising my readers, forty-five piano technicians from across the United States were recruited to participate in a written survey of the condition of new and almost-new pianos. The technicians' experience with servicing pianos ranged from about five to thirty-five years, averaging about fifteen years each, and nearly all were Craftsman-level members of the Piano Technicians Guild (although the Guild itself played no part in this survey). Pads of survey forms were distributed to the technicians, with instructions that they fill out one form for each piano five years old or younger that they serviced during the following three months. The forms had space for brand, model, age, place of service, and other identifying information; had a checklist of sixty-nine possible problems a piano might have; requested an overall evaluation of how highly the piano could be recommended for purchase; and asked that any additional information be provided on the back of the form. I want to emphasize that this survey was not intended as a precise scientific instrument, and its results cannot be considered statistically valid. Rather I considered it a fact-finding tool from which a limited amount of useful information might be extracted. It was also a way

of encouraging technicians to look more closely at the pianos they were servicing, and a way of opening up conversation with the technicians that would lead to the development of an accurate picture of each brand.

Over eleven hundred forms were returned by the forty-five technicians. (In a similar survey taken in 1983 for the first edition of this book, about one thousand forms were completed by thirty technicians.) Many forms contained additional comments that explained problems in more detail and effectively expanded the sample by indicating which problems were common to other pianos of the same model and which were just quirks. After reviewing the results, I interviewed most of the technicians (and others not involved in the written survey) at great length to find out how these results actually corresponded to their experience and opinions. I also "shopped" at piano stores, inspected new pianos, and spoke to dealers, salespeople, and other service technicians whenever the chance arose. All told, about sixty technicians contributed to the survey in written or oral form. To ensure maximum objectivity and prevent harassment by dealers or manufacturers, all technicians participating in this study were guaranteed anonymity.

Eleven hundred pianos may seem like a lot, but not all the manufacturers were represented well enough in the written part of the survey to yield usable results. For all other manufacturers, the reviews are based on interviews with technicians and, occasionally, on personal inspection of the pianos. I believe this information is reliable, but it is more limited in detail.

To make the most appropriate use of a survey of this kind, you need to understand its limitations. It was my intention to write fair and balanced, but candid, reviews that could serve as a guide to consumers, who otherwise have nowhere else to turn for advice. But this is not "God's word" on pianos. These are reviews of pianos as seen by a few members of a particular segment of the population—piano technicians—whose concerns may not always be the same as yours. I chose piano technicians, rather than musicians or dealers, because they have the widest exposure, the most technical knowledge, and the least bias of all those connected with the piano industry. But they are not entirely without prejudice. They often tend to see pianos more in terms of their serviceability than their playability. Many technicians, in fact, do not play the piano. In some cases, their assessment of tone may be based on how the piano sounds when it is being tuned rather than when it is played. (Some pianos are very difficult to tune, but when all closed up sound just fine—and vice versa.) So some pianos that technicians don't like may still be acceptable, especially for use by beginners.

The technicians differed in how closely they examined pianos, perhaps finding more fault with pianos they were predisposed not to like than with others. They also differed in their standards of quality. By keeping close tabs on the survey forms returned by each participant, and through interviews that revealed each participant's quality standards and degree of exposure to particular brands, I was able to compensate for these differences somewhat in the final results.

This brings me to my own role in the survey, which was far from that of a neutral observer. In addition to designing the survey and doing the interviews, I had to evaluate the credibility of my sources and in other ways process the information I received. Not to do so would have been unfair to everyone involved. I also had to inspect pianos personally in a few cases where data was insufficient. (I believe I was aided in this by my thirty years as a pianist, as well as my fifteen years as a piano technician.) I have done my best to state when opinions are strictly my own, but even those opinions attributed to other technicians ultimately represent only my own best assessment of their views, based on my research. Despite these limitations and the subjective nature of the reviews, I believe that when used with discretion, good judgment, and common sense, this guide will result in a better purchase and a little more peace of mind.

How to Use This Guide

Information of many different kinds is contained in these reviews, whose thoroughness varies, depending on the amount of information that was available to me, what information seemed to be most useful for the consumer, and other considerations.

Each review begins with the name, address, and telephone number of the company or its U.S. distributor. This is so you can contact the company to find out if there is a dealer near you, or to settle a warranty claim that cannot be satisfactorily settled with the dealer.

This is followed by the name of the actual owner of the company (or in the case of a distributor, the maker of the piano) and by the trade names the company has used during the past ten years (some of these companies own many more trade names than are listed, but have not recently used them). A listing of all trade names mentioned in this guide and the names of the companies under which they are reviewed can be found on page 76. Note that some foreign manufacturers with very limited distribution in the U.S., and some other assorted brands not requiring full listings, are listed under "Miscellaneous," page 109. Trade names that belong to dealers and distributors, not manufacturers, are known as "stencil pianos," explained on page 112.

A little bit of the history of some companies, especially their recent history, is included, partly for interest, partly to warn you when recent changes of ownership, management, location, and so on, may affect the products' quality.

A listing and evaluation of pianos follows, including data from the written survey where applicable. As I said earlier, the technicians completed a survey form for each piano five years old or younger that they serviced during a three-month period. I included pianos that were as much as five years old, rather than only brand-new pianos, because I believe a piano must demonstrate its ability to hold up with time and use before being considered acceptable. Some pianos that seem flawless when new may not pass muster a few years down the road. Other pianos may arrive from the factory needing much work, but once the work is done they may hold up beautifully. The written survey was an attempt to take a "snapshot" in time to discover how the pianos hold up and what problems seem to occur most often. In some of the reviews, these problems are mentioned.

It's important not to be too alarmed by these problems or take them too seriously. Many problems are minor and easily corrected. Since companies are continually solving old problems and discovering new ones, and because of differences between one instrument and another or between one production run and another, there is no guarantee that any of the problems listed would appear in your piano if you bought one of that brand.

Still, I believe that the written survey and the lists of problems do help provide a more accurate picture of each brand. The lists, taken in context with the rest of the review and in conjunction with the technical material presented in the last chapter, can be useful to you as you shop for a piano or when you or your technician examines the piano before you purchase it. It may point out potential problems that could make the piano unsuitable for you or may help you in making a list of problems that need to be corrected before you will accept delivery. And even though the manufacturer may have corrected some of the specific defects listed, or changed models, by the time you get around to shopping for a piano, the type and number of such defects or problems may give you a better general idea of what to expect from that brand of piano.

Because of the large time span covered in these reviews, this guide is also intended for those who are buying a used piano of recent origin. It is inevitable, though, that reviews of this kind are to some extent out of date by the time they are published. My apologies to those manufacturers whose products may be inaccurately described as a result.

Note: To save space, technical terms mentioned in the reviews may not be explained where they appear. They may be looked up in the Glossary/Index.

Ratings. In the first edition of this book, each model was given a numerical rating to indicate its technical quality and recommendability relative to other brands and models. Although this rating system was extremely popular, I have eliminated it in this edition for several reasons. First, despite the numbers, the ratings were very subjective. The survey and reviews contain enough subjectivity already and, in my opinion, do not benefit from more. Second, quality can differ even within the same brand and model, and it can differ from one dealer to another because of differences in service. Third, I believe the brand reviews, and the "Overview" beginning on page 73, give adequate information about the quality characteristics of each brand. Fourth, consumers, in their understandable search for certainty in a bewildering situation, tended to overuse the ratings and interpret them too literally, often ignoring other important information and their own common sense. Last, retailers, preying on their customers' vulnerability, often misused the ratings by making tiny differences between brands loom large.

NEED MORE HELP?

Making decisions about the purchase of a piano can sometimes be difficult and confusing. Sorting out the conflicting claims of dealers and manufacturers and deciding which piano represents the best value for you can often be aided by speaking to a sympathetic and knowledgeable person who is not trying to sell you something. In response to many requests for additional information and advice, I have developed a telephone consulting service to assist people shopping for a new piano.

For a fee of thirty dollars (subject to change) charged to your credit card, I will spend up to a half hour on the phone advising you on which piano brands and models best fit your particular needs, preferences, and budget. I can also tell you the approximate prices I consider fair for you to pay, and how to bargain for the lowest price. Finally, I can supply you with names of qualified piano technicians in your area and other information about piano maintenance. Many customers have reported that the advice they received saved them hundreds or even thousands of dollars on their purchase, as well as giving them greater peace of mind.

To make the best use of this service, I suggest you first read this book, as many of your questions may be answered here, and that you do some shopping to acquaint yourself with the various brands, dealers, and prices in your area. Then, to make an appointment, call the publisher, Brookside Press, at 800-545-2022 (617-522-7182 from Canada) and leave your name, address, phone number, credit card information, and the best time to reach you. I will return your call collect, usually within a day or two.

Note: The purchase of a *used* piano requires detailed, onsite inspection and evaluation. Telephone advice about such pianos, therefore, can only be of a very general nature.

NOTICE TO READERS*

Each manufacturer was sent a copy of the proposed review of its pianos prior to publication, along with an invitation to make comments and corrections and, if necessary, to write a response that would be printed in the book following the review. Many manufacturers were very gracious in accepting criticism, even when they disagreed with it, and had no problem with allowing the review to be published. Some, however, were extremely displeased with their reviews, felt them to be unfair, and suggested that legal action might be taken if the proposed reviews were published; or simply did not communicate with me in a timely and satisfactory manner. To avoid expensive legal entanglements, I have deleted those reviews. I regret any inconvenience to my readers.

---

*Please see "Addendum" following page 176.

THE PIANO INDUSTRY TODAY: AN OVERVIEW

The piano industry today, especially in the United States, is in a state of decline. Some foretell its doom; others predict it will simply stabilize at a new level. Whereas the number of new pianos sold in the United States (including imports) peaked in 1978 at over 282 thousand, by 1985 only a little more than 150 thousand were sold, and that volume has been maintained, give or take a little, through 1989. Yet despite these gloomy figures, a survey sponsored by the American Music Conference and carried out by the Gallup Organization reports that amateur piano playing is as widespread as it has ever been, and extrapolations from the survey suggest that nearly two million U.S. households bought a piano in 1984!

Although some of this discrepancy may be due to inaccurate estimates for those manufacturers who didn't report (reporting is voluntary) or to statistical error in the survey, clearly the vast majority of piano sales are of used pianos, and most of these are private transactions that therefore go unreported. Several factors contribute to the continued vigor of the used piano market. One is the perceived high price of new pianos—whose manufacture is labor intensive—compared to the lower and lower prices of electronic entertainment devices—televisions, VCRs, and electronic keyboards, among others. Another is the growing pool of skilled piano technicians who are rebuilding and reconditioning pianos, efforts fueled by the bad reputation earned by the junk piano makers of the last two decades.

The health of the used piano market certainly doesn't help the U.S. piano industry. Whereas sixty years ago there were literally hundreds of piano makers in the United States, and even a decade ago there were at least a dozen major firms, now only a few remain, five having ceased production in the first half of the 1980s alone. Some of the ones that remain are able to hold on only because they have diversified to other products that subsidize their meager piano sales.

Also contributing heavily to the drop in piano sales has been the explosion of the electronic keyboard and synthesizer market. Some of these instruments are now able to produce sounds that are virtually indistinguishable from those of a real piano, and when they are encased in piano-like cabinets and priced right, they may make a real piano a questionable purchase for some buyers. Already the electronic boom has decimated the home organ industry, causing many piano and organ dealers to fail or scurry for new products to sell.

Yet it is not used piano sales and electronic keyboards alone that are responsible for the decline of the U.S. piano industry. It is also, and perhaps primarily, the large influx of foreign-made pianos, and the currency imbalance that caused U.S.-made pianos to be more expensive than foreign pianos both at home and abroad for many years. For most of the past thirty years, some of the world's best raw materials for piano manufacture have been assembled in the United States using a combination of imprecise machinery, inefficient factory methods, and poorly managed human labor. Although some blame the American worker for the shoddy results, I believe that responsibility really lies with poor factory management, and with a culture in which the consumption of material goods is so rampant that anything that can be sold will be produced, regardless of its quality. From a business point of view, everything worked just fine as long as there was no competition from abroad. But since the late 1970s, American piano firms have increasingly been forced to compete with the efficient methods and low prices of foreign producers. These foreign companies—mostly Asian—have also been aided by lower labor costs, greater technical sophistication and automation, favorable tariffs, and the ability to more rapidly assess and meet changing consumer desires. At the same time, declining sales of U.S. pianos have precluded all but the strongest U.S. firms from making the investments in research and development necessary for effective competition; the others have gone under or are barely hanging on.

Changing consumer buying patterns and tastes also interact strongly with the growing international flavor of the U.S. piano market, both influencing and being influenced by it. Many adults of the baby-boom generation, having played piano as children, are returning to the instrument now that their families and careers are more settled. Although they may be buying pianos partly for their children to learn on, they are looking for good quality more than for low price, especially when their professions (such as computers, business, and medicine) make a better piano affordable. Japanese and Korean manufacturers were supplying these buyers with good large uprights and grands at very reasonable prices, while American manufacturers were still busy trying to sell spinets and consoles—until it was too late. So while the total number of new pianos sold dropped 9 percent in 1984, the number of imported grands increased by 37 percent. There has also been a turn away from decorator-style pianos toward the continental style, leaving behind those manufacturers whose pianos were primarily fancy furniture.

When you enter a piano store, you are going to find a greater international mix of piano brands than ever before, including pianos from the United States, West Germany, Japan, and Korea, and a smattering from other European countries, both East and West, and mainland China. Furthermore, some foreign manufacturers also own factories in the United States and some U.S. companies sell foreign-made pianos under their own (American) label. This makes the piano shopper's job more difficult and confusing than ever before, and some kind of guidance more essential. The following summary of the more detailed listings and recommendations contained in this chapter may help orient you at the start of your search. However, be sure to read the detailed listings before making a purchase.

During the past two decades, U.S.-made pianos have ranged from the sublime to the ridiculous. On the low end, and to be avoided, are the following companies who have passed away during the 1980s, but whose pianos may still occasionally be for sale: Aeolian (under numerous trade names—see listing), Kohler & Campbell, Marantz, Currier, and Lowrey/ Story & Clark. Kimball, formerly one of those whose pianos I would have suggested avoiding, has done quite a turnaround during the 1980s. Their studios are now quite respectable, their grands commendable. Baldwin, the country's largest piano manufacturer, now also owns Wurlitzer. Yamaha and Kawai, Japanese companies, also make or assemble pianos in the United States. Given that so many of the parts, machinery, and sometimes even the workers are imported from Japan, it's no wonder that these manufacturers' American-made products now often emulate the high quality of those made in Japan. Carrying on an American tradition of craftsmanship that never entirely disappeared are Sohmer, Mason & Hamlin, and Steinway. Don't forget to explore the lesser-known U.S. piano makers: the unusual Astin-Weight, the high-quality home and school pianos of Charles Walter, the concert-quality grands of Falcone, and the player pianos by Classic (now also reviving the Story & Clark name), among others.

Japan has been making pianos since about 1900, but began exporting them to the United States only about 1960. At first the pianos fell apart because the wood was not dried to meet the demands of our climatic extremes, but within a few years the quality improved and the price gave U.S. makers a run for their money. For a variety of reasons, including currency fluctuations and higher wages in Japan, the price of many Japanese pianos has become as high or higher than comparable American-made pianos. At the same time, sales of Japanese pianos have been severely undercut during the past few years by the Korean piano industry, forcing the Japanese both to tighten their belt and to market a more professional image to convince the public that their pianos are worth the extra money, which they most assuredly are. The two major Japanese piano makers, Yamaha and Kawai, are both recommended very often by piano technicians for general home and institutional use. Other Japanese instruments found here in recent years have been Tadashi and Tokai, the latter not recommended.

In Japan, industrial engineering is a highly respected profession and factory management is elevated to a high art. The Japanese factories are among the most automated anywhere, and Japanese pianos among the most uniformly made. This precision, and the intelligence with which the pianos are designed, especially for servicing, are the chief assets of Japanese pianos. But unlike the United States, Japan is poor in raw materials, especially wood, and must import most of it. Due to Japan's high volume of production, and the relative scarcity and high cost of fine woods, Japanese pianos usually contain cheaper woods, especially for the cabinets and possibly for other parts, too. This is thought to affect the tone of the pianos as well as their longevity (Japanese pianos have historically had a crisp, bright, brittle tone that was a little short on sustaining qualities). They seem to hold up reasonably well in our climate and piano technicians love to service them, but there is considerable speculation that over the long run (a generation or more), they aren't likely to hold up as well as some of the more expensive American-made pianos, especially under heavy use or adverse conditions.

Western European pianos are sold in the United States in relatively small (though increasing) quantities, probably due to their high price and low name recognition, but there is quite a list of them, and most are of high quality. They tend to lap at our shores like the tide, coming and going as the currency values fluctuate. Best known here are Bösendorfer (Austria), owned by Kimball; Bechstein (West Germany), until recently owned by Baldwin; and the popular Schimmel (West Germany); other Western European names include Grotrian, Ibach, Feurich, Seiler, and Sauter (all West Germany), and Knight (England), among others.

Eastern European pianos are also sold here. They usually have great scale designs, and the workmanship is often exquisite, too. But due to different working and business conditions, and sometimes shortages of high-quality raw materials, the pianos are a little less consistent in quality than the pianos from Western Europe and tend to need more preparation by the dealer. The best Eastern European brands are Blüthner and August Forster (East Germany). Petrof

(Czechoslovakia) is also very good; Zimmermann (East Germany) is of medium quality. The prices of all these pianos are much lower than that of their Western counterparts. With the liberation of Eastern Europe will undoubtedly come higher wages, but their effect on these pianos' prices may be offset by a lowering of the stiff forty percent duty on imports from some Eastern bloc countries. The rapidly changing political situation in Eastern Europe may affect product quality, so I advise checking on this at the time of purchase.

Most European piano factories are very small compared to the average American factory, and like a fly on an elephant compared to a giant like Yamaha. Interestingly, despite their size and contrary to their image, a few of them are also extremely automated and computerized. They also have access to the best woods and carry forth a tradition of impeccable craftsmanship and exquisite cabinetmaking. Given this combination of talent and resources, it would appear that European piano makers are the ideal source of quality instruments, and their reputation—and, yes, their prices, too—reflects this. Be aware, though, that for reasons of both tradition and design, some European pianos have a sweeter, less brilliant tone than American pianos, one that may not always be suitable when a more powerful sound is desired. And because they are built to very tight tolerances, there is also a slightly greater risk of small problems due to humidity changes than in comparable U.S.-made instruments.

The Korean piano industry is little more than thirty years old, and growing up as it did in an impoverished and war-torn economy, it has had to borrow all its technical know-how from Japan and West Germany. Like Japan, Korea has little in the way of natural resources, so the raw materials have had to be imported, too. When Korean pianos first entered the United States in the late 1970s, like the Japanese before them they experienced great humidity-related problems. By the mid-1980s, though, they were improving so rapidly that it appeared as if any day they would overtake the Japanese in quality. Based on some observations of Korean pianos in showrooms and at trade shows, and on scant evidence from technicians in the field, I gave rather rosy reviews and ratings to these pianos in the first edition of this book.

Unfortunately, this turned out to be premature. Not only did the pianos have many more problems than a casual inspection would reveal, but just as the book was going to press, an explosive Korean labor situation erupted into crippling strikes that left many Korean pianos in unsatisfactory condition. This situation has passed, and the pianos continue their slow march toward improvement. But given their short history, and the struggle just to build a piano that would hold up

under diverse conditions, it's not surprising that Korean pianos have not yet developed a consistent identity or "voice" of their own. As musical machines, they sometimes work acceptably, but to my ears, their tone tends to offer a variety of American, Japanese, and European elements that, at best, neither offends nor delights.

The Korean piano industry is now in the same state of transition that the Japanese industry was in only a decade or two ago: as wages rise rapidly, automation is proceeding as quickly as possible so the industry can remain competitive in the world market. Remaining competitive will be no easy task, though. Korean pianos are already almost as expensive as some Japanese pianos, whereas the quality, in my opinion, is not even close. As world-wide demand for pianos slackens and competition heats up, expect the Koreans to be paying more attention to quality control in the near future, and to marketing a more professional image. Of the three major Korean manufacturers—Young Chang, Samick, and Sojin—Young Chang is considered the more serious. But personally, unless price is the major consideration, I prefer not to recommend any of these brands, especially for high-use environments, until I'm sure they'll hold up well with time.

A number of piano makers, especially Samick, Young Chang, Sojin, and Kimball, also make pianos for other firms, marketed here under such names as Schafer, Schumann, Hyundai, and Weber. These are names of importers and distributors—not manufacturers—some of whom are just capitalizing on familiar names. It remains to be seen whether these names will become a long-term force in the piano market or if they will be dropped as the market becomes saturated with look-alike pianos.

Mainland Chinese pianos have also been appearing in piano stores on and off over the last few years. At first they had the same problems that the Korean and Japanese pianos once had—warpage due to inadequate seasoning of lumber and lack of climate control in the factories. For a while some stores actually employed unskilled labor just to unwarp piano keys and case parts, after which regular piano technicians performed normal service on the pianos. (Buying a piano like this—regardless of the warranty or the low price—is just asking for trouble.) But due to a growing demand for pianos in China, the Chinese government has recently decided to invest heavily in its country's piano industry, and Chinese pianos shown at a recent industry trade show seem quite a bit improved, though probably still not up to the quality level to which we are accustomed. I would recommend against buying one until they stand the test of time.

Any guesses about where the next pianos will come from?

INDEX TO TRADE NAMES

Trade Name	See Under
Acrosonic	Baldwin
Aeolian	Aeolian
Altenburg, Otto	Miscellaneous
Astin-Weight	Astin-Weight
Atlas	Tadashi
August Forster	Miscellaneous
Bach, Otto	Dietmann
Baldwin (D.H.)	Baldwin
Barock	Miscellaneous
Bechstein, C.	Bechstein
Becker	Kimball
Bernhard Steiner	Dietmann
Blüthner	Miscellaneous
Bösendorfer	Bösendorfer
Bradbury	Aeolian
Brambach	Kohler & Campbell
Brentwood	Miscellaneous
Cabaret	Wurlitzer (see also Aeolian)
Cable	Aeolian
Cable, Hobart M.	Classic (see also Lowrey/Story & Clark)
Call	Miscellaneous
Cambridge	Aeolian
Camilleri	Miscellaneous
Casino	Wurlitzer
Charles R. Walter	Walter, Charles R.
Chickering	Wurlitzer (see also Aeolian)
Classic	Classic
Conn	Kimball
Currier	Currier
Daesung	Miscellaneous (Lyon & Healy)
Daytron	Sojin
DeVoe & Sons	Kimball
Diapason	Kawai
Dietmann	Dietmann
Duo/Art	Aeolian
Ellington	Baldwin
Entertainer	Aeolian
Estey	Call
Estonia	Miscellaneous (Nordheimer/Estonia)
Everett	Yamaha/Everett
Falcone	Falcone
Fazer	Fazer
Fazioli	Miscellaneous
Feurich	Miscellaneous
Fischer, J. & C.	Aeolian
Forster, August	Miscellaneous
French, Jesse	Marantz/Pianocorder
Gershwin	Miscellaneous (Barock)
Grand	Marantz/Pianocorder
Grotrian (-Steinweg)	Miscellaneous
Gulbransen	Miscellaneous
Hallet & Davis	Aeolian
Hamilton	Baldwin
Hampton	Lowrey/Story & Clark
Handok	Miscellaneous
Hanil	Miscellaneous
Hardman (Duo)	Aeolian
Hardman, Peck	Aeolian
Harrison	Kimball
Hastings	Miscellaneous
Heintzman	Miscellaneous
Hinze	Kimball
Hoffmann, W.	Miscellaneous (Feurich)
Horugel	Samick
Howard	Baldwin
Hyundai	Hyundai
Ibach	Ibach
Ivers & Pond	Aeolian
Jasper (-American)	Kimball

Trade Name	See Under
Jonas Chickering	Wurlitzer
Kawai	Kawai
Kimball (W. W.)	Kimball
Kincaid	Marantz/Pianocorder
Knabe, Wm.	Mason & Hamlin/Knabe (see also Aeolian)
Knight	Miscellaneous
Kohler (& Campbell)	Kohler & Campbell
Krakauer	Krakauer
Kranich & Bach	Baldwin (see also Aeolian)
La Petite	Kimball
Lesage	Miscellaneous
Lowrey	Lowrey/Story & Clark
Lyon & Healy	Miscellaneous
Maeari	Hyundai
Marantz	Marantz/Pianocorder
Mason & Hamlin	Mason & Hamlin/Knabe (see also Aeolian)
Mason & Risch	Aeolian
McDermed-Rouse	Walter, Charles R.
Melodigrand	Aeolian
Miller, Henry F.	Aeolian
Monarch	Baldwin
Musette	Aeolian
Muzelle	Miscellaneous
Nordheimer	Miscellaneous
Otto Bach	Dietmann
Pearl River	Miscellaneous (Brentwood)
Petrof	Petrof
Pianocorder	Marantz/Pianocorder
Pianola	Aeolian
QRS	Miscellaneous
Rudolf Wurlitzer	Wurlitzer
Samick	Samick
Sauter	Sauter
Schafer & Sons	Schafer & Sons
Schiedmayer	Kawai
Schimmel	Schimmel
Schubert	Miscellaneous (Lyon & Healy/Schubert)
Schuerman	Kimball
Schultz & Sons	Schultz & Sons
Schumann	Schumann
Seiler, Ed.	Seiler
Sherlock-Manning	Miscellaneous
Sherman Clay	Miscellaneous
Sohmer	Sohmer
Sojin	Sojin
Steck, Geo.	Mason & Hamlin/Knabe (see also Aeolian)
Stegler	Samick
Steiner, Bernhard	Dietmann
Steingraeber & Sohne	Miscellaneous
Steinway & Sons	Steinway & Sons
Sting II	Aeolian
Story & Clark	Classic (see also Lowrey/Story & Clark)
Tadashi	Tadashi
Tokai	Tokai
Toyo	Miscellaneous
Vose	Aeolian
Wagner	Young Chang
Walter, Charles R.	Walter, Charles R.
Weber	Weber
Wellington	Aeolian
Whitney	Kimball
Whittaker	Kimball
Winter	Aeolian
Wurlitzer	Wurlitzer
Yamaha	Yamaha/Everett
Young Chang	Young Chang
Zimmermann	Zimmermann

For explanation of survey and review procedures, please see pages 69–72.

AEOLIAN

Aeolian Pianos
Memphis, Tennessee

No longer in business

Names used: Aeolian; Bradbury; Cabaret; Cable; Cambridge; Chickering; Duo/Art; Entertainer; J. & C. Fischer; Hallet & Davis; Hardman; Hardman Duo; Hardman, Peck; Ivers & Pond; Knabe; Kranich & Bach; Mason & Hamlin; Mason & Risch; Melodigrand; Henry F. Miller; Musette; Pianola; George Steck; The Sting II; Vose; Wellington; Winter; possibly others.

See also: Sohmer, Mason & Hamlin, Wurlitzer

Aeolian pianos is no longer in business, but its history, and the trade names it owned, will continue to be important to the piano industry for many years. Although Aeolian shut down operations in 1985, some of the pianos it manufactured may still be found on showroom floors.

Aeolian Pianos dates back to 1899, when it was founded as Heller & Co., a few years later changing its name to Winter & Co. Since that time, through numerous mergers, acquisitions, and name changes, Aeolian obtained ownership of dozens of illustrious piano trade names, such as Chickering, Knabe, Mason & Hamlin, and Ivers & Pond. Each of these brands by itself has an extremely colorful history, some dating back to the early 1800s, but too long to describe here. In 1983 Aeolian was sold by the Heller family, which had controlled it for eighty years, to Peter Perez, former president of Steinway & Sons. Aeolian owned a piano factory in Memphis, Tennessee, where its cheaper verticals were made; a Canadian subsidiary, Mason & Risch; and the company's Aeolian-American Division in East Rochester, New York, which manufactured all its grands and better verticals.

At the time Aeolian was acquired by Perez, the Memphis plant was known throughout the trade for making some of the worst pianos in the United States. In my first survey, taken at about the time Aeolian was sold, almost every one of the sixty Aeolian verticals examined was found to have from thirty to fifty of the sixty-nine possible problems listed on the survey form, and nearly all were rated "terrible" or "unsatisfactory" by the reviewers. The average number of manufacturing defects per piano was over ten (I lost count). Believe it or not, this was considered by many to be an *improvement* over previous years. (Aeolian also made player pianos, but according to informed sources, the player action was put together even more poorly than the piano was!) In addition, virtually identical pianos were being sold under a vast number of different trade names controlled by the company to give consumers the illusion of choice and to maximize market penetration by avoiding real franchise agreements, a tactic not uncommon among many large businesses today. (See "Stencil Pianos," page 112, for further explanation.)

While all this was going on in Memphis, the Rochester plant, long esteemed for its high level of craftsmanship, was turning out shoddy and disappointing products. Finally, in the midst of the recession of the early 1980s, this plant was shut down entirely, putting hundreds of loyal and talented craftspeople out of work.

When Perez bought Aeolian, he immediately undertook to reform the company's marketing strategy and image. He correctly recognized that the company's chief assets were the trade names it owned, especially Mason & Hamlin, Knabe, and Chickering, which were applied to pianos that had long been made exclusively at the Rochester factory. Chickering, a Boston piano maker of the nineteenth and early twentieth century, had the most colorful history and popular appeal of the three, and was therefore chosen as the centerpiece of the new strategy. By producing a line of low-price Chickering consoles in Memphis—as well as the higher priced version in Rochester—and selling piano dealers on the opportunity to put an "affordable" Chickering in every living room (a chicken in every pot?), Perez was able to turn the company's image around almost overnight.

Another part of Perez's strategy was a promise to improve product quality, but this was never realized. Perez was not a piano technician, and even had he been, it's possible that the Memphis factory was too far gone for the kind of reform that would have been necessary. Whatever brief success Perez had at Aeolian was due more to a change in marketing strategy and public relations than to anything else.

Perez also reopened the East Rochester factory under capable management. This factory had been making pianos under the illustrious names of Mason & Hamlin, Knabe, and Chickering in the same factory buildings since the 1930s. Each brand was originally made in a different building (the names are still on the buildings) to different quality specifications, but for many years their production had been combined in a single building with the same quality standards for all. Generally, the Mason & Hamlin design was considered to be superior to the other two, but through most of the production process all three were given about equal treatment. The Mason & Hamlin instruments were singled out for special care principally in the final stages of action and tone regulating. All were available in both grand and vertical styles. The Mason & Hamlin 50″ upright was, for about fifty years, the only tall upright being manufactured in the United States. The Knabe console had also been popular for many years. The new management at Rochester had plans to upgrade and modernize equipment and raise quality as resources would allow.

Unfortunately for Perez and company, the activity in Memphis and Rochester was cut short by cash-flow problems, and in 1985 Citicorp, Perez's primary lender, called in its loan, took over Aeolian, and closed the factories when Perez was unable to meet his financial obligations to their satisfaction. The Chickering name, patterns, equipment, and unfinished pianos, plus all other assets of the Memphis factory (including most of the trade names Aeolian owned), were sold to the Wurlitzer Co. (see ''Wurlitzer''). The Mason & Hamlin and Knabe names, patterns, equipment, and unfinished pianos were sold to Sohmer & Co. (see ''Sohmer'').

You may run across Aeolian pianos, both pre- and post-Perez, at a dealer's showroom or when looking at a used piano in a private home. Avoid like the plague the Aeolian pianos made in Memphis—they're junk—even though Sohmer and Wurlitzer reportedly will honor the warranties of the piano names they purchased. Most of the verticals made in Rochester were reasonably good. Grands made at the Rochester plant toward the end had improved, but probably not enough to warrant your purchase.

Sohmer, now owned by the same person who owns Falcone, is reissuing the Mason & Hamlin pianos, and eventually the Knabe, in their original designs. Wurlitzer, now owned by Baldwin, has occasionally been using the Chickering name on some inexpensive verticals.

ASTIN-WEIGHT

Astin-Weight
120 West 3300 South
Salt Lake City, Utah 84115
(801) 487-0641

Owned by: Ray Astin, Don Weight

Name used: Astin-Weight

The Astin-Weight piano, manufactured in a small plant in Salt Lake City, Utah, since 1959, is one of the oddest pianos made in this country. Even the owners of the company, Ray Astin and Don Weight, recognize that their piano is a bit strange, for they call it a ''cult'' piano, by which they mean that most purchasers of their piano had seen it before and specifically

asked for it, whereas those who see it in a store for the first time may be somewhat intimidated by it.

Several things make the Astin-Weight a unique piano. First, both vertical models—a 41″ console and a 50″ upright—have no wooden back posts. Instead they use a massive full-perimeter cast-iron plate to support the string tension. According to the company, this eliminates the destabilizing effect of wooden posts expanding and contracting with changes in humidity. Note that this is a true full-perimeter plate, not the imitation sometimes used by other companies.

This alone would not be so strange, for some foreign-made pianos are constructed this way. What really sets these pianos apart, however, is the way the soundboard is attached. On most vertical pianos, the soundboard extends only part way up the piano back, because room must be left for the pinblock. On Astin-Weight pianos, the soundboard takes up the entire back of the piano, behind the pinblock; therefore, the vibrating area is much larger, resulting (says the company) in a much larger volume of sound (Figure 4-1). The company claims that its 41″ console has a soundboard the same size as that of a conventional 54″ piano, and its 50″ upright the same as that of a 60″ piano. For the past few years, most Astin-Weight pianos have had solid spruce soundboards; previously, they were of laminated spruce (a few are still laminated, by dealer request, to lower the cost).

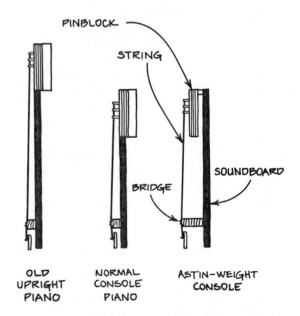

FIGURE 4-1. Astin-Weight vertical pianos have larger soundboards than do other pianos of similar size because the Astin-Weight soundboard is mounted behind the pinblock instead of under it. This arrangement requires the use of a very thick bridge to connect the soundboard with the strings.

For explanation of survey and review procedures, please see pages 69–72.

Critics of this design claim that a cast-iron plate alone, without wooden posts, cannot adequately hold a piano in tune (though the evidence tends to contradict this), and that positioning the soundboard behind the pinblock requires the bridges to be so thick (to contact the strings) that the harmonic content of the tone must be very distorted. Also, it should be kept in mind that while the volume of sound may be greater than from conventional pianos, the quality of sound depends more on the length of the bass and tenor strings and on the overall scale design than on the size of the soundboard, and the strings on these pianos are no longer than on other pianos of comparable size. So, as one might expect, the console sounds unexceptional, while the upright sounds more interesting.

Astin-Weights are also unusual in their cabinet designs and finishes. Most of the designs are extremely simple and the cabinets are finished in hand-rubbed oil finishes. Dealers report that some customers find this a refreshing alternative to the shiny lacquer and polyester finishes of every other brand.

Astin-Weight uses a Langer action in its upright. Most of the consoles also have a Langer action; a few continue to use Pratt-Win actions, when requested by a dealer to lower the cost.

Technicians seem to be divided in their assessment of Astin-Weight pianos. Most agree that Astin-Weights are well made. However, they produce a very rich spectrum of overtones that make them challenging for some technicians to tune, and which some consider to be odd-sounding. Of course, this richness is precisely what many Astin-Weight owners love about their pianos. As one technician who also sells Astin-Weights wrote:

"This piano, as you said in your first edition, is difficult to rate because of its unusual design and tone. We began selling them nearly ten years ago, and at that time I felt that it was one of the best pianos you could buy. However, in the past three to four years I have come to the conclusion that, while it seems to be sturdily built and have a fair degree of quality, it lacks the musical quality we find pleasing today, that being a clear, bright, full sound. Instead, it has a deep, unclear sound that, while pleasing to a small percentage of our customers, is not what the majority of the piano purchasers are looking for today. In addition to this, I personally find it very difficult to tune; no matter how precise a tuning I give it, I find myself disappointed with the results."

Another dealer, however, writes:

"We began selling the Astin-Weight piano in 1975 because we felt it to be superior in construction, quality, and tone to anything else on the market. We also admired the courage of the company for producing such an obvious improvement in a very tradition-bound industry. Upon first playing the piano our customers are stunned by the deep range of tonality not found in the 'tinny' conventional-type pianos. Our tuners report that because of their scale design Astin-Weight pianos have no false beats and are easier to tune. This is in addition to superior tuning longevity brought about by the full-perimeter frame. To quote one of them who is a musician with the local symphony, 'Astin-Weights tune as smooth as butter.'"

To the piano shopper considering the purchase of an Astin-Weight, I would say this: Astin-Weight pianos are made with more care and integrity than most pianos on the market, especially the mass-produced ones. If, after careful comparison with other brands, you find you prefer the tone, touch, and other features of an Astin-Weight piano, by all means buy it and ignore this controversy.

If you thought the verticals were strange, wait till you see the 5'9" grand, which has been produced in limited numbers for quite a few years. Instead of having a straight side on the left and a curved side on the right as all other grands do, it's shaped almost symmetrically. This allows the bass bridge to be repositioned so that the bass strings are 18 inches longer than normal for a piano that size, and increases the soundboard area by 45 percent, so the company says, resulting in the tonal equivalent of a 7'6" piano. Furthermore, the lid is hinged on the right (treble) side, instead of on the left (bass), a feature that Astin-Weight calls "Grand, American Style."

Warranty: Twenty-five years, parts and labor.

BALDWIN

See "Notice to Readers," page 72.

C. BECHSTEIN

Bechstein Piano Corp.
Eastern Representative: 251 Memorial Drive, Lititz, Pennsylvania 17543
Western Representative: 1701 Port Barmouth Place, Newport Beach, California 92660
(800) 426-3205

Pianos made by: C. Bechstein Pianoforte Fabrik GmbH,
Reichenberger Strasse 124, 1000 Berlin 36, West Germany

Owned by: Karl Schulze

Name used: C. Bechstein

Bechstein was founded in 1853 by Carl Bechstein, a young German piano maker who, in the exploding world of piano technology of his day, had visions of building an instrument that the tradition-bound piano-making shops of Berlin were not interested in. Through fine workmanship and the endorsement of famous pianists, Bechstein soon became one of the leading piano makers in Europe, producing over five thousand pianos annually by 1900. The two world wars and the Depression virtually destroyed the company, but it rebuilt successfully, and in 1963 it was acquired by Baldwin. This sale supplied Bechstein with a source of capital and supplied Baldwin with a source of piano service internationally for concert artists who play Baldwin pianos. However, Bechstein kept operating as an autonomous unit, continuing its tradition of impeccable craftsmanship.

In 1986, Baldwin sold Bechstein to Karl Schulze, a leading West German piano retailer and master piano technician who, with a team of experts, undertook a complete technical and financial reorganization of the company. The three factories in Berlin, Karlsruhe, and Eschelbronn were closed and combined into one new state-of-the-art factory in Berlin, opened in 1989. The entire product line, scale designs, and manufacturing techniques were re-evaluated with an eye to restoring the original scales and techniques of the founder, serving the market, and combining efficient factory methods with traditional craftsmanship. A 5'2" grand and a 48" upright were introduced, a new grand action was designed and built, and the 6'8" grand was redesigned (now 6'10").

The new owner's plans also call for gradually increasing production from the present 1,000 to about 1,500 pianos annually by 1995. To do this, new craftspeople will have to be trained. Working in the tradition of old German guilds, pianos are built at Bechstein by teams, each consisting of workers with different tenure at the company. This way, new employees have the benefit of learning from those more experienced. Bechstein expects to train enough new craftspeople in this manner by 1995 to meet their production plans without sacrificing quality.

Bechstein verticals come in three sizes, a 44" studio and 48" and 50" uprights. All have Renner actions, solid Bavarian spruce soundboards, full agraffes, and Delignit pinblocks. Two pedals are standard; a middle pedal with mute bar (practice pedal) is optional (sostenuto is optional on the 48" model). The pianos are available in many custom finishes. I must say that the Bechstein verticals I've played have consistently been the most beautiful sounding vertical pianos I've ever encountered.

Bechstein grands come in five sizes: 5'2", 5'11", 6'10", 7'3", and the 9'2" concert grand. They are available in many custom finishes. All have Renner actions, solid Bavarian spruce soundboards, full agraffes, beech rims, Delignit pinblocks, and three pedals (including sostenuto). The concert grand is single-strung. The agraffes used on Bechstein pianos incorporate a rounded bearing surface with a traditional agraffe in an effort to overcome some of the limitations of the traditional kind.

The tone of Bechstein grands is what one might call "classically European." It is very clean and thin in the treble and emphasizes the fundamental rather than harmonics in the bass. Those of us who grew up on the sound of American pianos may find the Bechstein sound somewhat alien, though interesting. I personally find it to be quite lovely at low volumes, the clearly articulated attack giving it a delicate character, but sometimes find it too bright for my taste at higher volumes. I also prefer a more pronounced singing quality and a heavier action than the Bechstein provides. These are, of course, a matter of personal preference; many pianists revere the Bechstein, and it is considered to be one of the world's pre-eminent pianos.

Warranty: Five years, parts and labor.

BÖSENDORFER

Bösendorfer Pianos
c/o Kimball Keyboard Products
P.O. Box 460
Jasper, Indiana 47549
(812) 482-1600

Pianos made by: L. Bösendorfer Klavierfabrik AG, Bösendorferstrasse 12, A-1010 Wien, Vienna, Austria

Owned by: Kimball International, Inc.

Name used: Bösendorfer

Bösendorfer was founded in 1828 in Vienna, Austria by Ignatz Bösendorfer. The young piano maker rose to fame when Franz Liszt endorsed his concert grand after being unable to destroy it in playing as he did every other piano set before him. Ignatz died in 1859 and the company was taken over by his son Ludwig. Under Ludwig's direction, the firm greatly prospered and the pianos became even more famous throughout Europe and the world. Ludwig, having no direct descendents, sold the firm to his friend Carl Hutterstrasser in 1909. Carl's sons Wolfgang and Alexander became partners in 1931.

For explanation of survey and review procedures, please see pages 69–72.

Until the Depression, Bösendorfer made about two to four hundred pianos a year, after the Depression only about a hundred a year, except during the final years of World War II, when production ceased during and after the bombing of Vienna. Bösendorfer was sold to Kimball—a U.S. manufacturer of low- and medium-priced pianos—in 1966. Since then, production has been gradually increased to about 750 pianos annually, made by about 300 employees.

Bösendorfer makes one vertical piano—a 52" upright—and six models of grand piano, from 5'8" to the 9'6" Imperial Concert Grand, one of the world's largest pianos. (The Bösendorfer catalog also shows a 48" vertical, but it is apparently not for sale in the United States.) All Bösendorfer pianos have three pedals, the middle pedal being a sostenuto.

One of the most distinctive features of the grands is that the largest four models have more than eighty-eight notes. The 7', 7'4" and 9' grands each have four extra notes in the bass, and the 9'6" grand has nine extra notes. The lowest strings vibrate so slowly that it's actually possible to hear the individual "ticks" of the vibration, and it's next to impossible to tune these strings accurately. They are also, of course, almost never used, except when playing some new music written expressly for them, but their presence, and the presence of the extra long bridge and larger soundboard to accommodate them, adds extra power, resonance, and clarity to the lowest regular notes of the piano. In order not to confuse pianists, who rely on the normal keyboard configuration for spatial orientation while playing, the keys for these extra notes are usually covered with a black ivorine material.

The rim of the Bösendorfer grand is built quite differently from that of all other grands. Instead of being made of veneers bent around a form as one continuous rim, the rim is made in solid sections and jointed together. It is also made of spruce instead of the maple, beech, or other hardwoods usually used. Spruce transmits sound well, making the Bösendorfer case become an extension of the soundboard, but is sometimes said not to be as good at reflecting sound back to the soundboard as those other woods. These factors, as well as the scale design, are probably responsible for a sweeter, less powerful treble and a bass that features the fundamental tone more than the higher harmonics. It is an interesting and beautiful sound, but some think it may be better suited to Mozart than Rachmaninoff. To some extent, the largest grands make up for this difference simply by virtue of their size.

Perhaps to add a little "guts" to the treble, especially for the American market, in 1990 Bösendorfer added a 7' grand with duplex scaling to their line. The duplex scaling makes the treble tone more complex; it sounded to me like a cross between a Bösendorfer and a Steinway. Duplex scaling may in time be added to other models if this experiment is deemed successful.

There are a few other Bösendorfer features that are either unique to it or are shared with only a few other brands. One is the removable capo d'astro bar in the treble. This facilitates rebuilding of the instrument and, Bösendorfer says, provides greater acoustic separation from the plate, thus less tonal absorption. Another is leather key bushings, which have a longer life than felt bushings. A third is single-stringing, in which each string has its own individual hitch pin on the plate instead of being connected to a neighboring string. This may slightly improve tuning stability, and is an advantage in case of string breakage.

Kimball has made extensive use of its ownership of Bösendorfer, both to promote Kimball pianos and to improve Kimball quality. All Bösendorfer pianos bound for U.S. dealers are first air-freighted to the Kimball factory in Indiana for inspection and adjustment. Given these facts, potential buyers sometimes question whether Bösendorfers are still as good as their reputation and price suggest. Apparently they are, as there have been no reports of radical changes in their quality. Technicians consider the Bösendorfer grand to be one of the finest pianos in the world. It is also one of the most expensive.

Also offered by Bösendorfer is their Computer-Based Piano Performance Reproducing System, a very sophisticated reproducing (player) piano that allows the user to digitally record, play back, and edit every nuance of a piano performance. It does this by optically scanning every key, hammer, and pedal 800 times a second. Using the computer and software that come with the system, even the volume, duration, and position of a single note can be edited. The system is being promoted for such uses as recording and playing back recordings of master artists or students for study purposes, and for use in recording studios, where mistakes can be edited out without rerecording. The system package includes the piano, all the electronics, a tape recorder, and a dedicated computer. The system doesn't alter the touch of the instrument. Note that it is only available with the 7'4", 9', and 9'6" models, and is not MIDI-compatible (see page 113 for an explanation of the acronym MIDI).

Warranty: Ten years, parts only.

CLASSIC

Classic Player Piano Corporation
Quaker Drive
Seneca, Pennsylvania 16346
(814) 676-6683

Owned by: Edward E. Keefer

Names used: Classic Player Pianos, Story & Clark, Hobart M. Cable

Classic Player Piano Corporation is a relatively new company that manufactures player pianos under the name "Classic" and normal acoustic pianos under the names "Story & Clark" and "Hobart M. Cable." The Classic player pianos are made with piano parts supplied by Baldwin and a player mechanism formerly made by Universal. In the past Universal had installed its mechanism in pianos made by Lowrey/Story & Clark and by Kohler & Campbell. When those companies ceased production, Edward Keefer obtained the rights to update and manufacture the Universal mechanism. Classic markets its players under its own name, and also manufactures player pianos for Baldwin (identical to the Classic except for cabinet) and for Wurlitzer (previously manufactured by the Aeolian player group), as well as other private-label brands.

Classic players are built around a vertical back, plate, and pinblock supplied by Baldwin. These are the same components Baldwin uses for its Hamilton studio pianos. Classic installs the tuning pins, strings, and a modified Pratt-Win action and keys (also made by Baldwin), adding the hammers and dampers in its own facility. Classic manufactures the highly stylized 47" player piano cabinet. After a bit of a rough start, these pianos now seem to be satisfactory (at least I haven't heard any complaints). A limiting factor may be the quality of parts supplied by Baldwin (see "Baldwin"). No Classic pianos were included in the present survey.

Of the Universal player mechanism, one expert writes, "Indeed, all of the modern players with the exception of the Universal have the earmark of something engineered by bullheaded people who think they can invent something better than a product of the late 1920s that already had twenty-five years of experience behind it! The Universal was an exception, being engineered by people well-experienced in the strong and weak points of all the old brands of player actions."

In 1990 Classic purchased the Story & Clark and Hobart M. Cable names and scale designs from the Bergsma Furniture Company (see "Lowrey/Story & Clark") and announced plans to make 42" Story & Clark consoles. Classic will manufacture its own strung back for these pianos, using a modified version of the old Story & Clark plate. The keys and compressed console action will be from Pratt-Win and modified by Classic. When requested by a dealer, the Hobart M. Cable name may be used on versions of these pianos. The Story & Clark studio piano is scheduled for introduction in the near future. (Note: A few dozen Story & Clark consoles and studios are being made by the Walter Piano Co. using some parts left over from the old Story & Clark operation.)

Classic provides prompt technical service and support to its dealers and customers.

Warranty: Ten years, parts only on the piano; two years, parts only on the player mechanism. Labor ninety days on both. All apply to the original purchaser only.

CURRIER

Currier Piano Co.
Marion, North Carolina

Out of business

Owned by: Kaman Corporation

Name used: Currier

Currier was founded in 1958 under the name of the Westbrook Piano Co. Westbrook sold the company in 1970 and the name was changed to Currier. In April 1970 the Currier factory was struck by lightning and burned down (on Friday the 13th), but production continued in a nearby facility. In 1972 Currier was purchased by the Kaman Corporation, whose music division also makes Ovation guitars and other music products. In 1982, citing a depressed domestic piano market, Kaman closed Currier.

Currier's chief claim to fame occurred in 1981, when it introduced the "Strataphonic String Panel," a laminated panel of steel and medium-density fiberboard that replaced the traditional cast-iron plate in Currier pianos. The idea, though interesting, apparently didn't go over well enough to prevent Currier's continued decline.

Currier made spinets, consoles, and a studio piano. The spinets and consoles were very inconsistent in quality, but generally a little to one side or the other of satisfactory. The studio with the new Strataphonic String Panel was said to have "possibilities," though the tone was a bit loud and metallic.

For explanation of survey and review procedures, please see pages 69–72.

DIETMANN

Dietmann Pianos Ltd.
5840 Alpha Rd.
Dallas, Texas 75240
(214) 233-1967

Pianos made by: Dietmann Klavier, Bollen, Horsterdamm 345, 2050 Hamburg 80, West Germany (but assembled in South Africa)

Names used: Dietmann, Otto Bach, Berhard Steiner

These pianos, available in 42 ½″, 46 ½″, and 48″ sizes, are made in South Africa by a German company. They use solid spruce soundboards and are available with either Renner or Langer actions. Plans are in progress to open a factory in Dallas, Texas to assemble these pianos here for the U.S. market. No information is currently available about their quality. The names Dietmann, Otto Bach, and Bernhard Steiner are applied according to dealer request; they are exactly the same piano.

FALCONE

Falcone Piano Co.
35 Duncan Street
Haverhill, Massachusetts 01830
(508) 372-8300

Owned by: Bernard Greer

Name used: Falcone

Falcone Piano Co. was founded by Santi Falcone (pronounced Fahl-KON-eh), a piano technician, rebuilder, and retailer in the Boston area who, in the early 1980s, began to build his own grand pianos. Originally from Sicily, Falcone came to the United States at the age of fourteen and began tuning pianos at sixteen, eventually owning a chain of seven stores that sold and leased new pianos and rebuilt older ones (he was also the U.S. importer of Barock pianos from Japan). Troubled both by the inferior, mass-produced character of most pianos today and by the incredibly high price of the high-quality pianos, he set out to build an instrument that was at once of the highest caliber and affordable.

To do this, he gradually sold all of his stores and set up a workshop adjacent to one of them in Woburn, Massachusetts. In 1984, after several years of research and development, he began production, and in 1985 he and the eleven craftsmen he employed made about thirty pianos. With a large backlog of orders, Falcone moved to a much larger factory space in Haverhill, Massachusetts in the spring of 1986 with the in-

tention of sharply increasing production over the next several years.

Although production did increase somewhat, raising capital, increasing production, and maintaining quality were not as easy as anticipated. Falcone eventually decided to sell a substantial amount of stock in the company to outside investors to raise needed capital, and hired Lloyd Meyer, former president of Steinway & Sons, as a consultant. The major investor was Bernard Greer, a wealthy Seattle businessman who became interested in the company after purchasing a Falcone piano for himself. In 1989 Greer purchased the remaining shares in the company and named Meyer chief executive officer. Falcone was offered a post in the company, but declined. He is now operating a chocolate candy-making business with his wife out of their home, but says he may eventually re-enter the piano business on a smaller scale.

Under the new management, the factory has been reorganized for greater efficiency, and investments have been made in new machinery, climate control, and conditioning rooms for wooden parts. Sources inside the factory indicate that these changes are genuine improvements, but that they may entail some loss of the small-business feeling that formerly prevailed. Production is gradually increasing and morale seems to be positive.

Falcone (the company) makes three models of grand piano: 6′1″, 7′4″, and 9′. All three are loosely based on the scale design of the three corresponding models of Steinway—A, C, and D—but many refinements borrowed from European designs, as well as some of their own, have been gradually added, and experimentation continues to produce improvements. All Falcone pianos have a maple rim, solid spruce soundboard, and action parts made by Renner on an action frame of the Steinway design. Keys are by Kluge. The finish is polyester, available in high-polish ebony, satin ebony, and rosewood. Other woods and decoratively carved cases are available. All models have three pedals, including sostenuto.

I've been impressed with the quality of the Falcone pianos I've played or about which I've received reports, with only minor flaws noted here and there. There seems to be some agreement that the 7′4″ model is the most successful model tonally, followed by the 9′, with the 6′1″ model being good but not superlative. The few pianos examined for this review were made while Santi Falcone was with the company. He personally supervised the construction of about two hundred pianos (to about serial number 1200). Little quality information is available about current Falcone pianos, except from dealers, who say they are happier with them than ever. Note that some earlier Falcones had problems with veneer coming loose. Those pianos have been repaired under warranty and the problem has been corrected.

One development that may help insure Falcone's success is Greer's recent purchase of Sohmer, which also owned the Mason & Hamlin and Knabe names. Sohmer studios and Mason & Hamlin uprights are being made at the Sohmer plant in Pennsylvania, and Mason & Hamlin grands are just beginnning to be made at the Falcone factory in Massachusetts. See "Sohmer" and "Mason & Hamlin/Knabe."

Warranty: Ten years, parts and labor.

FAZER

Oy Musiikki Fazer Musik AB
Halkia, Finland

No longer being imported into the U.S.

Owned by: Hellas Piano, Finland

Name used: Fazer

This marvelous 43" studio piano was imported into the U.S. by Coast Wholesale Music Co. for several years. It had a four-ply laminated soundboard made of woods I've never heard of, a particle-board cabinet, and sold for $3,000 or so. But despite this unflattering description, the piano was beautifully made, worked perfectly, and sounded great! Here are several comments about the piano from technicians: "Best bass sound on a piano this size with a laminated soundboard I've seen." "Beautiful piano—once again Fazer impresses! Smooth sound and action, gorgeous case." The piano also used a Langer action, and was considered a real bargain. Unfortunately, Fazer pianos are no longer available. In 1989 the wholesale price of the piano abruptly rose by forty percent, making it no longer worthwhile to import it.

HYUNDAI

Hyundai Corporation (USA)
Piano Division
One Bridge Plaza North
Fort Lee, New Jersey 07024

Distributed by: North American Music, 126 Rt. 303, W. Nyack, New York 10994
(914) 353–3520

Pianos made by: Samick

Names used: Hyundai, Maeari

Best known in the United States for its automobiles, Hyundai Corp. is one of Korea's largest industrial conglomerates, and makes or distributes many kinds of consumer goods. Hyundai is counting on name recognition from its automobile advertising to separate its pianos from those of its Korean competitors. You should know, however, that Hyundai does not make its own pianos. All Hyundai pianos are made by Samick. See "Samick" for a review of these pianos and for information on how these pianos may or may not be different from pianos sold under Samick's own name.

Hyundai also sells pianos under the name "Maeari," which means "echo." The name is well-chosen because the Maeari pianos are the same as the Hyundai pianos.

Warranty (Hyundai): Twelve years, full; lifetime on soundboard.

IBACH

Rud. Ibach Sohn
Mittelstrasse 34,
5830 Schwelm/Westf.
Postfach 405
West Germany

Owned by: Ibach Family

Name Used: Ibach

Established by Johannes Adolf Ibach in 1794, Ibach has the distinction of being the oldest existing manufacturer of fine pianos in the world. For perspective, in 1794, Haydn was writing his last works while Beethoven was writing his Opus 1 piano trios. Also, in contrast to this ever changing industry and world, Ibach is still owned and managed by the original family, Messers. Christian and Rolf Ibach, the sixth generation.

Ibach has been notable in the development of both piano construction and the piano industry in general. The second generation saw Ibach lead piano builders in replacing the wooden plate with one made of cast iron to produce a more powerful piano tone. Carl Rudolf Ibach also developed the world's first production vertical piano in 1838–39—a 44" studio upright. During Ibach's third generation, Rudolf Ibach departed from the factory retail showroom system to establish the retail dealer system as we know it today. The fourth generation of Ibach developed the world's first tonally successful 40" console piano.

One of the smaller piano builders of the world, Ibach manufactures approximately 1,000 vertical

For explanation of survey and review procedures, please see pages 69–72.

pianos and 250 grands a year for world consumption. Although not as well known in North America as some other European manufacturers, Ibach has quietly built a solid reputation in Europe over the last two centuries through fine craftsmanship and by supplying pianos to a long list of famous composers and artists, such as Wagner, R. Strauss, Liszt, Bartok, Schoenberg, and others.

Verticals. Ibach verticals come in five sizes, though the smaller sizes are less often imported into North America. The 47" model C is Ibach's standard-bearer vertical piano, found in many European conservatory practice rooms. The 50" model D is the professional upright for musicians requiring the largest tonal response from an upright piano. The 51" model H is a slightly larger professional upright with an elegant, turn of the century cabinet design. All verticals are available in either continental cabinet style or with casters and toe construction. Two pedals are standard, with a third pedal available to activate a muffler rail (practice pedal mechanism).

Grands. Ibach currently builds grands in four sizes. The model F-I S, 5'5", produces a high quality tonal response for a small grand. The model F-II S, 6', is Ibach's standard-bearer and is used in many of the world's music conservatories. The model F-III S, 7'1", is the model named after Richard Strauss, whose Ibach piano was of this size. It has a very large open sound that might normally be associated with a larger instrument. The model F-IV S, 7'9" half-concert grand, is the model named after Richard Wagner, whose Ibach was of this size. This piano is designed as a concert instrument for average-sized and smaller recital halls that do not require a 9' concert grand. Only four to six of these 7'9" pianos are made annually. The model F-V, 9' concert grand, is being redesigned to incorporate recent innovations and will be introduced again in regular production during Ibach's bicentennial in 1994.

Followers of the Ibach piano report that Ibachs are very consistent in their characteristics. Due possibly to a very hard, heavy beech rim, Ibachs have a long tonal sustain and exhibit a bit more power than some other European pianos when played fortissimo. The scale design is very even throughout the keyboard and with proper voicing, the hammers elicit a very large range of tonal color and volume. The high-quality action is built by Renner to an Ibach design. All models come with three pedals including a full sostenuto, and are available in a variety of high-gloss polyester, satin rubbed, or satin matte finishes.

Warranty: Five years parts and labor to the original purchaser only. For warranty assistance, contact the Ibach North American Technical Service Center, 5780 Celi Drive, East Syracuse, NY 13057.

KAWAI

Kawai America Corporation
2055 E. University Drive
P.O. Box 9045
Compton, California 90224
(213) 631-1771

Owned by: Kawai Musical Instrument Mfg. Co., Ltd., Hamamatsu, Japan (publicly owned in Japan)

Names used: Kawai, Diapason, Schiedmayer

Kawai, Japan's second largest piano manufacturer, was founded in 1927 by Koichi Kawai, an inventor and former Yamaha employee who was the first Japanese to design and build a piano action. When Kawai first began exporting pianos to the United States in the sixties, they were a relative unknown, and many dealers took them on only if they couldn't get the Yamaha dealership. While Kawai pianos are still second to Yamaha in size, they have a well-deserved reputation all their own for quality and innovation.

Kawai makes a complete line of console, studio, and upright pianos from 41" to 52" in height, and grand pianos from 5'1" to 9'1" in length. All Kawai grands and uprights, and the upper-level consoles and studios, are made in Japan, while the less expensive consoles and studios are assembled in Kawai's new plant in Lincolnton, North Carolina.

Verticals. Kawai offers a confusing array of vertical pianos—confusing because the model letter and number designations and the sizes do not make clear what the differences are between one model and the next. Even some Kawai dealers admit this to be so, and add that constantly changing models and specifications, and the difficulty of getting up-to-date model information from the manufacturer, can sometimes make it hard for them to give proper guidance to the customer.

Kawai consoles come in two basic levels of quality, each level in both continental and furniture styles. The 41" continental style CX-5 (updated from the CX-4) is Kawai's least expensive piano. It has a laminated spruce soundboard and only two pedals. In place of a practice pedal, it has a manually operated mute bar that can be placed between the hammers and the strings. Despite its size and construction, this piano has a surprisingly big sound in the bass. It's made in Japan and, though simple, is well put together.

The 42″ 500 and 600 series (currently 502 and 602) are Kawai's lower-level furniture-style console models. The 600 series is technically identical to the 500 series, but has fancier furniture. These two models are assembled in the U.S. from a Japanese-made strung back and action and a U.S.-made cabinet. A 700-series furniture-style console made in Japan was formerly offered, but was not received well and was dropped from the line. These lower-level verticals are priced to compete with Korean and less expensive American products. They are simplified in construction and features and not the best Kawai can make, but they are put together reasonably well.

The 44″ continental-style CE-11 (updated from the CE-10) and the 44″ furniture-style 804 are Kawai's upper-level consoles. They are both entirely made in Japan. The CE-10 was technically identical to the 804, but the CE-11 has been slightly upgraded in scale design and hammer quality, and has synthetic ivory keytops. One additional model, the 45″ CS-9 (now CS-11), appears to be a studio, but actually contains a console action and is technically identical to the CE-11.

Kawai's 46″ studio line consists of its traditional school model, the UST-7, made in Japan (a few were recently assembled in the U.S. on a trial basis), and a less expensive version, the UST-8, assembled in the U.S. The UST-8 was designed to be more competitive in school bidding situations. Although it fulfills school requirements, its cabinetry is not as substantial as that of the UST-7, and the scale design and action are also not quite as good. (The new model UST-8A has a thicker cabinet and weighted keys for better touch, and a scale design similar to that of the UST-7.)

The upright line has three levels of quality. The 48″ CX-21 is the least expensive, the 49″ and 50″ NS series uprights are the middle level (the 50″ was just discontinued), currently with solid spruce soundboards, but sometimes in the past with laminated ones; and the 52″ US series is the top level. The US-6X (formerly the US-55) is the regular model of this series. The US-75 is the same as the US-55 but has a full sostenuto pedal. It also has two extra strings, but no keys or hammers to strike them, below the lowest regular notes on the piano on the theory that the extended bridge will make the lowest regular notes sound better. The KL-70W (now the US-6X WP) is the US-6X with a styled polished walnut case. All these uprights are made in Japan.

In the survey for the first edition of this book, very few problems were found in Kawai verticals. In fact, they had the lowest "defect" rate of any major brand examined. For the present review, eighty-one Kawai verticals were examined. While there were no major problems reported, there were many more small complaints, mostly with the lower-priced pianos. The early 500 and 600 series pianos and the UST-8, all assembled in the U.S., had many small problems with cabinet design, finish, and the fitting of cabinet parts. The pianos also were insufficiently tuned and regulated at the North Carolina factory. Follow-up interviews indicate that this situation is steadily getting better and the new models are very acceptable, though still not as well put together as those entirely made in Japan. The 700 series pianos, low-priced but made in Japan, also were problematic. The model 706 had many problems with poorly weighted keys and consequently poor repetition, as well as poor tone and a drab cabinet. The model 708 that replaced it was an improvement technically, but apparently was not aesthetically pleasing to dealers or customers. The console models CE-7, 10, and 11—each a slight improvement over the one before it—and the model 804 were all basically problem-free and very much liked, as was the UST-7 school studio, considered a real "workhorse."

In the uprights, the inexpensive model CX-21 was disliked by nearly all the technicians who were familiar with it, an unusual response to a Japanese upright, though it sells well, I'm told. Bad tone was the principal problem, but there were also complaints about workmanship and materials. The other uprights were well-liked and no unusual problems were reported.

Grands. There are three types of Kawai grands: GE, KG, and GS. The 5′1″ model GE-1 was originally intended as a lower-cost alternative to the 5′1″ model KG-1. The GE-1 had, according to Kawai, thinner structural parts, a lower-quality soundboard, and less expensive cabinetry, among other differences. But most people couldn't tell the difference between the two models and bought the less expensive one, so Kawai changed the size of the KG-1 to 5′4″ (and renamed it the KG-1E) and upgraded the quality of the GE-1 to match that of the KG series. The KG-2 and the GE-2 are, likewise, two different sizes but the same quality, Kawai says.

The 5′10″ KG-2 is one of the largest-selling grands in the United States. It now comes in several varieties. The KG-2D was a very popular piano, with a sound that was on the "mellow" or "warm" side. Kawai recently replaced it with the KG-2E, a much brighter, jazzier sounding piano (perhaps more like a Yamaha?), which had an improved action design. Dealers complained a lot because they really liked the sound of the KG-2D, so Kawai came out with the KG-2S, which has the new action design but also the "warmer" sound.

For explanation of survey and review procedures,
please see pages 69–72.

The GS series pianos start at the 6'1" size (model GS-40). Kawai people tend to be a little vague about the differences between the KG and GS pianos. My sense is that the GS pianos "sing" a little better. There may be some differences in design, materials, and workmanship that contribute to this characteristic, but Kawai says the principal difference is that much more time is spent voicing and adjusting these pianos. The GS series grands (and some of the upper-level verticals) have keytops made of a natural cellulose material that mimics the properties of ivory.

Three other Kawai grands are the RX-A, a very mellow and exotic sounding 6'5" piano; the R-1, a less expensive version of the RX-A with a thinner rim and some cabinetry differences; and the EX concert grand, a very expensive, limited-edition piano. These pianos, and the GS-100, are built in a separate portion of the factory and get much more hand-crafted attention.

Sixty-four Kawai grands were examined for this review. As with the first survey, few major problems were found, but there were a certain number of smaller complaints. The GE-1 was judged to have a poor tone in the top and bottom octave or octave-and-a-half. This model was liked least of the Kawai grands. The GE-2 was better, but there were also some complaints about the scale design. The KG-2 and all the GS grands received very favorable comments. Problems found rarely, but just often enough to mention, include: loose hammer heads, rattling bass strings, broken treble strings, and repetition springs on new pianos being too strong and needing adjusting. (I believe all these have been corrected.)

A review of Kawai pianos would not be complete without a comparison with Yamaha pianos, as the two are as competitive with one another as any two brands could be (see also "Yamaha" for some general comments about Japanese pianos that could apply equally to Kawai). I found technicians to be surprisingly articulate and consistent in their comments about the two brands, and in their assessment of the direction in which Kawai seems to be heading. Generally, the two brands are very similar in quality and price, and the distinctions between the two are subtle ones. But historically, technicians say, Kawai pianos have had a slightly warmer, mellower tone that held up a little better with time than Yamaha's before turning bright. Yamaha's tone has tended to be brighter and jazzier and thus more appealing to some people, but did not stay pleasant as long. Lately, though, Kawai tone has become brighter, and the hammers have gotten harder, in both verticals and grands, and many technicians who have favored Kawai in the past now say they are a little disappointed. (Yamahas have also gotten brighter, the technicians say, but the gap between the two has narrowed.)

There may also have been, over the last few years, a small deterioration in the quality of Kawai cabinets and general workmanship due, I'm sure, to competition with the Koreans and a worldwide decline in the demand for pianos. This deterioration has been most obvious in the less expensive verticals, especially in the problems, mentioned earlier, associated with the start-up of the North Carolina factory. But it has also shown up to some degree throughout the line in the form of a little less preparation at the factory. Yamaha has also had to tighten its belt, but seems to have been able to do so a little less obviously and more gracefully. I want to emphasize that Kawai's problems are still very small compared to most mass-produced pianos, and any Kawai dealer who services his or her pianos even a little will correct them. Furthermore, Kawai's service department is very competent and stands behind its pianos one hundred percent. Nevertheless, this trend is worth noting.

Comparing specific models, the technicians I interviewed generally preferred the Yamaha vertical line over the Kawai vertical line, especially with the smaller, less expensive pianos made by both makers in the U.S. Yamaha's U.S. manufacturing has been perfected to a greater degree than Kawai's. However, the top-level Kawai consoles (CE-11 and 804) and studio (UST-7), made in Japan, are as good as Yamaha's U.S.-made products, if not better (though the Yamaha P22T studio is hard to beat for value). Kawai's uprights are very good (except the CX-21), but Yamaha's just have that keen edge of finesse in design and workmanship that makes them a little superior. In the grands, Kawai's model GE-1, though no gem, is preferred over Yamaha's GH-1, which is not particularly recommended. The Kawai KG series may also be favored just a little over the Yamaha G series. With the larger grands, each brand has its fans, and I don't think I can determine any favorite.

I want to say again that these differences are subtle and may well be overshadowed by variations that exist among instruments of the same model or among dealers in the service they provide. Some dealers will probably try to make mountains out of these differences, but you should pay no attention. Only if price, personal preference, and other factors are all equal should you take the above comments into consideration.

Diapason and Schiedmayer

Over the past few years, Kawai has also sold pianos in the U.S. under the names Diapason and Schiedmayer. The Diapason is a line of pianos Kawai has sold in Japan for many years. Its scale design is said to be a little "warmer" than that of the Kawai. The Diapason line is now being discontinued in the United States.

Schiedmayer is a German company, owned by Ibach, that makes celestes and pianos. Ibach has licensed Kawai to produce and market pianos of Ibach design under the Schiedmayer label. Just what this design is, how much it actually resembles an Ibach, nor whether this is desirable are not known, but it is obviously meant to capture some of the growing market for anything "German" in pianos. Anyway, what's important is that the Schiedmayer is basically made to the same quality standards as the Kawai. (Another variation on the Kawai, upgraded from all other models Kawai makes, is "Schultz & Sons," available in some locations. See separate listing.)

Warranty: Ten-year full warranty. Note that the warranty does not cover replacement of broken strings, which is considered to be "normal maintenance."

KIMBALL

Kimball Keyboard Products
P.O. Box 460
Jasper, Indiana 47546
(812) 482-1600

Owned by: Kimball International, Inc., Jasper, Indiana (publicly owned)

Names used: Kimball, Conn, Jasper-American, W. W. Kimball, Hinze, Harrison, Schuerman, DeVoe & Sons, Whittaker, Becker, La Petite, possibly others; private-label brands also made (see "Stencil Pianos"). No longer used: Whitney

Kimball Keyboard Products (formerly Kimball Piano & Organ Co.) began in 1857 under the name of W. W. Kimball & Co. when Kimball, a poor Maine farmboy who had set up a business selling real estate and insurance in Iowa, moved to Chicago and opened up a piano store, convinced that there was money to be made supplying goods to "Western" pioneers. He soon became one of the largest merchants of keyboard instruments in the country. The 1880s saw a critical shortage of merchandise for Midwestern merchants, so in 1886 Kimball began to manufacture his own pianos, becoming a leading manufacturer within a short time. Kimball's company reached its peak in the early 1900s, but a combination of changing consumer desires, the Depression, and poor managerial decisions on the part of Kimball's heirs and successors caused the company's decline toward insolvency. It was finally sold to the Jasper Corporation, an Indiana

plywood and cabinet manufacturer, in 1959, and piano production was moved to Indiana.

During the next two decades, Jasper, now called Kimball International, purchased the renowned Austrian piano manufacturer Bösendorfer in 1966 (see "Bösendorfer"); the highly respected U.S. piano maker Krakauer in 1980 (see "Krakauer"); supplier companies such as the English maker of the Schwander and Langer actions, Herrberger Brooks; and timber lands, lumber mills, and firms in other industries necessary to its operations. Kimball International is a Fortune 500 company with involvements in furniture making, contract cabinetry, electronic subassembly, and plastics.

Throughout the 1960s, '70s, and early '80s, Kimball produced mostly low-priced pianos. In the survey for the first edition of this book, taken in 1983, technicians found many problems in Kimball pianos and considered them difficult and unpleasant to service. Details about pianos from this period can be found in the first edition, available from the publisher. Although these pianos may have filled a valid need in the market of their day, I would suggest not purchasing a used Kimball from this period.

In response to changing consumer desires in the piano market, over the last five to ten years Kimball has impressively upgraded its factory equipment and operations, and consequently the workmanship of Kimball pianos has improved considerably. In addition to improving its quality, Kimball has been working to improve its image, producing promotional events that would put Madison Avenue to shame. These have included becoming supplier to various World's Fairs and Olympics and taking part in TV extravaganzas and telethons. For purposes of both image and quality improvement, Kimball has also upgraded the features in its pianos, in particular replacing the laminated soundboards it had used exclusively for almost thirty years with solid spruce soundboards in most of its pianos. At the same time, to continue to service the low end of the market, Kimball sells its less expensive pianos through a subsidiary under different names.

Verticals. Until just prior to this writing, Kimball manufactured a 42″ promotional console, "W. W. Kimball," and several versions of a 42″ console that differed primarily in the sophistication of their cabinetry. (New models just released will be described later.) It also makes a 46″ "Classic" school studio piano. In addition, through the "Jasper-American Manufacturing Co.," Kimball sells inexpensive console pianos with a variety of trade names on them (see "Names used") and private-label brands for a number

For explanation of survey and review procedures, please see pages 69–72.

of dealers and distributors (see "Stencil pianos"). The W. W. Kimball and Jasper-American pianos are manufactured in Kimball's plant in Renosa, Mexico, where its Schwander actions are assembled. All other pianos are made in Kimball's Indiana factory. Note that Kimball no longer makes spinets.

Since 1986, Kimball has made some significant changes to the vertical pianos it sells under the Kimball name. In some models the laminated soundboards have been replaced by solid spruce ones, the Pratt-Win actions replaced by Schwander actions in the consoles and by a Langer action in the studio, and a portion of the console scale design that gave tuners difficulty was rescaled.

Kimball pianos were represented in the 1989 survey by only about two dozen instruments, mostly consoles. Noted most often were tuning pins that were too tight or uncontrollable, loose key bushings (Kimball key bushings used to be too tight—perhaps they went too far in correcting this), some poor hammer spacing, and some regulation and tone complaints. Pianos made under one of the Jasper names, especially Conn, were found to have, in addition, poorly spaced strings, poor key weighting, poor tone throughout, insufficient preparation in the factory, and some examples of less careful workmanship.

In follow-up interviews in 1990, most of the technicians consulted about Kimball pianos said that the consoles had improved, but that they still did not care for the tone. Many suggested that the scale design and the hammers could be improved. It was not clear to me from their comments that the solid spruce soundboards were necessarily an improvement over the laminated ones. It's possible that any such improvement would be masked by other tonal problems, or it could be that Kimball's long-time claim that its laminated soundboards are as good or better than solid spruce ones may be true. Since the pianos seem to be mechanically and structurally satisfactory, they would probably be okay for those whose musical needs are less demanding. I would still not recommend the private-label and stencil pianos, however, because they seem to be less carefully made or prepared for sale.

Kimball has just announced a new series of consoles to replace the present line. These 43" consoles in three levels of quality and cabinetry include new scale designs, weighted keys, full-length sharps, and improved hammers. The less expensive models will have laminated soundboards, the top model a solid spruce soundboard. Kimball says these new models represent an evolution of the quality improvements that began with the grands and have gradually migrated down the line to the consoles. The private-label and stencil pianos will also benefit from these changes, Kimball says, as they will use the same scale design.

Most of the technicians interviewed about Kimballs were not as familiar with the "Classic" studio as with the consoles, but those who knew it usually thought well of it. The scale design of this piano, especially in the bass, may also need some work (or perhaps the pianos I played just needed voicing), but the new Langer action is quite remarkable. This version of the Langer contains the "B.P. Jack System," an auxiliary spring that assists the jack in returning under the hammer butt faster for the next stroke of the key. The action on this piano is exceptionally fast and nimble. I found that I could play music on this piano that I cannot play on most other verticals. The Kimball studio is a piano worth taking a look at.

Grands. Kimball makes five sizes of grand piano: the 4'5" "La Petite" grand, and the 5'2", 5'8", 6'7", and 9' "Viennese Classic" grands. The concert grand is made in the Bösendorfer factory in Vienna, and its scale design is a new one made exclusively for Kimball. The "La Petite" is the smallest grand ever made. (Grand pianos like this, actually wider than they are long, are usually not recommended by piano technicians.) This piano uses a simplified version of the Pratt-Win action and the middle pedal operates a bass sustain. The "Viennese Classic" grands all use a Schwander action and offer a true sostenuto.

In the first survey, Kimball grands were found to be plagued with many small action and cabinet problems that should never occur in a quality instrument. These problems were complicated by the fact that fourteen screws had to be removed just to access the action. Despite these defects, a number of technicians admitted they were impressed with the 5'8" and 6'7" grands, then called "Viennese Edition," and said that though their tone was unexceptional, they were good enough to be recommended for those with less demanding musical needs.

Since the first survey, Kimball has redesigned these grands, including replacing the laminated soundboards with solid spruce ones. It has also received some coaching from Bösendorfer, probably a more important factor than the soundboard replacement. The pianos now arrive from the factory needing some regulating and voicing but little remedial repair by the dealer, and the case parts have been redesigned to make servicing easier. Those who plan to raise and lower the lid often should take note of its heavy weight. Kimball says, though, that the medium-density fiberboard it uses for the lid is less likely than conventional materials to warp when the lid is kept open for long periods of time. Technicians once again report being very impressed with the 5'8" and 6'7" grands, but this time also find the tone to be quite pleasing. The 5'2" grand, limited by its size and not yet upgraded into the Viennese Classic series at the time of the survey, was not favored as much by those who were familiar with it. In early 1990 I played several examples of all three models (including an upgraded 5'2" model), and found them to be quite musical and a pleasure to play.

Kimball uses some less traditional materials and features in its grands than do other makers. Instead of blindly following tradition, Kimball looks for the most suitable material for the job, even when it turns out to be a non-traditional material like medium-density fiberboard. The poplar it uses in its grand rims may be less highly regarded by those who make instruments of the highest quality, but it has long been used by others and works quite satisfactorily. The soundboard ribs, although full-length, are not tightly fitted into notches in the inner rim, as they would be in more traditional pianos (I discuss this feature in Chapter 3). As a result of its research into non-traditional materials and features, Kimball is able to offer an instrument that performs well at a lower cost.

The Kimball Viennese Classic grands are priced somewhere in between the Japanese and the Korean grands. This is right about where I would place their value. The Kimballs, though they seem reasonably well made, lack some of the finesse in workmanship characteristic of the Japanese instruments. The Korean pianos, though perhaps potentially more sophisticated or traditional in design and materials than the Kimballs, so far appear not to be as consistent and, in any case, do not sound as good as the Kimballs. Most of the technicians I interviewed who were familiar with the Kimball Viennese Classics said they would recommend them over most Korean grands.

Warranty: The Kimball "Full Diamond Warranty" is a fifteen-year full warranty (parts, labor, transferable) that covers Kimball grands, studios, and the newest line of consoles. The Jasper-American pianos have a ten-year, parts-only warranty, seventy years on the laminated soundboard.

KOHLER & CAMPBELL

Kohler & Campbell, Inc.
Granite Falls, North Carolina

Out of business

Names used: Kohler & Campbell, Kohler, Brambach

Founded in 1896 in New York City as a partnership between Charles Kohler and J.C. Campbell, Kohler & Campbell was for many years a leading piano and player piano manufacturer. The company moved to Granite Falls, North Carolina in 1954, and went out of business in 1985.

Kohler & Campbell made verticals and grands in various sizes. The spinet and the console were actually of identical scale design, with the console plate simply positioned in its cabinet to accept a console action. Most of the pianos had laminated soundboards. The pianos came in a wide variety of furniture styles and levels of sophistication in cabinetry.

In the earlier survey, technicians found that the verticals were mechanically fairly well made and came out of the factory in decent regulation. The big complaint, especially about the spinets and consoles, was that the tone, and the ability of the pianos to be accurately tuned, was very bad, due to deficiencies in the scale design. In addition, technicians found the case parts to be very poorly designed for servicing. Technicians were very consistent and specific in their opinions about these pianos and found the majority of them to be unacceptable. The grands, not included in the written survey, seemed to be very average instruments, with a poor bass tone.

In 1984 Kohler & Campbell changed the name on its pianos, for marketing purposes, to Kohler. The name Brambach was put on its "budget" line of spinets and consoles. The company also made pianos for Universal Player Piano Co., which installed its own player mechanism in them.

KRAKAUER

Krakauer Pianos
Berlin, Ohio

No longer in production

Owned by: Kimball International, Inc., Jasper, Indiana

Name used: Krakauer

Founded in 1869 by Simon Krakauer, this company was controlled by the Krakauer family all the way to 1977. In that year Howard Graves, a successful engineer who had always dreamed of owning a piano company, bought Krakauer and moved it from New York City to the small Amish town of Berlin, Ohio, where labor was cheaper and of high quality. But the costs of starting a new company, combined with a national economic recession, were too much, and

For explanation of survey and review procedures, please see pages 69–72.

Krakauer was acquired by Kimball in 1980. The manufacturing facilities remained separate from Kimball's and the standards much higher, and Graves was retained as manager. Kimball closed the Krakauer factory in 1985, citing market factors as the reason.

The old Krakauer upright made in the early part of this century was a highly esteemed instrument. In keeping with the times, the company switched to a mediocre console in its later years. After buying the company in 1977, Graves changed to a different console design. This 41" instrument, made in a variety of furniture styles, was about as hand-crafted as a piano can be, with especially meticulous care taken in the cabinetry and finish. Piano technicians tend to be oblivious to the furniture aspects of pianos, but the Krakauer, alone in my survey, received rave reviews for its finish.

Krakauer made fewer than a thousand pianos a year, and only seven were represented in the survey. The problems cited were quite consistent from one piano to another: rattling bass strings, overly tight tuning pins, not enough tuning and regulating at the factory (or too much tendency to go out of tune and regulation when new), squeaking trapwork, and manufacturing debris left in the piano. Concerning the tone, the Krakauer was found by most of the technicians to have an especially lovely sounding treble, but a poor transition from the treble to the bass strings and a poor low bass tone (as most consoles do). Once the minor defects were fixed and adjustments made, the Krakauer was considered to be quite a good console piano.

LOWREY/STORY & CLARK

Story & Clark Piano Co.
c/o Lowrey Industries, Inc.
La Grange Park, Illinois

No longer in business

Owned by: Bergsma Furniture Co., Grand Rapids, Michigan

Pianos made by: Bergsma Furniture Co.

Names used: Lowrey, Story & Clark, Hampton, Hobart M. Cable

Note: The names Story & Clark and Hobart M. Cable, and the pianos designs associated with those names, were purchased in 1990 by Classic Player Piano Corporation. See "Classic." The review below is of these pianos under their former ownership.

Hampton Story began making pianos in 1857 and was joined by Melville Clark in 1884. The business settled in Grand Haven, Michigan, in 1901, where it remained until recently. After a number of confusing business transactions, both Story & Clark and Lowrey Organ Co. ended up belonging to Norlin Industries, a large manufacturer of diverse products. In 1984 Norlin sold the organ and electronic keyboard division to two former piano company executives, who formed a company called Lowrey Industries, now owned by Kawai. The Story & Clark Piano Co. was sold to the Bergsma Furniture Co. of Grand Rapids, Michigan, which had all along been making cabinet parts for Story & Clark. Bergsma consolidated the Story & Clark operation into its own factory and contracted with Lowrey Industries to market the pianos, but the newly organized piano business apparently never got off the ground, and piano manufacturing ceased about 1986.

Lowrey and Story & Clark vertical pianos made under Norlin's ownership in Grand Haven were made in the same factory. The Lowrey had fancier cabinetry, and the two had some relatively insignificant technical differences to differentiate them for marketing purposes, but they had the same scale design and were essentially the same piano. As one technician summed up the difference: "Lowrey pianos are sold by businessmen in suburban mall stores, and Story & Clark pianos are sold by technician-owned businesses." Hampton was the name of the "budget"-model Lowrey; Hobart M. Cable the "budget"-model Story & Clark. These models had basswood laminated soundboards, instead of the spruce laminated "Storytone" soundboard of the regular models, cabinets of particle board instead of lumber-core plywood, and cheaper construction in many other parts, too. The survey technicians found that Lowrey and Story & Clark verticals had many problems with cabinetry, hardware, pinblock, stringing, action regulation, and tone, and the pianos could not be recommended. A year later, the pianos were rescaled and reportedly had an improved tone.

Lowrey and Story & Clark grands were also made at the Grand Haven factory until about 1984, when they were discontinued. The two differently-named grands were otherwise identical. They were apparently satisfactory instruments, with a sprinkling of minor problems, but nothing serious.

MARANTZ/PIANOCORDER

Marantz Piano Co., Inc.
Morganton, North Carolina

Out of business

Owned by: Superscope, Inc., Chatsworth, California (publicly owned); Pianocorder now owned by Yamaha

Names used: Marantz, Grand, Kincaid, Jesse French, Pianocorder

Marantz Piano Co. was a division of the same Marantz that makes stereo equipment. In fact, a small portion of the piano factory in Morganton, North Carolina was used for making stereo speakers. Marantz bought this factory from the Grand Piano Co. in the late 1970s. Although Marantz stopped making pianos in 1984, it continued making the Pianocorder Reproducing System for a few more years, until the rights to the Pianocorder were finally sold to Yamaha and the product was discontinued in 1987. The Pianocorder is an electronic player piano mechanism that, by means of a casette tape, can record or play a "live" performance on any piano in which it's installed. Marantz used to make some of its pianos with the Pianocorder already installed, some without, and separate Pianocorder kits that could be installed in any piano. Although the pianos and the kits have been discontinued, a few technicians and dealers may still have kits to install. More advanced digital player piano systems are gradually supplanting the Pianocorder.

Until 1984, Marantz made a 39" spinet and a 42" console. The names Marantz, Grand, Kincaid, and Jesse French were used on them interchangeably, depending on the preference of the dealer to whom they were being sold. These pianos were quite possibly the worst pianos ever made in the United States. One piano examined had so many defects and problems that the technician had to add three pages of explanatory notes to describe the disaster he was witnessing. A few comments give the flavor of his exasperation with them: "This company is also often sloppy with glue in the action, dripping glue on bass strings, butt felts, catchers, in between action parts, etc. I found two 'dead' bass strings glued together." "They often come in a half-step flat, or with the bass almost a half-step sharp, and won't hold a tuning even after several pitch raises and a few fine tunings." "Front legs are very precarious, and will break off easily if the front caster rolls across even a small crack in the floor."

The Pianocorder System, however, was reasonably well-made. It came in two forms—a kit installed in the piano and a separate unit that wheeled up to the piano. With the kit, most of the electronics and player action go in the bottom, with parts sticking up through a slot in the keybed to impart motion to the keys. In a grand, the system resides in a box attached to the bottom of the keybed and sticks through a slot cut in the keybed. The installation, especially in grands, is very time-consuming and quite tricky to do right. When choosing an installer (if you can still find someone who installs them), experience in doing these installations and access to spare parts should count heavily. The biggest mistake you could make would be to try to save a few hundred dollars by having a less experienced person do the installation. The price of the kit, including installation, is about $2,500 for verticals and $3,500 for grands. Yamaha has said it will continue to make spare parts for these systems.

The second kind of Pianocorder, not made for some time, was called a "Vorsetzer." It was a completely separate unit that was wheeled up to the keyboard, its eighty-eight rubber plungers positioned over the keys to play the piano. An extension rod activated the sustain pedal. (The unit looked sort of like a headless robot.)

The Pianocorder System is run by cassette tapes with computer signals on them, still available. A large catalog of tapes includes every kind of music. The system works well if properly installed and adjusted in a good piano (these are big "ifs"). The Pianocorder also comes with an optional record feature that doesn't work well and is not recommended.

MASON & HAMLIN/KNABE

Mason & Hamlin Corp.
35 Duncan Street
Haverhill, Massachusetts 01830
(508) 372-8300

Owned by: Bernard Greer (who also owns Falcone Piano Co.)

Names used: Mason & Hamlin; not presently used: Knabe, George Steck

Mason & Hamlin was founded in 1854 by Henry Mason and Emmons Hamlin. Mason was a musician and businessman and Hamlin was an inventor working with reed organs. Within a few years, Mason & Hamlin was one of the largest reed organ manufacturers in the country. The company began making pianos in 1881, and soon became, along with Chickering, among the most prestigious of the Boston piano makers. With the rise of the radio and phonograph as the dominant forms of entertainment in the late 1920s, and then the Depression, the piano market declined and many piano names were bought out and consolidated. Mason & Hamlin, Knabe, Chickering, George Steck, and many others became part of the Aeolian American Corp., which located in East Rochester, N.Y. The Winter Piano Co., originally established in 1899, acquired Aeolian American in 1959, and was renamed Aeolian Pianos Inc. Over the next twenty-five years, the quality of these piano brands declined. (See "Aeolian" for details of this company's recent history.)

When Aeolian Pianos went out of business in 1985, the Mason & Hamlin, Knabe, and George Steck brand names and scale designs were sold to Sohmer, by then owned by Pratt, Read and operating in Ivoryton, Connecticut (see "Sohmer"). Pratt-Read left the piano business shortly thereafter, selling Sohmer to an investor. Sohmer tried to revive Mason & Hamlin, but due to a lack of skilled labor and other problems, very few Mason & Hamlin pianos were built. In 1988, Sohmer moved its manufacturing facilities to Elysburg, Pennsylvania in a final attempt to continue manufacturing. In 1989 Sohmer and the Mason & Hamlin, Knabe, and George Steck names and scales were sold to Seattle businessman and philanthropist Bernard Greer, who had just purchased the Falcone Piano Co. (see "Falcone").

The 50" Mason & Hamlin upright, which for many years was the only tall upright being produced in the United States, continues to be made in the Elysburg plant, along with Sohmer verticals. Two sizes of Mason & Hamlin grand, the model A (5'8 ½") and the model BB (7') are being made at Falcone's Haverhill, Massachusetts factory. These are excellent piano designs with long and illustrious histories, and Falcone is one of the few piano companies in the United States capable of giving them the attentive handcrafting they deserve. Rather than just exploiting the names, as is so common, Falcone will be using the original scale designs, as the company acquired all the tooling and patterns for those pianos along with the rights to the names. Actions will be made by Renner. Current plans are to make about 300 Mason & Hamlin grands in the first year of production, sold through a small network of dealers. Due to the tumultuous recent history of Mason & Hamlin and the lack of field

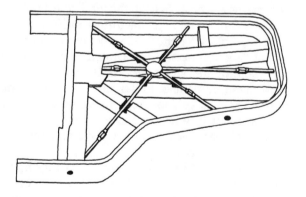

FIGURE 4-2. The Mason & Hamlin *tension resonator* is a series of turnbuckles connecting parts of the inner rim. In theory, this prevents the rim from expanding with age and therefore preserves the crown of the soundboard.

reports, it is not possible to report on the quality of the Mason & Hamlin pianos at this time, but I fully expect them to be top-rated pianos, similar in quality to the Falcone.

Mason & Hamlin grands have a unique construction feature called a tension resonator, which consists of a series of turnbuckles that connect various parts of the inner rim (Figure 4-2). In theory this web of turnbuckles, nicknamed the spider, locks the rim in place so that it cannot expand with stress and age, thereby preserving the crown of the soundboard. (The soundboard is glued to the inner rim and would collapse if the rim expanded.) There is no modern-day experimental evidence to confirm or deny this theory, but many technicians believe in its validity nevertheless.

The Knabe and George Steck designs and names are not currently being used.

Warranty: Ten years, parts and labor.

PETROF

**Geneva International
200 Larkin Drive
Wheeling, Illinois 60090
(800) 533-2388**

Pianos made by: Petrof Pianos, Musicexport, Vaclavske nam. 18, 11227 Prague, Czechoslovakia

Name used: Petrof

The Petrof piano factory was founded in 1864 by Antonin Petrof in Hradec Kralove, an industrial town located 100 kilometers east of Prague in Czechoslovakia. Three generations of the Petrof family owned and managed the business, during which time the company kept pace with technical developments and earned prizes for their pianos at international exhibitions. In 1965, Petrof joined the Industrial and Commercial Group—Czechoslovak Musical Instruments (Musicexport), the state-controlled import-export company. In 1970, a new main factory for production of vertical pianos utilizing an automatic assembly line was built, and in 1989, a new grand piano factory was opened. Currently Petrof manufactures about 26,000 verticals and 1,000 grands a year, with a goal of eventually producing 2,000 grands a year. Petrof maintains an educational facility to train new craftsmen, with current enrollment at 180 apprentices.

Grands. Petrof manufactures five sizes of grand piano, from 5'3" to 9'3". The majority of components are produced in Petrof's own factories, including actions, hardware, plates, and cabinetry. The grand pinblocks and rims are of laminated European beech, the soundboards of native-grown spruce. All grand models except the 5'3" size come with full sostenuto pedal and are available in a variety of interesting veneers and finishes, both high-polish polyester and open-pore satin.

Petrof grands are very sturdily built instruments and are known for their warm, rich, singing tone, full of color, though perhaps somewhat lacking in the tonal projection of the famous northern German pianos. Workmanship varies in the pianos; it is not uncommon to find beautiful cabinetmaking alongside less than careful attention to detail in action assembly, the fitting of case parts, regulation, and voicing. The hardware is not as well made as that available to Western piano makers.

Although they arrive from the factory in somewhat rough condition, after careful preparation and voicing, Petrof grands can sound and feel quite beautiful and hold their own against some of the better-known European pianos. For this reason, they are sometimes called "technicians' pianos." Most piano dealers are not prepared to put the time into these pianos that it takes to bring them to their potential, but dealers with strong service departments, especially those who are also technicians, can. Best of all, despite a very high duty, the price of these pianos is only about half that of many other European pianos and often at similar prices to the Japanese pianos. When properly prepared, they are a very good value.

Verticals. Petrof verticals are available in three sizes: a 42" console, a 45" studio, and a 50" upright. Most of the comments regarding workmanship, preparation, quality, and value of the grands also applies to the verticals, except that the verticals are more mass-produced and, being verticals, have less potential. There have also been some problems with loose bass string windings and loose action centers, and a tendency for the polyester finish in the lower panel of the verticals to make creaking noises. All these are easily correctible during pre-sale service by the dealer. At this time, the 42" console in the style called "Antik" is made in a different factory and more attention to detail is present in this model.

Warranty: Ten years, parts and labor, from Geneva International.

SAMICK

Samick Music Corp.
18521 Railroad St.
City of Industry, California 91748
(818) 964-4700

Pianos made by: Samick Musical Instrument Mfg. Co. Ltd., Incheon, South Korea

Names used: Samick; no longer used: Horugel, Stegler; private-label brand names; Samick also makes pianos for various distributors, such as Hyundai and Schumann.

Samick was founded by Hyo Ick Lee in 1958. Facing an immense challenge in impoverished and war-torn South Korea, Lee began to build and sell a very limited quantity of vertical pianos using largely imported parts. As the Korean economy improved in the 1960s, Lee expanded his operation, and Samick is now one of the world's largest piano manufacturers (as well as the largest maker of fretted instruments), making most parts of the piano in house. Samick also makes one model of console piano in the United States.

Samick entered the U.S. market in the late 1970s under a variety of trade names, including Horugel and Stegler. These first pianos reacted very poorly to the climatic extremes of North America, as have the first imported pianos of every other Asian manufacturer, with wooden parts warping, cracking, and binding. Many of them had to be sent back to Korea.

By the mid-1980s, Samick pianos were rapidly improving and were considered by some to be satisfactory. Insufficient information at the time I did the research for the first edition of this book led me to report, "Samicks now arrive from the factory in very good condition, needing relatively little servicing by the dealer, and no significant field problems are reported." At that time I gave them "tentative" ratings very close to that of the major Japanese pianos.

Unfortunately, this turned out to be premature. Verbal reports received after the book was published showed that the pianos were very erratic in quality, and many were plagued with problems, requiring hours of repair and adjustment by the dealer. To make matters worse, just at the time the book was published (fall of 1987), labor unrest in Korea culminating in strikes resulted in some highly defective pianos being shipped to the United States. Interestingly, most of the worst reports I received were of pianos made by Samick under other names. Samick says that "Samick" pianos were inspected at their California warehouse, whereas pianos entering the country under other names may have gone directly to distributors unscreened.

By the spring of 1988, Samick-made pianos had returned to about the same level of quality as before the strikes, and not much progress was reported during the following year. Pianos made during this period were very inconsistent; some had a lot of problems and some came through in relatively good shape.

Although most technicians who were interviewed did not recommend these pianos, some who were given latitude in servicing them and who were very experienced with them said they could be made into satisfactory instruments.

With the rising cost of Korean labor and the general world-wide decline in the demand for pianos, Korean pianos can no longer compete on price alone. Many are now almost as expensive as some Japanese pianos (about 12 to 15 percent less). Recognizing this, during 1989 Samick upgraded some of its manufacturing facilities and greatly improved its quality control. Follow-up interviews in early 1990 indicate that since the fall of 1989, Samick-made pianos have come through with far fewer problems and needing, for the most part, much less preparation by the dealer. The tone quality still needs improvement, and because the product has only recently been improved and still needs to stand the test of time, there is still, at the time of this writing, a question in my mind about how the regulation, voicing, and construction will hold up. Therefore I recommend a Samick-made piano with caution, and only if price is the major consideration and the dealer thoroughly services the piano prior to sale.

If you shop for a Korean piano, one potential source of confusion will be the conflicting claims of dealers as to whether pianos sold under the names Hyundai and Schumann (and other names belonging to distributors and dealers) are the same as those sold under Samick's own name. Samick dealers will usually say that their pianos have an improved scale design and a better soundboard, while dealers of the other brands will usually say that their pianos are exactly the same as Samicks.

To understand how this confusion can continue to exist, keep in mind that "Samick" pianos are distributed by the American subsidiary of the manufacturer, whereas Samick-made pianos distributed under other names are obtained from the factory via different channels. Due to communications and public relations barriers, it has sometimes been difficult to obtain reliable technical information concerning the differences between these brands.

According to Samick Music Corp., the Samick piano scales were redesigned by noted German scale designer Klaus Fenner in the mid-1980s to improve them, which also had the effect of differentiating them from Samick-made pianos sold under other names. Samick then said these new models had "Imperial German Scale Designs." After a while, some of these scales began to appear under other names. A casual comparison of the plates of the variously named pianos suggests that most of the scales now used are identical from one name to another. However, many aspects of scale design require very careful and extensive measurement to compare, so it's possible that some that look the same are actually different in certain ways.

Samick Music also says that its soundboard is made of a solid core of spruce surrounded by two extremely thin veneers of spruce and therefore, though technically laminated, behaves virtually like a solid spruce soundboard, except that it won't crack. The company also claims that Samick pianos sold under other names have other types of soundboard. My own inspection of all these pianos reveals that the situation is much more complex than that. Samick Music does admit that a variety of different kinds of soundboard, including the kind described above, soundboards with three equal layers or five layers, and sometimes even solid spruce soundboards, have at times been installed in its pianos and in those of its competitors by the factory. Samick Music now says that it is "tightening up its ship" and that henceforth technical differences will be more consistently enforced.

I have gone to some length to discuss this confusing situation only to illustrate the difficulty of getting accurate technical information from Asian manufacturers (Samick is not alone in this), the elaborate lengths to which companies will go to differentiate pianos that are basically similar, and the folly of paying any attention to the technical song and dance the dealers will give you about them, since even the most sincere dealer may well be mistaken. To be honest, any small technical differences that may actually exist between these brands are probably, for all practical purposes, insignificant. If you buy a piano made by Samick, you should make your choice between brands based on price, personal tonal preference, how well the piano has been serviced by the dealer, and if all else fails, which name you prefer.

Warranty (Samick): Lifetime, parts and labor for original purchaser on soundboard, plate, and pinblock; ten years, parts and labor, on rest of piano.

SAUTER

C. Bechstein America Corp.
425 Hayes Street
San Francisco, CA 94102
(415) 255-0284

Pianos made by: Carl Sauter, Pianoforte Factory
7208 Spaichingen, West Germany

Name used: Sauter

The Sauter piano firm was founded by Johann Grimm, stepfather to Carl Sauter I, in 1819, and has been owned and managed by members of the Sauter family to this day. It produces about 2,500 pianos a year in its factory in the extreme south of Germany, at the foot of the Alps. Structural and acoustical parts are made of high-quality woods, including solid Bavarian spruce soundboards, and actions are made by Renner. Sauter makes its own keys, and the keybed is reinforced with steel to prevent warping. The verticals use an action, designed by Sauter, that contains an auxiliary jack spring to aid in faster repetition. Sauter calls this the "R2 Double Escapement Action," but it is not really a double escapement action as the term has historically been used, though it has some of the same effect. Sauter also makes a MIDI grand called the "Picco." Grands and verticals are available in a variety of finishes and styles.

The Sauter grands I played had a lush, full, singing tone, more like an "American" sound than most other European pianos. Sauter is considered in Europe to be a medium-high quality piano.

Warranty: Ten years, parts and labor.

SCHAFER & SONS

Schafer & Sons
P.O. Box 691
Dana Point, California 92629
(800) 227-1189

Distributed by: American International Buyers Association, P.O. Box 15086, Santa Ana, CA 92705

Pianos made by: various manufacturers—see text

Name used: Schafer & Sons

Presided over by Vern Schafer, Schafer & Sons grew out of the Southern California chain Colton Piano & Organ. After selling pianos with the name Schafer out of these stores quite successfully for a number of years, Schafer expanded his marketing efforts across the United States. The Schafer personnel with whom I spoke were somewhat reluctant to say where their pianos are made, preferring to refer to them instead as the Korean Schafer and the American Schafer. The most reliable information I have (in early 1990) is that through 1989 the Korean Schafers were all made by Samick; beginning in 1990 they are being made by Sojin. The American Schafers are now made by Kimball. I do not know to what extent, if any, the Schafer versions of these pianos differ from those built under the manufacturers' own names.

Warranty: Schafer offers its own "Lifetime Limited Warranty" on all these pianos. It covers the piano, including both parts and labor, except the cabinet, for the lifetime of the original purchaser, and is not transferable. Important: the warranty may be voided if you use the services of a technician not authorized by a Schafer & Sons dealer without written permission.

SCHIMMEL

Schimmel Piano Corp.
Eastern Representative: 251 Memorial Drive, Lititz, Pennsylvania 17543
Western Representative: 1701 Port Barmouth Place, Newport Beach, California 92660
(800) 426-3205

Pianos made by: Wilhelm Schimmel Pianofortefabrik GmbH, P.O. Box 4860, D-3300 Braunschweig, West Germany

Name used: Schimmel

Wilhelm Schimmel began making pianos in 1885, and his company enjoyed steady growth through the late nineteenth and early twentieth centuries. The two world wars and the Depression disrupted production several times, but the company has gradually rebuilt itself over the past forty years with a strong reputation for quality. Today, Schimmel is owned and managed by Nikolaus Schimmel, the grandson of the founder. Schimmel makes about 7,500 verticals and 1,500 grands a year, and is the largest piano maker in Western Europe. About two-thirds of its pianos are for foreign export, to countries including the United States. A 24.9 percent share of Schimmel is owned by Yamaha.

The Schimmel piano line includes several sizes of studio and upright piano and three sizes of grand. The smaller verticals have a very big bass for their size. The 51" upright also has a very large sound, and listening to it, it would be easy to think you were in the presence of a grand. The 5'10" and 6'10" grands are great pianos; the smaller of the two is especially powerful for its size. The larger grand also comes in a style called "Unikat", or "Unique", which features decorative medallions and Mr. Schimmel's signature on the plate, brass-plated tuning pins, and other deluxe features. (The 6'10" grand is also available in "Traditional Plexiglass" for $72,000.) Schimmel plans to introduce an 8'4" grand in 1991.

For explanation of survey and review procedures, please see pages 69–72.

Twenty-one Schimmel pianos were inspected in the present survey and interviews with technicians brought several observations. Basically, Schimmels are terrific pianos with great sound and workmanship. But, typically European, the manufacturing tolerances are very tight, and when the pianos first arrive at the dealer, most have tight key bushings and balance holes that need easing. Sometimes, too, humidity changes will have caused some case parts to bind or a few action centers to tighten. But the technicians said these problems are not serious, and once taken care of at the dealer they rarely return. Furthermore, the technicians say, the pianos need little other servicing.

Schimmels probably received more rave reviews than any other brand in the survey: "One of the best sounding uprights I've ever heard." "Absolutely beautiful! Tone bright and pure. Action feels quick and light like Bosendorfer. Piano in almost perfect tune right out of the box." "This is an incredible piano. Yamaha-like precision with a great bass." "Uncanny tuning stability." "Absolutely inspiring."

Schimmel dealers usually bill Schimmel pianos as exotic, "handcrafted" instruments, and the comments above would seem to support that. Indeed, compared to most pianos for sale in this country, Schimmels are exquisite. But readers may be interested in knowing that, in fact, the Schimmel factory combines computer-controlled machinery with its handcraftsmanship, and my European contacts tell me that in Europe, where superbly crafted pianos are commonplace, Schimmels are considered very good but not the very best possible. At this level of quality, however, the differences between a piano like Schimmel and "the very best possible" become rather subtle, each slight quality increase raising the price substantially. It's not surprising, then, that I receive many calls from worried piano shoppers who, after trying out all the "best" pianos and finding they prefer the Schimmel at half the price, wonder what they might be "missing" by buying one. My advice is usually that if they don't perceive a difference in quality (and I don't blame them if they don't), then for their purposes there is no significant difference and they should buy the less expensive piano. Even those who do recognize the subtle differences between these brands, though, find the Schimmel to be a very good deal. As one technician wrote, "Schimmel has been my favorite grand for the past ten years, beating out Bechstein, Grotrian, Ibach, and the rest by virtue of its value."

Warranty: Ten year, limited.

SCHULTZ & SONS

Schultz & Sons International, Ltd.
171-A Milbar Blvd.
Farmingdale, New York 11735
(800) 2-Pianos
(516) 756-0222

Owned by: Gary Haig Schultz

Pianos made by: various manufacturers—see text

Name used: Schultz & Sons

Gary Schultz, a well-known and highly respected piano technician and retailer on Long Island (NY), puts his family name on pianos made in cooperation with a variety of manufacturers. These really shouldn't be called "stencil pianos," but since this manufacturing concept is somewhat unique and innovative in the industry, for ease of categorization I'll call them that, but with a difference! Schultz starts with pianos that are either the same as, or in some cases better than, the pianos sold under a manufacturer's own name, and then makes substantial and meaningful technical modifications to further enhance the pianos' quality and value. Another benefit to this process is that the pianos receive a quality control check and preparation both in the original factory and in the Schultz & Sons factory. Also unlike most stencil pianos, these pianos are sold with both the original manufacturer's warranty and the Schultz & Sons warranty. No attempt is made to deceive the customer as to the actual identity of the original manufacturer.

At present the Schultz & Sons line consists of a 42" console originally made by Kimball and a 46" studio originally made by Sohmer. Shortly, it will also include 42½" and 44" consoles by Kawai, a 52" upright by Kawai, and 5'7", 6', and 6'11" grands by Kawai. Other "joint venture" products are on the drawing board. Modifications and upgrades vary by product, but include such things as rescaling, key weighting and balancing, and action and trapwork modification where needed; and installation of Renner hammers, solid spruce soundboard, and simulated ivory keytops in some models. Schultz says his aim is to pack more meaningful features into the pianos at each price level to provide the best value possible, combining American ingenuity, German parts, and Japanese precision to that end. Schultz also says he is bringing together top experts in piano design and construction on an ongoing basis to advise him as the Schultz & Sons line evolves.

Although it is not possible to evaluate these pianos

at this time because of their relatively small distribution, it would probably be safe to say that they are of higher quality than pianos of the original manufacturer to an extent that varies according to the particular enchancements made.

Warranty: Original manufacturer's warranty plus Schultz & Sons fifteen-year full warranty.

SCHUMANN

Schumann Piano Co.
700 Willow Lane
West Dundee, Illinois 60118
(800) 541-2331

Pianos made by: Samick, Kimball

Name used: Schumann

All pianos with this name are made by Samick except for the least expensive console and grand, which are made by Kimball.

Warranty: Ten years, parts only; seventy-five years, parts only, on pinblock, soundboard, and plate in Samick-made pianos.

SEILER

Seiler America, Inc.
2363 South Hamilton Rd.
Columbus, OH 43232
(614) 868-1877

Pianos made by: Ed. Seiler Pianofortefabrik, Schwarzacher Strasse 40, 871 Kitzingen, West Germany

Name Used: Seiler

Eduard Seiler, the company's founder, began making pianos in Liegnitz, Silesia, Germany in 1849. The company grew to over 435 employees, producing up to 3,000 pianos per year in 1923. Seiler was the largest piano manufacturer in Eastern Europe at that time. In 1945 and after World War II, the plant was occupied by Poland and the Seiler family left their native homeland with millions of other refugees. In 1951 Steffan Seiler re-established the company in Copenhagen under the fourth generation of family ownership, and in 1962 moved it to Kitzingen, West Germany, where it resides today. Seiler has over 200 employees and produces approximately 5,000 pianos annually.

Seiler makes high quality pianos using a combination of traditional and modern scientific methods. The scale designs are of relatively high tension, producing a brilliant, balanced tone that is quite consistent from one Seiler to the next. Although brilliant, the tone also sings well due to, the company says, a unique soundboard feature—a groove running around the perimeter of the board—that gives the soundboard flexibility without losing necessary stiffness. The pianos feature Bavarian spruce soundboards, multilaminated beech pinblocks, quarter-sawn beech bridges, and Renner actions.

Seiler's piano line includes 45", 46 ½", 48", 50 ½", and 52" verticals, and 5'11", 6'9", and 7'9" grands. The 5'11" grand is also available in models with beautiful wood inlays. An extraordinary "Showmaster" grand designed for show business is available in the 5'11" and 6'9" grand sizes and can be equipped with MIDI, as can the "Showmaster Junior" 45" and 46 ½" verticals.

Warranty: Ten years, parts and labor.

SOHMER

Sohmer Corp.
35 Duncan Street
Haverhill, Massachusetts 01830
(508) 372-8300

Owned by: Bernard Greer (owner of Falcone Piano Co.)

Name used: Sohmer

Founded by German immigrant Hugo Sohmer in 1872, Sohmer & Co. was owned and managed by the Sohmer family in New York City for 110 years, most recently by the founder's grandsons, Harry and Robert Sohmer. Getting old and having no descendents willing to take over the business, the Sohmer brothers sold the company in 1982 to Pratt, Read & Co., a leading manufacturer of piano keys and actions. Due to the decline of the U.S. piano industry and foreign competition, Pratt, Read had excess manufacturing capacity and a skilled work force, so the match seemed like a good one, and Sohmer & Co. was moved to Ivoryton, Connecticut. The Sohmer brothers moved, too, and for a while continued to play a part in managing the company, but most of the labor force and the rest of the management stayed behind in New York. In 1986, continuing its withdrawal from the piano business, Pratt, Read sold Sohmer to a group of investors headed by Robert McNeil, former chief of McNeil Laboratories (creators of Tylenol). At the same time, McNeil purchased the Mason & Hamlin and Knabe names and assets from Citicorp, the owner of the bankrupt Aeolian Pianos. (See "Mason & Hamlin/Knabe" for more information.) McNeil sold Sohmer (and Mason & Hamlin/Knabe) to Bernard Greer, owner of Falcone Piano Co., in 1989.

During its many years in New York, the Sohmer piano was known as a fine handcrafted instrument. Sohmer had a close informal association with the other major New York piano maker, Steinway, and many of Sohmer's manufacturing methods have been similar to Steinway's. The new management in Connecticut was technically knowledgeable and sought to maintain and even improve the product, which was generally considered to be one of the finest pianos made in the United States. After a few years, though, the Connecticut labor market became so tight that it was almost impossible to find the skilled labor necessary to build the pianos, which by this time also included the Mason & Hamlin line (Sohmer officials sometimes said they were competing with McDonald's for help). Finally, in 1988, Sohmer moved its manufacturing facilities to Elysburg, Pennsylvania, an area with a large pool of skilled but unemployed woodworkers and craftspeople. Since the sale of Sohmer to Greer, production of Sohmer pianos in the Elysburg plant has gradually increased back to normal levels as the new workers have been trained.

Until 1988, Sohmer made 42" consoles, 45" studios, and 5' and 5'7" grands. The consoles and grands have been discontinued and only a 46" studio is now made (the same piano an inch taller). This is the model for which Sohmer has always been best known. It has a solid spruce soundboard, no particle board in the case, has individually weighed-off keys, and a Pratt-Win action.

In the survey for the first edition of this book, it was found that although Sohmer was highly regarded among piano techncians, some felt that the pianos excelled more in their cabinetry and structural integrity than in their tone. Poor hammer quality was often cited as a principal problem. Others praised the pianos in all respects. It should be noted that the scale design of the studio is similar to that of the console, which explains why technicians have long complained that the tonal transition from treble to bass (the "bass break") in the studio model is not as good as should be expected in a studio piano. Poor string spacing was also frequently cited in the verticals. Nevertheless, the Sohmer studio has long been a popular and successful school piano.

In the survey for the second edition, poor string spacing was again cited, but so was insufficient tuning, regulating, and voicing at the factory. Apparently

pianos made during the last year in Connecticut, though structurally sound, often were not finished (prepared) properly. Although not included in the survey, early reports say that the new Sohmers being made in Pennsylvania are a much improved product.

About their grands, Sohmer was always very low-key, perhaps because in New York they were overshadowed by the pianos of neighbor Steinway. Or perhaps because the grands weren't particularly noteworthy. Basically, Sohmer grands were adequate instruments for casual use inside of nicely made cabinets. Sohmer says it has no plans to manufacture its grands in the future.

Warranty: Twelve years, parts and labor.

SOJIN

See "Notice to Readers," page 72.

STEINWAY & SONS

Steinway & Sons, Inc.
Steinway Place
Long Island City, NY 11105
(718) 721-2600

Owned by: Steinway Musical Properties, Inc.

Name used: Steinway & Sons

Henry Englehard Steinweg, a cabinetmaker and piano maker in Seesen, Germany, emigrated to the United States around 1850 with his family. After first taking jobs with other piano manufacturers to learn the American way of doing business, he and his sons established Steinway & Sons in 1853. This came at a time when interest in the piano, already well established in Europe, was undergoing explosive growth in America, and the Steinways, with twenty-five years of piano making already under their belt, were in a prime position to exploit the commercial, artistic, and technological potential of the piano in their adopted country.

Within a short time, the Steinways were granted patents that revolutionized the piano, and which were eventually adopted or imitated by other makers. Most of these patents concerned the quest for a stronger frame, a richer, more powerful sound, and a more sensitive action. Theodore Steinway, a scientist and engineer, was assisted in his acoustical research by association and correspondence with prominent scientists of the day, including the noted German physicist Hermann von Helmholtz. The business grew rapidly due to good management, to high-quality products, to technical innovations, and to artist endorsements, which were actively sought, a practice still used today with great success. By the 1880s, the Steinway piano was in most ways the modern piano we have today.

In the late 1800s, Steinway gradually moved its manufacturing facilities from Manhattan to Queens, and built a company village there for its employees, who were largely German immigrants. The Steinways were very active in New York civic affairs, and the role of the Steinways is still remembered through the businesses, streets, and even a subway station named after them. In 1880, Steinway established a branch factory, still in operation today, in Hamburg, West Germany.

In the early 1900s, there were fewer technical changes to the instruments, and the quality standards set by the previous generations were strictly adhered to. As Steinway's worldwide dealer network became established, its concert and repair services became widely accessible. The fame of the Steinway continued to spread, and ownership of Steinways with elaborately carved cases became a symbol of wealth and culture. The Depression and the rise of the radio and phonograph both caused sweeping changes in the piano industry. Steinway survived this period by cutting back production, by selling pianos to radio (and later television) stations, and by producing smaller grands and verticals that would appeal to smaller homes and budgets.

In the 1960s, the fourth generation of Steinways found themselves without any heirs willing or able to take over the business, and with a lack of capital with which to finance much needed equipment modernization, so in 1972, Steinway & Sons was sold to CBS. CBS sold Steinway to its present owners in 1985.

Steinway's new management is a departure from its recent past. Steinway's head of manufacturing is a highly credentialed engineer, formerly with General Electric, and he has brought in other engineers without previous piano background. Steinway's present view is that the piano is a manufactured object and, as such, can be treated to a certain extent like any other manufactured object. Problems can be investigated in a scientific manner and manufacturing procedures can be standardized. Many factory processes are being reviewed and reorganized, and new machinery designed, with an eye toward greater precision, especially in the area of action part manufacturing, which had long been problematic. Steinway's challenge right now is to find the right balance between modern engineering and old-world craftsmanship that will preserve the integrity of its construction process.

Verticals. Steinway currently makes two kinds of vertical piano in three sizes—a 45″ studio (model 45), a 46½″ studio (model 1098), and a 52″ upright (model

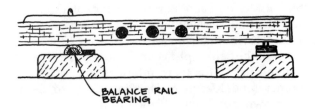

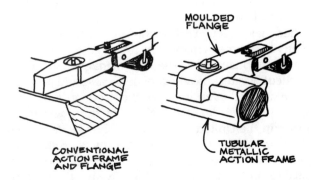

FIGURE 4-3. Two features of Steinway pianos: (Top) Accelerated action. The key balances on a half-round bearing instead of a flat surface, which, Steinway says, increases the speed of repetition. (Bottom) Tubular metallic action frame. The unique shape of the flange and rail virtually prevent movement of the flange, thus helping maintain proper alignment of action parts.

K-52). The model 45 and model 1098 have identical scale designs—only the cabinet is different—the former being in a period style for home use, and the latter for school use or less furniture-conscious home use. The model K-52 upright is a reissue (in 1981) of the model K piano that Steinway discontinued in 1929. Until 1986, Steinway also made a 40″ console (model F). The studio and upright models all have three pedals, the middle one a true sostenuto. The console had only two, sustain and soft. All Steinway verticals use a solid spruce soundboard, have no particle board, and in many other ways are similar in design, materials, and quality of workmanship to Steinway grands.

Sixteen Steinway verticals were examined for the present survey. By far, the biggest complaint was that the pianos were extremely hard to tune, particularly in the treble section. This concern was expressed in one way or another by almost every technician who was interviewed about them. There seem to be several reasons for this tuning problem. First, the tuning pins are quite tight, although this alone would probably be an asset rather than a drawback. Second, unlike most other brands of piano, Steinways do not have plate bushings that surround each tuning pin where it passes through a hole in the plate. These bushings normally support the pin, preventing it from bending much as it is turned during tuning. On a Steinway,

For explanation of survey and review procedures, please see pages 69–72.

the pins tend to "flagpole" (bend), making it more difficult to control and set them. Third, the strings do not move smoothly over their bearing (friction) points when the tuning pins are turned; as a result the strings will suddenly jump out of tune at some point after being tuned.

Other than a little bit of squeaking trapwork, few mechanical problems were found, and none with any regularity. But the opinions about these pianos varied a lot, especially about the consoles and studios. Most technicians felt the tuning problem, combined with what they considered the not-so-special tone of the console and studio models, made them hard to highly recommend, especially considering the price. Some recognized that the tuning was difficult, but sometimes liked the tone of the studio. These opinions are a little different from those expressed in the first survey, when most technicians interviewed considered the studio, at least, to be worth the tuning hassle. The K-52s were more highly favored. Some of these K-52s were said to sound very much like small Steinway grands, while others sound unexceptional.

Grands. Steinway makes five sizes of grand piano at their New York factory: 5'1" (model S), 5'7" (model M), 5'10 ½" (model L), 6'10 ½" (model B), and 8'11 ¾" (model D).

The model S is billed as being "for the home where space is at a premium." Though very good for a small grand, it's frankly too small to be a really worthwhile instrument. Steinway introduced this model in 1935, when all the manufacturers were building smaller pianos in the hopes of reviving the depressed piano industry. Not very many S's are sold, and Steinway doesn't push them very hard.

The model M is a full six inches longer, but costs little more than the S. This is the most common model of Steinway grand, the one found in living rooms across the country. Although its medium size makes the tone in certain areas slightly less than perfect, it's an excellent home instrument.

The model L is only 3 ½" longer than the M, but the scale design and tone are far superior. This instrument is suitable for the more advanced player, larger living room, and many school and teaching situations.

The model B is my favorite of the New York-made Steinways, and the best choice for the serious pianist, recording or teaching studio, or small recital hall.

The model D, the concert grand, is the flagship of the Steinway line and the piano of choice for the overwhelming majority of concert pianists. It's too large for most places other than the concert stage.

Steinway grands were represented in the present survey by sixty instruments, including all sizes, but mostly models M, L, and B. While few problems were found with great frequency, the ones most often checked on the survey forms included: key bushings too tight (when new) or occasionally too loose, since corrected; rattling bass strings, occasional loose key leads, tight action centers in jacks (in several three-year-old pianos), no longer a problem; some dampers not damping properly, a variety of small trapwork problems, hammers poorly spaced to strings or shanks traveling, manufacturing debris in the piano, action needing regulating, and tone too soft in the treble. There were also a couple of more serious problems: the beginnings of soundboard cracks in two model B pianos, and one concert grand the technician said could not be regulated properly, possibly because of an incorrect relationship between hammers and strings.

Concerning the comment that the tone was too soft in the treble, technicians report that many Steinways sound muffled in the treble because the hammers are not hard enough. Salespeople often tell customers that after playing the piano for a while, the hammer felt will pack down and the piano will sound brighter. This is true, of course, but depending on how much you use the piano, it could take a very long time for this to happen. Hardening the hammers to brighten the tone is a relatively simple operation; don't hesitate to request it, if necessary.

Follow-up interviews indicated that the pianos are quite inconsistent in how they arrive from the factory. There are almost always some problems, but the particular problems differ from piano to piano. Occasionally a piano arrives from the factory needing little work, but usually the technicians said that about six to ten hours of troubleshooting, regulating, and voicing is needed to make an instrument suitable for the average good player. An additional day or two of service might be needed to do the highest level of work on the very best pianos. Despite the garden variety of problems they presented when new or later on, technicians usually said they liked the pianos. There were many comments to the effect that the rumor that Steinway was no longer capable of making great instruments is simply untrue, but that it takes a good bit of service to uncover the pianos' potential. Most technicians interviewed about Steinways expressed confidence in the new Steinway management and felt that the pianos were continually improving.

When shopping for a Steinway, I would suggest hiring a piano technician who is very experienced in servicing modern Steinways. Very careful inspection and selection with the help of such a technician should help you sidestep most problems.

Warranty: Five years, parts and labor.

TADASHI

Tadashi Piano Corp.
Mississauga, Ontario, Canada

No longer in business

Pianos made by: Atlas Piano Manufacturing Co., Hamamatsu, Japan

Names used: Tadashi, Atlas

Despite the Japanese name, Tadashi was a North American company, headquartered in the Toronto area, that imported Atlas pianos from Japan. Atlas was started in 1955 by Tadashi Yorikane as a technical joint venture with Kunitachi College of Music in Tokyo, which has a Musical Instrument Research Institute. The pianos were initially marketed in North America in the late 1970s under the tradename Atlas as was used in Japan, but American rights to this name turned out to be already owned by another music-related company, so the piano's name was changed here to Tadashi. (It's ironic that in Japan the piano went by an English name and in the United States by a Japanese name, but I'll bet it sold better that way.)

Tadashi pianos were an interesting blend of European-style design and Japanese precision, and quite nicely made for the most part. But the vertical pianos varied a lot in quality. On some the tone in the upper treble was quite dead and the action parts were not as perfectly aligned as is expected in a Japanese piano. Other pianos were free of these problems. The grands were more consistent and had a lovely singing treble and an even tone across the scale. Like other Japanese pianos, though, they could become quite bright with time.

In 1986, due to the sudden change in international currency values, importers of Japanese products scurried to find less expensive alternatives that would be more competitive in the U.S. market. Rather than go the Korean route like everyone else, Tadashi briefly tried importing pianos from Taiwan and from Canada, but was not able to survive and went out of business in 1987.

TOKAI

Tokai Piano
126 Route 303
West Nyack, New York 10994
(914) 353-3515

Pianos made by: Tokai Gakki Co., Ltd., Hamamatsu, Japan

Name used: Tokai

We often assume that everything made in Japan is well made, but in the case of Tokai this is not so. In the first edition of this book I reported that Tokai pianos needed a lot of servicing by the dealer before being presentable, and that the tonal quality, cabinet finish, workmanship, and materials in their pianos seemed closer to Korean quality than to Japanese. In the most recent survey, the examination of several grands made between 1985 and 1987 served to confirm this. Follow-up interviews found little acquaintance with Tokai pianos, but among those who knew the brand, most of the opinion was unfavorable. There were, though, a couple of undocumented reports of nicely made Tokai grands, so perhaps the company has improved a bit in recent years.

Distribution of Tokai pianos in the United States was dropped in 1989.

CHARLES R. WALTER

Walter Piano Company, Inc.
700 West Beardsley
Elkhart, Indiana 46514
(219) 293-8242

Owned by: Charles R. Walter

Names used: Charles R. Walter, Janssen

Charles Walter, an engineer, was head of Piano Design and Developmental Engineering at C. G. Conn in the 1960s, when Conn was doing important research in musical acoustics. In 1969 Walter bought the Janssen piano name from Conn, and in 1975, he brought out the Charles R. Walter line of consoles and studios, based on his continuing research in piano design. Fewer than two thousand of these pianos are made each year.

The Walter Piano Co. is fairly unique among U.S. piano manufacturers in that it is a family business, staffed by Charles and his wife, several of their grownup children and various in-laws, in addition to unrelated production employees. The Walters say that each piano is inspected by a member of their family before being shipped, and that person's signature can be found on the top of the piano back, underneath the lid. Dealers and technicians report that doing business with the Walters is a pleasure in itself.

The Walter line consists of 43″ and 45″ studio pianos in various decorator and institutional styles. The 43″ versions are called "consoles" for marketing purposes because of their styling, but both are really studios (as I define the term) by virtue of their studio-size actions, and are actually identical pianos in different sized cabinets. Because of the larger action, the "console" will outperform many real consoles on the market.

For explanation of survey and review procedures, please see pages 69–72.

Although Mr. Walter is not oblivious to marketing concerns, his piano bears the mark of being designed by an engineer who understands pianos and strives for quality. Exceptionally long, thick keys that are individually lead-weighted provide a very even feel across the keyboard. The scale design is well thought out and the bass sounds good all the way to the bottom. When at its best, the treble sings beautifully. The piano has a solid spruce soundboard, Delignit pinblock, and uses no particle board in the cabinetry, which is very substantial and beautifully finished. Since the first edition of this book, a Langer action has replaced the Pratt-Win action in most of the pianos. (Occasionally a dealer requests the cheaper action to reduce the price of the piano, but this is a false savings in my opinion.) Perhaps most appreciated by technicians is that most Walter pianos arrive at the dealer meticulously tuned and adjusted.

Forty-two Charles Walter pianos turned up in the present survey, an unusually large number considering the size of the company. Few problems of any consequence were found, but the following items were noted occasionally: minor cabinet finish problems, some tight key bushings and action centers (in Pratt-Win action), squeaking trapwork, manufacturing debris left in the piano, bass dampers not damping effectively, and tone too bright. Most of the pianos were rated as very good or excellent, but some technicians did not care for the tone and rated the pianos only satisfactory or good. Follow-up interviews found the same spread of opinion, most technicians praising the Walter pianos in every way, and a small but significant number less enthusiastic about them. In addition, several technicians who were also Walter dealers said they had seen a slight variation in the quality and consistency of the piano over the last few years, though they stressed that it was still one of the best-made pianos manufactured in this country.

Puzzled over the spread of opinion about these pianos, I decided to examine some Charles Walter pianos myself, and doing so, found a tremendous difference in the tone quality from one piano to another. Some sang beautifully just like the ones I inspected and reported on for the first edition of this book. Others, though, had a poor tone. It's sometimes difficult to isolate the various tone-producing elements to determine the cause of poor tone, but in this case, my instincts told me it was the hammers. A call to Mr. Walter seems to confirm this. He said that a change in ownership and management of one of his suppliers resulted in hammers of inconsistent quality for a time, but that the problem is on the way to being corrected. Given some effort, he said, the irregular hammers can be successfully voiced.

I strongly recommend checking out the Charles Walter pianos if you're shopping for a vertical in the middle to upper price range. Be sure to check several instruments to find the ones with the best tone. Although perhaps not quite up to the quality of some of the exquisite European verticals available today, the Walter, at half the price or less, is a very good value.

(For a short time in the mid-1980s, some Charles Walter pianos were outfitted with a player piano mechanism by another company and sold under the name "McDermed-Rouse.")

There may also be a few dozen console and studio pianos sold by Walter under the names Story & Clark and Janssen, left over inventory purchased from the old Story & Clark Piano Co., and not to be confused with the Story & Clark pianos being sold by the Classic Player Piano Corp. (see "Classic"). In 1991, Walter plans to introduce his own 6'3" grand piano.

Warranty: Twelve-year full warranty

WEBER

Weber Piano Company
51 Hartz Way
Secaucus, New Jersey 07094
(201) 902-0920

Owned by: Weber Piano Co. is a division of Samsung America Inc.

Pianos made by: Young Chang Akki Co., Ltd., Incheon, South Korea

Name used: Weber

The present-day Weber Piano Co. was started by Young Chang, a Korean piano manufacturer (see "Young Chang") in 1986, at a time when protectionist sentiment was growing in the United States and there was a possibility that quotas might be placed on imported pianos. By spawning a second piano line, Young Chang hoped to garner a larger market share and therefore increase whatever quota might later be imposed on its products. (This tactic is used by many foreign companies.) About a year later, Young Chang sold the Weber name to Samsung, a large Korean industrial conglomerate. Young Chang continues, however, to manufacture all Weber pianos.

The original Weber Piano Co. was founded by Albert Weber in 1852. The name later became part of the Aeolian group and was eventually purchased by Young Chang when Aeolian went out of business. Today's Weber pianos have no connection or resemblance to the original Weber pianos except for the name.

At first, all Weber pianos were identical to the Young Changs except for slightly cheaper cabinets. Now, although some of the models are a little different, they are all generally considered to be of the same quality as the Young Changs and sell for about the same price.

Weber says that some of its scale designs (the design of all tone-producing elements) are taken from those of a German manufacturer of high-quality pianos, which other sources suggest is Ibach. Weber uses this "German" connection as one of its principal selling points to differentiate its product from Young Chang's. To the degree that the difference in scale design results in a discernible difference in tonal quality, it may be of practical significance to the buyer. However, the manufacturing quality of these Webers should be considered, for all practical purposes, to be identical to that of Young Changs.

A Weber official said that, as a rough rule of thumb, Weber piano models that are of the same size as Young Chang models are probably of identical scale design. Even the ones of identical scale design, though, may be different in furniture design. For instance, Weber grands are finished on the inside of the rim with mahogany when it is cosmetically an advantage to do so, and there are also other cabinetry differences between the two brands that may interest you.

See the listing for Young Chang for information about the quality of Weber pianos.

Warranty: Twelve-year full warranty; lifetime warranty on action and case parts.

WURLITZER

See "Notice to Readers," page 72.

YAMAHA/EVERETT

Yamaha Corporation of America
6600 Orangethorpe Ave.
Buena Park, California 90620
(714) 522-9011

Owned by: Yamaha Corporation, Hamamatsu, Japan

Names used: Yamaha, Everett

Yamaha was founded in 1887 and has been making pianos since 1900, currently making about 200 thousand pianos annually. Yamaha also makes a wide variety of other consumer products, such as electronic keyboards, sporting goods, and guitars. Yamaha began exporting pianos to the United States in about

1960. In 1971 it acquired the Everett Piano Co. in South Haven, Michigan.

Until mid-1986, Yamaha made a complete line of verticals and grands in Japan and a completely different line of verticals at the Everett factory in Michigan, where it also made a line of Everett pianos (see also the listing for Everett at the end of the Yamaha review). The U.S.-made instruments were satisfactory, but not nearly as well made as those from Japan. The only model you need to be warned about is the P202 studio, which was very problematic, and eventually was replaced by the much-improved P22. (More detailed information about other models from that period can be found in the first edition of this book, available from the publisher.)

In mid-1986, Yamaha closed the Everett factory and moved all its U.S. piano manufacturing to a plant in Thomaston, Georgia where some of its electronic musical instruments were made. This was undoubtedly due to the decline of the U.S. organ industry, which had left the Georgia plant with excess capacity, and a decline in sales of decorator-style verticals, which is what Everett primarily made. At first the Georgia plant simply put Japanese parts inside of U.S.-made cabinets, but now the wooden back, soundboard, and pinblock are also made in Georgia, while the plate, action, keys, and other parts come from Japan. Eventually, Yamaha plans to make in Georgia all the vertical pianos it sells in the United States. At the time of this writing, though, only the consoles and studios are made there; the uprights are still made in Japan, as are the grands. You can tell which Yamahas have been made in Thomaston, Georgia because they all have the letter T in front of the serial number.

Verticals. Yamaha's console line consists of the M1E in continental style, the M300 series in furniture style with a basic, plain cabinet, and the M400 series with a fancier furniture cabinet. All three are 43″ tall and similar in musical design to the very popular M1 series of consoles Yamaha used to make in Japan. During the first few years in Georgia, Yamaha also made the popular 42″ LU-11, which had a particle board cabinet made in Japan and assembled in Georgia.

The studio piano line consists of the P22T, which is the school studio model, and the P2E, a descendent of the P2 formerly made in Japan (and later replaced by the P116). The school model P22T is one of the best bargains in the entire Yamaha line because the furniture isn't fancy, but the piano is sturdily constructed for school use (or abuse) and priced low to compete for bids from school systems.

The upright line consists of the U series and the WX series, both in 48″ (U1E and WX1) and 52″ (U3E,

WX3, and WX7) sizes. The WX series has a radial back design (see Figure 3-6 on page 29), "tone louvres," and fancier furniture; the U series has a less massive, traditional back post design, and a less expensive cabinet. The WX3 and WX7 have a full sostenuto. The WX7, which is the same size as the WX3 but of a different scale design, also comes with keytops made of Ivorite® (a material Yamaha developed to imitate the properties of ivory, which is now difficult to obtain) and a duet-size bench, among other features.

In the present survey, 125 Yamaha verticals were examined, most made in Georgia or Japan, about a dozen in Michigan. The most common complaints about the Michigan pianos were squeaky key bushings at the balance rail (Yamaha will replace these key bushings under warranty), squeaky pedals, and poor tone. As I said before, these pianos were considered satisfactory but not great.

The Japanese and Georgia pianos had few problems mentioned with any regularity. The most commonly reported problem was that of hammers in the low tenor section double-striking on a soft blow. In fact, this is probably the most often cited complaint about Yamaha verticals and should be taken seriously by pianists who play with a soft touch. Also mentioned often were a lack of clarity and power in the low bass on most models, and a tendency for the tone to become unbearably bright within a short amount of time. Otherwise, technicians liked the tone, especially on the uprights. Some of the four- to five-year-old verticals had key bushings worn on one side, causing lopsided keys due to the key design and poor quality cloth, a problem frequently found on older or well-used Yamaha verticals. Some of the larger uprights exhibited cabinet groans and squeaks when the bottom panel rubbed against the cabinet; this was eliminated easily by the application of a small amount of lubricant on the edge of the bottom panel. Follow-up interviews indicate that the workmanship in the Georgia-made consoles and studios is much better than in the ones formerly made in Michigan and about as good as in the ones formerly made in Japan, though sometimes a little more lightly constructed than they used to be. The only place where the Japanese pianos are said to excel is in the color matching of cabinet parts.

Technicians are enthusiastic about servicing Yamaha verticals, especially the uprights, which are considered rather spectacular pianos. The 48" model U1 is considered by many to be one of the best values among pianos. Two technicians speak for most when they write: "It is hard to find anything wrong with these Yamahas. I think the Yamaha U1 Professional Upright is, without a doubt, the best piano on the market in its category, save the Steinway. Considering the price, it's the best deal, I think, in pianos. The tone and action are both extremely even and consistent." And: "Excellent on all counts. Exceptionally good tunability and very little inharmonicity. I look forward to tuning these pianos. I wish more of my customers owned a Yamaha!"

Grands. There are two basic types of Yamaha grands—the G series and the C series. The G series, also known as the Classic Collection, consists of the G1 (5'3"), G2 (5'7"), G3 (6'), and the GH-1 and GH-2, less expensive versions of the G1 and G2. The C series, also known as the Conservatory Collection, consists of the C3 (6'), C5 (6'6"), C7 (7'6"), CF (9' concert grand), and the CF III (a version of the 9' concert grand under continuous development). In addition, there is the strange model S-400B (6'3"), rarely seen, which is a very mellow and beautiful sounding piano, unlike any other Yamaha grand (it is sometimes nicknamed the Hamburg Yamaha, after the Hamburg Steinway, a German-made Steinway that is supposedly mellower and more beautiful than its American-made counterpart). Notice that the G series and C series overlap only at the 6' size.

The model GH-1, the less expensive version of the G1, used to be considered substandard by technicians, having an inferior action and a horrible tone in the tenor. The GH-1 and GH-2 have been rescaled and upgraded and now have the same scale as the G series and the same action except for part of the key frame. They also have lighter plates and fewer braces, though, which could affect their tuning stability, a bass sustain pedal instead of a sostenuto, no duplex scaling, no locks, and plainer cabinetry.

The C series grands differ from the G series in that the former have rims made of harder woods, plates of a slightly different composition, and different scaling. There are also some cabinetry differences and the C series grands have keytops made of Ivorite®.

The differences in rim, plate, and scaling, are especially interesting, as they are designed to give the C series a more powerful and sustained tone than the G series. One of the criticisms of Yamaha and most other Asian pianos is that they are substantially made of softer and cheaper woods, such as lauan (also known as Philippine mahogany). The best thinking on the subject is that grand piano rims must be made of very dense woods, such as the maple and beech used on most of the best American and European grands, in order to reflect sound energy back to the soundboard for a more sustained tone. Unfortunately, the Japanese do not have access to the quantities of these woods that would be required for mass production, so they use the inferior and more energy-absorbent woods. As a result, so the theory goes, the Yamaha grand tone tends to be "brittle" and lack sustaining qualities. Many jazz pianists, desiring a crisp, clear sound for runs up and down the keyboard, actually prefer this kind of tone. But players of other kinds of music requiring a singing melodic line above an accompaniment may be frustrated by the piano's inability to produce it. Because the Yamaha has a tone which is rather pleasing in its own way, the problem may not be entirely obvious until one places a Yamaha and a Steinway side by side and plays the same music on both. The refinements in the C series grands may be an attempt to overcome these tonal limitations by making a harder rim and a less energy-absorbent plate.

A related problem with tone concerns the dampers and sustain pedal which (leave it to the Japanese!) work too efficiently. Possibly because the sound energy dissipates too quickly, and perhaps because this tendency is exacerbated by the pedal leverage, I find that the dampers cause the sound to cut off too abruptly, making the music sound choppy, and making me work harder to play legato. On many other fine pianos, such as the Steinway, even when the dampers are working perfectly, a slight echo or reverberation of the instrument gives the impression that the tone is being slightly sustained, and the sustain pedal can be worked up and down in small gradations to produce the effect known as "half pedaling." To the extent that the Yamaha is unable to produce these effects, its versatility as a musical instrument is limited.

The Yamaha model CF III concert grand has been in the news a great deal recently, as it has been vying for a place among the world's greatest pianos. Yamaha now has a concert and artist program like Steinway's and Baldwin's, with hundreds of concert grands stationed around the country ready for Yamaha artists to use in concert. This is part of Yamaha's effort to elevate its image so it can appeal to the more upscale buyers who form a large part of today's piano market, and so it can justify the higher price of Japanese pianos versus Korean. The CF III has gotten some great reviews and is really a very impressive instrument.

Sixty-six Yamaha grands were examined in the present survey. Comments about the older model GH-1 were unprintable. The rescaled version had several mentions of excessive seasonal pitch change and poor tone in the tenor and low bass, and follow-up interviews indicated problems with tuning stability on this model, especially when new. It was considered satisfactory, but not good. Tuning instability was also found on some recent G1s, but much less fre-

quently. Other than this, very few problems were noted on the grands. Most problems were in pianos three or more years old, usually G series pianos, and consisted of excessive false beats and some buzzing in the treble, poor tone in the bass, squeaking trapwork, and damper problems. These problems were not serious, but they do reinforce the opinion often expressed by technicians in follow-up interviews that Yamaha and other Asian pianos tend to deteriorate a little more rapidly than the more expensive American and European pianos. The C series pianos received many compliments. Most of the G series models were well-liked, but praise was not effusive.

One problem Yamaha had with its C series pianos, potentially very embarrassing, instead turned into an opportunity for the company to show off its outstanding service department. Concerning a small percentage of pianos with Ivorite™ keytops (synthetic ivory substitute), complaints were received from customers and technicians that the keytops were getting dirty and the dirt could not be washed off. Apparently the pore structure of this material was absorbing not only sweat, but dirt as well. After several tries, Yamaha succeeded in redesigning the Ivorite™ so it would filter out the dirt, which could then be wiped off in a normal fashion. Whereas some piano companies might have given customers the runaround or paid local technicians a pittance to replace the keytops, in each case Yamaha has quickly and cheerfully sent a factory-trained technician to the customer's home to replace the keytops, sometimes tuning and regulating the piano for free as well. This kind of service, and other cases like it, left several astonished technicians to say that if for no other reason, they would recommend a Yamaha because of the incredible support the factory provides. (Note: It is not clear why this problem affected only a small percentage of pianos with Ivorite™ keytops; individual differences in body chemistry, personal hygiene, and conditions of use are probably factors. Yamaha requests that anyone experiencing this problem immediately contact Yamaha or a Yamaha piano dealer so the keytops can be replaced. Those not experiencing a problem need not do anything.)

Yamaha also makes electronic player pianos called Disklaviers. This cleverly designed mechanism allows the piano to play by itself a large repertoire of musical favorites from a library of pre-recorded standard computer floppy disks, or for you to record your own playing on disk. It is MIDI-compatible and velocity-sensitive and capable of many interesting tricks, such as tempo changes and transposition. Right now it's available already installed in the U1 upright, the M1 console, and in the G1, G2, C3, and C7 grands. The C3 and C7 grands are available in MIDI-compatible models, but without the playback feature. (See page 113 for more information on MIDI.)

In closing, I should say that it is my impression that for general home and school use, piano technicians recommend Japanese pianos—especially Yamaha—more often than any other brands. The precision and intelligence with which they're made, the lack of service problems, their good performance, and their reasonable price make them an extremely good value for a consumer product. At the same time, many technicians express doubt about the long-term durability of their cabinets, pinblocks, and tone due to some of the lower quality materials used, as well as the lesser quality workmanship in some places that don't show, such as the fitting of the pinblock. They warn that this is likely to limit the lifetime of these pianos to twenty-five or thirty years, possibly much less under heavy use or adverse conditions, and that the tone quality is likely to be at its best when the piano is first purchased, not later on. Of course, a generation of good use is nothing to laugh at, especially when compared to most other consumer items, and the estimates of these pianos' longevity has been increasing. But those who buy a Yamaha (or other Asian piano) as a lower-cost substitute for a high-quality piano based on its price and how it sounds in the showroom—and many do—should understand that there is a real tradeoff between cost on the one hand, and performance and durability on the other, that may not become apparent for a number of years.

See also the review of Kawai pianos for some comparisons between the two brands.

Warranty: Yamaha has a limited ten-year warranty on all its pianos. It covers parts and labor and is not transferable to future owners within the warranty period. Yamaha also has a "Service Bond" that comes with each piano. It pays for two tunings and an action regulation and maintenance check during the first six months of ownership.

Everett

The Everett Piano Co. originated in Boston in 1883 and moved to South Haven, Michigan in 1956. It was acquired by Yamaha in 1971. Until mid-1986, Yamaha made a line of Everett vertical pianos in this factory alongside its U.S.-made Yamaha pianos. The Everett line consisted of a 41" console in several levels of quality and cabinetry, a 45" studio that was for years very popular in institutions, and very briefly a 48" upright similar to the Yamaha U1. There was also for a short time a 6' "Everett" grand, made in Japan, that was basically a copy of a Yamaha G3. The Everett verticals, like the U.S.-made Yamaha verticals of the time, were considered reasonably good, but by no means outstanding. In the first edition of this book, I list a variety of silly, nuisance problems found in these pianos that could easily have been solved if anybody had cared enough to spend a little time on it.

When Yamaha moved its U.S. piano manufacturing to Thomaston, Georgia, Everett did not go with it. Pianos bearing the name Everett thereafter were built by Baldwin using Yamaha scale designs, plates, and actions and Baldwin backs. These new models, distributed through the old Everett dealer network, could be identified by the letter C at the end of the model number. In 1988 the models were changed back again to the old Everett designs and built entirely by Baldwin (and the letter C designation dropped), and distributed through the regular Yamaha dealer network.

The first of the two Baldwin-made Everett models was not bad, but according to some dealers and technicians, the second left something to be desired. Little information on Baldwin-made Everetts appeared in the written survey, but of four Everetts I inspected in a store, two were average pianos and two had serious tonal problems. The contract under which Baldwin was manufacturing these pianos for Yamaha ended in 1989 and the Everett name and piano line was dropped permanently.

YOUNG CHANG

Young Chang America, Inc.
13336 Alondra Blvd.
Cerritos, California 90701
(213) 926-3200

Owned by: Young Chang Akki Co., Ltd., Incheon, South Korea (publicly owned in South Korea)

Names used: Young Chang, Wagner (no longer used); also makes pianos sold under the names Wurlitzer and Weber

In 1956, the three brothers Kim began selling Yamaha pianos in Korea under an agreement with that Japanese firm. Korea was recovering from a devastating war, and only the wealthy could afford pianos. But the prospects were bright for economic development, and as a symbol of cultural refinement the piano was much coveted. In 1964, due to competition and an extremely stiff tariff on Japanese goods (resulting from an age-old animosity between the two nations), Young Chang began importing partially completed instruments from Yamaha, doing final assembly work itself, to reduce import duties. This led to an agreement with Yamaha by which Yamaha helped Young Chang set up a full-fledged manufacturing operation. Doing so was no easy task, as restrictions and tariffs made it almost impossible to import basic industrial equipment, so Young Chang began making its own equipment and, thereafter, most of its own piano parts. In 1975, Yamaha and Young Chang parted company when the latter decided to expand to serve the world market, thus becoming a competitor.

Young Chang is now one of the world's largest piano manufacturers. In addition to making pianos, Young Chang also makes guitars, harmonicas, reed and electronic organs, and industrial woodworking machines.

The first Young Chang pianos to enter this country (some of which bore the name Wagner), around 1980, experienced humidity-related problems (as did all other Asian pianos before them), due to inadequate seasoning of the wood for our climatic extremes. Many of these pianos were sent back to Korea. Young Changs no longer experience any significant humidity-related problems.

By the mid-1980s, Young Chang pianos were rapidly improving and were considered by some to be satisfactory. Insufficient information at the time I did the research for the first edition of this book led me to write, "Technicians report an almost complete absence of significant problems with them." At that time I gave Young Chang pianos "tentative" ratings very close to that of the major Japanese pianos.

This turned out to be premature. Verbal reports received after the book was published indicated that the pianos were more inconsistent than previously thought, and some had problems that required a great deal of repair and adjustment by the dealer. Technicians sometimes reported being dissatisfied with the tone of the instruments, and the pianos were said to go out of adjustment in a relatively short amount of time. Unlike some other Korean-made pianos, however, I did not find a large increase in problems following the Korean labor strikes of 1987.

Young Changs today arrive at the dealer needing much less work than in previous years. Most need thorough, but fairly routine, servicing, such as key easing, regulating, voicing, and minor adjusting; some need more. Pianos not properly serviced by the dealer are likely to need a technician's attention soon after delivery. The larger pianos (studios, uprights, grands over six feet) seem to have fewer problems than the smaller models and are often quite nice after proper servicing. The tone does seem to get quite bright and require voicing in a relatively short amount of time (in a manner similar to some other

Asian pianos), and I personally still have some question about how the pianos will hold up with time and high use. However, the pianos are acceptable for many whose budget precludes buying a more expensive piano.

Young Chang is generally considered to be a more serious piano maker than the other Korean companies. Its pianos seem to have marginally better materials and workmanship than pianos of other Korean makers, and though not always consistent, there seems to be a greater percentage of Young Chang pianos that are acceptable or even, occasionally, admired. Unlike the other Korean companies, Young Chang maintains a visible presence in the technical community, and its service department is considered good.

Warranty: Twelve-year full warranty; lifetime limited warranty to original purchaser on case and action parts. Also covers institutional or commercial applications.

ZIMMERMANN

Performance Pianos, Inc.
9730 Town Park, Suite 102
Houston, Texas 77036
(713) 774-4402

Pianos made by: Zimmermann, Moelkin, German Democratic Republic (East Germany)

Name used: Zimmermann

One of the Leipzig area piano builders, Zimmermann was started by two brothers, Max and Richard Zimmermann, under the name of Leipsiger Pianofortefabrik in the town of Moelkin, Germany in 1884. By 1895, the enterprise had grown to 120 skilled workers, and future years brought branches in nearby towns. The factories were destroyed in World War II, but afterward several of the top managers set about reorganizing the company. Operations were first started to replace furniture destroyed by the war. Later piano manufacturing was resumed, with many older craftsmen returning to their former occupation. In 1951, Zimmermann instituted a formal three-year training program for apprentices under the direction of master craftsmen. This program provides extensive training and even includes a demand that each apprentice learn how to play the piano to achieve his certificate.

Grands. Zimmermann only produces one size of grand piano—a 4'9" model in three case styles, Traditional, Chippendale, and Chippendale/Antique, and

For explanation of survey and review procedures, please see pages 69–72.

in several finishes. The Chippendale/Antique is especially beautiful with its highlighted panels and carved mouldings on the rim. Zimmermann soundboards and keys are of Bavarian spruce, the actions are manufactured by the German company Fleming, and the pinblocks and bridges are of multilaminated European beech, the latter with a solid maple cap.

When Zimmermann pianos first arrived in North America in the early 1980s, they had a lot of problems, among them action problems due to humidity (sometimes severe), and the workmanship was just not up to the standards normally expected here from European instruments. The company was very responsive to calls for improvements, however, and by the mid- to late-1980s, most of these problems were reduced to the normal ones encountered by other manufacturers, such as tight key bushings and occasional tight action centers. There also continue to be reports of some dampers in the tenor section not damping well, and buzzing noises have been noted periodically, most often due to rattling case hardware, especially the fallboard lock. Zimmermann reports that it has changed its lock installation, so this should no longer be a problem.

Piano technicians do not generally recommend grand pianos under five feet in length because of their seriously compromised scale design, especially in the tenor and low bass. The Zimmermann is no exception. But for those who insist on purchasing a piano of this size anyway, the Zimmermann grand would, in many situations, make a reasonable purchase. The furniture is handsome; the scale design, though compromised, is not bad for a piano of this size; the action performs satisfactorily; and the piano is extremely affordable.

My only caution is that this piano is quite lightly constructed, both in case parts and in the action. It is definitely better suited for lighter music like baroque, classical, and other less bombastic styles. I would not suggest this piano for institutional, commercial, or professional use, or for those who plan to practice Rachmaninoff concerti six hours a day. But it would be acceptable for the casual player or amateur pianist who wants a nice piece of furniture and a small, inexpensive musical instrument in the home.

Verticals. Zimmermann makes two sizes of vertical piano, a 43″ console and a 46″ studio, both in a variety of styles and finishes. The treble in these pianos is clear and sweet, while the bass is shallow and light. The 43″ console has recently been redesigned, and now has a more powerful bass. As with the grands, these instruments are rather lightly constructed and best suited to lighter musical styles.

Warranty: Ten years parts and labor. Must return warranty registration card within ten days of purchase.

MISCELLANEOUS

Listed here are a variety of piano names that for one reason or another do not require a full listing. Some are names of foreign companies with very small distribution in the United States or about which I have little to say, some are brand names that are found only in one chain of pianos stores, and some are names that are no longer used or pianos that are no longer being made or imported. A listing in this section, however, does not imply that a piano brand is inferior in any way.

Altenburg, Otto. This is the house brand of Altenburg Piano House in Elizabeth, New Jersey. The Altenburg family has been in the piano business about 150 years, at one time as a manufacturer as well as a dealer. Altenburg pianos are now all assembled by Samick in Korea. Mr. Altenburg says, however, that all Altenburg grands 5′10″ and larger have complete Renner actions and damper actions, assembled in Germany and shipped to Korea, where they are installed in the pianos. The smaller grands have Renner actions as an option. Mr. Altenburg says that high-quality German Kluge keys have been requested for his grands and that Renner actions have been requested as an option for his 48″ and 52″ uprights. All the other Altenburg verticals are regular Samick models.

August Forster. Made in Lobau, East Germany since 1859, this is considered one of Eastern Europe's highest quality pianos. Models exported to the U.S. include 46″ and 49″ verticals and 6′4″, 7′4″, and 9′2″ grands. Due to lower labor costs in East Germany, prices are quite moderate compared to comparable quality pianos from Western Europe. Distribution in the U.S. is quite limited. Imported by Performance Pianos, Inc., 9730 Town Park, Suite 102, Houston, Texas 77036; (713) 774–4402.

Barock. This Japanese piano, also sold under the stencil name "Gershwin," was imported at one time by Santi Falcone, but is no longer available. It was basically a good piano, but had humidity-related problems.

Blüthner. This firm has been making highest quality pianos in Leipzig, East Germany since 1853 and, though nationalized in 1972, is still under the management of the Blüthner family. Until 1900, Blüthner was Europe's largest piano factory. During World War II, the factory was bombed, but after the war the East German government allowed the Blüthner family and workers to rebuild it because the Blüthner piano was considered a national treasure (and because the Soviet Union needed quality pianos). With the liberation of Eastern Europe, Blüthner expects again to be privately owned in 1990, and has entered into an agreement with the other great German piano company, Bechstein, for collaboration in certain areas of production and promotion. The two firms can work together well, for they appeal to different "ears." Whereas the Bechstein has a clear, transparent tone, the Blüthner could be said to have a warm, romantic, lyrical tone that is generally deeper and darker. Blüthner builds about 150 verticals and 350 grands per year. Three vertical and six grand piano models are imported into the U.S. For nearly thirty years, the U.S. Blüthner importer has been Kasimoff-Blüthner Piano Co., 337 North Larchmont Blvd., Hollywood, California 90004; (213) 466-7707.

Brentwood. This name is now being used on a line of pianos made by the Guangzhou Piano Co. of Guangzhou (Canton), People's Republic of China. The "Pearl River" pianos formerly exported by this manufacturer were not acceptable here, but the Brentwood pianos are of a different design and, judging by the ones I saw at a trade show, the quality seems to have improved. I would still be cautious, however, about buying any pianos from China until they have proven themselves in the field for several years. Brentwood pianos are distributed by Westbrook Piano Co., 5470 Oakbrook Parkway, Suite H, Norcross, Georgia 30093; (404) 441-9574.

Call. In 1978, Jack Call bought the rights to the Estey piano design and started making Call pianos—identical to the Estey—in Charlotte, North Carolina. Call had been a leading piano and organ bench manufacturer and piano retailer. Estey had been making pianos since 1869 under changing owners and in various locations, most recently in Pennsylvania. Until 1982 Call produced about twelve hundred pianos a year, selling them through his piano retail stores in the Charlotte area and elsewhere in the southeastern United States. In 1982 the factory was struck by lightning and burned down. It was going to be rebuilt and reopened, but now seems to have gone out of business permanently. The Call piano was a 40" console and said to be reasonably well made, similar in quality to other medium-priced American-made pianos.

Camilleri. Sam Camilleri, a New York piano technician with thirty years experience, and one of the most respected piano rebuilders in the country, manufactured his own pianos for a brief period until his death in 1986. Camilleri had hoped to move the piano manufacturing operation to the island of Malta, his birthplace, off the coast of Italy, where the government reportedly had offered him generous terms. Camilleri's piano, a 7' grand, was patterned after the Steinway model B, with modifications. It had been in production only a few years, with an initial production run of only about thirty instruments. In the planning stages had been several other Steinway-like models. Lloyd Meyer, a former president of Steinway & Sons and now head of Falcone Piano Co., purchased the Camilleri operation, which is primarily a piano rebuilding shop, and has said that no new Camilleri pianos would be built in the future.

Fazioli. Musician and engineer Paolo Fazioli of Rome, Italy began designing and building pianos in 1978 under his own name with the object of making the finest quality pianos possible. Now even the most accomplished piano makers of Western Europe are praising them and artists throughout the world are using them successfully on the concert stage and elsewhere. Fazioli builds grands only, in the following sizes: 5'2" (F 156), 6' (F 183), 6'9" (F 212), 7'4" (F 228), 9'2" (F 278), and 10'3" (F 308). The 10'3" model is the largest grand piano being made in the world today. It also has the distinction of having four pedals. Three are the usual sustain, sostenuto, and una corda; the fourth is a "soft" pedal that brings the hammers closer to the strings, just like on verticals and some older grands, to soften the sound without altering the tonal quality as the una corda often does. Fazioli produces about a hundred pianos a year, and availability in the U.S. is extremely limited. Fazioli Pianoforti S.R.L., Via Ronche 47, 33077 Sacile (Pordenone), Italy; tel. 39/434/72026. Promoting Fazioli pianos in the U.S. is International Brokers Inc., Rt. 6 Box 253A, North Little Rock, Arkansas 72118; (501) 753-8616.

Feurich. This is a high-quality West German piano made since 1851. The few reports about it I've received have been very favorable. Feurich also makes pianos under the name of W. Hoffmann. Julius Feurich Pianofortefabrik GmbH, Carl Muller Str., 8821 Langlau, West Germany. U.S. distributor is Premier Piano Corp., 700 Willow Lane, Dundee, Illinois 60118; (800) 541-2331.

Grotrian (also known as Grotrian-Steinweg). This piano is considered to rank with such makes as

Bechstein and Bösendorfer as one of the highest quality European pianos. U.S. availability is very limited, but a new U.S. distributor has just opened its doors: Lyon & Healy, 168 Ogden Ave., Chicago, Illinois 60607; (312) 786–1881.

Gulbransen. Established in 1906, Gulbransen made first player piano actions and then pianos until about 1970. In the seventies the company was bought by the CBS Musical Instrument Division; it was then sold to Mission Bay Investments in 1985. Gulbransen now makes organs and electronic keyboard products. Pianos bearing the name Gulbransen, however, are now made by Samick and are identical to pianos made under the Samick name. Gulbransen pianos are only sold in stores owned by Mission Bay Investments.

Handok. This is a medium-quality Korean manufacturer whose name means "Korea-Germany." Distribution in the U.S., very limited, is through the Moro Trading Co., 6040 Dawson Blvd., Suite C, Norcross, Georgia 30093; (404) 840–9877.

Hanil. This is a low-quality Korean manufacturer. No other information available.

Hastings. This line of vertical pianos is assembled in Macao, a Portuguese colony off the coast of Hong Kong, largely from parts made by the Guangzhou Piano Co. of Guangzhou (Canton), People's Republic of China. See comments for "Brentwood," above, about Chinese pianos. Hastings pianos are imported by Coast Wholesale Music Co., 1215 West Walnut St., P.O. Box 5686, Compton, California 90224; (213) 537–1712.

Heintzman. Many technicians recall the old Heintzman piano, a high-quality upright made in the early part of this century. In the decades that followed, the Heintzman, like so many other brands, was gradually cheapened in quality. In 1981 Sklar-Peppler, a large Canadian furniture maker, bought Heintzman from the Heintzman family, and made very good quality Heintzman pianos for several years. In 1986 the Heintzman name was sold to The Music Stand, a piano dealer in Oakville, Ontario. The Music Stand has been applying the Heintzman name to inexpensive pianos from several U.S. makers, probably Kimball and Wurlitzer. The Gerhard Heintzman name is used on promotional 42″ consoles and 4′6″ grands, and the Heintzman name is used on 42″ and 43″ consoles and on 5′2″ and 5′8″ grands.

Knight. This remarkable English vertical piano is not well known in this country, but is very highly regarded in Europe and among piano designers. In addition to impeccable workmanship throughout, Knight pianos have a few technical features that are fairly unique for a vertical piano, such as the mounting of the pinblock in a pocket cast in the plate, and the use of exceptionally hard phenolic tuning pin plate bushings, both of which enhance tuning stability; and the lack of plate struts interrupting the treble bridge, which enhances the treble tone. The piano's tone is warm and singing; the action is the Langer design. The Knight piano company was founded by Alfred Knight in 1936. Today the firm is managed by Knight's daughter and her family. They make about six hundred pianos a year, all verticals, in 42″ and 44″ sizes. Alfred Knight Limited, Langston Road, Debden Estate, Loughton, Essex, England 1G10 3TL. U.S. agent is Warfield Piano Service, 821 Kent Ave., Catonsville, Maryland 21228; (301) 747–7700.

Lesage. This hundred-year-old Canadian piano maker was bought by the former owner of Sherlock-Manning, another Canadian piano company, in 1986, then closed soon after. A Mr. Rosch then built pianos under the name Rosch-Lesage for another year or so, the last ones made in 1988.

Lyon & Healy/Schubert. The original Lyon & Healy company, established in 1864, is best known for its harps, still the best in their field today. Lyon & Healy also made pianos from 1880 to 1930, as well as other musical instruments. The company eventually became part of the CBS Musical Instrument Division in the 1970s, was sold in 1985 along with Steinway and others to Steinway Musical Properties, Inc., and then was sold again in 1987 to a Swiss maker of harps and other musical instruments. The new owner is now distributing pianos made by the Dutch piano maker Rippen with the Lyon & Healy name on them. Rippen pianos are considered medium-quality by European standards. Distribution of this make has just begun, so no field information is available yet.

Lyon & Healy is also distributing pianos made by the Korean piano maker Daesung under the name Schubert. Daesung has not had much experience making pianos for this climate, so I would use caution in purchasing one of these pianos until they have proven themselves in the field. Lyon & Healy, 168 Ogden Ave., Chicago, Illinois 60607; (312) 786–1881.

Muzelle. This name is put on player pianos and nickelodeons. The pianos themselves are made by Sojin, Daesung, or Kimball, depending on the model. Distribution is by Resource West, Inc., 2295 E. Sahara Ave., Las Vegas, Nevada 89104; (702) 457–7919.

Nordheimer/Estonia. The name Nordheimer is being used on 44" and 47" studio pianos from Latvia and the Soviet Union, and the name Estonia on 6'2" and 9' grands from Estonia, that are being imported into Canada. Distribution is by Oxford International in Toronto; (416) 297-0304.

QRS. This firm is known worldwide as the oldest and largest manufacturer of player piano rolls. It has also developed an electronic player piano mechanism (described elsewhere) that can be retrofitted into any piano. QRS also sells new pianos already fitted with this device. These pianos are made by Samick. QRS Music Rolls, Inc., 1026 Niagara St., Buffalo, New York 14213; (716) 885-4600.

Sherlock-Manning. This hundred-year-old Canadian piano company stopped making pianos around 1988.

Sherman Clay. This is the name of a national chain of piano stores. Until 1989, pianos bearing the name Sherman Clay were made by Sojin; now they are made by Kimball. Sherman Clay, 851 Traeger Ave., Suite 200, San Bruno, California 94066; (415) 952-2300.

Steingraeber. This is a good-quality West German piano, made since 1852, by a very small firm. It makes several sizes of verticals and grands for export. In addition to its regular line of pianos, Steingraeber makes a piano that can be used by physically handicapped players who don't have use of their legs. A switch in a backrest cushion operates the sustain pedal and a switch under the keybed operates the soft pedal. This mechanism can be installed in pianos of other makers if certain technical requirements are met. Steingraeber & Sohne, Friedrichstrasse 2, Postfach 110117, 8580 Bayreuth, West Germany.

Toyo. A Japanese piano no longer imported into this country. It was considered a good piano, especially in the larger models.

STENCIL PIANOS

Stencil pianos are those bearing a name that is not the manufacturer's, or a trade name owned by the manufacturer, but rather the name of a dealer or distributor. The practice of selling stencil pianos, also known as "private-label" or "house" brands, must be at least a century old. The term comes from the stenciled name on the fallboard of a piano. This is usually the name of the manufacturer, but a buyer who purchases a certain minimum number of pianos can often request that a different stencil be applied instead. Historically this practice has been carried on by dealers, but during the past decade many importer-distributors have sprung up to import look-alike Asian pianos, and I believe that the various names used by these firms can rightly be called stencil names as well. In recent years, large dealers and distributors have succeeded in even having their chosen name cast into or attached to the iron plate.

Why would a manufacturer and dealer want to do this? For a manufacturer, it means selling more pianos to more dealers ("increasing the market share") without having to worry about breaking franchise agreements. One dealer can sell "Jones Bros." pianos and the dealer next door can sell "Smith Bros." pianos, and the customer who is trying to decide which to buy doesn't realize they're the same. For the dealer, a private-label brand can be prestigious, has no competition, appears to offer the customer a larger choice, and can fill a low price point without forcing the dealer to promote a brand name that may be associated with poor quality or sold by a competitor.

Some manufacturers own a variety of trade names that they will put on pianos at the request of dealers. On one of my factory visits, I was shown a large drawer full of stencils with various names I had never heard of that were being applied to pianos according to dealer's requests. These are not stencil pianos as I've defined the term above, because the names are all owned by the manufacturer, but the purpose and effect are the same. (Some technicians feel that well-known pianos names of the past now being applied to cheap promotional pianos by the manufacturers who own these names should be considered stencil names, but I have not labeled them as such.)

This and similar tricks are used extensively in marketing all kinds of goods, from electronics to laundry detergents. In my opinion, using stencil names is one of those marketing tactics that goes far beyond simply informing or persuading people about products, and, though not illegal, borders on the unethical. It is also extremely confusing to the consumer and leads to distrust of the entire industry.

The stencil pianos most widely distributed in the United States are included in this book, either in the main listings or under "Miscellaneous." Stencil names generally confined to one or a few stores are too numerous to list (an exception being those few pianos that are distinctly different from pianos sold under the manufacturer's name). If while shopping for a piano you find one with the name of the dealer or a name that you don't recognize or that is not listed in this book, ask whether it is a stencil piano and, if so, who makes it. Many salespeople will not want to tell you. If they claim ignorance or say the dealer manufacturers it, they are probably lying. Usually they will admit it is made by someone else (they may not say by whom), but they'll add that it is made to the dealer's "specifications," implying it is somehow better than the manufacturer's regular model. The truth is that, with only a few exceptions, it's probably the same as the regular model, except possibly for the particular style and finish and the name on it, and it may well be an inferior model. Stencil pianos usually carry a warranty from the dealer or distributor, not from the manufacturer. If the real manufacturer is a recommended one and you trust the dealer's warranty, there is no particular reason not to buy a stencil piano. However, stencil pianos tend to be made by manufacturers whose products are not recommended very highly. In the recent past, most stencil pianos found in the United States were made by Aeolian and Kimball. With the demise of Aeolian, most are now made by Kimball, Wurlitzer, Samick, Young Chang, and Sojin.

OTHER ITEMS OF INTEREST

Should I Buy a Digital Piano?

Digital pianos are electronic musical instruments, often built to look like pianos, that electronically reproduce authentic piano sounds. Digital pianos have no hammers, strings, or soundboard; instead they have electronics and speakers. They also usually have a number of features that make them attractive to certain buyers, such as several different types of piano, harpsichord, and other instrumental sounds to choose from; built-in rhythm capabilities, a headphone jack for playing late at night, recording capabilities, and so on. Digital pianos never need tuning and are much easier to move than regular acoustic pianos. They also cost less in most cases.

The problem with digital pianos is that despite their fascinating array of features, they cannot really duplicate the tone and touch of a piano. Although the tone of individual notes is authentic, these instruments' technology is still not advanced enough to duplicate the sound of all the strings and other tone-producing elements resonating together. Thus most music, except for the simplest pieces, sounds rather sterile played on a digital piano. The "action" of a digital piano, though much improved over earlier models, is still a far cry from that of even a rather mediocre acoustic piano. It does not provide the same feedback and responsiveness and is not as suitable, in my opinion, for learning piano technique as an acoustic piano would be.

There is no doubt that digital pianos have features that may make them preferable to an acoustic piano for some people. But before you run out to buy one for Junior to start taking lessons on, think about the following: Will Junior still be interested in the gadgets a month from now, or will the digital piano go the way of countless computer and video games and other electronic toys? How well will the digital piano hold up with use, and will it be continually repairable, and spare parts available, for decades, as is true for an acoustic piano? Does Junior's piano teacher emphasize piano technique or general musicianship in the early years? If the former, a digital piano may be a hindrance to learning; if the latter, it could be an advantage, but only if the teacher knows how to make use of the electronic features. Keep in mind also that an acoustic piano represents a connection with a three-hundred-year-old tradition and a large body of literature, and provides certain intangible benefits of ownership that accrue from that connection, whereas a digital piano is still seen as a novelty.

MIDI Interfaces for Pianos

A few years ago, the major synthesizer manufacturers got together and agreed upon an electronics standard for their industry that would allow several synthesizers to be connected together and controlled from one synthesizer keyboard. This interconnecting standard is known as MIDI, for Musical Instrument Digital Interface. MIDI also allows a keyboard to be connected to a personal computer equipped with a MIDI interface, so that, using appropriate music-processing software, a musician can compose at the keyboard, then edit the composition at the computer terminal before printing out the final score on the computer's printer. In principle, any MIDI-compatible device can be interfaced with any other MIDI-compatible device.

Several MIDI interfaces are available for acoustic piano, allowing a piano keyboard to be used as the keyboard controller for synthesizers or for entering music into a computer. The oldest and best known is the **Forte MIDI-MOD** (Forte Music, 1951 Colony

Street, Suite X, Mountain View, CA 94043; (415) 965-8880). It consists of eighty-eight sensitive switches placed beneath the piano keys and a switch activated by the piano's sustain pedal. The key switches are velocity-sensitive, which means that the faster you press a key, the "louder" will be the output, just as on the piano. The installation does not affect the tone, touch, or normal operation of the piano. Hundreds of installations have been performed, mostly for recording studios, performers, and producers, but also for an increasing number of amateur musicians, and it has a very good record for trouble-free service. Additional features allow for transposition, programmable split keyboard, and selection of MIDI channel from the keyboard.

A new product that appears to be based on a similar principle, but with fewer features, is the **Solton Piano MIDI Kit** (Bell Duovox Corp., 126 Route 303, W. Nyack, NY 10994; (914) 353-3515).

Another product in the field of piano MIDI interfaces is the **Crystal KS2 MIDI Keyboard Controller** by Gulbransen (3132 Jefferson Street, San Diego, CA 92110; (800) 677-7374). Installation of this device also involves putting an electronic strip under the keys, but the Gulbransen product senses key position and velocity with optical sensors instead of with switches. This allows for finer gradations (and control by the user) of velocity sensitivity, the programming by the user of the exact point in the key travel when the MIDI signal is triggered (or re-triggered for a repeat stroke of the key), and the automatic adjustment of the mechanism to any keyboard in a matter of seconds, drastically cutting down the installation time. The Crystal KS2 boasts twenty-one functions, such as split keyboard, transposition, program change, inputs for foot-pedal controllers, and much more. Crystal also has available several other models of keyboard controller with fewer functions, and other devices that interface with pianos.

Electronic Player Pianos

The original electronic player piano was the **Pianocorder**, made by Marantz (see "Marantz/Pianocorder"). By means of a casette tape with computer signals on it, this device played a "live" performance on the piano. A large catalog of music was available for it, including repros of the old Ampico and Duo/Art reproducer rolls. Rights to the Pianocorder were purchased by Yamaha and it was discontinued in 1987.

At about the same time, Yamaha brought out its own series of electronic player pianos, known as **Disklaviers** (see the review for Yamaha). These mechanisms are built into several of Yamaha's regular piano models. They operate with computer floppy disks, are MIDI-compatible, both record and play back using a combination of key switches and optical sensors, are velocity-sensitive, and are capable of transposition and tempo changes, among other features. Reports from the field about the Disklaviers have been consistently positive.

If you want many of the same features as the Disklavier but already own a piano, you might try the retrofit system known as **PianoDisc** (2444 Marconi Ave., Sacramento, CA 95821; (916) 973-8710). It can be installed in virtually any piano, is MIDI-compatible and velocity-sensitive, uses standard computer floppy disks, and comes with a hand-held remote controller. At the time of this writing, a record feature is about to be introduced. The PianoDisc library has about one thousand titles at this time.

Probably the most sophisticated of all electronic player systems is the **Bösendorfer SE** system (see "Bösendorfer"), invented by Wayne Stahnke. It has over a thousand levels of expression in the keys and hammers, over five hundred in the pedals. The basic system is not MIDI-compatible (MIDI has only 128 levels of expression), but a MIDI translation program is available. The system is only available in certain models of Bösendorfer and comes with a computer terminal for editing the recordings, if desired.

Stahnke has adapted the SE system for **QRS Pianomation** (1026 Niagara St., Buffalo, NY 14213; (716) 885-4600), a retrofit system that can be installed in any piano. Although the electronic hardware is similar to that of the SE system, QRS says that at this time it does not have the ability to make recordings with expression to play on its system, so the large QRS library of cassettes and compact discs play without expression. The system does not currently have record capabilities.

One of the problems with installing player piano retrofits into grand pianos is that an unsightly box containing much of the hardware must hang down below the piano. Often modifications must also be made to the trapwork to accommodate it. Larry Broadmoore of the **Autograph Invisible Action Co.** (1709 First St., Suite C, San Fernando, CA 91340; (800) 266-7529) has invented a solenoid rail (player mechanism) that fits neatly inside the piano, eliminating the need for the box and the trapwork modifications, and eliminating much unwanted mechanical noise as well. Broadmoore says this arrangement may soon become available as part of one of the other player systems on the market.

Perhaps the simplest and most creative electronic player system is the **Piano Midi-Matic** (H&K Automated Musical Creations Co., Ltd., 295 West Shore

Drive, Massapequa, NY 11758; (516) 797-7790). This system uses the best of both old-world and modern technology by combining traditional player piano pneumatic action with a solenoid rail. Because the solenoids are used only to activate pneumatic valves, not to push keys, they use much less power and generate negligible heat. The system is MIDI-compatible and has a transpose feature, but like traditional player pianos, does not play back with expression. The large Micro-W library (which also supplies QRS) of music on cassette is available for the Piano Midi-Matic. A unit called "Octet" can be used to interface the Piano Midi-Matic with a regular player piano so the owner can play both traditional music rolls and cassettes on the same piano.

Caution: All player piano systems, regardless of design, tend to place great demands on a piano, at least in part because their use is not limited in duration or physical power by the normal limits of human endurance. These systems should be installed only in pianos of good quality and condition that can withstand such use, and their owners should expect the need for more frequent and extensive service than the pianos would otherwise require.

Advances in Piano Technology

It is well known that a vertical piano action, in principle, is not as responsive or expressive, and does not repeat as fast, as a grand action. The U.S. Patent Office is full of experimental designs that purport to improve the vertical action, mostly the speed of repetition, that never made it into production. Perhaps the most promising new design, just patented, is the **Fandrich Vertical Action** (Fandrich Design Inc., 210 Third Ave. S., Seattle, WA 98104; (206) 623-6493) by Darrell Fandrich and Chris Trivelas. The Fandrich action is promising because it concerns itself with not just the issue of repetition, but deals in an integrated fashion with all of the major differences between grand and vertical actions. These differences include the lack of continuous contact, in a vertical action, between the hammer and the jack (which pushes the hammer), producing a characteristic loose and disconnected feeling; the difficulty of the jack getting back under the hammer for a repeating stroke of the key, causing less certain repetition; and the lesser inertia in the vertical action, producing an insubstantial feel.

The Fandrich action solves these problems largely with the use of an ingenious repetition spring connecting the jack and the hammer butt, keeping them in contact with one another except when separation is necessary to allow the jack to return under the hammer butt. The hammer return spring is also strengthened and made adjustable to simulate the gravity return of the grand action, and the keys are weighted and balanced to simulate the grand's inertial characteristics. The result is a vertical piano action that really does feel like a grand. Fandrich and Trivelas are now in discussion with several manufacturers about producing this action.

The grand piano action has been in its current configuration for over a hundred years and has long been considered to be just about as perfect as it can get. But there are still some improvements to be made, particularly in the areas of inertia and friction. Both are often uneven from note to note, and flange friction changes seasonally. Piano technician David Stanwood has invented the **Stanwood® Action** for the grand piano (Stanwood & Company, RFD 340, Vineyard Haven, MA 02568; (508) 693-1583) to solve these thorny problems. Stanwood first modifies regular grand action parts to remove unwanted mass and friction, then weights and balances the keyboard by a method that factors friction out of the key-balancing equation, and finally concentrates most action friction in a variable-friction hammer flange. The touch weight and inertia in the Stanwood Action are both perfectly uniform from note to note, for perfect responsiveness, and the touch can be adjusted in a matter of minutes to compensate for seasonal changes in friction or to accommodate the wishes of the pianist. Stanwood is currently licensing and training technicians around the country to install his actions, which have received strong endorsements from concert artists and technicians.

Less complicated, perhaps, but no less practical is **Quiet Keys®**, the universal mute for vertical pianos (Quiet Keys®, Rt. 3, Box 179, Austin, MN 55912; (800) 777-5397). Piano owners often ask for a way to quiet down their pianos so they can play late at night and not disturb others. Many old uprights and some new vertical piano models have a mute ("practice") pedal, but owners of other pianos either go without this feature, or have their technicians install retrofits. Until now, most retrofit mute mechanisms have been difficult to install and even more difficult to remove when the piano is to be serviced. Quiet Keys®, however, installs by slipping right over the tuning pins, which are, of course, standardized from piano to piano. Removal and reinstallation take a matter of seconds, and the unit adjusts to fit any vertical piano. A cable connects to an on/off knob placed beneath the keybed. The cost, including installation by a technician, should be around a hundred dollars, though the instructions are simple enough for a do-it-yourselfer.

CHAPTER FIVE
Buying a Used Piano

IF YOU READ NO FURTHER IN THIS CHAPTER than just this first paragraph, remember this: the most important thing you should know about buying a used piano is that you should have it inspected by a piano technician before putting your money down. Each year countless people, thinking that the piano in question "just needs tuning," throw away hundreds or even thousands of dollars on "instruments" that would be better put to use as firewood and baling wire. This is not to say that the seller necessarily tries to defraud the buyer. Usually the seller is as ignorant of the piano's condition as the buyer. But this experience does tend to lead to "fraud," as the buyer, on being informed by the technician that the piano is untunable or unrepairable, often tries to get his or her money back by selling the piano to another unwary buyer, sometimes seeking the technician's help in doing so. The "hot potato" thus passes from hand to hand until someone finally either accepts the loss and junks the piano or shells out the money to have it repaired properly. These people could have saved themselves a lot of grief and money if they had only consulted a technician before buying.

Of course, it's impractical and too expensive to take a technician along to inspect *every* piano you check out. You want to inspect most of them yourself as best you can, and then hire a technician to look at the one or two most likely candidates for purchase. This chapter is largely about how to inspect a piano yourself—to avoid the worst catastrophes, to anticipate future problems, and to estimate repair costs. However, depending on the pianos you encounter and your ability to use the material presented here to inspect them, you may find it necessary to hire the services of a technician several times before you settle on a satisfactory instrument, so you should budget enough money to cover that possibility. Most technicians charge a fee similar to their tuning fee to inspect a piano.*

One important note: Both extreme dryness and extreme dampness can seriously damage a piano, particularly in regions where the weather annually swings from one extreme to the other and back again. Such regions include most of the United States and Canada. Usually the most severe problems will show up during the dry season, in the form of cracked wooden parts, broken glue joints, and loose tuning pins that won't hold the piano in tune. These problems may be absent or disguised during the damp season, and may be especially severe when pianos previously stored in damp places or humid climates have been moved to drier places or climates. I would

_____

*See page 16.

therefore advise you to do your piano shopping at the driest time of the year. This way you can see the piano at its worst before purchase and avoid unpleasant surprises later on.

WHAT'S OUT THERE

Before you go out into the "cruel world" of used pianos, you might want me to tell you something about what you're going to find out there. The best way I can do this is to give you a *very* brief, and *very* selective, history of the piano.

The piano was invented about 1700 by an Italian harpsichord maker named Bartolomeo Cristofori of Padua. Cristofori replaced the plucking quill action of a harpsichord, which could pluck only with unvarying force and hence unvarying volume of sound, with a newly designed striking hammer action, whose force and volume could be precisely controlled by the player. Thus was born the *Gravicembalo col piano e forte* or "keyboard instrument with soft and loud." This later got reduced to *pianoforte*, then *fortepiano*, and finally just *piano*. (Considering some of the harsh-sounding instruments today, perhaps it's time to change the name to *forte*.) During the 1700s the new instrument, made mostly by craftsmen in their shops, spread quietly through upper-class Europe. A number of different forms of piano action and structure were invented, such as the "Viennese action," the "English action," the "square piano," and so on. (Replicas of early fortepianos are now popular among certain musicians who prefer to play music of that period on the original instruments for which the music was written.)

During the 1800s, the piano spread more quickly through the middle classes and across the ocean to North America. Riding along with the Industrial Revolution, piano making became an industry, as opposed to a craft. Many important changes took place during the century. The upright piano was invented; the modern grand piano action was invented, incorporating the best aspects of the previous rival actions; the cast-iron plate was invented, vastly strengthening the structure and allowing for the strings to be stretched at a higher tension, increasing their power and volume of sound; the range of the instrument was extended from about five octaves to the present seven-plus octaves; cross-stringing was invented, improving the bass tone; and, toward the end of the century, the square piano died out, leaving just grands of various sizes and the full-size upright. By 1880, most of these changes were in place, and the pianos made today are not very different from those of a hundred years ago.

In your searching for a piano, you're unlikely to run across instruments made before 1880. There are two possible exceptions that I want to warn you about. One of them is the **square piano**, or square grand, as it is sometimes called—really a rectangular box—which was so popular as a home piano during the nineteenth century (Figure 5-1). Stories about these pianos are stock-in-trade among technicians. A typical story goes something like this: A person shopping for a used piano stops into an antique store where a square piano is on display, and, charmed by the ornate legs and unusually shaped case—highly polished for the occasion—the shopper plunks down her money and drags the beast home. How lovely it will go with the pseudo-Victorian furniture! Then begin the phone calls to piano technicians to get the charming antique "tuned up." Well, the first five technicians called politely decline the work. They don't know anything about square pianos, they say, or they find them too much trouble to work on. The sixth technician needs the work badly, and so agrees to do the best he can to patch up the musical innards using a hodgepodge assortment of antique and modern parts he manages to scrounge up. After several months of futile tinkering, the piano still does not work right, and phone calls to the technician are no longer being returned, so a seventh technician is called. This one, a wise and compassionate soul, assesses the damage and calmly tells the owner the sad truth. This piano, she says, like most other squares, has little or no historical, artistic, or financial value, would cost thousands of dollars to repair correctly, and even then would be unsuitable to practice on, even for a beginner. Indeed, especially for a beginner—unless that beginner is to lose all interest in music!

Another kind of piano to avoid is a type of upright made primarily in Europe from the middle to the end

FIGURE 5-1. The square piano—or square grand, as it is sometimes called—should be left to antique collectors. It is not suitable for practice purposes, even for beginners, and may be next to impossible to repair properly.

of the nineteenth century. The dampers on this piano are positioned *above* the hammers and are actuated by wires in *front* of the action, unlike in a modern upright, in which the damper system is entirely behind and beneath the hammers. This "over-damper" system has been nicknamed the "birdcage action," and you can see why in Figure 5-2. Besides being very difficult to tune and service through the "bird cage," these pianos are usually so worn out that they will not hold a tuning longer than about ten seconds, and their action works erratically at best. Many of these pianos were cheaply made to begin with, but they often have fancy features, such as candlesticks, that make them attractive to antique collectors. In recent years, hundreds of these and other useless antique pianos have been dumped on uninformed buyers in the United States and Canada, often at extravagant prices. (Note: Serious collectors of antique musical instruments and musicians with specialized performance needs requiring those instruments should use the services of a technician who specializes in them. These technicians are a rare breed, but can generally be located through museums and universities with antique instrument collections.)

The years from 1880 to about 1900 were a transitional period, as some old styles were slow to fade. But some pianos from this period may be suitable for you. A piano with only eighty-five notes instead of eighty-eight may be perfectly satisfactory if you don't anticipate ever

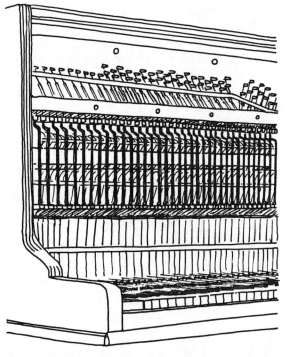

FIGURE 5-2. The "bird cage" action on some old Victorian uprights makes servicing very difficult. Also, these pianos are usually too worn out to be usable.

needing the highest three notes. The resale value of such a piano may be slightly lower than its more modern equivalent, but so should be the price you pay for it. A piano with an old-style cast-iron plate that, while extending the full length of the piano, leaves the pinblock exposed to view is, for all practical purposes, just as structurally sound as one in which the plate covers the pinblock. In fact, some European manufacturers still make instruments in this style today. Avoid, however, the so-called "three-quarter plate" piano, with a plate that ends just short of the pinblock. These pianos have a high rate of structural failure. Pianos with actions that are only very slight variations on modern actions are fine as long as the parts are not obsolete and absolutely unobtainable. Most pianos this old will need a considerable amount of repair and restoration to be fully usable, so the best candidates from this period will be those instruments that justify the expense involved, such as Steinway, Mason & Hamlin, Bechstein, and Blüthner grands, or in rare instances a more ordinary brand that has been exceptionally well preserved. With occasional exceptions, the vast majority of uprights and cheaper grands left from this period are not worth repairing, unless for historical or sentimental reasons.

The period from about 1900 to 1930 was the heyday of piano manufacturing. Thousands of small firms turned out millions of pianos during this time; in fact, far more pianos were made per annum then than are made today. If you are shopping for a used full-size upright or a grand, probably most of the pianos you see will be from this period. Smaller pianos were not introduced until later on.

You may wonder whether it's advisable to buy a piano that is sixty to ninety years old. What you must remember is that pianos age more as people do than as present-day automobiles and appliances. With proper care and some replacement of parts, a piano well made sixty years ago may have many years of use left in it. Of course, a good deal of junk is left over from this period too, but the average level of quality is surprisingly high, and your chances of finding an instrument in satisfactory condition or worth putting in shape are quite good.

People in the market for used pianos often ask me to recommend specific brands. This is a problem, because the present condition of the piano, the kind of use you will be giving it, and the cost of the piano and repairs are far more important factors than the brand when considering the purchase of an old piano. Even a piano of the best brand, if poorly maintained or badly repaired, can be an unwise purchase. Time and wear are great levelers, and a piano of only average quality that has not been used much may be a much better buy. Nevertheless, since this answer never satisfies anyone, I offer the following list of some of the brand names of the period which were most highly regarded. Please note that this list, which is by no means complete—or universally agreed upon—includes only pianos made before about 1930, since in many cases the same names were later applied to completely different pianos made to entirely different (usually lower) quality standards.

Steinway	Baldwin	Mason & Hamlin
Knabe	Chickering	Bechstein
Bösendorfer	Blüthner	Sohmer
Ivers & Pond	Henry F. Miller	McPhail
Steinert	Jewett	Hume
Emerson	Vose	Chas. Stieff
Apollo	A.B. Chase	Packard
Weber	Wing	Haines Bros.
Krakauer	Hallet & Davis	Lester
Everett	Hamilton	Kimball
Ibach	Heintzman	

The piano industry was full of mergers and acquisitions during the early 1900s. During the Great Depression many piano makers, both good and bad, went bankrupt, and their names were bought up by the surviving companies. In some cases, the defunct company's design continued to be used, but most of the time, as I've said, only the name lived on.

To revive the depressed piano market in the late thirties, piano makers came up with a new gimmick—the small piano. Despite the fact that small pianos, both vertical and grand, are inferior in almost every way to larger pianos, marketing experts managed to convince the public that spinets and consoles were to be preferred to larger pianos because they would look better in the smaller homes and apartments of the day. This involved a major change in the perception of the piano from a musical instrument to a piece of furniture, a view that lasts to this day. Because of their perceived value as furniture, used spinets and consoles will usually cost more than used full-size uprights of comparable condition. (An exact comparison is not really possible because when the manufacture of spinets and consoles started, the manufacture of full-size uprights almost entirely ceased.) Please see page 44 for the technical differences between vertical pianos of different size.

Piano making in the 1930s, though reduced in quantity from earlier years, was of a similar high quality in most cases. During World War II many piano factories were commandeered to make airplane wings and other wartime products, and what piano making there was fell in quality because of a lack of good raw materials and skilled labor. Things changed for the better in the fifties, and then reversed again in the sixties as some companies came under management that sought to expand the industry at the expense of quality.

Brief Notes on a Few Old Piano Brands

Steinway. Steinway grands built since about 1880 are almost always worth buying and restoring, both because a conscientious restoration job will usually result in a superior instrument and because the market value of the restored piano will justify the cost of the restoration. Old Steinway uprights, on the other hand, are worth buying and restoring only if the action is in good condition. Although good replacement action parts are available for old Steinway uprights, due to a lack of standardization these parts will not always precisely fit. The extra labor required to make them fit can render this job impractical. When in good condition, these uprights are great instruments.

Mason & Hamlin. Old Mason & Hamlin grands are often considered the equals of old Steinways. Especially prized are the smaller models, such as the model A (5'8½"). For a couple of decades in the early 1900s, Mason & Hamlin also made pianos known as "screwstringers." These had an unusual tuning mechanism using machine screws instead of tuning pins. Although this mechanism required different tuning tools and techniques, it worked extremely well. Many of these old screwstringers, both grands and uprights, are still around, some in good condition. The only drawback to buying a screwstringer is that the parts for the tuning mechanism are obsolete and hard to obtain, and some of the parts, if broken, may be difficult even for a machinist to duplicate.

Chickering. Chickering was an illustrious and innovative piano maker who liked to experiment. Sometimes it seems as if each Chickering was a one-of-a-kind instrument. The grands were known for their terrific bass tone . . . and for their lackluster treble. Chickerings have a lot of charm and history and a very loyal following, especially in New England. But the unusual technical features in some of them, especially the earlier ones, make them a pain in the neck to rebuild, and in the end many a rebuilder has wondered whether it was, musically speaking, worth all the trouble. Later ones were usually more conventional.

Steinert. Steinert was a Steinway dealer who, until 1932, also manufactured his own pianos. Steinert grands were basically "budget" copies of Steinways. Steinert also made pianos under the names Jewett and Hume. All are considered good pianos and are frequently rebuilt. They are rarely found, however, outside the Northeast.

Also in the sixties, the Japanese began exporting pianos to the United States in large numbers. Although at first they had some difficulties building pianos to the demands of our climate, by the mid-seventies their quality was so high and their price so low that they threatened to put all the domestic makers out of business. In response, the quality of most domestic brands has risen greatly over the last ten years, despite the financial restrictions brought on by the recession of the early 1980s. Also, while the Americans were busy making spinets, the Japanese were supplying the country with larger verticals. Demand for and production of spinets is now on the decline as a result and American makers are starting to bring out larger models to compete with the foreign imports. (In some cases, these larger models are actually made for the domestic companies by their foreign competitors!) Please see page 73 for information on the piano market today.

(Note: Large numbers of used Japanese pianos are now being dumped on the U.S. market, sold by both dealers of new pianos and used. You should know that these pianos, many of them twenty or thirty years old, or older, were built for the Japanese market and used in Japan, often in schools. They vary tremendously in quality and condition, and are often different in style and design from Japanese pianos made for the U.S. market. It's possible that they may not have been built to withstand the climatic extremes of this continent. Some of them bear the same familiar Japanese names found on pianos normally sold here, such as Yamaha and Kawai; others bear names found only in Japan. Be cautious when shopping among these imported used pianos. Have the piano carefully inspected and make sure the warranty is adequate.)

Purchase of a used piano made within the past few decades can often be a very good deal (the cautionary note above notwithstanding), as these pianos may still show very few signs of age and wear but may be priced far below a new piano. In some cases a warranty may still be in effect. General information on piano quality that will be of use to you if you are buying a used piano made within the past couple of decades can be found in Chapter 3, "Buying a New Piano." Chapter 4, "A Consumer Guide to New and Recently Made Pianos," may be useful if you want to look up a particular brand and model made since the late 1970s (or, in some cases, even earlier).

Though in each decade both good and bad pianos have been produced, and each piano must be judged on its own merits, this brief historical overview may give you some idea of what to expect to see as you shop for a used piano. You can determine the age of a piano by finding its serial number and looking it up

in a book called the *Pierce Piano Atlas*. (See page 139 for where to find the serial number of a piano.) Most piano technicians and many libraries have copies of this invaluable reference book, which lists serial numbers, dates, and other historical information for thousands of piano brands, as well as a lot of irrelevant personal data about the publisher. Your technician will probably be happy to look up information for you without charge.

Players and Reproducers

The success of the piano industry in the early part of this century was partly due to the popularity of the **player piano**. The player piano (Figure 5-3) is a regular piano, usually an upright, with a slightly deeper cabinet into which is installed a player mechanism that enables the piano to play by itself. This mechanism is operated by reduced air pressure (vacuum) created by a foot-operated bellows or an electric pump. Figure 5-4 shows how this works. All player pianos can also be manually played just like a regular piano, if desired.

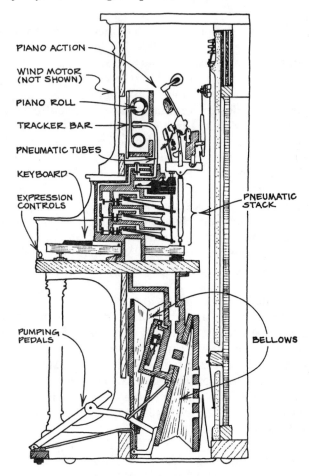

FIGURE 5-3. Cross-sectional view of a typical player piano.

Most player pianos were made between 1910 and 1925, when their popularity was so intense that more than 85 percent of all pianos made in the United States were players—over 2.5 million in all. After 1925 the player piano declined in popularity, due first to the rise of the radio and phonograph as the dominant forms of entertainment, and then to the Depression. In the decades that followed, many people removed their piano's player mechanism as it fell into disrepair, or to make the rest of the piano easier to service. Since the

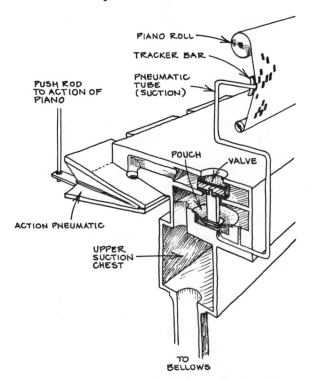

PIANO ROLL
TRACKER BAR
PNEUMATIC TUBE (SUCTION)
PUSH ROD TO ACTION OF PIANO
POUCH
VALVE
ACTION PNEUMATIC
UPPER SUCTION CHEST
TO BELLOWS

FIGURE 5-4. How each note in a player piano works. Suction created by the foot-operated pumping bellows normally pulls the valve downward, causing it to close off the lower opening, as shown in the drawing. When a punched hole in the paper piano roll passes over a corresponding hole in the tracker bar, normal atmospheric pressure is allowed to enter the pneumatic tube for that note. The pouch, a flexible diaphragm, still under the influence of suction from above but no longer from below, rises. The valve, attached to a valve stem that sits on the pouch, also rises, uncovering the lower opening and closing the upper one. This allows the suction from the bellows to enter the action pneumatic, which collapses, causing a push rod to push up on the corresponding note of the piano action. When the hole in the piano roll moves away from the tracker bar, the opening is again sealed, restoring suction underneath the pouch, which allows the valve to again be pulled downward. Air enters the upper opening and rushes into the action pneumatic, which opens, and the push rod returns to its normal position. A wind motor, using the very same vacuum pressure, winds and rewinds the piano roll. Expression controls allow the user to manually vary the tempo and dynamics as the roll plays.

1960s player pianos have become quite the fad again, and many an unwary buyer purchases an old player, complete with music rolls, with the intention of making it work again.

There are a number of things you should think about before investing in an old player piano. A player piano is, in a sense, two pianos in one—a regular piano, with its thousands of parts and their potential problems, and a player action, with *its* thousands of parts and *their* potential problems. It's vital that the regular piano be in good condition, or worth putting in good condition, before you even consider restoring the player action. Beware of any player piano advertised as "partially restored" or just needing a little work. Restoring a player piano that has been poorly or partially repaired is sometimes more expensive than restoring one that has never been touched at all, so if you don't know for certain that the piano has been completely restored, consider it completely unrestored. Also, don't waste your money on a former player piano that is now missing the player action in the hope that you will be able to find one that fits. You may wait forever.

Very few piano technicians know or care anything about player pianos. In fact, many won't even consent to tune them because the player mechanism is in the way and makes tuning difficult. (Actually, a knowledgeable technician can often remove the parts that are in the way quite quickly, but most aren't that knowledgeable.) Restoring the player mechanism is probably not something you should attempt yourself, so you will have to locate someone fully qualified to do the job. The restoration will be very time consuming and expensive, possibly exceeding the value of the regular piano itself. Because of these considerations, I would advise that you locate the qualified technician before shopping, then use his or her advice to secure a piano. Buying a fully restored player piano from such a technician might be the safest route to take.

Though some kinds of folds and tears are repairable, old music rolls with torn and brittle edges can be hazardous to your player piano. They won't track properly, and small bits of paper can get sucked into the mechanism, clogging it up hopelessly. Many fine old piano rolls are still in excellent condition, however, and thousands of tunes unavailable on new rolls can be found on these old ones. There are several mail-order piano roll auction firms, the best known being Mike and Fred Schwimmer Piano Roll Center, 325 E. Blodgedt, Lake Bluff, Illinois 60044. New piano rolls are abundantly available from many piano dealers and mail-order sources (for more information write to QRS Music Rolls, Inc., 1026 Niagara St., Buffalo, New York 14213, or Play-Rite Music Rolls, P.O. Box 1025, Turlock, California 95380).

The player mechanism in a player piano imparts the same amount of force to every note, so every note sounds at the same volume. This is, of course, different from the way (most) people play. The constant volume is part of what gives a player piano that machine-like sound that lets you know it's a player piano and not a real person, even without looking. During the same period that player pianos were being made, another, much more sophisticated mechanism was being installed in high-quality grand pianos. These mechanisms, called **reproducers**, were capable of copying every nuance of an artist's playing, and many of the greatest pianists of the late nineteenth and early twentieth century recorded music rolls for them.

The most famous reproducer brands were Ampico, Duo-Art, and Welte, which were installed in many top-name grand pianos, such as Steinway and Mason & Hamlin. Some of these pianos were made several inches longer to accommodate the mechanism; others housed the mechanism in a drawer. Usually slots or holes were cut through the keybed to connect the portion of the reproducer action below with the piano action inside. Witnessing one of these marvels in action is an experience you'll not soon forget. Unfortunately, reproducers in good working condition are very rare. And if you think it's hard to find a competent player piano technician, just try to find someone to service or rebuild a reproducer! Music rolls for reproducers were never standardized, but rolls for a few makes are again being commercially made.

If you are seriously thinking of buying an old player or reproducer, you should definitely read *Player Piano Servicing & Rebuilding* by Arthur Reblitz (The Vestal Press Ltd., Vestal, New York 13850). This well-written, thorough, fully illustrated book will tell you in more detail how player and reproducing pianos work, how to inspect one—restored or unrestored—before buying, and how a serious hobbyist or professional should restore them. The Vestal Press also publishes numerous other books on player pianos and other automatic musical instruments.

It's possible, too, to buy *new* player and reproducing pianos. Some of these function similarly to the old ones; others are largely electronic. According to player piano experts consulted, however, a properly restored player or reproducer from the 1920s will always play circles around a modern one.

HOW TO FIND A USED PIANO

Here are some of your options—you may be able to think of others:

- Contacting piano technicians and rebuilding shops
- Visiting new piano dealers (who sometimes have used pianos for sale as well)
- Visiting used piano dealers
- Answering ads or notices offering pianos for sale
- Hunting up a piano by placing an ad yourself or by contacting places that might have pianos they would like to get rid of
- Buying a piano from friends or relatives or accepting one as a gift

Let's discuss these options one at a time:

Contacting technicians and rebuilding shops. The first thing to do as you start looking for a used piano is to call your piano technician (or the technician you plan to use when you find a piano). He or she may know of, or have, used pianos for sale, or may be able to refer you to someone who does. He or she can also inform you about local market conditions and prices, what stores to patronize or avoid, and so on. Most technicians are glad to give you this advice over the phone without charge or obligation.

If at all possible you should visit a technician's shop and look at pianos that are being, or have been, repaired, reconditioned, or rebuilt. Ask exactly what has been done to the pianos and why. Ask what you should be looking for in a used piano. This is an invaluable opportunity to supplement the technical information contained in this chapter so that you'll feel confident in using it to inspect a piano on your own if necessary. You'll also meet some fascinating people and see a slice of life in your community you might not otherwise encounter. There's more to this piano business than meets the eye.

If you decide to buy a piano from a technician, you will probably pay quite a bit more than you would for an equivalent piano from a private owner. The advantages are that the piano has (presumably) been carefully checked over and repaired, a warranty is given (see "Warranty," page 143), and you may save yourself the hassle of shopping in the private market, where you might or might not find an "equivalent" piano. You will also have the satisfaction of patronizing a local craftsperson.

Even if you buy from a technician you trust, it's not a bad idea to have the piano inspected first by another, independent technician. This may be a little awkward for everyone concerned, but even the best technicians can differ in their opinions. Also, a technician who has a considerable amount of money and time invested in an instrument must sell it even if it hasn't turned out so hot, which happens often and unpredictably, and it makes good sense to protect yourself. Make sure the technician you hire determines that the repair or rebuilding work claimed to have been performed has actually been done. If a technician balks at having you bring in another technician to appraise a piano, shop elsewhere.

When considering buying a rebuilt piano from a piano technician, the amount of experience the technician has had should count heavily in your decision. The complete rebuilding of a piano requires many dissimilar skills. That is, the skills required for installing a soundboard, for example, are very different from those required for installing a new set of hammers or for regulating the action. Mastering all these skills can take a very long time. In a sense, you should be shopping for the rebuilder as much as for the piano.

It may occur to you that you could save a lot of money by buying an unrestored piano—a "wreck"— and having a technician completely restore it, rather than buying the completely restored piano direct from the technician. This is often true. But as I said, the results of restoration jobs are unpredictable. If a lot of money is involved and you are particular in your tastes for tone and action, you would be better off letting the technician make the profit—and take the risks. If you're interested in a particular piano, a technician might be willing to buy it and restore it and give you the first chance at it when it's done. If you do go ahead and buy the "wreck," by all means make sure a technician inspects it first and ascertains that it's worth restoring. Sometimes the price of the "wreck" plus the cost of the restoration far exceeds the value of the restored piano. (Hint: If the technician won't buy the piano, that may be why.) At the time this is being written, a complete rebuilding of a grand piano could cost from eight to more than twelve thousand dollars.

Visiting new piano dealers. Dealers of new pianos sometimes rebuild pianos too, or at least recondition used pianos that they take in on trade. Because these pianos take up valuable floor space and compete with new pianos for the customer's attention, their prices are usually rather high. But visiting one of these dealers is a convenient way to shop for a used piano, especially if you are not sure whether you will be buying new or used. An independent technician you hire to inspect a used piano here may be able to tell you whether you are getting good value. Sometimes these used pianos are just bait to get you into the store, and may be vastly overpriced compared to what you would pay to a private owner, or even to an independent rebuilding shop. Be sure the technician you hire is unconnected with, and owes no favors to, the dealer.

Visiting used piano dealers. Here I am referring to dealers who are basically entrepreneurs without technical skills, out to make a buck. Even if they have a few

Repair, Reconditioning, and Rebuilding

Three terms are often used when discussing restoration work on pianos: repair, reconditioning, and rebuilding. There are no precise definitions of these terms, and any particular job may contain elements of more than one of them. It's therefore vital, when having work done on your piano or when buying a piano that has been worked on, that you find out exactly what jobs have been, or will be, carried out. "This piano has been reconditioned" or "I'll rebuild this piano" are not sufficient answers. One person's rebuilding may be another's reconditioning.

Generally speaking, a *repair* job involves fixing isolated broken parts, such as a broken hammer, a missing string, or an improperly working pedal. That is, it does not necessarily involve upgrading the condition of the instrument as a whole, but attends only to specific broken parts.

Reconditioning always involves a general upgrading of the whole piano, but with as little actual replacement of parts as possible. For instance, the reconditioning of an old upright piano might include resurfacing the hammers (instead of replacing them) and twisting the bass strings to improve their tone (instead of replacing them), as well as cleaning the whole instrument and regulating the action. If parts are broken or missing, of course, they must also be repaired or replaced, so this particular reconditioning job might also include replacing a set of bridle straps and other relatively minor parts, if needed.

Rebuilding is the most complete of the three levels of restoration. Rebuilding involves restringing the piano and usually, replacing the pinblock in a grand and repairing or replacing the soundboard. In the action, rebuilding would include replacing the hammer heads, damper felts, and key bushings, and possibly replacing or completely overhauling other sets of parts as well. Refinishing the piano case may also be done as part of a rebuilding job. Ideally, rebuilding means putting the piano into "factory-new" condition. In practice, however, it may involve much less, depending on the needs and the value of the particular instrument, the amount of money available, and the scrupulousness of the rebuilder. The bottom line is the restringing. If a piano has not been restrung, it really cannot qualify as a rebuilt instrument. Indeed, many technicians would assert that a piano has been rebuilt only if the pinblock has been replaced.

Due to the varied and sometimes unwarranted use of the word *rebuilding*, some rebuilders have come up with a new term—*remanufacturing*—to indicate the most complete restoration job possible, with special emphasis on the fact that the soundboard has been replaced, which may not be included in a regular rebuilding job. In my opinion, this new word only confuses the issue and, in time, it too will become tarnished. There is no substitute for requesting an itemization of the work performed.

tuners working for them, their instructions are generally just to "make all the keys work." My first job was for a place like this. It was a small storefront that sold used pianos and refrigerators. Each time a piano was delivered to a customer, I was sent out to tune it and to fix anything that the customer wasn't happy with. Considering the pitiful state of some of these pianos, it was often difficult to satisfy the customer, especially since I was paid only a flat fee for each piano I serviced. And when I would suggest to the manager, who didn't know a hammer from a bridle strap, that a piano might need more than fifteen dollars' worth of repair, he would accuse me of wanting "to rebuild the damn thing." I lasted only a month there.

Places like this are often well disguised. They may appear quite respectable and advertise widely in the media. In some cases they may have extensive repair facilities, but do very sloppy work. The best way to tell is to ask some reputable technicians which places to avoid—they will tell you. Interestingly, once in a while these stores will have a few pianos of high value selling for very low prices simply because the owners are unaware of what they have, or they need the cash. But do you really want to patronize a place like this?

Furniture stores and antique dealers sometimes take in pianos on consignment. These establishments tend to be ignorant about what they're selling—or are selling the instrument for its antique or furniture value—rather than dishonest. Their pianos are, at best, overpriced, or, at worst, defective and overpriced.

Answering ads. This is probably the most common way to buy a used piano. Classified ads for pianos can be found in big city daily and Sunday papers, local weekly papers, and in the "alternative press." Especially useful are the little booklets of want ads that appear weekly or biweekly, usually found at supermarket checkout counters and newsstands, published under such names as *Want Advertiser*, *Bargain Hunter*, *Buy Lines*, and *Pennysaver*. You'll also find ads or notices posted anywhere people congregate—laundromats, churches, synagogues, community centers, food co-ops, and so on. Most of the people who place these ads will be private individuals selling the piano from their home. A few, though, will be dealers and technicians who advertise a couple of their pianos this way and then invite you to come see the rest of their wares when you call. (Some may be trucking companies; see the cautionary note on page 63 about buying a "repossessed" piano from the back of a truck.)

Most ads say very little. When you call, you'll want to find out some more, such as: What brand is it? What size is the piano? Is it a spinet? When was it made? What condition is it in? When was it last tuned or otherwise serviced? What additional work needs to be done on it? You may be shocked to find out how little people know about their piano. Often they don't even know the brand name without looking, though they can tell you the location of every scratch on the case. Nevertheless, using what scanty information you have, as well as your hunches, you must decide which ones are worth your while to visit.

Hunting up a piano. This is the more aggressive approach. Place a "piano wanted" ad in the classifieds or post a note to that effect on a bulletin board. Someone who never got around to doing something about that old piano that's been sittin' around unplayed for years just might give you a call.

Another approach that falls into this category is to call around to all the churches and private schools in your area to see if they have any pianos they want to get rid of. But you must be very careful here. Pianos in institutions suffer incredible abuse, either from constant pounding by players (especially in "gospel" churches), from vandalism, from neglect by administrators charged with their care, or from the ravages of winter dryness and overheating in cold climates. By the time institutions are ready to get rid of their pianos, they are usually ready for the junk pile. You will therefore want to check them very carefully. An exception may be once wealthy churches and schools that are now in need of funds and may still have some healthy pianos.

Movers and storage warehouses are another potential source of pianos. These places sometimes get stuck with pianos that won't fit through the door or up the stairs and which for these or other reasons their customers abandon. Conditions for inspecting these pianos may be less than ideal.

Another audacious approach is to go to an auction where a piano is up for bid. The problem here is that you may not have enough time beforehand to inspect the piano and have a technician inspect it, and if yours is the winning bid, you have to pay for it, like it or not. Also, if the piano is one of much value, you're likely to be competing with piano technicians for it. Don't get carried away and end up paying more than the piano's worth.

One last idea—I've never tried it, but it might work if you're in no hurry—is to leave your card with lawyers and others who handle the disposition of estates, letting them know you're in the market for a piano. If one comes by their desk, they might give you first crack at it just to save themselves the trouble of having to advertise it.

Obtaining a piano from friends and relatives. It's nice when pianos remain in the family. I got my piano this way. But pianos purchased from friends and relatives or received as gifts are as likely as any others to have expensive problems you should know about. It's very hard to refuse a gift, and perhaps embarrassing to hire a piano technician to inspect it before you accept it, but for your own protection you should insist on doing so. Otherwise you may spend a lot of money to move a "gift" you could have done without.

Which of these routes you end up following will depend on your situation and what you are looking for. If you have a lot of time and transportation is no problem, you may get the best deal by shopping around among private owners or in out-of-the-way places. If you are busy or without a car, but have money to spend, it may be more convenient to shop among piano technicians, who may be able to show you several pianos at the same time and spare you from worrying about future repair costs and problems. The best route also depends on where you live, as some communities may have a brisk trade in used pianos among private owners but few rebuilding shops, or vice versa, or have an abundance of old uprights but few grands.

CHECKING OUT THE PIANO

Unless you're very rich and can afford to keep a piano technician on retainer full time, chances are that at some point in your searching for a used piano you're going to have to go it alone. Knowing that you'd rather not stare dumbly at the piano, I've prepared a little inspection routine for you here. A thorough inspection of a piano must really be a joint effort with a technician, because some crucial parts of the piano, such as the pinblock, can be tested only by feel or with special tools, and an overall judgment of the condition of the piano requires some experience. At the very least, though, this inspection will teach you a lot about the piano, enable you to talk intelligently with your technician, and make you feel a useful and involved participant instead of a passive bystander. And while in many cases a decision about purchase involves a balancing of pros and cons rather than a clear yea or nay, this routine may help you to weed out those occasional catastrophes that do not deserve your, or your technician's, further attention.

In addition, I've tried to give some idea of the relative significance of each part as I cover it, and, in very general terms, of the probable cost of repairing it, if necessary. As such, I've used the terms "cheap" and "inexpensive" to refer to repairs that are likely to cost

less than $50, "moderate" to mean $50 to $200, and "expensive," over $200. This value system is more likely to apply to inexpensive uprights than to other pianos, but you can make the translation as needed.

Much of the information you need can be found in previous chapters. Basic descriptions of piano parts and how they work are in Chapter 1, which you may want to review now. Page references are given to sections of Chapter 3, "Buying A New Piano," and other chapters that contain more helpful technical material. The information on how pianos differ in quality and features, also in Chapter 3, applies to used pianos too, especially those made since about 1960.

The tools you should bring with you are: a flashlight; a soft brush, such as a paint brush, for brushing away dust; a small screwdriver (with about a ⅛-inch tip) and a large screwdriver (with about a ⁵⁄₁₆-inch tip), for removing outer case parts, if needed; a tuning fork or pitch pipe, obtainable from a music store, to determine if the piano is up to standard pitch; paper and pencil for taking notes; this book; and someone to play the piano, if you don't, and to lend moral support.

Looks, styling, and finish. Look the piano over. Imagine it in your home. Could you live with it? If not, you might as well not go any further. A grand can be partially restyled by changing the legs and music desk, and any piano can be refinished, but both of these are expensive (refinishing a piano can easily cost one to two thousand dollars.)

If you're thinking of refinishing the piano yourself, let me warn you: stripping and refinishing a piano is much more work than refinishing other furniture, and most do-it-yourselfers give up long before this job is done. Some take short cuts, and end up sealing the piano shut or painting the strings. But if you're prepared for the long haul, hire a technician first to remove all the outer case parts and the action and to cover the strings; then get a good book on furniture refinishing.

Also check for loose veneer and other signs of water damage along the bottom edge of verticals. In general, loose veneer is found on pianos that have undergone extremes of both dryness and dampness. If you're going to refinish the piano, of course, the veneer will first have to be reglued; otherwise, it's up to you.

Beware of old uprights that have been restyled in nonstandard ways, such as by cutting down the height of the upper panel, installing mirrors, and so on. Sometimes this work is done by people who haven't thought of the consequences and who turn out pianos that are henceforth difficult or impossible to service. If the work has been done by an experienced piano technician, though, it's probably all right.

Play the piano a bit to get some sense of what this instrument is all about and to relax a little before the next step. Make mental or written notes about anything you think needs looking into.

Open up the piano. First ask the owners to remove anything (other than music) that's on the piano. Let *them* break their knickknacks, not *you*. If they look askance as you start to take their piano apart, remind them that they wouldn't buy a used car without first looking under the hood, would they? Following Figures 5-5 through 5-13, for a grand, very carefully open the lid (after checking to make sure that the hinges and hinge pins are in place) and prop it up, and remove the music desk. You might also want to remove the fallboard, which may require removing the keyslip and keyblocks too. On a vertical, open the lid; remove the upper panel, music shelf, and music desk (depending on the style); and remove the bottom door. (Note: Removal of these parts is usually not difficult and is mandatory if you expect to do any reasonable inspection of a piano, so don't be shy.) No need to remove other parts at this time.

Opening the Piano for Inspection

Removing the cabinet parts of a piano is seldom difficult and will usually follow the directions outlined below. However, sometimes you will have to play detective to find an elusive screw or latch. If you understand the general principles involved in these instructions, you will probably be able to handle the exceptions.

When removing screws, be sure to identify them and return them to the same holes from which they were taken. Even screws that look alike can sometimes make slightly different holes in the wood. One method piano technicians sometimes use to keep screws organized is to punch them through a piece of cardboard and write on the cardboard the name of the cabinet part from which they were taken and their position.

Take special care not to scratch or otherwise damage the cabinet parts, especially if the piano doesn't belong to you. These parts can sometimes be unwieldy to handle, so I suggest that these procedures always be followed by two persons working together.

Grand

Open and prop up the lid (Figure 5-5). Fold the front part of the lid back onto the main lid. Then prop the lid open with the longer of the two propsticks. *Caution:* Before opening the lid, be sure the lid hinges are attached and the hinge pins are in place or your lid may fly away like the one shown in the inset.

FIGURE 5–5.

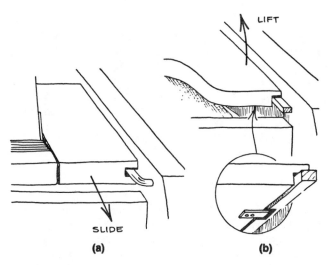

FIGURE 5–6.

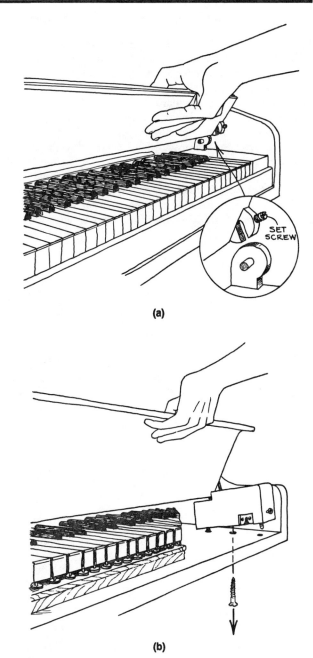

Remove the music desk (Figure 5-6). Try sliding the music desk out as shown in 5-6a. If it won't slide all the way out, then it's possible that a tab on the bottom of the desk must be lined up with a space in the slide rail, after which the desk can be lifted out, as in 5-6b. Some music desks are held in place by screws or hinge pins instead.

Remove the fallboard (Figure 5-7). (Note: Removing the fallboard from a grand piano can be tricky, and has the highest potential for scratching the case of all the operations described in this section. What you can see with the fallboard removed is helpful, but not essential, to your inspection of the piano.) There are two kinds of fallboard: One kind can be removed by itself, as shown in 5-7a. The other kind is attached to the keyblocks in such a way that the fallboard and keyblocks must be removed together as a unit, as in 5-7b.

Tilt the fallboard toward you at about a 45-degree angle, and, with both hands, try lifting the fallboard up and out of the piano. If there are set screws at the pivot points of the fallboard, as shown in the inset of (a), unscrew them several turns, then try lifting the fallboard up and out. If this doesn't work, try unscrewing the set screws another turn or two, but don't remove them entirely. Some fallboard pivot systems are very visible, as in (a); some are more hidden or of a slightly different design.

If there are no set screws, and the fallboard cannot be removed by just lifting, then it is probably type (b). You will need to skip ahead to "Remove the keyslip (Figure 5-8)" to complete that operation; then return here.

Look at the underside of the keybed, directly under the center of each keyblock, for a large screw that holds the keyblock down. Remove the two screws (one for each keyblock). Then lift up on the front of each keyblock to disengage its dowels (if any) from their holes in the keybed. Tilt the fallboard toward you and lift up on the whole

FIGURE 5–7.

fallboard-keyblock system. If it feels entirely loose and ready to be lifted out, do it. If not, check to see what's holding it in place (usually the dowels on the bottom of the keyblocks will still be stuck in their holes in the keybed). Lift the system out and place it on the floor. (Note that the keyblocks may not be fastened to the type (b) fallboard and may fall off once clear of the case, possibly landing on the floor or scratching the case. Be prepared to catch them or remove them before they fall.)

Opening the Piano for Inspection (*continued*)

To return the fallboard to the piano when the inspection is finished: If the fallboard is type (a), be sure to notice how the pin in the case side (or in a metal bracket attached to the keyblock) lines up with the slot in the fallboard (or vice versa, depending on the particular piano). Sometimes this is tricky to do. Tighten the set screws, if any. If the fallboard is type (b), when you removed it from the piano and set it down on the floor it's possible that the keyblocks fell off. Not to worry. Set the fallboard in place on the keyboard, then, one at a time, reattach each keyblock to the metal stub at the end of the fallboard. Push each keyblock down so its dowels are firmly seated in their holes in the keybed. Then screw the keyblocks down with their large screws. Replace the keyslip (see Figure 5-8).

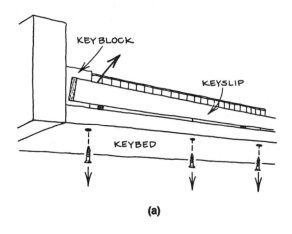

(a)

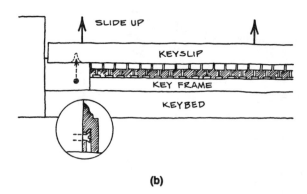

(b)

FIGURE 5–8.

Remove the keyslip (Figure 5-8). (For the purpose of this inspection, you need only remove the keyslip if you are removing a type (b) fallboard, as previously described.) Most keyslips are removed as in 5-8a, by taking out three to six screws located under the keybed. On Steinway and Mason & Hamlin grands (and occasionally others), the keyslip is held in place by the *heads* of two screws, one projecting from the front of each keyblock, that fit into slots in the back of the keyslip (5-8b). Slide the keyslip up to disengage it; sometimes the fit is tight. When removing a keyslip, be sure to save any cardboard shims you find between the keyslip and the key frame and return them to the same position later.

Vertical

Open the lid (Figure 5-9). Most lids open one of the three ways shown in the drawing. The example on the right is a "grand style" lid, hinged on the left side, found on some contemporary verticals. To inspect the piano, remove the hinge pins on the grand style lid and take the lid off. (Note: Some studio pianos, such as the Baldwin Hamilton, open differently; see Figure 5-12.)

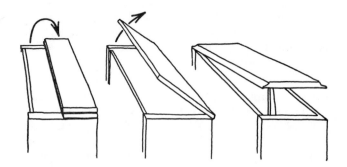

FIGURE 5–9.

Remove the upper panel (Figure 5-10). If the piano is an upright, first close the fallboard down over the keys. This is done because on some uprights the fallboard mechanically interlocks with the upper panel, or leans against the upper panel, and makes disassembly difficult when open. The upper panel either is secured by a latch on each end, a common type of which is shown in 5-10a, or swings on screws or stout pins sticking out from the cabinet sides, as in 5-10b. Sometimes these methods may be combined, in which case you should proceed as for the first type. On some spinets and consoles, the upper panel–music shelf assembly is attached to the cabinet sides with screws. After removing the upper panel, try opening the fallboard. On some pianos the fallboard, when open, hits the action when the upper panel is not in place. Usually this kind of fallboard assembly can be removed by simply lifting it straight up and out of the piano. Otherwise, it's generally not necessary to remove the fallboard to inspect the vertical piano.

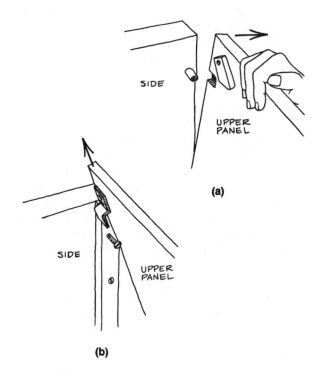

(a)

(b)

FIGURE 5–10.

Remove the music shelf (Figure 5-11). Some old uprights have a separate music shelf, which must be removed. Sometimes the music shelf just slides out, or slides and then lifts, and sometimes it is held in by screws. The screws may be hidden under decorative moldings that must first be removed by unscrewing them from the cabinet sides.

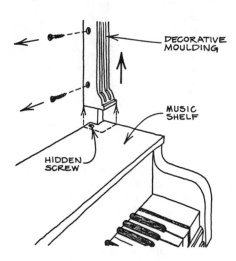

FIGURE 5–11.

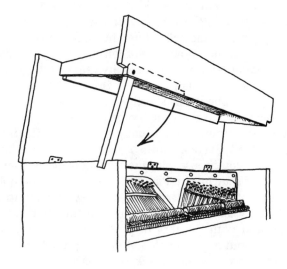

FIGURE 5–12.

How to open some studio pianos (Figure 5-12). On some studio pianos, especially the Baldwin Hamilton, the lid, upper panel, and music shelf are all contained in one bulky piece. A propstick swings down to support this assembly on the cabinet side.

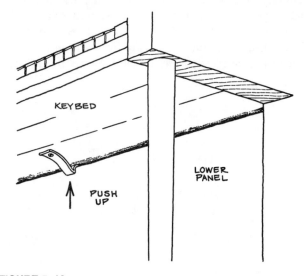

FIGURE 5–13.

Remove the lower panel (Figure 5-13). The lower panel is usually held in place by a leaf spring or two. Simply press the spring(s) up toward the keybed and pull the panel out. Sometimes a rotating wooden latch is used instead. When replacing the lower panel, be sure the bottom edge of the panel is lined up correctly with the bottom rail on which it sits.

Pitch and tuning. Does the piano sound more or less in tune? When was it last tuned? If the piano is so far out of tune that some individual notes sound like chords—that is, the two or three strings of a single note [7] are at radically different pitches from each other—then nine times out of ten that spells trouble. Even pianos left untuned for many years rarely go out of tune in that manner unless the tuning pins are loose (more about this shortly).

Now take out your pitch pipe or tuning fork (Figure 5-14). Tuning forks usually sound A or C; pitch pipes usually have a choice of notes to sound. Whatever note you choose, play the same note on the piano and see if they match. Play the same letter-name note at different octave intervals up and down the piano to see if they all sound pretty much in tune with each other and with the fork or pipe. If they are mostly within about a quarter step of being on pitch, fine. If a substantial portion of the piano is a semitone or more flat, this may or may not mean trouble—we don't know yet—but it *will* mean extra tuning work to bring it up to pitch—if it *can* be brought up to pitch. Make an ominous note in your notebook.

The pinblock. The condition of this crucial part of the piano's structure determines whether or not the piano will stay in tune [30]. Unfortunately, it's the part of the piano you can tell the least about yourself, as the experience and tools of a professional are needed to determine if the tuning pins are tight enough to hold the strings at their proper tension. Nevertheless, you

can read a few clues. Look at the tuning pins (Figure 5-15). When the piano is new, the pins are set so the coil of wire around each pin is about 3/16 inch above the plate. If pins get loose, they can be driven further in to tighten them—if necessary, until the coils are almost touching the plate. That 3/16 inch acts as a safety margin: even if the tuning pins on the piano you are inspecting turn out to be loose, the piano may still be worth buying if there is still sufficient space left between the coils and the plate to drive the pins in further to tighten them. (However, this repair doesn't always work, and repinning the piano with larger tuning pins is preferred when economically feasible.) Conversely, if the piano is dreadfully out of tune and far below standard pitch *and* the tuning pins have already been driven in as far as they can go, the chances are fairly good that that piano would require extensive rebuilding to bring it back to life. A new set of larger tuning pins could cost at least several hundred dollars, and a new pinblock, if necessary, could cost a few thousand by the time all the work necessitated by it was completed. These are just clues; a final judgment on the matter must await the technician.

Also look around the tuning pins and on nearby areas of the plate for ugly, dark brown, gummy-looking stains that indicate the pinblock has been doped with chemicals to tighten the pins. On a grand, also look on the underside of the pinblock for the stains and for signs of cracking (Figure 5-16). Don't

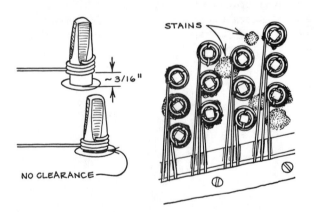

FIGURE 5-15. The distance between the plate and the coil of wire around each tuning pin gives a clue about the condition of the pinblock. When the piano is new, the tuning pins are set so the coils are about 3/16 inch above the plate. If the coils are close to the plate, this means that the tuning pins were once loose and were hammered in further to tighten them, and that if they should still be loose or should get loose again in the future, there will be no room to hammer them in again. Also look around the tuning pin area, and around the wooden plate bushings surrounding the tuning pins, for ugly, dark brown, oily-looking stains that indicate the pinblock has been chemically treated.

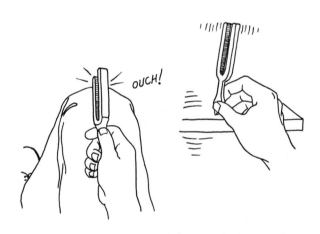

FIGURE 5-14. Hold the tuning fork by the stem and hit one of the tines on your knee good and hard (ouch!), *not* on the piano. Then touch the stem to a wooden part of the piano. The wood will amplify the sound of the fork. The note that the fork sounds, usually A or C, is printed on the side. Compare the fork to the same letter-name notes up and down the piano keyboard to see if the piano is up to standard pitch.

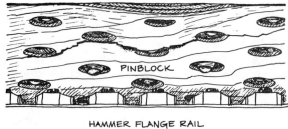

FIGURE 5-16. On a grand piano, with the fallboard off, look at the underside of the pinblock for chemical stains or signs of cracking. The pinblock shown here is in extremely poor condition. Notice especially that the bottom lamination is separating from the rest of the pinblock. Most ruined pinblocks are not this obvious, but you might as well recognize the ones that are. Also: if the tuning pins are sticking out the bottom of the holes, beware. This usually means someone installed the wrong size pins; if they should require hammering in, it will be impossible to do so. The protruding ends of the tuning pins may interfere with the action if there is not much clearance between them.

confuse dirt and rust with the chemical stains. Unless the piano is otherwise in very good condition, the price is right, or you plan to replace the pinblock anyway (a major rebuilding job), you would probably do best to steer away from a piano that has been doped.

Strings. How rusty are the strings? Some tarnish or a very light coating of rust is normal for an old piano. What you want to avoid is heavy, encrusted rust on the strings and pressure bar that will make the tone bad and cause the strings to break during tuning (although strings sometimes break even if they aren't rusty). Has this piano had a string breakage problem? Look carefully at the strings, which are arranged in sets of one, two, or three called *unisons* [7], to see if any are missing (Figure 5-17a). Are there many new-looking, untarnished strings on the piano? Some new strings—how nice, right? Wrong. Those new strings were installed to replace ones that broke, so their presence amidst the rusty ones indicates a possible string breakage problem, especially if several strings are missing too. Occasional string replacement (an inexpensive item) can be tolerated, but the expense and nuisance add up if strings break often. The presence of spliced bass strings, an alternative to replacement of broken bass strings, can also indicate a possible string breakage problem (Figure 5-17b).

Now play some bass notes. Do they "resound"? Or do they sound like they're underwater or being struck through a heavy blanket (thud . . . thud)? The copper

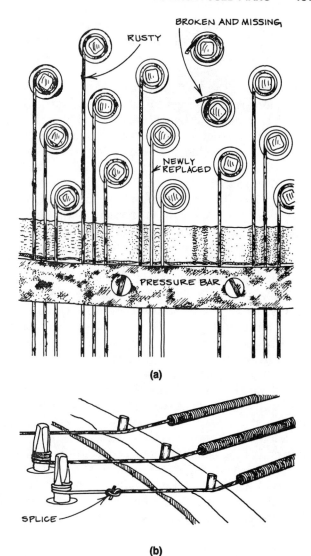

FIGURE 5-17. (a) The presence of several broken strings and several new, untarnished strings (meaning that some broken ones were recently replaced) among otherwise rusty or tarnished strings may indicate the piano has a string breakage problem. (Remember that in the treble section of most pianos each length of wire forms two strings, as shown in Figure 1-13.) (b) Broken and replacement bass strings may also indicate a string breakage problem. Sometimes a new piece of wire is spliced to the remains of a broken bass string as an alternative to replacing it.

or iron windings [33] on these strings loosen with time and also become clogged with dirt, which diminishes their flexibility. Replacing an entire set of bass strings, a moderate expense, is generally worth doing if the piano is otherwise in reasonable condition. Twisting and cleaning the old bass strings to make them sound better costs about half as much, but doesn't always work satisfactorily, and can make marginally tight tuning pins too loose to hold the strings in tune. If the bass strings need replacing and the piano is one of some value, you should consider restringing the entire piano at one time.

The bridges. The treble and bass bridges transfer the vibration of the strings to the soundboard [38]. Of special interest to us here is the bass bridge, which has a strong tendency to form cracks around the bridge pins due to the side pressure of the strings against them. Follow the bass strings toward their far end (on a vertical, to their bottom end) to find the bass bridge. As you look for cracks around the bridge pins you may need your flashlight to chase away the shadows and your brush to chase away the dust. Now, you may see some tiny hairline cracks around some—maybe even all—the bridge pins. This is very common and usually not a problem. The problem begins when the cracks get big enough so the bridge pins are actually pushed aside. This can cause a severe deterioration or loss of tone in the affected notes. Then the problem worsens when the cracks around adjacent pins run together, resulting in a perforated bridge ready to fall apart (Figure 5-18). If the pitch of the piano must be raised much to get it up to standard pitch, the resulting increase in string tension may exacerbate this condition.

A loose bass bridge will also cause a loss of tone. If one end of the bass has a much weaker tone than the other end, you might try pushing that end of the bridge down toward the soundboard while someone else plays the keys. If the tone noticeably improves, then the bridge is coming loose from the soundboard.

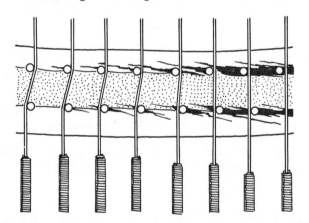

FIGURE 5-18. The strings exert sidebearing pressure against the bridge pins—pressure that is necessary for good tone, but that may eventually cause cracks in the bridge. This is especially a concern with the bass bridge. The bass bridge shown here is worse toward the right, where the hairline cracks are larger and have merged, allowing the bridge pins to be pushed out of line until there is no more sidebearing. A bridge like this would probably have to be replaced.

The treble bridge can also develop cracks, usually in the highest octave. On a vertical piano these can be hard to see because the action is in the way. Try peering down behind the action with your flashlight. If the bridge appears to be badly cracked, check the tone of these notes by plucking individual strings with your fingers. Do they give off a tone of a definite pitch, or is the pitch indistinct? The treble bridge on a grand piano can easily be viewed throughout.

Bridge repairs, unless very minor, tend to be moderately to very expensive, and are usually unjustified for the cheaper pianos, although it is not uncommon for a good upright to be fitted with a new bass bridge cap [38]. If the damage is not too severe, sometimes a less expensive repair can be made to a cracked bridge by removing bridge pins, filling cracks with epoxy, and then reinstalling the pins. A loose bass bridge can often be reattached by stuffing glue under the loose part and securing with a screw from the back of the soundboard.

One more bridge-related concern should be mentioned. On some pianos, both verticals and grands, made in the early part of this century (or earlier), the upper bearing point (the end of the vibrating portion of the string that is closer to the tuning pins) for the bass strings is made of wood instead of being an integral part of the cast-iron plate. This wooden "upper bridge" tends to have the same cracking problems that the lower bridge does, sometimes worse. Be especially cautious about buying a piano with serious cracks in this area.

Structural integrity. This refers to the condition of the cast-iron plate [30] and the supporting wooden case, posts, and beams [28]. Once in a great while, a crack will develop in one of these parts, most often the plate, usually rendering the piano useless (and usually unrepairable). In a grand, the plate can be seen in its entirety from above, and the rest of the supporting structure from below. In a vertical, much of the plate is hidden from view; the wooden structure, though, can easily be examined by moving the piano away from the wall and looking at the back. (Note: When pulling a vertical piano away from the wall, watch for wooden blocks under the back if the casters are missing.) In a vertical, look especially at the back of the top horizontal beam, and, if exposed, the top of the piano back (under the lid), for anything other than minor surface cracking. Also make sure the case sides are not coming unglued from the vertical back structure. To be honest, I'm including these items only for the sake of completeness; your chance of finding a major structural problem of this sort is probably very tiny. (An important exception is when a piano has been moved from a humid climate to a very dry one. In this situation it is more common to find wooden structural parts coming unglued.) An indication that a structural problem should be looked for might be, for example, that a piano only recently tuned has gone quickly and drastically out of tune for no apparent reason (although there are certainly lots of other reasons why this could happen). Major structural problems, especially a cracked plate, are very risky to try to repair. The risk should be left to a rebuilder, not you.

Another, more likely, structural problem—this one unrelated to tuning—is the condition of the legs. The front legs of spinets and consoles very frequently crack or become loose [26]. Usually they can be repaired or replaced at not too great a cost. Check also for visible (or invisible) cracks in the legs of grands. Push on the piano gently both forward and sideways to see if it rocks unduly. Installing a new set of grand legs or leg plates (which hold the legs on) is a bit costly, but usually worth doing if the piano is otherwise worth buying. Last, check for cracks in the lid of a grand, or loose lid hinges. A cracked lid could necessitate an expensive lid replacement, but only for aesthetic reasons. Damaged lid hinges should be repaired or replaced for safety.

Soundboard and ribs. While you're underneath the grand piano or behind the vertical looking at its structural components, you should also check out the soundboard and ribs [39]. Cracks in the soundboard, while unattractive, are not necessarily important, as long as the tone has not suffered. (This runs contrary to popular thought on the subject, I realize.) Very extensive cracking, however, can be taken as an indication that the piano has suffered great dryness or climatic extremes, and that its life expectancy may be short. (The more expensive the piano, the more important is the consideration of life expectancy.) Usually in such a case, the symptoms of dryness will be evident elsewhere in the piano as well. If the cracks are fitted with wooden shims, this means the piano was rebuilt at some time in the past (Figure 5-19a). Also check around the perimeter of the soundboard to make sure it isn't coming unglued from the piano.

The ribs run perpendicular to the grain of the soundboard, and therefore perpendicular to any cracks. Check each point where a rib crosses a crack to see if the ribs are still firmly glued to the soundboard or if they have separated (Figure 5-19b). Rib separations are potential sources of buzzing noises. Again, how important this is to you depends on the severity of the problem, whether buzzing sounds are currently present, and how expensive the piano is. In any case, this is rarely a fatal problem, and often (though not

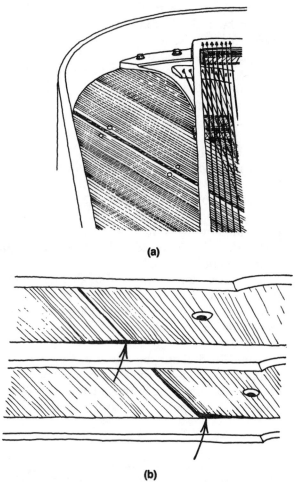

(a)

(b)

FIGURE 5-19. (a) When a piano is rebuilt without replacing the soundboard, the soundboard cracks are fitted with shims of wood, mostly for aesthetic reasons. In this drawing, the circles on either side of the shimmed crack are wooden plugs that cover the heads of screws used to reattach loose ribs. (b) Ribs often come unglued where they cross cracks in the soundboard (and sometimes elsewhere as well), causing buzzing sounds. They can usually be reattached with glue and screws.

always) ribs can be reattached to the soundboard with glue and screws at reasonable cost without "rebuilding" the piano.

When manufactured, the soundboard has a curvature or *crown* built into it to help resist the downbearing pressure of the strings on the bridges and to enhance the tone [39]. Over time, principally because of the drying out of the wood, the soundboard loses some or all of its crown. In theory, a soundboard with no crown shouldn't sound good, but actually many fine-sounding pianos have no measurable crown. This is one of those grey areas of piano technology, where every technician has a different opinion on the role that soundboard crown plays in determining the quality of tone.

My sense is that a measurement of soundboard crown can be useful in conjunction with other data. For instance, if the tone in the treble lacks sufficient sustain [42], there is no measurable downbearing of the strings on the bridges [38] (to be measured by the technician), and the soundboard has no crown, then the tonal problem may be due to a worn-out soundboard that needs replacing. But if the soundboard has plenty of crown, we might look elsewhere for the cause of the problem.

To measure soundboard crown, hold a long piece of thread, *pulled taut*, against the back of the soundboard parallel to the longest ribs (Figure 5-20). See if there is a space between the thread and the soundboard created by the soundboard crown. How much space? *Any* amount is considered sufficient. An eighth of an inch would be excellent.

Again, measuring crown, although much talked about, is of uncertain value. It's probably worth paying attention to when inspecting high-quality grands, but don't bother on verticals.

The action. Read about the action in Chapter 1 and also in Chapter 3 [44–47]; there's plenty to know about it. We won't be removing the action. It may be okay to do that (with proper instruction) when inspecting

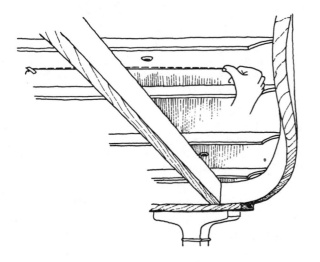

FIGURE 5-20. To measure soundboard curvature or *crown*, stretch a thread against the back of the soundboard parallel to the longest ribs. You can either tape one end of the thread to the soundboard, get someone else to hold it there, or try to hold both ends yourself. You may have to pass the thread over one of the case beams. Look for a space between the thread and the soundboard indicating that the soundboard is curved. A flashlight might be handy for this operation. Theoretically, crown is necessary for good tone, but actually many fine-sounding pianos have no measurable soundboard crown.

your own or perhaps a friend's piano, but *not* when examining a piano you are considering buying from a stranger—it's too easy to break parts. (You may legitimately ask to look under the hood of a used car before buying, but unless you're a trained mechanic, the owner may justifiably complain when you start to remove the transmission.) Fortunately, in most cases you can inspect a vertical piano action very thoroughly without removing it. If you're inspecting a grand piano, though, you'll have to be content with what you can see looking down through the strings or in through the front with the fallboard removed. If you're seriously interested in the piano, your technician can do a more complete inspection of the action later.

Do a general inspection of the action. Do the action parts look evenly spaced and uniform in appearance? Does every note work? Do any keys stick or do any dampers not damp properly? Are the hammers, dampers, and other felt parts badly moth-eaten? Check the condition of the bridle straps (vertical pianos only). If they are old and brittle or show signs of deteriorating (Figure 5-21), they need to be replaced. This is a relatively inexpensive repair that is important and very common.

There are thousands of parts in an action and *zillions* of things that can go wrong. I wish I could go into all of them here, but obviously that's not possible. If you enjoy playing detective, trace down the cause of malfunctions by comparing notes that work properly with ones that don't. The action diagrams and explanations in Chapter 1 should help you. Also make an inventory of any broken parts and strange noises (Figure 5-22).

Buyers of used pianos are often scared away from instruments with one or more notes that don't play. Actually, broken or missing action parts are usually among the easiest and cheapest repairs to make. Unless the action is utterly worn out or there has been wholesale destruction of parts, problems in this area of the piano are usually much less cause for alarm than some of the other, less obvious problems previously discussed. However, if a lot of wooden parts are broken or loose or appear to have been repaired, and the breakage occurred through normal use, this may indicate that the wood is overly dry and brittle and that future breakage may occur. Such a piano should be avoided by pianists who plan to make heavy demands on the instrument, but it may still be suitable for others, as long as it's humidified during the dry season. (Note: If a vertical piano was made before 1960 and some of the action parts are made of plastic, don't buy the piano. The old plastic breaks easily and the piano is likely to require wholesale replacement of parts.)

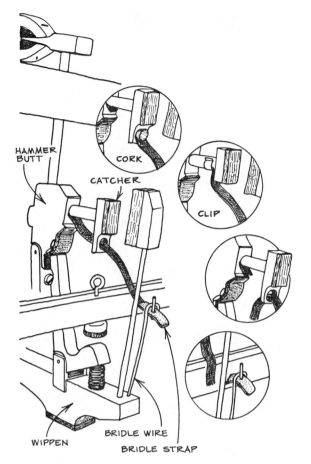

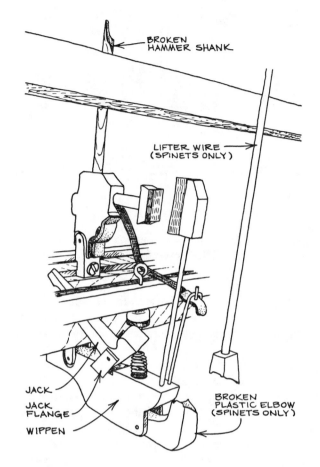

FIGURE 5-21. Bridle straps are cloth tapes with leather or vinyl tips that connect the wippen assembly to the hammer assembly on vertical pianos. There are eighty-eight of them. They are among the first parts in a piano to become worn out and may be replaced several times in the life of a piano. They are always worth replacing if the piano is worth keeping. The bottom two insets show how bridle straps may break at the end attached to the bridle wire or closer to the end attached to the hammer butt. The top two insets show two common types of replacement bridle straps: one with a cork that fits into the hole in the catcher, and one with a spring clip that clips to the catcher shank when the catcher is a type with no hole.

Keys [47]. Look at the keytops. Are they ivory or plastic [51]? Ivory usually has an irregular, natural-looking grain; plastic has no grain or a simulated grain of straight lines. Are any keytops missing or chipped or cigarette-burned (Figure 5-23)? Don't let a bad-looking keyboard scare you away. A few missing keytops can be replaced inexpensively and a new set of plastic keytops is available at moderate cost.

Do the keys rattle? Press a key down at the front and wiggle it left and right (Figure 5-24). Does it move a lot and make noise? The keys pivot on a key frame with metal guide pins underneath the front and sticking through the balance point of each key. Pieces of

FIGURE 5-22. This drawing shows three of the most common action problems that would cause a note on a vertical piano to not play at all: (a) The jack flange has come unglued from its slot in the wippen and has fallen over, so the jack can no longer push against the hammer butt. This is especially common in old uprights during the dry season. The repair is simple—clean out the old glue joint and reglue. (b) The hammer shank has broken and the hammer head has fallen into the piano somewhere. If it can be found, it may be possible to splice the shank back together. If the break was jagged or occurred too close to the top or bottom of the shank, the remains will have to be drilled out and the shank replaced. An inexpensive repair. (c) On spinets made during the 1940s and 1950s, the plastic elbows that connect the lifter wires to the wippens deteriorate and break. Once one or two break, the rest will soon follow, so it's most economical to replace the whole set at once with elbows made of wood or durable modern plastic. This is a moderate expense.

cloth called **key bushings** buffer the key wood from the guide pins. The key bushings in the most-used center area of the keyboard get the most wear. A new set of key bushings is another moderate-cost repair, but one that returns great value in the form of a quieter, smoother-feeling action. Also check the balance point of the key for excessive side-play in those bushings and for cracked key buttons.

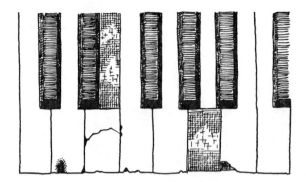

FIGURE 5-23. Missing, broken, and cigarette-burned ivory and plastic keytops can be unsightly, and jagged edges can be dangerous to the fingers. Replacing a few keytops is inexpensive, but if many are missing or broken, it's best to have the whole set recovered with plastic, a moderate expense.

Hammers [51]. Of all the parts in the action, the hammers are the most important for you to inspect. In them, too, can be read some of the history of the piano. First look at the string-cut grooves on the striking point of the hammer. Unless the hammer heads have been replaced at some point in the life of the piano, or the hammer felt resurfaced to its original shape by filing off a layer of felt (which would eliminate the grooves), the depth of the grooves will tell you something about how much use the piano has gotten over the years. More importantly, the deeper the grooves or the flatter the striking face of the hammer, the sooner you will need to have the hammers resurfaced, a low to moderate expense. But if there isn't enough felt left for resurfacing, the hammer heads will have to be replaced. This is expensive (at least a few hundred dollars, possibly much more) but worth doing on most grands, but a questionable investment for some of the cheaper verticals. Look especially at the hammers in the mid-treble section. These tend to experience the greatest wear in comparison to the amount of felt on them. Imagine these hammers restored to their original rounded-point shape by filing felt off the shoulders and the striking point. Is there enough felt left on the hammers to do this without just about reaching wood (Figure 5-25)?

The presence of deep grooves adversely affects the tone of a piano. Of course, on many pianos, particularly cheaper ones that won't be getting serious or fussy artistic use, the presence of grooves on the hammers—even deep ones—isn't of great importance. But it becomes more important in conjunction with certain other hammer problems. Look at the grooves again. Does each of the hammers that are supposed to strike three strings have three well-defined grooves approximately centered on the hammer? Or have some of the hammers

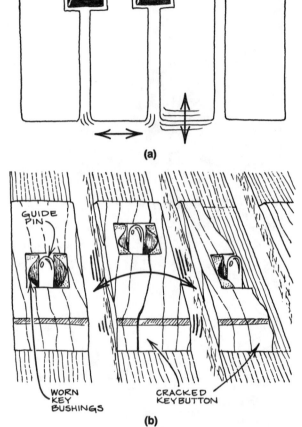

FIGURE 5-24. (a) Press a key down at the front and wiggle it left and right. There should be a very small amount of side play. If the key moves a lot and makes noise, it's time to get the front key bushings replaced. Also grab at the front of a key and try moving it forward and backward. Any play at all here is too much; it indicates abnormal wear of the balance hole at the bottom of the key at its balance point. (b) At the top of the keys at the balance point on most pianos are key buttons, inside of which are another set of key bushings. Like the key bushings at the front, these wear too, allowing the keys to wobble too much and make noise. Also check for cracked key buttons. Replacing an individual cracked key button or repairing an occasional worn balance hole is an inexpensive job.

moved over a bit, now striking only two of the three strings (Figure 5-26)? You can also check the alignment of vertical piano hammers by pushing hammers toward the strings with your hand (see Figure 3-32 on page 53). On a grand, pressing down keys will lift hammers closer to the strings for viewing from above. Moving a hammer over a bit to realign it with the strings is usually a simple matter, but if the hammer has become grooved in the misaligned position, the misaligned grooves will constantly "seek" the strings, attempting to move the hammer back into the wrong position every time you play the note. Eventually this will weaken or break the hammer at its pivot point. This problem can be avoided by

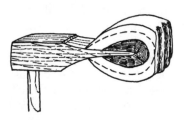

FIGURE 5-25. When hammers are flattened and deeply grooved, for best tone they should be reshaped by sanding off a layer of felt. But too little felt on the hammer—both at the striking point and on the shoulders—can make the tone ugly and hard. Imagine restoring the hammer to its rounded-point shape (indicated by the dotted line). Would there still be a reasonable amount of felt left? Not on this hammer.

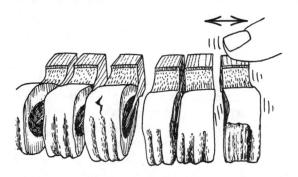

FIGURE 5-26. Unless the piano is brand new or the hammers have recently been reshaped, they will probably have some grooves in them. The grooves should be well defined and approximately centered on the hammers. In this drawing, the fourth hammer from the left has moved so it is hitting only two of its three strings (the third string appears to have worn away the very edge of the hammer). The right-most hammer has only a broad worn spot indicating, as does the finger test, that the hammer is wobbly. Realigning or repairing misaligned or wobbly hammers is not in itself a big job, but the realignment or repair could be temporary unless hammers are resurfaced or, in some cases, replaced.

resurfacing the hammers to eliminate the grooves, but, as I said, if there isn't enough felt left to resurface, the hammer heads will have to be replaced. Thus, in appraising the condition of the hammers, the presence of deep grooves becomes critical if many hammers are misaligned with the strings.

Look at the grooves one last time. Do any of the hammers have poorly defined grooves—just a broad flat spot at the striking point? This indicates that the hammer has been wobbly from side to side, striking the strings at a slightly different point with each stroke. You can also check for wobbly hammers by running your fingers lightly over the tops of the hammers, wiggling them slightly from left to right as you go. Each hammer should be fairly rigid at its pivot

point, snapping back quickly to its central position as you let go of it. The wobbly hammers will stand out quite easily. (*Caution:* Don't try to move a non-wobbly hammer to the left or right more than about ⅟₁₆ of an inch, or you may damage the action center [pivot point].) Wobbly hammers are caused by either loose hammer flange screws (the screws that attach the hammer assemblies to the action rail) or by loose or defective action centers. Tightening loose screws is a simple, inexpensive, and normal maintenance procedure [163]. Repinning or repairing action centers is also relatively simple and inexpensive if only a few need to be done, but can turn into a major expense if a large number of hammers are involved. Whether the problem is due to loose screws or defective action centers (or both) will be hard for you to determine by yourself. But regardless of which it turns out to be, the result is usually badly misshapen hammers which, if you're lucky, will need only to be resurfaced, and at worst, will need to be replaced.

The action centers on which the hammers pivot are sometimes too *tight*. On a vertical, push groups of five or six hammers at a time toward the strings with your hand, release them, and watch for any slow returners. You won't be able to do this on a grand until the action is removed, but you can watch the hammers through the strings as you play several keys at a time. A few sluggish action parts are usually not a major problem. If many hammers, or even a whole set of hammers, are sluggish, repair can be moderately expensive, but sometimes not out of the question, even for an old upright. The advisability of doing this will depend on the cause and severity of the problem and whether wholesale replacement of parts is necessary or if simpler remedies will suffice.

One last hammer problem and we'll move on to something else. Hammer *heads* sometimes become loose on their shanks due to drying and cracking of the glue joint, and will make a slight clicking sound at the moment the hammer hits the string. Test for this by wiggling the hammer heads up and down (in relation to the shank). If they wiggle at all, they're loose (Figure 5-27). Regluing loose hammer heads is about the same size job as repairing loose or tight action centers.

Dampers. Dampers are the felt pads and wedges that rest against the strings to keep them from vibrating when they're not supposed to (Figure 5-28). Are they doing their job? Play each note and release it, making sure that it stops ringing promptly. (Note: The strings in the top couple of octaves don't have dampers and are supposed to keep ringing.) Do many of the dampers buzz when they come back down on the strings?

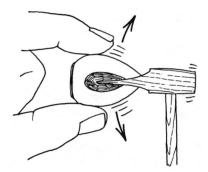

FIGURE 5-27. A loose hammer head will make a slight clicking sound at the moment it hits the strings. Test for this by gently trying to move it up and down. Any looseness is too much. A loose hammer head can be removed and reglued inexpensively.

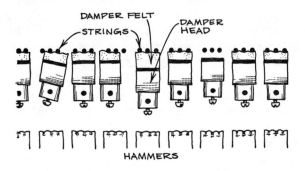

FIGURE 5-28. A row of vertical piano dampers resting against their strings, as seen from above. Notice that the felt on the damper in the center of the drawing has been replaced, and that the other damper felts, in contrast, appear to be quite worn. Some of the dampers are also misaligned and may not be damping all of their strings. One damper felt is missing.

It may be time for a new set of damper felts if they do, usually a moderate-cost repair. Press the right-hand pedal slowly and see if all the dampers rise off the strings at precisely the same moment. If not, they may need regulating. Damper problems are sometimes difficult to solve, but not usually so expensive or severe that they should prevent you from buying a piano that has them.

Pedals. Do all the pedals work? If not, investigate to see why not (see page 53 and Figure 3-33 for a description of how the pedals and trapwork operate). In a vertical, often a dowel will be missing or out of place or the pedal will need minor adjustment. The vertical piano's pedal system is very simple, and usually inexpensive to fix or adjust. The grand's pedal system is a lot more complicated, and since some of it is located behind the action, you may need a technician to inspect it. One thing you *can* check on a grand is whether the pedal lyre is coming apart at the joints, or

falling off the piano (Figure 5-29). Both conditions can be fixed at moderate expense. Loose and noisy pedals are usually relatively minor problems on both grands and verticals. However, on verticals, do check to make sure that the board to which the pedals are attached isn't cracking, bending, or falling off the bottom of the piano (this, too, can be fixed at low to moderate expense).

Is there a middle pedal? What does it do? If you are buying a grand and are a serious player of classical music, you may desire a true sostenuto pedal. You probably won't need it often, but when you do, there is no substitute for it. Some cheaper grands have a middle pedal that just lifts the bass dampers—a fairly useless feature. This feature is standard for many verticals. Some verticals don't have a middle pedal, or have one that never worked or no longer works—no great loss!

As discussed on page 54, the left pedal of a vertical piano makes the sound quieter by pushing the hammers closer to the strings, but in doing so it puts the action out of adjustment. Some old uprights were outfitted with a "lost motion compensator" mechanism (Figure 5-30) that allowed the action to remain in proper adjustment when this pedal was used. Vertical pianos with a lost motion compensator or a true sostenuto mechanism, or both, were usually among the best old uprights made and are often still in good condition.

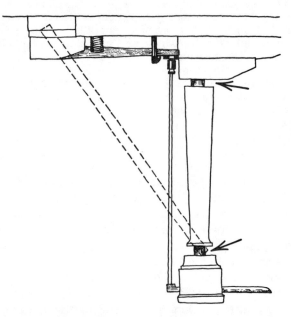

FIGURE 5-29. A grand piano pedal lyre seen from the side. The arrows point to where it's coming apart at the joints. Lyres on old pianos, particularly ones that have been moved many times, are often missing their diagonal lyre braces, shown here by dotted lines. These braces help the lyre to withstand the constant pressure of the feet on the pedals. They can be replaced inexpensively.

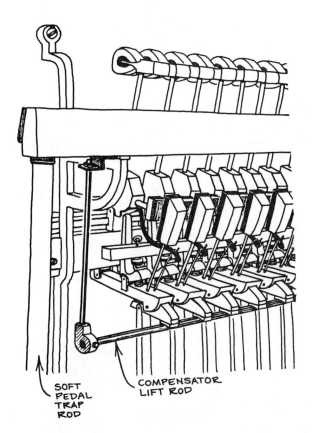

FIGURE 5-30. A lost motion compensator in an old upright piano. This mechanism took up the slack, or "lost motion," in the action that was created when the hammers were pushed closer to the strings.

Regulation. *Regulating* is the process of making technical adjustments to the piano action to compensate for the effects of wear and atmospheric changes on the wood and cloth parts that have occurred over the months and years of use, and to restore the functioning of the action as close as possible to the original factory specifications. The cost can vary from very cheap for minor amounts of regulating to moderate (one to two hundred dollars) for a complete vertical piano regulation to very expensive (three to six hundred dollars) for a complete grand action regulation. A full technical discussion of regulating would be too lengthy to be included here, but to give you an idea of what regulating involves, a few examples are included in Figure 5-32. Your technician can more fully evaluate the piano's regulation needs later. How much importance you should place on proper action regulation depends on how fine an instrument you're buying and on your level of technical skill. However, playing on a piano that is grossly out of regulation can be very frustrating, and possibly harmful to the piano.

Serial number. Find the serial number of the piano so you can look up its year of manufacture in the *Pierce*

Piano Atlas [120]. Usually four to eight digits, the serial number is most often located near the tuning pins, either printed directly on the plate or engraved in the wooden pinblock and showing through a cut-away portion of the plate. Or the number may be printed somewhere else on the plate or soundboard, printed or engraved on the top or back of a vertical piano back, or printed or engraved on the front edge of a grand piano key frame (Figure 5-31). (Sometimes a three- or four-digit number used in the manufacturing process also appears on various case parts; don't confuse this with the serial number.) When no serial number can be found or if the year of manufacture isn't listed in *Pierce*, sometimes a technician can estimate the age within about ten years just by looking at the case styling or technical details.

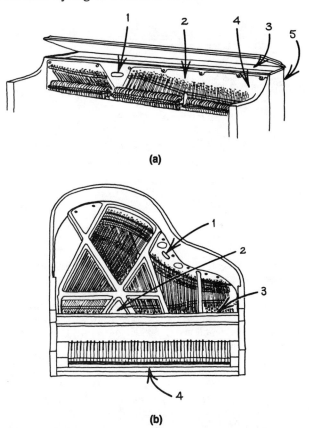

FIGURE 5-31. (a) The serial number of a vertical piano can usually be found in position 1, either stamped on the plate or engraved in the pinblock and showing through a cut-away portion of the plate. Positions 2 and 4, also on the plate, are other possibilities. On newer pianos, the serial number is sometimes on the top of the piano back (position 3) or stamped on the back of the piano (position 5). (b) The serial number of a grand piano is usually in position 2, stamped on the plate or engraved in the pinblock; elsewhere on the plate or soundboard (such as positions 1 and 3); or stamped on the front of the key frame (position 4). Access to the key frame is gained by removing the keyslip (for directions, see Figure 5-8).

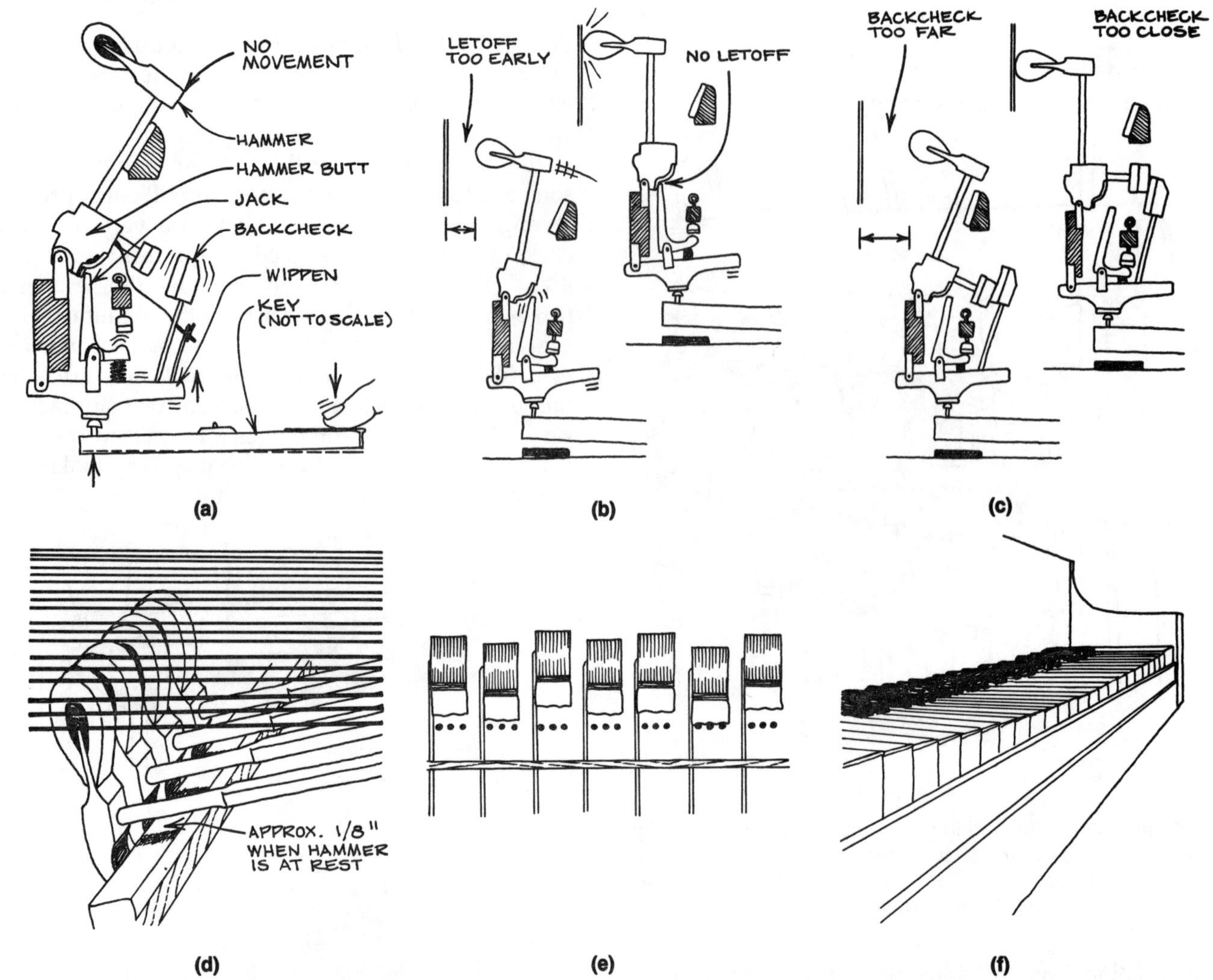

(a)

(b)

(c)

(d)

(e)

(f)

FIGURE 5-32. A few examples of what is meant when an action is said to be "out of regulation." See Chapter 1 for details of action operation. (a) When you just begin to press a key down on a vertical piano, the hammer should respond immediately. Sometimes the wippen and attached parts (such as the backcheck), will move a lot before the hammer will respond. This is due to a space between the top of the jack and the hammer butt, which causes slack in the action known as *lost motion*. This wasted motion can cause the action to malfunction. (b) The jack, which imparts power to the hammer, should disengage when the hammer is about ⅛ inch from the string (sometimes a little more on spinets and consoles and a little less on concert grands). This allows the hammer to go the rest of the way to the string on its own momentum and then freely rebound. You can test for this disengagement by pressing a key down very slowly and watching a hammer. (If you press slowly enough, the hammer won't even reach the string because of a lack of momentum.) The point of disengagement is known as *escapement* or *letoff*. When letoff occurs too early (that is, when the hammer is too far from the string), the hammer won't have enough momentum to reach the string when a key is played softly and will "miss." If letoff occurs too late (when the hammer is too close to the string), there is a risk it won't occur at all and the hammer will jam

against the string, damping its sound and possibly breaking it. (c) When a note is played normally, the backcheck should catch the hammer on the rebound roughly ⅝ inch from the string. If the hammer is caught too far from the string, the ability to repeat notes may be affected. If the hammer is caught too close, the hammer may jam against the string. If the backcheck doesn't catch the hammer at all, repetition may be affected, the hammer may double-strike the string, and the touch may feel strange. (d) Hammers seen through the strings of a grand piano. When grand piano hammers are at rest, the hammer shanks should be suspended about ⅛ inch (sometimes a little more) above the hammer rest rail or rest cushions. If the shanks are actually resting on the rail or cushions, the action may not function correctly. This applies to a grand piano action only. (e) When the sustain pedal, grand or vertical, is pressed, all the dampers should rise simultaneously as if made of one piece of wood and felt. Press the pedal very slowly to test for this. The drawing shows grand dampers rising at different times to different heights. (f) The keyboard should be perfectly level from one end to the other (although some are regulated slightly higher in the center in anticipation of settling). Over time, the well-used center area settles due to compacting of the key frame cloth under the keys. The drawing, slightly exaggerated, shows what this might look like as you sight down the keyboard from one end.

Close the piano now, reversing the instructions in Figures 5-5 through 5-13. Play the piano again and listen to the tone. Is there a smooth transition in tone from one end of the keyboard to the other, or are some sections completely different in character from the others? Do the bass strings sound full and alive, or dead and muffled? Do the few lowest and highest notes have a definite pitch and pleasing sound, or are they indistinct and essentially useless? Are you pleased with the tonal quality, brightness, and volume? Remember that: (1) room acoustics have a significant effect on tonal quality; (2) if the piano is out of tune, you may not be able to make an informed judgment about the tone; and (3) to some extent, tone can be altered by a technician through a process known as *voicing* or *tone regulating*. Read about all this in Chapter 3 [41] and in Chapter 7 [163].

This concludes the portion of the inspection that you can do yourself. If you later have a technician look at the piano, he or she will go over much the same ground you did, in addition checking the tightness of the tuning pins with a tuning hammer or a torque wrench, removing and inspecting the action of a grand piano, evaluating the state of the action regulation, and possibly measuring the downbearing of the strings against the bridge to check for possible soundboard and tone problems. Some technicians prefer to check out a piano alone, later issuing a written or oral report, whereas others wouldn't mind your presence and might be happy to answer your questions as they work.

HOW MUCH IS IT WORTH?

Ultimately, something is worth only as much as someone will pay for it. There is no "Blue Book" for used pianos, and their prices vary capriciously depending on the locale and the particular situation.

The value of a piano also depends very much on how knowledgeable the seller and potential buyers are. For every piano, there is what I would call an "informed value" and an "ignorant value." The informed value takes into account the technical quality and condition of the piano, whereas the ignorant value does not, being based primarily on how the piano case looks (if even that). Unfortunately, the ignorant value is more often than not what the piano actually sells for.

For example, I was recently called to inspect an old upright piano that the prospective buyer, my client, said had a beautiful case, seemed to need only tuning, and was "about fifty years old." The asking price was $700. As soon as I took off the upper panel, I knew that only the part about the "beautiful case" was accurate. The piano, in fact, was ninety-five years old and had almost every problem a piano could have and still play. The sellers were clearly as surprised as we were about the age and condition (don't ask me how they arrived at the asking price) and as we were leaving asked me how much I thought it was worth. I thought a moment and then said, "To a private buyer, I couldn't recommend it at any price, so it's worth nothing. But it's possible that a rebuilder would give you $50 or $100 for it." Then I added, somewhat reluctantly, "If you hold out awhile, though, you'll probably get $700 for it from someone who doesn't bring a technician along to inspect it." And with that, I left them to ponder the ethical dilemma of whether to continue asking $700 for the piano.

So how much was that piano actually "worth"? The value I assigned to it was an artificial one, based on my moral and technical sense and expertise. The seller's value was based (at least theoretically) on an observation of market conditions. The piano was clearly worth something very different to each party. In practice, when a piano is worth buying but the informed value and the market value differ substantially (such as with spinets), I will usually suggest some sort of compromise value. When the transaction is between friends, or where the seller isn't interested in making money, my figure is usually accepted. But if there is competition for the piano, the buyer may have to pay more.

My experience is that, in most private transactions, the seller hasn't the foggiest notion of what the piano is worth, and the asking price is vastly overinflated, often based on such considerations as that "Uncle Joe liked this piano, and he played all his life, so it must be a fine instrument." I'm not exaggerating! In these cases, there's plenty of room for negotiating. If the piano needs considerable repair, encourage the technician to tell you this in front of the seller, as it will better your bargaining position. Even where the seller knows the informed value of the instrument, the asking price is usually set high in the expectation of bargaining, and you can generally expect to agree at a price of from 10 to 30 percent less.

As I said, prices for used pianos vary greatly from place to place, time to time, and situation to situation. Nevertheless, as many readers of this book are undoubtedly looking for at least some general price information, I have compiled a list of the approximate selling prices of various ages, makes, and types of piano, gathered from my contacts around the country. Twenty-five technicians returned a questionnaire in which they listed the average low and average high selling prices (*not* asking prices) in their area for the pianos described here. The descriptions were, of necessity, brief and vague, but all the pianos were said to be in salable condition, and, unless otherwise noted, were for sale by a private owner, were not rebuilt, and were not Steinways.

I was not prepared for the incredible variation in prices that exists from place to place. To try to make some sense out of this situation, I have calculated three sets of prices for each item, rounded off and sometimes adjusted slightly for consistency. The first set is the very lowest average low and average high prices reported by anyone; the second set is the average reported average low and average high prices; and the third set is the very highest average low and average high prices reported. (Note that the extremes listed are not isolated aberrations, but actual average low and average high prices in some communities.) Your community may not neatly fall into one of these categories, but places with a depressed economy, little musical life, or a glut of pianos will probably tend toward the lower end, while locales with a high standard of living, a brisk piano trade, and a scarcity of good pianos, technicians, and rebuilders (or some combination of these factors) will tend toward the higher end. Or at least so it should be in theory. Obviously this list will be useful only in a most general way. You should consult your technician about prices and availability in your area.

Prices of Used Pianos

	Low Range	Average Range	High Range
Upright, pre-1930, average worn condition	$ 0–100	$ 200–400	$ 500–800
Upright, pre-1930, better condition (has received minor repair, cleaning, etc.)	75–300	300–600	750–1,000
Upright, pre-1930, very good condition (has received major reconditioning)	100–500	650–1,050	1,000–1,800
Studio, 1930–1950, fair condition	100–450	450–800	1,000–1,500
Studio, 1950–1970, good condition	300–500	600–1,200	1,200–1,800
Studio, 1950–1970, very good condition	500–1,000	900–1,450	1,500–2,200
Console or spinet, 1930–1950, fair condition	100–400	400–600	700–900
Console or spinet, 1950–1970, good condition	200–500	500–900	800–1,200
Console or spinet, 1950–1970, very good condition	500–800	750–1,300	1,100–1,600
Grand, pre-1930, average brand, average worn condition, 5' +	200–500	650–1,300	1,200–3,000
6'	300–500	900–1,800	2,500–4,000
Grand, pre-1930, better brand, (e.g., Knabe or Chickering), well-maintained, 5' +	600–1,400	1,300–2,100	3,000–3,500
6'	800–1,500	1,650–2,700	3,500–4,500
Grand, 1930–1950, better brand, good condition, 5'	800–1,500	1,800–2,900	4,000–5,000
6'	800–1,500	2,250–3,550	5,000–6,000
Grand, 1950–1970, mediocre brand (e.g., Aeolian), good condition, 5'	700–1,100	1,200–2,100	2,000–3,000
6'	800–1,200	1,500–2,500	3,000–4,000
Grand, 1950–1970, better brand, very good condition, 5'	1,000–1,800	2,200–3,450	4,000–6,000
6'	1,000–1,800	2,900–4,500	5,000–7,000

Note: Add 10 to 30 percent (sometimes up to 50 percent) for an "equivalent" piano from a technician instead of a private owner.
Steinway pianos usually sell for one-and-a-half to three times (sometimes as much as four) times the above prices.

Depreciation. The "fair market value" method of appraising pianos, presented above, is actually only one of three methods commonly used by professional appraisers. A second is the "depreciation" method, especially useful for appraising pianos of recent make when the models are still in production. To use it, one needs to find out how much a new piano of the same or comparable make and model would cost now, and then look up the age of the subject piano on a depreciation schedule. The percentage given represents what the piano is worth relative to the cost of a new one. There is no universally agreed-upon depreciation schedule for pianos, but one such schedule is provided below. This method works fairly well for pianos of average quality which have had a normal amount of wear. For better quality pianos, or pianos that have had either very little or far too much use, the values produced this way must be adjusted accordingly.

Depreciation Schedule for Pianos

Age in Years	Percent of New Value	Age in Years	Percent of New Value
1	85	20	43
2	82	25	34
3	80	Verticals only:	
5	74	30	27
8	67	35 to 70	20
10	62	Grands only:	
15	52	30 to 70	30

Depreciation schedule courtesy of Stephen H. Brady, RTT, Seattle, Washington

A third appraisal method is the "idealized value minus cost of restoration" method. If a rebuilt piano of the same or comparable model costs $15,000, and it would cost $10,000 to restore your piano to like-new condition, then according to this method your piano is currently worth $5,000.

These three methods of appraising will typically yield three very different values. Which you choose to use will depend to some extent on your reason for having the piano appraised (buying, selling, insurance appraisal, etc.). Professional appraisers will sometimes use all three methods and then take an average to obtain a final value.

AFTER THE SALE

Moving. If you buy from a private owner, moving costs are your responsibility unless the seller agrees otherwise. If you buy from a technician, rebuilder, or dealer, moving charges may be included in the price of the piano or may not be; you should inquire. See Chapter 6 for more information about moving.

Warranty. You receive no warranty, of course, when you buy from a private owner. All other sellers should provide at least a one-year warranty covering parts and labor for all repair work other than that needed to correct normal changes in tuning, regulation, and voicing. Be sure to get the warranty in writing. If the seller doesn't have enough confidence in the piano to guarantee it for at least one year, don't buy it. Pianos that have had extensive reconditioning or rebuilding work are customarily guaranteed for longer periods. It's not unusual for a completely rebuilt piano to be guaranteed for five years. A technician's warranty, however, is only good as long as he or she is in business. One rule of thumb might be that every two years a technician has been in business gives value to one year of warranty. Be sure to follow the terms of the warranty as to proper maintenance and climate control or you may void it.

If you have bought a piano from a commercial source (such as a technician or dealer), did not receive an adequate warranty, and are having problems with the piano that are not being solved to your satisfaction by the seller, you may still have legal recourse. Some states have *implied warranty laws* on the books that protect you even though you were not given a warranty in writing.

In Massachusetts, for instance, there are implied warranties of "merchantability" and "fitness for a particular purpose." Under the implied warranty of merchantability, a piano that will not hold its tune due to a defective pinblock is not merchantable (salable). Under the implied warranty of fitness for a particular purpose, the consumer relies on the seller's skill or judgment to select goods that are suitable. An antique square piano sold as a practice instrument would probably be judged as unfit for its particular purpose. These warranties come automatically with every sale and the seller cannot disclaim them by saying they don't apply in your case. Check with your state office of consumer affairs or a similar state agency for details.

Tuning. Most dealers and technicians include one home tuning in the sale price. This tuning should be done no sooner than two weeks after delivery, as it takes at least that long for the piano to adjust to the new conditions. Note also that if you are buying a piano that has recently been restrung, it may need more frequent tuning during the first year.

SELLING YOUR PIANO

Much of the information in this chapter about buying a piano is equally applicable to selling one. Use it to determine where, how, and for how much to advertise your piano. But one more piece of advice remains: tune your piano before you advertise it. You are probably thinking that since the buyer will have to have the piano tuned after moving it anyway, you might as well save money by not having it tuned now. But most prospective buyers know so little about the piano that when an instrument they encounter is out of tune or has some keys that don't work quite right, they have no way of knowing whether the problem is major or minor, or how the piano would sound after being tuned. Buyers will often reject out of hand a perfectly good piano because of relatively insignificant problems. By having the piano tuned and minor repairs made before selling it, you will eliminate any problems that would distract or confuse a prospective buyer. In my experience, piano owners who do this sell their pianos much faster and at a higher price than those who don't, easily recovering their expenses several-fold.

ADDENDUM: BUYING A USED STEINWAY

A question frequently asked is "Should I buy a new or a used Steinway?" or, put another way, "Is a fully rebuilt Steinway as good, or better, than a new one?" These questions are important, because a rebuilt Steinway usually costs from 25 to 50 percent less than a new one, and an older, used Steinway in playing condition (but not rebuilt) often sells for half the cost of a rebuilt one.

There are no clear answers to these questions. Naturally, technicians who are primarily rebuilders will point you in one direction and those who primarily sell or service new pianos will point you in the other. But technicians who both rebuild old Steinways *and* sell or service new ones are torn between the two options, and say that it really depends on the particular new and rebuilt pianos being compared, and on the use the piano will be getting. As I said in Chapter 5, a piano considered by one technician to be rebuilt might be considered by another technician to be only reconditioned, and the technical competence of rebuilders varies considerably. So does the condition of new pianos.

A rebuilt piano is not the exact equivalent of a new one. Even a fully and competently rebuilt piano will still retain the original case, cast-iron plate, keys, key frame, and action frame, and possibly the soundboard and some of the action parts, too. (Some technicians would say that the piano has not been *fully* rebuilt if the soundboard has not been replaced, but there is no general agreement about this.) These original parts will probably not give any trouble for the next twenty or thirty years if the piano was properly rebuilt and is well maintained, but it's hard to say for sure, especially about the soundboard and action parts, if not replaced, and about the keys, which may get brittle.

If you're considering the purchase of a model B or D Steinway grand for professional or institutional use, and an older piano to which a new one is being compared was manufactured before about 1900, my sense is that the age of the older piano, the heavy use the piano will be getting (probably with little climate control), and the fact that new model B and D Steinways contain German-made action parts and get extra care at the factory, would all tip the balance a little in favor of buying the new one. But if you're buying one of the smaller models, primarily for casual use in the home, the purchase of a used or rebuilt Steinway would be a very reasonable way to save money, and, if you buy wisely, it's unlikely you would ever regret having made the purchase. These two situations are, of course, at opposite extremes. If you're buying a larger model for casual use or a smaller model that will be getting heavy use, the choice between new and used will be more difficult.

List of Steinway Models

As an aid to those buying a used Steinway, I have listed below all models of Steinway piano made in New York City since the firm's inception in 1853.* Since this list has never before been published, I have, for the record, given a much more complete list than most piano buyers will ever need. Hopefully, piano technicians and historians will also find the list useful. (Square pianos and other pianos made before about 1880 are listed for academic purposes only; see page 117 for information on buying square and antique pianos.)

Note that entries in the list refer to models in regular stock manufacture only, as they appeared in catalogs and price lists. There are no listings here of the different furniture styles available in each model, or of custom cases or experimental variations that were made from time to time. During the formative years of Steinway & Sons, an immense amount of experimentation and development was in progress. Hence, some details are elusive, especially concerning pianos built during the first twenty-five years of manufacture. This list is based on the best available information to date, but should not be considered infallible.

The keyboard compass (range) began at seven octaves (eighty-five notes, AAA to a'''', unless otherwise indicated) and was gradually expanded to seven and a third octaves (eighty-eight notes, AAA to c'''''). Because most of the dates listed here are from catalogs, whereas the serial numbers are from production records, dates and serial numbers may not match each other exactly, and dates may differ by a year or so from other versions of this list in circulation. Also, a given model may have been manufactured or sold in limited quantities after the time it was officially discontinued.

Steinway & Sons piano manufacture officially began on March 5, 1853, but the first illustrated catalog did not appear until 1865. Until 1861 piano styles were identified by name (plain, fancy, double round, middle round, prime, and so on). In that year Steinway began to assign style numbers to their pianos and by 1866 each piano was designated in this way. These early style numbers, however, referred to both differences in scale design and differences in furniture styling. Furthermore, the style to which each number referred changed from year to year, and so the numbers cannot be relied upon for identification. An 1878 catalog lists pianos by style *letter* as well as style number for the first time, and letters and numbers appeared together in the catalogs through 1896, after which letters were used exclusively. During the nineteenth century some letters, like the numbers, were used to designate more than one scale design or style, but in the twentieth century a given letter has been applied to only one scale design regardless of the case styling. In 1932 the term *style* was replaced by *model* in price lists and catalogs. In the list below, to avoid confusion, only the word *model* is used and, as I said, furniture style variations are omitted.

*I gratefully acknowledge Mr. Roy Kehl, piano technician, of Evanston, Illinois for generously sharing with me the results of his research into the history of Steinway scale designs, from which this list was largely developed. Additional information was received from Arthur Reblitz in Colorado Springs, and from Henry Z. Steinway, Peter Goodrich, and William Garlick, all of Steinway & Sons in New York.

Steinway (New York) Models — 1853 to Present

	Compass	Size	Dates	Serial No.
SQUARE PIANOS				
Early scales	7 (CC to c''''')		1853–c. 1856	(First) 483
	7⅓ (AAA to c''''')		1853–c. 1863	(First) 495
	6¾		1854–c. 1863	(First) 499
	7 (AAA to a'''')		1854–c. 1863	
	6¼		1855–c. 1859	(First) 587
	6⅞		1856–c. 1862	(First) 891
Small scales	7	6'8"	c. 1865–1881	
	7⅓	6'8"	1881–1885	
Medium scales	7⅓	6'8½"	c. 1865–1873	
Large scales	7⅓	6'11½"	c. 1865–1888	(Last) 62,872
GRAND PIANOS				
Model D Concert Grand (and ancestors)	7 (parallel-strung)	c. 8'	1856–1859	(First) 791
	7 (overstrung)	8'5"	1859–1864	(First) 2,522
	7⅓	8'5"	1865–1877	(First) 9,326
	7⅓	8'9"	1876–1883	(First) 33,449

The model D pianos above have a 17-note bass section; those below have a 20-note bass section.

	Compass	Size	Dates	Serial No.
	7⅓	8'10"	1884–1913	
	7⅓	8'11¼"	1914–1966	
	7⅓	8'11¾"	1967–	(First) c. 178,700
Model C Parlor Concert Grand (and ancestors)	7	7'1"	1861–1869	(First) 2,485
	7	7'2"	1870–1883	
	7	7'3½"	1884–1886	

The model C pianos above have a 21-note bass section; that below has a 20-note bass section.

	Compass	Size	Dates	Serial No.
	7⅓	7'5"	1886–c. 1933	(First) 58,952 (Last) 276,811

Model C was listed in the catalog and price list through 1905 and said to be discontinued in 1913, but was reportedly made or sold as late as 1933 in New York. This model is still made in Steinway's Hamburg factory.

	Compass	Size	Dates	Serial No.
Model B Music-Room Grand (and ancestors)	7	6'8"	1872–1883	(First) 24,xxx
	7	6'10½"	1884–1892	(Last) 75,473
	7⅓	6'10½"	1891–1913	(First) 73,212
	7⅓	6'11½"	1914–1917	
	7⅓	6'11"	1917–1966	
	7⅓	6'10½"	1967–	

	Compass	Size	Dates	Serial No.
Model A Drawing-Room Grand	7	6'1"	1878–1893	(First) 38,887
	7⅓	6'1"	1892–1897	(First) 74,766

The model A pianos listed above have 57 wound strings, including two two-string unisons and seven three-string unisons strung over a separate tenor bridge. The pianos listed below have 42 wound strings, including five two-string unisons in the tenor, but no separate tenor bridge. The pianos above have round tails, those below have square tails. The squared-off tail allows for more soundboard vibrating area near the bass bridge. The pianos above, although officially listed in catalogs of the period as being 6', usually measure between 6' and 6'1", and are known in the trade as being 6'1". The one listed below as 6'1", also officially given in catalogs as 6', usually measures between 6'1" and 6'2". This is the model A currently made at Steinway's Hamburg factory as 6'2". The versions of model A below are considered to be of a superior scale design to those listed above. The 6'4½" model A is sometimes known as model A III.

	Compass	Size	Dates	Serial No.
	7⅓	6'1"	1896–1913	(First) 86,272
	7⅓	6'4½"	1913–1947	(First) 163,422
				(Last) 321,289
Model O and Model L Living-Room Grand	7⅓	5'10" (O)	1900–1913	(First) 96,766

Earliest specimens have two-string wound unisons on the two lowest tenor notes; later ones have all steel wire three-string unisons in the tenor. Early specimens have a straight bass bridge; later ones have a curved bass bridge.

	Compass	Size	Dates	Serial No.
	7⅓	5'10½" (O)	1914–1923	(Last) 221,xxx

The model O, above, has a round tail. The model L, below, has a square tail. The squared-off tail allows for more soundboard vibrating area near the bass bridge. This is the only difference between the model O and model L. The model O is still made in Steinway's Hamburg factory.

	Compass	Size	Dates	Serial No.
	7⅓	5'10½" (L)	1923–	(First) 219,684
Model M Medium Grand	7⅓	5'6"	1911–1914	(First) 149,500
	7⅓	5'6¾"	1914–1917	
	7⅓	5'7"	1917–	(First) 178,001
Model S Baby Grand	7⅓	5'1"	1935–1965; 1977–	(First) 280,900

GRAND REPRODUCING (PLAYER) PIANOS

From 1909 to 1932, Steinway made grands with extended cases for the Aeolian Piano Co., who installed the Duo-Art reproducing mechanism. (In Hamburg, reproducing mechanisms were installed by both Aeolian and Welte.) Reportedly, the suffix "Y" was used instead of "R" on some pianos repossessed from Aeolian in the early 1930s when Steinway removed the reproducer and shortened the case.

Model XR   6'1¾" or 6'2"

The model XR used the 5'6", 5'6¾", or 5'7" model M piano. Rarely encountered "UR" and "XU" designations are the same as the XR.

Model OR   6'5"

The model OR used the 5'10½" model O (and later, model L) piano. The rarely encountered "XO" designation is the same as the OR.

Model AR   6'8½"
                                                                                 6'11¼" or 6'11½"

The first model AR listed above used the 6'1" model A piano; the second used the 6'4½" model A.

Model D or DR   9'5¾"

The model D or DR reproducer used the 8'11¼" model D piano.

	Compass	Size	Dates	Serial No.

UPRIGHT PIANOS—NINETEENTH CENTURY (1862 TO 1898)

The first upright was made in 1862, serial number 5,451, and had a compass of seven octaves. Information is incomplete for 1862 to 1864.

Model E (and ancestors)	7	45"	c. 1865–1868	
	7	48"	1869–1871	
	7	46"	1872–1883	
	7	48"	1884–1892	
	7⅓	50"	1891–1898	(First) 73,333
Model F (and ancestors and successors)	7	52½"	c. 1865–1866	
	7	52"	1869–1873	
	7	52¼"	1878–1881	
	7⅓	53¾"	1882–1883	
	7⅓	53½"	1884–1898	

Other letter-named style variations on model F include N, O, L, R, T, X, H, and S.

| Model G (and ancestors and successors) | 7⅓ | 56" | 1874–1883 | |
| | 7⅓ | 56¾" | 1884–1898 | |

Other letter-named style variations on model G include M, P, Q, S, U, K, and T.

UPRIGHT PIANOS—TWENTIETH CENTURY (1898 TO PRESENT)

Model I	7⅓	54¼"	1898–1913	(First) 91,702
	7⅓	54"	1914–1923	
Model N	7⅓	52"	1900–1912	(First) 95,105
Models K and K-52	7⅓	52"	1903–1913	(First) 107,181
	7⅓	51½"	1914–1929	
	7⅓	52" (K-52)	1981–	(First) 472,970
Model V	7⅓	49"	1913–1934	(Last) 279,xxx

Earliest specimens of model V have 52 wound strings; later ones have 46. This model is currently made in Steinway's Hamburg factory.

STUDIO AND CONSOLE PIANOS (1938 TO THE PRESENT)

Models P and 45	7⅓	45½" (P)	1938–1960	(First) 291,575
	7⅓	46½" (45, Sk. 1098)	1952–	(First) 335,580
	7⅓	45" (45, Sk. 45-10)	1959–	
Models 40, 100 and F	7⅓	40" (40)	1939–1953	(First) 297,092
	7⅓	40" (100)	1953–1971	(Last) 418,392
	7⅓	40" (F)	1967–1987	(First) 402,637
				(Last) 502,807

Ages of Steinway Pianos

To determine the year of manufacture of a particular Steinway piano, find the serial number on this list that is closest to, but higher than, the serial number of the piano. The year listed next to it is the approximate year of manufacture.

1,000 1856	35,000 1877	125,000 1907	215,000 1923	281,000 1936	340,000 1953	423,000 1971	
2,000 1858	40,000 1878	130,000 1908	220,000 1923	284,000 1936	343,000 1954	426,000 1972	
3,000 1860	45,000 1881	135,000 1909	225,000 1924	289,000 1937	346,500 1955	431,000 1973	
5,000 1861	50,000 1883	140,000 1910	230,000 1925	290,000 1938	350,000 1956	436,000 1974	
7,000 1863	55,000 1886	145,000 1911	235,000 1925	294,000 1939	355,000 1957	439,000 1975	
9,000 1864	60,000 1887	150,000 1911	240,000 1926	300,000 1940	358,000 1958	445,000 1976	
11,000 1865	65,000 1889	155,000 1912	250,000 1927	305,000 1941	362,000 1959	450,000 1977	
13,000 1866	70,000 1891	160,000 1913	255,000 1927	310,000 1942	366,000 1960	455,300 1978	
15,000 1867	75,000 1893	165,000 1914	260,000 1928	314,000 1943	370,000 1961	463,000 1979	
17,000 1869	80,000 1894	170,000 1915	265,000 1929	316,000 1944	375,000 1962	468,500 1980	
19,000 1869	85,000 1896	175,000 1916	270,000 1930	317,000 1945	380,000 1963	473,500 1981	
21,000 1870	90,000 1898	180,000 1917	271,000 1931	319,000 1946	385,000 1964	478,500 1982	
23,000 1871	95,000 1900	185,000 1917	273,000 1932	322,000 1947	390,000 1965	483,000 1983	
25,000 1872	100,000 1901	190,000 1918	274,000 1932	324,000 1948	395,000 1966	488,000 1984	
27,000 1873	105,000 1902	195,000 1919	275,000 1933	328,000 1949	400,000 1967	493,000 1985	
29,000 1874	110,000 1904	200,000 1920	276,000 1933	331,000 1950	405,000 1968	498,000 1986	
31,000 1875	115,000 1905	205,000 1921	278,000 1934	334,000 1951	412,000 1969	503,000 1987	
33,000 1876	120,000 1906	210,000 1922	279,000 1935	337,000 1952	418,000 1970	507,700 1988	
						512,600 1989	

Teflon bushings. All moving piano action parts pivot on small metal pins, called **center pins**, that rotate in tiny holes in the wooden parts. Traditionally, these holes have always been lined, or *bushed*, with wool cloth. These cloth **flange bushings** (flanges are the hinges to which action parts are attached) are amazingly durable and resilient, and it is not unusual for a hundred-year-old piano to have flange bushings that are almost as good as new. The only problem with them is that, like the wood around them, they respond to humidity changes, swelling up in damp weather and shrinking in dry weather, causing the attached moving parts to become alternately sluggish or loose.

To minimize the servicing that its pianos needed from one season or climate to another, Steinway in 1962 introduced its "Permafree" action, in which all the cloth bushings were replaced with Teflon bushings. Teflon, created by DuPont, is a very slippery inert plastic, immune to temperature and humidity changes. The bushings were tiny, hollow cylinders of Teflon; the center pins would rotate in these instead of in cloth (Figure 5-33). Switching to Teflon bushings involved changing more than just the bushings themselves, though. To accommodate the new bushings required manufacturing the wooden parts differently, making a new kind of center pin, supplying new tools and supplies, and teaching new techniques to technicians who had to service these actions.

Several unforeseen problems with these bushings eventually caused their downfall. First, although they themselves did not respond to humidity changes, the wood around them continued to expand and contract with the seasons. This had the unexpected effect of causing some of the bushings to become loose in their wooden parts during the humid season (the opposite of what one might guess), resulting in a clicking sound whenever those particular notes were played. The remedy was to replace the offending bushings—not particularly difficult, but with approximately a thousand bushings in a piano action, there were plenty of potential trouble spots. The wood could also squeeze the bushings in the dry season, causing the action parts to become sluggish, which completely defeated the

purpose of the Teflon bushing. A second problem—annoying but not as serious—was that Teflon, unlike cloth, was an "unforgiving" material: when dented it did not bounce back, but remained dented. This meant that the slightest mishandling of an action part might cause the center pin to dent and ruin a bushing. The technical problems of Teflon bushings were magnified by bad press and the conservatism of piano technicians, and Steinway finally gave up and began a return to cloth bushings in 1981.

If you are buying a used Steinway made between 1962 and 1981, you may not need to be as concerned with the presence of the Teflon bushings as the previous discussion might suggest, especially if your piano will be receiving only average use in the home. According to technicians with extensive experience servicing these pianos, there are usually few problems with these bushings after those that give trouble during the first few seasons are replaced. But the bushings (or, rather, the wooden action parts into which the bushings are inserted) are very sensitive to humidity changes, and the technician, when servicing these bushings, must be very careful to take into account the humidity conditions at the time of servicing. Because of the bushings' sensitivity, and the fussy service they require, pianos under heavy use or in adverse conditions, such as in some schools and concert halls, will probably benefit by changing to cloth-bushed action parts. Also, if a piano with Teflon bushings is in the shop for rebuilding, it would make sense to rebuild the action with cloth-bushed parts. Note that it is not possible to replace the Teflon bushings with cloth bushings without replacing all the action parts as well.

Verdigris (pronounced *VER-di-gree*). *Verdigris* is a green-colored substance produced by a chemical reaction between the metal center pins and chemicals in the bushing cloth or in lubricants applied to the cloth. The effect of this green "gunk" is to make the action parts move sluggishly or, in the worst cases, to prevent their movement altogether. Although certainly not unique to Steinways, the verdigris problem is frequently found in Steinways from the 1920s and to a lesser extent in pianos made during the several decades before and after that period. If you encounter an older Steinway with an extremely heavy touch or one in which the keys and hammers appear not to return to their rest position quickly, there is a good chance the piano has a verdigris problem.

Technicians have attempted many solutions to this problem, using chemical, mechanical, heat, and electrical methods, and some of these methods appear to provide at least temporary relief when the problem is not severe. But because verdigris may penetrate the wood as well as the cloth, the only really permanent solution, especially in severe cases, seems to be replacement of all the action parts affected. This makes verdigris an expensive problem to correct, so be aware of it when inspecting a used Steinway prior to purchase.

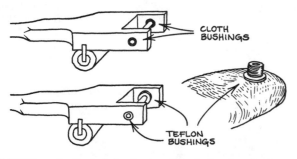

FIGURE 5-33. A cloth-bushed and a Teflon-bushed grand hammer shank with center pin inserted. The flanges that the center pins attach to the shanks are not shown (see Figure 4-3). A Teflon bushing is shown actual size on a finger.

CHAPTER SIX

Piano Moving and Storage

Why *Not* to Move a Piano Yourself

Movers like to tell stories like this one:

A young woman asked her father to help her move a piano from one place to another in her house. Her father got a couple of his friends to come along and they brought a dolly. While they were lifting the piano—a full-size vertical—it tipped back too far and got away from them. While it was falling, its upper corner dug down through the wall. The trench it made was deep enough to sever an electric conduit, which shorted and began to burn. The "movers" were unable to stop the fire, which also spread to the floor below, another person's apartment. After the fire department was done, there was little left of the two apartments and the piano.

Obviously, this is an extreme example of the damage that can be inflicted when moving a piano in do-it-yourself fashion. But even if you don't burn down your house, there is a substantial risk of personal injury, not to mention damage to the piano.

Pianos are very heavy. The average spinet or console weighs in at from three hundred to five hundred pounds, full-size uprights at about seven hundred, but sometimes as much as a thousand. Grands vary from about five hundred to a thousand pounds, though a concert grand may weigh as much as thir-teen hundred. If it were simply a matter of weight, though, all it would take would be enough strong people to do the job. Unfortunately, along with the weight come problems of balance and inertia, knowledge of which can make all the difference in doing a moving job safely and efficiently. Piano moving may conjure up images of men with monstrous arms and huge torsos, but actually two or three people of average build can do most piano moving jobs—even grands—if they have some brains, experience, the right equipment, and a knowledge of just when and where to apply a little force.

How Pianos Are Moved

Anyone with even a little bit of curiosity inevitably wonders how pianos get moved. How do you fit a grand piano through a door? How do you get a piano up to the fifth floor?

Unless the piano is very small and light, it is almost always placed on a special skid called a piano board. The piano is covered with blankets and strapped to the board. If the piano is to be moved over a level surface for any distance, the piano board is put on a dolly—a small platform on wheels—and rolled to its destination, such as a truck or a stairway. At the stairway, the dolly is removed and the piano board is slid in a very slow and controlled manner up or down the stairs.

As shown in Figure 6-1, a grand piano is moved on its side, straight side down. First the lid and the pedal lyre are removed. Then the leg at the straight side of the piano is removed and the piano is carefully lowered down to the piano board. (Some movers unscrew and remove the lid hinges because they overhang the case side and would otherwise cause damage to the case when the piano is put on its side. Others prefer to position the piano so the hinges overhang the edge of the piano board.) After the remaining two legs are removed, the piano is covered with blankets and strapped to the board. Stripped down in this manner, a grand piano is quite thin and will actually fit through a door or other opening very easily.

When a piano must be moved to or from a floor other than the first, many movers prefer to hoist or rig it (Figure 6-2) rather than move it up or down stairs. Believe it or not, moving a piano by stairs is actually

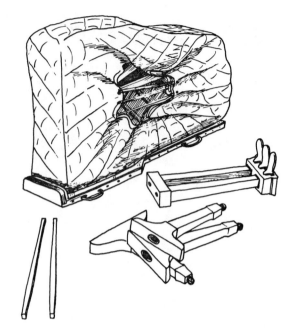

FIGURE 6-1. Grand pianos are moved on their side, with legs and lyre removed.

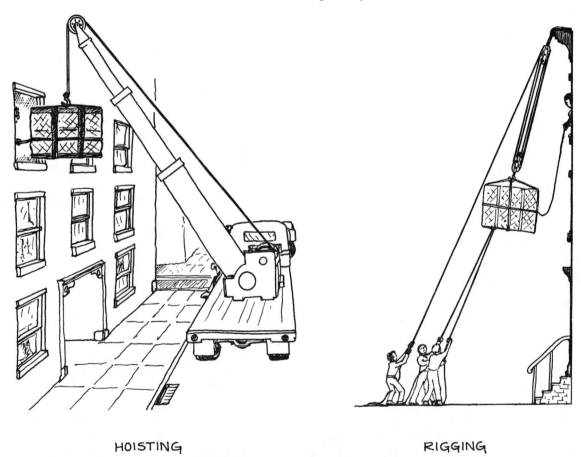

HOISTING   RIGGING

FIGURE 6-2. Hoisting is done with a crane. When the house is set too far back from a road or driveway or for some other reason the window isn't accessible to a crane, the piano can be rigged. Rigging involves using a block and tackle, supported from the window above or from the roof, to lift the piano.

more dangerous, both to the piano and to the movers, than hoisting it through an upper-story window with a crane. Most movers will consent to moving by stairs when only one flight is involved, or when no other alternative is possible. Of course, if the building has a freight elevator that can support the piano, that method is preferred over all others.

Basically, it is the customer's responsibility to make sure the piano will fit in its new location. This means not expecting a piano to be hoisted in a window that's too small or carried down a stairway with too low an overhang or moved around a corner that's too tight. Figure 6-3 shows how the dimensions of the piano relate to some common moving situations. Corners are the hardest to judge because they can't be easily measured. An experienced mover can usually judge these situations pretty accurately by eye and may prefer to visit the moving sites prior to moving day if there is any question about the difficulty of the job. This probably won't be possible if the move is a long-distance one. If the piano won't fit in its intended location, the customer will have to pay for its delivery back to its point of departure, to an alternate destination, or to storage.

Note that some movers like to "keyboard" a vertical piano—that is, remove the front part (keybed, keys, action)—to get the piano around a tight corner when there is no other alternative. You should know that this is not recommended, as it can sometimes result in permanent damage to the piano and make it difficult or impossible to get the piano working properly again.

Moving a Piano Around a Room

It's understandable that you might not want to hire a mover just to move a piano around a room, but these small moves can be surprisingly dangerous. With both grands and verticals, it's primarily the legs you want to watch out for. Breaking a leg on a vertical may just be an inconvenience, but on a grand it can be disastrous. I was once called twice in a single month to repair a grand piano that had been dragged across a floor. Both times a leg had gotten caught in the grate of a heating duct, causing the piano to crash to the floor. Of course, the pedal lyre broke too. Dragging a grand piano across carpeting can also be too much for the legs to handle. If you insist on moving the grand yourself, three to five strong people should gather around its circumference and lift while moving. Don't actually try to lift it off the floor; just relieve the strain on the legs.

At least two people should always move a vertical piano. Spinets and consoles with free-standing legs should have their legs protected by lifting or tilting

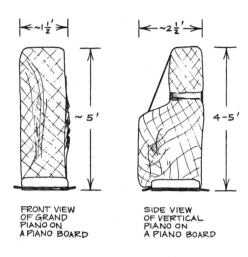

FRONT VIEW
OF GRAND
PIANO ON
A PIANO BOARD

SIDE VIEW
OF VERTICAL
PIANO ON
A PIANO BOARD

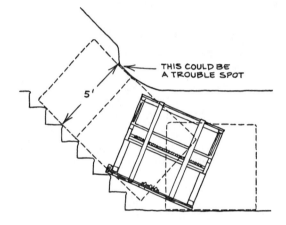

THIS COULD BE
A TROUBLE SPOT

FIGURE 6-3. The top drawings show the approximate dimensions of pianos on skids, which you might want to know if moving a piano through a window or a door. These dimensions vary by a few inches from piano to piano. Note that a grand piano on a skid is almost always very close to 60 inches tall, regardless of the length of the piano (remember, this is the keyboard end of the piano standing up). A standard-size window is also about 60 inches tall, so you will have to measure carefully here to avoid disappointment. Movers routinely remove window sashes, window frames, storm window frames, and just about anything else they have to to get a piano through a window. However, pianos will not usually fit through garret or attic windows or windows with sashes that can't be removed. The bottom drawing shows a problem that can occur when moving a piano up or down a stairway. The important measurement is the *minimum* clearance between the edge of the steps and the ceiling, measured *perpendicular to the plane of the stairs.* The fact that people can walk down the stairs without hitting their head does not necessarily mean the piano will fit, because people do not walk perpendicular to the plane of the stairs! Grands and large verticals will not fit down cellar bulkhead stairways, except, sometimes, when the bulkhead stairs themselves are removable.

the piano back ever so slightly while moving. But remember that most of the weight of the piano is in its back, so be sure you have a firm grip on it and don't tilt so far that the piano is in danger of falling over. Larger verticals and smaller ones without legs can simply be rolled, although this may be hard to do on carpeting. Piano casters can sometimes get stuck unexpectedly, so move slowly with one person on each end of the piano. When making turns, keep the back of the piano on the *inside* of the turn. And be careful not to push a stubborn vertical piano over your helper's foot!

Casters and trucks. If you're going to be moving a piano around a room or stage, or from room to room, often, be sure the piano is properly equipped. Grand pianos should be mounted on a piano truck or fitted with special casters. Small verticals are best not moved around much, but there are special piano trucks for them, too. (See Figure 6-4.) Larger verticals often come with heavy-duty casters, but casters that are too small or old cast-iron casters can be replaced by your piano technician with double rubber-wheel ones that move easily and don't mar the floor. (Note: These replacement casters may sometimes lift your piano an inch further off the floor, making the pedals hard to reach. A piece of thick carpeting or wood placed in front of the pedals for the heel of your foot to rest on will remedy this problem.)

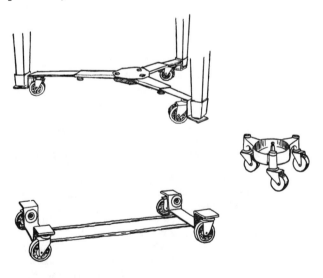

FIGURE 6-4. Grand pianos that are going to be moved around a lot can be mounted on a truck or carriage like the one shown at top. These are a bit ugly, though classier ones than that shown are available. The three-wheeled caster at right is less obtrusive. One of these casters under each grand piano leg will support the piano quite well. The truck shown at bottom is for vertical pianos.

Hiring a Piano Mover for a Local Move

Finding a piano mover. As with most other services, the best way to find a piano mover is by word-of-mouth referral from another piano owner or from your piano technician. A piano dealer can also recommend a mover. Some movers move pianos only, some move all kinds of household goods but specialize in piano moving, and some otherwise competent general movers don't know the first thing about piano moving. Since piano moving requires some specialized knowledge and equipment to do properly, always have the piano moved by a specialist.

Licensing and insurance. Most states require that anyone offering to move household goods for hire be licensed by the state department of public utilities or similar state regulatory agency. To get a license in those states that require one, a moving company must show that there is a need for its services, that it has the proper equipment, and that it has at least the minimum amount of cargo insurance required by state law. In addition, the mover's rates must be approved by the regulatory agency. We've all seen ads of the "two men and a truck—$40/hr." variety, but in regulated states these ads are illegal unless the firm is licensed, and newspapers are not supposed to carry ads for unlicensed firms. Ads for licensed firms will usually be accompanied by their license number. Since the deregulation of the interstate trucking industry in 1980, there has been an increasing tendency on the part of the states to deregulate, too. You should therefore check with your state regulatory agency about the current status of moving regulation in your state.

Most regulated states require that movers carry around five or ten thousand dollars worth of cargo insurance, the amount varying from state to state. But this is simply an upper limit or aggregate amount. It does *not* mean that each item moved is insured for that much. A careful reading of the moving contract will reveal that your piano (for instance) is insured for only so much per pound, the amount again varying from state to state, but usually somewhere between fifty cents and one dollar. This may be fine for your funky old upright, which is very heavy but not worth much, but won't help much if your expensive Baldwin grand is dropped from a third-story window.

To protect yourself against the latter kind of loss, you can buy extra insurance either from your insurance company or from the mover (the mover simply acting as an agent for its insurance company). The cost can run from as little as five cents to more than a dollar per $100 of declared value, depending on whether the piano is insured for replacement value minus depreciation or full replacement value with no deduction for depreciation, and on what deductible is chosen, if any. Even if your instrument is insured for less than its full value, you still may be able to sue the mover for the unreimbursed part of the damage if you can show that it was due to gross negligence.

Some states may not require it, but you should also be sure that your mover carries personal liability and worker's compensation insurance. The former will protect you in case, for instance, your walls are damaged. Without the latter you may be responsible for hospital bills if a mover is hurt on your property.

Prices. Most piano movers charge by the hour and are willing to give only a rough estimate of the total charge, if that. At least you should assume it's an estimate unless otherwise told. It's definitely worth getting several estimates for a piano moving job because prices often vary enormously, even among equally reputable movers in the same locality. However, be sure you are dealing with a skilled piano mover; the lowest estimate is not necessarily the best choice.

The hourly rate for a moving job will depend on the type and size of piano and the complexity of the job, because the larger pianos and more complex jobs require more workers. A first-floor-to-first-floor move of a small vertical or small grand usually requires only two people. Moving a full-size vertical or a smaller piano up or down stairs requires three, and moving a large grand may require more than three.

Phone calls around the country revealed the usual wide spread of prices, from about twenty-five dollars per person per hour (including truck) in the rural Midwest to as much as seventy-five dollars in the large metropolitan areas. For a simple one-hour first-floor-to-first-floor move of a spinet or console, this translates to a charge of from fifty to one hundred fifty dollars. A full-size upright might be about 50 percent more and a medium-size grand roughly double. Each staircase could add from fifteen to forty dollars to the cost. Hoisting and rigging might cost from one to three hundred dollars additional. These are intended only as approximate figures and obviously don't include unusual situations and complications. Be aware that what to you may seem only "a few steps up" to the front door may be significant to a mover and could result in an extra charge. Also, some movers have minimum charges.

Damage. Before the piano is moved, both you and the mover should inspect it carefully and note any pre-existing damage, such as scratches, dents, and loose veneer, on the bill of lading. Then, after the piano is moved to its destination, inspect it again and note any new damage on the bill of lading. Most damage to pianos in local moves is quite small and is repaired or touched up by the mover or by a piano technician or refinisher hired by the mover. Only in rare cases, or with some large interstate movers, will you need to file an insurance claim, but if you do, the mover is required to furnish you with the claim forms and process them for you (unless you obtained your insurance coverage independently).

Although damage to pianos from moving certainly does occur, piano owners also tend to imagine or suspect a lot of damage that doesn't exist. One reason is they probably examine their piano far more carefully after a move than at any other time in its life, and so discover scratches and marks that have been there for years unnoticed. This is why it's so important to agree on pre-existing damage before the move. Another reason for the suspicion is simply a lack of knowledge about the technical and maintenance needs of pianos. When I tune a piano after a move, and in the process notice the need for some additional maintenance, I'm invariably asked if the need for the extra work wasn't, after all, caused by the movers and therefore subject to reimbursement by them. In most cases the maintenance was needed before the move, too, but was never mentioned or not noticed by previous technicians. Usually, a piano has to be handled quite roughly for internal damage to occur.

Interstate, Long-Distance, and Household Moves

Interstate movers must be licensed by the Interstate Commerce Commission (ICC), a regulatory agency of the U.S. government. As with the regulated states, applicants for an ICC license must have the proper equipment for the job, a minimum of $10,000 worth of cargo insurance, and $750,000 worth of liability insurance.

When you dial the phone number listed for a major van line, you're actually calling its local agent. The agents book the moves and own a fleet of trailers. They hire drivers, called owner-operators, who own tractors to pull those trailers. It's an owner-operator who actually hauls your goods. (Sometimes the agents own the tractors, too, and just hire drivers.) Since the partial deregulation of the trucking industry in 1980, thousands of additional owner-operators have received ICC licenses, bringing the total to about twenty-five thousand nationwide.

Many people contemplating a major move automatically call a major van line whose name is a household word. But in most localities there are also smaller moving companies, sometimes with many years of experience, that specialize in moves to certain regions of the country. For instance, in Boston there are companies that specialize in moves within the New York–New England area and others that specialize in moves to Florida, where many New Englanders spend the winter. These smaller firms sometimes offer more personal service, more flexible scheduling, and lower prices.

The price of moving a piano alone a long distance is prohibitively expensive. For instance, several movers quoted prices of $1,200 to $1,500 for moving a 1,000-pound piano (such as a medium-size grand) from New York to California. The price is computed from both the weight and the distance, but the higher the weight, the lower the price per pound. This means that a piano moved with a typical 8,000-pound load of household furniture might cost from less than one-third to one-half as much as when moved alone. Also, most long-distance movers have a minimum charge, usually based on a weight of 1,000 pounds, but the minimums could range from 500 to 2,500 pounds. If a piano being moved alone weighs less than the minimum, it will be charged at the rate for the minimum weight. If you live in New York and are considering sending your old upright piano to your child in California, you might be better off selling it locally instead and sending your child the money to buy one in his or her area.

In addition to the rate quoted you for moving your piano long distance—with or without other household goods—there may be other hidden costs that you should inquire about. Because a piano requires special packing, a handling charge is usually added on to the bill. This is typically from forty to seventy dollars or so. In some cases the moving price includes only the trucking of the piano and not the cost of moving it in and out of the house. This may be so when the long-distance mover is equipped to haul pianos but not to handle them and must hire local piano movers on both ends of the trip. You may be required to pay the piano movers directly, which could add several hundred dollars to the moving cost if you thought all this was included in the bill.

If you are moving your household goods long distance yourself in a rented truck, the safest and most economical way to move the piano is to hire local piano movers at both ends to load and unload the piano.

For more information on interstate moves of household goods, I suggest you read the article on moving companies in the September 1986 issue of *Consumer Reports*.

International Moving

Who does it? International moving is one of the services that many regular movers provide. The actual overseas shipping is done by a "freight forwarder," who consolidates the goods from a number of different customers or movers into crates or containers (large metal boxes that are hauled by trucks and ships) and deals with the steamship line. Freight forwarders require a license from the Freight-Maritime Commission to do this. Your mover may or may not be a freight forwarder, but if not, it will have a relationship with one. The mover will pick up your goods and deliver it to them; you don't have to deal directly with the freight forwarder or the steamship line at all. The mover will tell you (or you should ask) what steamship line your goods will take, what port they will leave from, the container number, dates of departure and arrival, and ports of call on the way. Your mover does not need to have an ICC license to provide this service for you unless it will be moving your goods interstate in the process.

Some foreign manufacturers wrap their pianos in airtight plastic when shipping overseas to avoid having the pianos exposed to excess humidity. You should inquire of the mover whether this would be possible for your instrument.

Shipping costs. International moving is priced either by weight or by volume. Pianos are heavy and so should be priced by volume. My sources quoted somewhere between seven and fourteen dollars per cubic foot as a typical shipping cost, depending on the size of the shipment and the destination port. (For example, India cannot accept containers because people move into the empty ones as they are waiting to be used again, so shipments to India must be crated, increasing the cost.) This translates to a cost of roughly three hundred to seven hundred dollars for a small vertical and five to thirteen hundred dollars for a large vertical or small grand. The usual minimum charge is based on a weight of five hundred pounds or forty cubic feet, which most pianos will exceed.

Import duties. While the shipping costs described above are considerable, higher still are the import duties and taxes assessed by the foreign governments once the shipment has arrived. These duties are frequently 100 to 150 percent, and sometimes as much as 200 percent, of the replacement value of the piano *at its destination*, which may be much higher than at its origin. With these duties, governments seek to prevent the import of pianos for resale, presumably to protect their own local piano industry. Some countries have exclusions from duties for professionals in the music field, and some require proof of ownership of six months to two years to avoid duties. A call to any international mover will provide country-specific information on duties.

Insurance. Movers are not required to provide insurance coverage, but generally make it available. Insurance is always on the replacement value at the destination. One price quoted was $3 per $1,000 of value, with a minimum value of $1,000. A special point mentioned by my sources was that the insurance should be an "all-risk marine policy," which includes what is known as a "general average clause." This will insure against any extra costs the shipper might otherwise have to pay if damage is sustained to the ship en route and the cargo is impounded in a port other than one that is scheduled. These extra costs can be huge.

Shipping times. Shipments to Europe and the Middle East are made from the East Coast, and to Australia and the Far East from the West Coast. Shipping charges from your locality will include "land bridge service" to one coast or the other as appropriate. "Around the world" service may also be available, which allows goods to be shipped by sea anywhere in the world from either coast via the Panama Canal. Door-to-door shipping of a piano from the East Coast will usually take about thirty days to Europe, thirty-five to forty days to the Middle East, and forty-five to fifty-five days to Australia and the Far East. Shipping times from the West Coast will differ from those from the East Coast accordingly. Shipping to Canada and Mexico is usually by land, although reaching certain coastal cities may sometimes be cheaper by sea. Overland shipping for pianos should be by air-ride vans; rail flatcar shipping can be hard on pianos.

Arrival. The customer or the customer's designee will be notified by the shipper's agent when the piano has arrived at the destination port and he or she must go to the agent's office to file the necessary paperwork. Various forms are needed to establish the value of the piano, including the insurance company's valuation, so that any duty may be paid. (Shipping fees and insurance premiums are paid in advance at the point of origin; only duties are due on arrival.) The duty must be paid before the agent can complete the delivery to the house. If the customer is not at the destination when the piano arrives, it will have to be stored, which is expensive. It's better to delay shipping the piano than to have it wait at the destination port.

Damage claims. If there is damage, the customer should file a claim form, available from the mover's claims personnel at either end of the move. The customer must also arrange to have the insurance agent inspect the damage, usually after delivery to the new residence, obtain an estimate for repairs from any qualified technician, and submit it to the claims personnel of either the mover or the insurer, depending on the usual procedure used by the mover. If the customer doesn't have any idea of who to call for repair estimates, which could be the case in a foreign country, the names of local businesses are usually available from the insurance company or the mover.

Storage

The best advice about storing a piano is not to do it if you can help it, or to store it with a friend who will use it and take good care of it. Storing a piano involves extra moving and an uncertain environment and certainly doesn't improve the instrument, to say the least. Still, there are times when storing a piano is unavoidable, such as when you have to move out of your house before the movers are scheduled for the long-distance haul (in which case they will pick up and store your goods for you) or when you arrive in a new city before you've found a permanent place to live.

Most cities and towns now have self-storage places that offer cubicles of various sizes for rent by the month. When choosing one, it's preferable that it be at least minimally heated, though an unheated space is by far better than one that is overheated. The smallest-size cubicle in which you can store the piano will probably be determined by the size of the door, rather than by the size of the cubicle. Typical cubicle sizes might be 8x8x6 feet or 5x10x8 feet. Smaller sizes may not have a big enough door. Also be sure that the cubicle you're given is not upstairs and does not have an overhead entrance requiring a ladder, movable stairs, or forklift.

Monthly rates for the sizes mentioned above vary enormously. Phone calls around the country revealed rates as low as twenty dollars a month in some rural Midwestern towns and as high as a hundred dollars or more a month in the larger cities.

Storage in an unheated space. Many people keep pianos in summer homes and wonder how to protect the piano in the winter when the place is unheated. The conventional wisdom is that pianos should never be allowed to freeze, but any technician will tell you that pianos left unheated year after year are often in better condition than those in well-heated houses, the latter usually suffering from the effects of overdryness. Some experts advise stuffing the piano with rolled-up newspaper to absorb the dampness that often accompanies low temperatures. But my sources in the Maine woods tell me that, more often than not, those newpapers just end up as nests for mice, and the torn up, soggy newsprint is hard to extricate from the piano come spring. Their advice? Place some mothballs in the piano (but don't let them touch the finish), close up the piano, and leave it as is. (Alternatively, says the Maine woodsman, put some chewing tobacco in a cheesecloth sack and hang it inside the piano.)

The Effects of Moving and Storage

Tuning. The piano is hoisted out of a third-story window, trucked across the state, and later that day hoisted into a fifth-floor apartment. After the movers leave, the pianist sits down to play, and is surprised to find the piano in very good tune. Two weeks later, the piano sounds terrible. This common scenario is due to the fact that it is not generally the physical moving of the piano that puts it out of tune—it is the change in humidity from one location to another, and this change takes anywhere from a few days to a few weeks to show its effect. For this reason, you should wait at least two weeks after moving before having the piano tuned. Only with some of the cheaper spinets and consoles will the actual physical moving affect the tuning directly.

Pedals. Grand piano pedals are frequently out of kilter after a move. Shims of leather or cardboard used to take up slack in the trapwork often fall out when the lyre is removed. Also, less careful movers sometimes mix up the order of the pedal rods that rise from the back of the pedals. These rods are not always equal in length and so may not be interchangeable. Pedal dowels in verticals also sometimes fall out of place. It is a fairly simple matter for your piano technician to correct these problems when he or she comes to tune the piano. *Special note:* If your grand piano has lyre braces (which it should), be sure the movers remember to put them back on. Movers often forget and leave them in the truck, never to be seen again (see Figure 5-29, page 138).

Other effects. The effects of moving, except those mentioned above, are very unpredictable, especially if there is a large difference in humidity between the old and new locations. *Warning:* A piano that has been in a damp or unheated place for many years should never be moved to a dry or well-heated location. Such pianos are known to self-destruct in a short time.

One additional item to check on a grand piano before moving: Because a grand is placed on its side to be moved, a narrow wooden rail called a **key stop rail** is mounted on top of the keys, behind the fallboard, to prevent the keys from falling off the key frame during moving. If the key stop rail is missing or not securely installed, as sometimes happens, the keys will be in terrible disarray and completely unplayable after moving. A technician can fix this, but it may take a while even to extricate the action from the piano. If you know you're going to be moving, have your technician check for the key stop rail before the move. Otherwise, see Chapter 5 for instructions on removing the grand fallboard to look inside. Although less common, a similar problem can occur in a vertical if it has to be upended to get it around a tight corner.

CHAPTER SEVEN
A Beginner's Guide to Piano Servicing

SINCE THIS BOOK MAY BE ALL YOU WILL EVER read about the technical aspects of pianos, it would be a mistake to let you go without giving you some basic information about the kind of service your piano will need in the months and years after you buy it. If you have read this far, you probably appreciate by now that, as sturdy as a piano may look, it actually contains some ten thousand parts, many of them quite delicate, and needs much more servicing than most people realize. To maintain your piano in top condition, you should attend to its servicing with the same kind of diligence and thoroughness that you would with any other major purchase, such as an automobile. And as with an automobile, if you can't afford to service your piano, you really can't afford to buy it.

TUNING

Tuning is the most basic kind of piano maintenance there is, yet it is perennially misunderstood. What is tuning? Why do pianos go out of tune? How often and when should my piano be tuned? How can I minimize its going out of tune? These are some of the questions I and every other piano technician get asked constantly, and which I'll take up in this chapter.

What Is Tuning?

As explained elsewhere in this book, the more than two hundred strings in a piano are stretched at high tension across a cast-iron frame, one end of each string being attached to a hitch pin and the other end coiled around a tuning pin. The pitch of each string when vibrating depends, among other things, on the tension at which it's stretched. By turning the tuning pin, the tension can be tightened or slackened, and thus the pitch altered, according to the wishes of the tuner, who performs this operation with a socket wrench confusingly called a "tuning hammer." Tuning, then, means adjusting the tension of each of the piano strings, using a tuning hammer to turn the tuning pins, so that the pitch of each string sounds pleasingly in harmony with every other string according to certain known acoustical laws and aesthetic rules and customs. Note that whereas most tuners are also capable of providing other kinds of piano maintenance, tuning, properly speaking, is only the operation defined above, and does not include repairs and adjustments, fixing squeaky pedals, cleaning, and so on, as is often thought to be the case.

Why Do Pianos Go Out of Tune?

By far, the most important factor causing pianos to go

out of tune is the change in humidity from season to season that occurs in most temperate climates, affecting all pianos, good and bad, new and old, played and unplayed. The soundboard, glued down around its perimeter and bellied like a diaphragm in the center, swells up with moisture in the humid season and pushes up on the strings via the bridges on which the strings rest. This causes the strings to be stretched at a higher tension, raising their pitch. In the dry season, the opposite happens. The soundboard releases its moisture to the air and subsides, releasing the pressure on the strings, which then fall in pitch. Unfortunately, the strings don't rise and fall in pitch by exactly the same amount at the same time. The process is more random than that, with the result that the strings no longer sound in harmony with one another and need retuning.

To make matters worse, the change in pitch tends to be most pronounced in the tenor and low treble areas of the piano, whose bridges are located on the flexible center area of the soundboard (Figure 7-1). It's not at all unusual to find that the high treble and low bass, whose bridges are located near the more stable perimeter of the soundboard, have remained virtually unchanged in pitch despite a huge change in the center. Any octaves or chords that, for example, span the bass and tenor at these times will sound especially out of tune.

If the piano has been properly tuned, moderate playing will not, by itself, have a large effect on the tuning. Rather, its effect is to accelerate whatever changes in tuning are happening due to humidity fluctuations. A vibrating string more easily slides over its friction points than a stationary one, and thus is more apt to go randomly out of tune when its tension is being altered by the movement of the soundboard. Obviously, the harder and more frequently the piano is played, the faster this process will happen. But an unplayed piano will still go out of tune with the seasons.

Although all pianos go out of tune, some do so more than others. Some pianos, including some very well-made ones, have soundboards that are very responsive to humidity changes and go through large seasonal variations in pitch. Other pianos, particularly some of the cheaper spinets and consoles, have weak structures that actually twist slightly from season to season or even while the pianos are being tuned, making stable tunings all but impossible. These pianos go out of tune chaotically, in addition to showing large seasonal variations in pitch.

How Often and When Should I Have My Piano Tuned?

When to tune your piano obviously depends on your local climate and how responsive your piano is to humidity changes. But, in general, you should avoid times of rapid humidity change and seek times when the humidity will be stable for a reasonable length of time. Turning the heat on in the house in the fall and winter, and then off again in the spring, both cause major indoor humidity changes, and in each case it may take several months before the piano soundboard fully stabilizes again at the new humidity level.

In Boston, the tuning cycle goes something like this for most pianos (Figure 7-2):

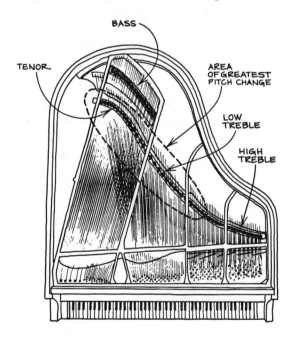

FIGURE 7-1. The area of greatest pitch change from season to season is in the tenor and low treble sections of the piano.

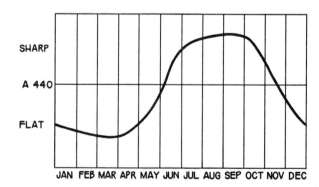

FIGURE 7-2. The pitch of the piano in the tenor and low treble range closely follows the annual indoor humidity cycle. The diagram shows how a typical piano in Boston might behave. Most areas of the country that have cold winters will show a similar pattern.

A piano tuned in April or May when the heat is turned off in the house will probably be out of tune by late June. If it is tuned in late June or July, it may well hold its tune until October or later, depending on when the heat is turned on for the winter (although sometimes extreme humidity in August will do it in). If you have the piano tuned right after the heat is turned on, say in October or November, the piano will almost certainly be out of tune by Christmas. But if you wait until after the holidays (and of course, everyone wants it tuned *for* the holidays), it will probably hold pretty well until April or even May. In my experience, most accusations of tuner incompetence occur in November or December, and then to a lesser degree in June, and are caused not by the tuner at all, but by poor timing of the tuning with the seasonal changes.

If you have the piano tuned four or more times a year, you don't have to worry too much about the "right" time to tune it. Any seasonal tuning changes will be corrected soon enough. It's those who tune their pianos twice a year who have a problem. For these people, there will be at least two times per year when the piano is noticeably out of tune but when it will not yet be the right time to tune it. If you are in this group, you will have to decide then whether to go ahead and have it tuned—knowing it may go out of tune within a month or so—or to suffer until the "right" time. At those times of year, I try to inform customers who call for a tuning about the consequences of having the piano tuned then, and let them decide how badly they want it done.

There is an additional problem for the twice-a-year people. The times of rapid humidity change—spring and fall—are also the times of most moderate indoor humidity levels, while the times of stable humidity—summer and winter—are the times of most extreme humidity levels. As shown in Figure 7-2, the pitch of the middle range of the piano follows the humidity changes and is therefore most sharp and flat at the "recommended" tuning times. Pianos tuned at these times may have to undergo large pitch changes to bring them back to standard pitch. As any tuner can tell you, large pitch changes are the bane of stable tuning, as structural forces within the piano tend to make a piano tuning creep back in the direction from which it was moved. Pianos showing large seasonal pitch variations may require extra tuning work, at greater expense, and may not stay in tune as well. Thus, ironically, the tuning times recommended in response to climatic factors are the least recommended times in relation to structural stability, and vice versa. Unfortunately, there is no solution to this problem except to have the piano tuned more often.

If you tune the piano only once a year, you should do it at the same time each year so the tuner will not have to make much pitch adjustment. Some pianos actually go back into almost perfect tune each year around the anniversary of their tuning (but don't count on this happening).

How often you have the piano tuned will depend not only on the piano and the humidity inside your house, but also on your ear (how much out-of-tuneness you notice and can tolerate) and on your budget. Four times a year is ideal, but impractical for most folks. The "official line" is twice a year. Where the piano is rarely used, once a year may suffice, but less than that is not recommended. The average cost of a piano tuning is currently from forty-five to seventy-five dollars, depending on where you live. The cost could be higher if a "double tuning" (a rough tuning followed by a fine tuning) is required to compensate for large seasonal variations in pitch, or if for some other reason the piano was not at standard pitch. In some areas of the country, a double tuning is required almost every time a piano is tuned. Also, as mentioned in Chapter 3, new pianos (or pianos that have been restrung) may need to be tuned more frequently the first year or so as the new strings continue to stretch.

You may legitimately ask how important it is to have a piano tuned; that is, will harm be done to the instrument if it isn't tuned? This is a subject piano technicians don't discuss much. When they do, they offer a variety of pseudoscientific explanations to convince their customers (or themselves) of the necessity for tuning. The truth, as I see it, is that in most cases no harm will be done. The harm is mostly to one's aesthetics—an out-of-tune piano can be painful to listen to. It can also be discouraging and distracting to a student. In the extreme case where a piano is being tuned after, say, twenty years of neglect, raising the pitch of the piano back to standard pitch will entail a good deal of extra work and could result in some broken strings or split bridges, but I'm not convinced that these problems wouldn't have occurred anyway, and possibly sooner, if the piano had been maintained. Raising the pitch of a piano can also alter the positions of the strings in relation to their bearing points, introducing tonal irregularities (false beats), but this can often be corrected, and in any case is not what I would call "harmful." Suggestions that the piano will be structurally harmed if it is not precisely at standard pitch and in tune are, in my opinion, spurious.

HUMIDITY AND PIANOS

When you consider that a piano is made largely of wood, it's not surprising that the subject of humidity plays such an important role in piano technology.

Relative Humidity

Relative humidity is a measurement, expressed as a percentage, of the amount of water vapor in the air compared to the maximum amount the air could possibly hold at a given temperature. The relative humidity of the outdoor air depends on the nature of the air mass—that is, how moist or dry it is—and on the temperature, because the ability of the air to hold moisture increases with increasing temperature. So if we take a "parcel" of air with a certain amount of moisture in it and we heat it up, the relative humidity will decrease, because the amount of moisture in the air will have decreased *in comparison* to the amount the air is now capable of holding. Alternatively, if we cool that air, again without adding or subtracting moisture, the relative humidity will increase, because the capacity of the air to hold moisture will have diminished.

The relative humidity of the outdoor air can be high or low from day to day, regardless of the season. The reason such a fuss is made about low winter humidity is that in climates that have cold winters, the *indoor* relative humidity is artificially lowered by heating the air with a furnace system without supplying any additional moisture. If, for example, the outdoor temperature is 32 degrees Fahrenheit and the outdoor humidity is 100 percent (an extreme example), by the time the air is heated to 68 degrees indoors, the indoor relative humidity will have dropped (theoretically) to only 28 percent (the actual amount may be a little higher due to human respiration, plants, and other factors).

A continuous exchange of moisture goes on between the air and the wooden piano parts and other porous objects around the house, as the moisture level attempts to reach a state of equilibrium. Since the air is usually a much greater reservoir of moisture than the objects, it tends to dictate the terms of this interchange. When the relative humidity is low, the air sucks up moisture from the piano, causing the pitch to fall, tuning pins to loosen, and parts to rattle (not to mention causing plants to wither, furniture joints to loosen, skin to crack, and throats to get sore).

Piano manufacturers suggest that the ideal humidity level for pianos is about 40 to 50 percent, whereas studies show that for people, 50 to 60 percent is best. Actually, as far as pianos are concerned, the particular humidity level is not nearly as important as the change in humidity through the seasons. In most cases, a piano can be adjusted to exist quite well at any reasonable level of humidity as long as it doesn't change much. But when, as happens in most of North America, the indoor humidity goes from very high to very low and back again, year after year, the alternate expansion and contraction has the net effect of shrinking, cracking, and warping even wood that has been well seasoned prior to manufacturing. One of the most important parts of good piano maintenance is keeping the humidity as constant as possible.

Where to Place the Piano

There are several ways you can protect your piano from extremes and fluctuations of humidity. The most important of these is putting the piano in the right place. *NEVER* put a piano near or against a working radiator, next to or over a hot-air vent, or under a ceiling vent. If you can't observe this one simple rule, there's no point to even buying a piano. You'll be throwing your money away. A concert pianist who is a customer of mine insisted, over my objections, on situating her fifteen-thousand-dollar grand over a large heating vent in her living room. "It doesn't look good any place else," she said. Her piano is now almost untunable. Priorities, please!

Some tuners advise their customers not to place a piano near a window or a door because of possible drafts, or against an outside wall that may get cold. This is undoubtedly good advice, but following it may severely restrict your ability to have a piano at all. Use your judgment. My experience is that these factors are often not too significant unless the conditions are extreme (Figure 7-3). If in doubt, and an inside wall is not available, move your piano six inches away from an outside wall to provide an insulating air space, or try putting a sheet of styrofoam insulation behind the piano. Remember, too, not to place your piano in an unusually damp place, such as a damp basement.

Direct sunlight on a piano should be diffused with curtains or venetian blinds. Besides damaging the finish of a piano, sunlight can wreak havoc on the tuning. I remember the time I was called by a grand piano owner who claimed his piano seemed to go out of tune at certain times of the day and back in tune at other times.

FIGURE 7-3. Where *not* to put your piano. (Illustration by Rick Eberly, © 1986 GPI Publications, Cupertino, CA. Reprinted by permission.)

"Sure," I thought skeptically, but agreed to check it out. Not finding anything obviously wrong, I proceeded to tune the piano. Halfway through the tuning, I discovered, to my dismay, that the piano was already going out of tune. Then I noticed that while I had been tuning, the sun had shifted its position in the sky and was now shining directly on the soundboard. I quickly got up and closed the blinds. After five minutes, to my relief and amazement, the piano was back in almost perfect tune.

Temperature

Another way you can keep the humidity up in the wintertime is to keep the temperature at a moderate level. Temperature alone does not affect a piano very much unless extreme, but it decidedly affects relative humidity. A temperature difference of just 5 degrees can make the difference between a house that is hazardously dry and one that is moderate and comfortable. Some of the best-preserved pianos I have seen have been in rooms that were relatively poorly or indirectly heated. Some of the worst have been in houses heated to over 70 degrees. Some piano manufacturers state that the ideal temperature for a piano is 72 to 75 degrees. In my opinion, this is ridiculous. Not only would this be a waste of expensive energy resources, but it can be nearly impossible to keep an adequate humidity level when a house is heated to such temperatures in the wintertime. Studies have shown that the best temperature for most physically active people is around 64 degrees, although there is, of course, a certain amount of variation from one person to another (for instance, people who are elderly or ill usually need a much higher temperature to avoid hypothermia). Obviously you need to strike a balance between your health and comfort needs and the requirements of your piano. Fortunately, this balance is usually not hard to find if you are willing to be flexible and wear a sweater indoors from time to time.

Humidifiers and Climate Control Systems

Recognizing the importance of an adequate humidity level to their health and possessions, including their piano, households in increasing numbers are artificially raising the humidity during the dry months by using humidifiers. These come in three kinds: a central humidifier directly connected to your forced hot-air heating system (if you have this kind of system), a portable unit that can humidify one or several rooms, and a miniature climate control system installed right in your piano.

If you do heat with forced hot air, connecting a central humidifier is by far the best route. A heating and cooling contractor can install one for four or five hundred dollars. This may cost more than the smaller portable models, but it will take care of the entire house with no additional noise or clutter of extra appliances. Central humidifiers are usually designed to refill themselves with water automatically, but you must clean them often to remove mineral deposits, especially in hard-water areas, and to prevent the growth of bacteria.

If you heat by other means than forced hot air, you should consider buying a portable humidifier, usually priced from one hundred to two hundred dollars. These, however, require a lot of maintenance. Like the central kind, they must be cleaned often (weekly, or at least monthly) to avoid the growth and spread of airborne diseases. They must also be filled with water quite often (on the average, daily), the frequency depending on the capacity and output of the humidifier, the temperature of the house, and how well the house is insulated. If you go away for a few days and the humidifier runs out of water, the house could get dry and the piano could go out of tune. Also, these appliances tend to make a lot of noise, something to which a musician is likely to be sensitive. Last, when the temperature is very low outside, indoor humidity must also be kept low—often lower than is acceptable for your piano—to prevent water vapor from

Buying Tips: Shopping for a Humidifier

When shopping for a portable console humidifier, be prepared to see big, ugly plastic boxes in fake Mediterranean styling. You may have to pay more to be offended less. Be sure to ask the following questions: How many gallons does it hold? (The more it holds, the longer between fillings.) How many square feet is it rated to cover in the average house? (If your ceilings are very high, adjust this figure downward accordingly.) Does it have a water-level indicator? A low-water warning light? Automatic shutoff when it runs out of water? An automatic humidistat? (If it doesn't have an automatic humidistat, it will keep running until the house becomes a tropical rain forest.) Check how accessible the tank is for cleaning and filling, as these tasks will occupy most of the time you spend on maintenance. Does the tank lift out of the cabinet for easier cleaning? Are there casters so you can roll it to the sink? Is a hose provided? Check how much noise the fan makes; the larger models, and models with more than one fan speed, sometimes make less noise.

The new ultrasonic humidifiers work on a different principle than the evaporative type and don't require as much in the way of cleaning. Ease of filling and cleaning aren't problems because the units are so small, but their capacity and output are limited, so they won't cover as large an area. Also—very important—if you live in a hard-water area, ultrasonic humidifiers may spread a fine white dust over all the surfaces in your house.

condensing on windows and other cold surfaces. In fact, too much humidification can result in moisture seeping into the walls and, over time, causing structural damage to the house. If you would like to avoid this risk, would be bothered by the motor noise of a console humidifier, want to avoid the nuisance of frequent cleaning and filling, go away for long periods of time, live in an area that is too *damp* all the time, or just want to give extra special attention to protecting your piano, the best route is to have a climate control system installed right inside your piano (Figure 7-4). These systems can be ordered and installed by your piano technician. The system consists of a humidifier (a bucket of water with a heating element and cloth wicks), a dehumidifier (a long heating element that raises the temperature and thus lowers the relative humidity), a humidistat (senses the humidity level and turns on and off the humidifier and dehumidifier as needed), a low-water warning light mounted under the keybed, and an easy-fill tube so you can refill the humidifier without having to open up the piano. In a vertical piano, the system is installed right inside the lower panel, near the pedals. In a grand, it fits under the soundboard. The cost for the system and installation is about $200 to $250 in a vertical and $250 to $350 in a grand.

The advantages of this system are that it makes no noise at all, requires filling (extremely easy) only every one to four weeks, depending on conditions, and needs cleaning and changing of the humidifier wicks only once a year, which your technician can do. Since the system covers only a small area, it can control the humidity in that area very closely. The drawback is that it can't reach the entire piano, only the inside of the vertical and the underneath of the grand. In both cases, it will help to stabilize the tuning, and in the vertical it will protect the action as well, but in a very dry room, it may not provide the kind of total protection that the room humidifier can. I highly recommend these systems for both vertical and grand pianos, but sometimes suggest that they be supplemented by a room humidifier, especially for grands, if the piano owner doesn't mind the inconvenience.

OTHER KINDS OF PIANO SERVICE

Action Regulating

Action parts need periodic adjustment to compensate for wear, compacting and settling of cloth and felt, and changes in wooden parts due to atmospheric conditions. Making these adjustments is called *regulating*. Regulating is also discussed in Chapter 3, page 56; some examples of regulating adjustments are shown in Chapter 5, page 140. Most new and rebuilt pianos will need to be regulated to some extent within six months to a year of purchase because of initial settling of cloth parts. Thereafter, frequency of regulation will depend on the amount of use. A piano in the home played an hour a day might need a full

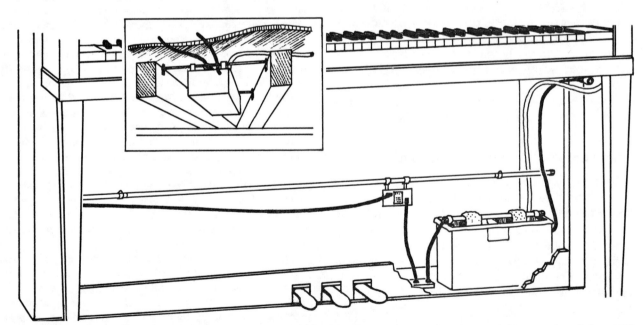

FIGURE 7-4. The Dampp-Chaser climate control system includes a humidifier (tank in lower right corner), a dehumidifier (long heating rod), a humidistat (box hanging from dehumidifier), and a low-water warning light and filling tube mounted under the keybed. The inset shows how the system is mounted under the soundboard of a grand piano, supported by the wooden braces.

regulation only once every five to ten years, whereas one played all day by a professional might benefit by a full regulation every year. Small amounts of regulating done as necessary at each tuning will put off the day when a full regulation is needed. A full regulation of a vertical piano action usually costs between $150 and $250; a grand regulation between $300 and $600. The price spread partially reflects the lack of agreement about what particular procedures regulation should include. Some adjustments, such as hammer filing, may not be included in a standard list of regulating procedures, but are often performed in conjunction with regulating nonetheless.

Although letting your piano go out of tune may not harm it, letting it go badly out of regulation may. For instance, hammers that block against the strings instead of releasing could break, or cause strings to break. Excess space or "lost motion" between two contacting parts could make one part punch the other instead of pushing, causing unnecessary wear.

Two other operations I would like to call your attention to are screw tightening and hammer spacing. The hinges, called **flanges**, on which all the action parts move, are screwed to the action frame. These screws—some two to three hundred of them—loosen with time due to vibration and wood shrinkage. When they get loose, the parts get noisy and move out of alignment. Have your technician check the tightness of these flange screws once a year, preferably during the dry season when they're loosest.

When flange screws get loose, or when wooden parts warp, hammers and other parts may go out of proper alignment. Figure 3-32, on page 53, and Figure 5-26, on page 137, show what misspaced hammers look like. As explained in Chapter 5, once hammers are left misspaced for a length of time, spacing them correctly can be more involved, requiring reshaping or replacement. A little time spent at each tuning checking and adjusting hammer spacing can lengthen the life of the hammers considerably and can also provide benefits in evenness of tone.

Voicing

Voicing, or tone regulating, is the adjustment of the tone of the piano, mostly by changing the density or hardness of the hammer felt. To put it simply, hardening the felt will make the tone brighter, softening it will make the tone mellower. Sometimes other, more complex, changes in tone can be accomplished, too. Voicing techniques include proper alignment of the hammers with the strings, filing or sanding a layer of felt off to reshape the hammer and eliminate grooves, ironing the hammer felt or treating it with chemicals to harden it, and pricking it with needles to soften it. To eliminate any other variables that could affect the tone, a piano must be in perfect tune and regulation before it can be voiced.

New and rebuilt pianos may sound quite bright after six months or a year of use and may need some voicing to compensate for the packing down of the hammer felt. After that, frequency of voicing should depend on how much you use the piano and on how often you think the tonal quality is no longer optimum.

A hint: I find that 90 percent of complaints about tonal quality disappear after the piano is tuned.

Cleaning and Polishing

Polishing the case. Most piano manufacturers recommend *against* the use of furniture polish. The best way to clean dust and finger marks off the piano, they say, is with a soft, clean, lintless cloth (such as cheese cloth) slightly dampened with water and wrung out. Fold the cloth into a pad and rub in the direction of the grain of the wood, using long straight strokes. Then repeat with a dry cloth pad to remove any remaining water droplets. If you insist on using furniture polish, make sure it contains no silicone. Some piano supply companies sell polish especially made for piano finishes, available from your technician.

Cleaning the keys. Use the same kind of soft, clean cloth to clean the keys. Dampen the cloth slightly with water or with a mild white soap solution. Don't let water run down the sides of the keys. If your keytops are made of ivory, be sure to rub each key with a dry cloth right after cleaning it. Don't let the water stand on the ivory for any length of time. Since ivory absorbs water, the keytops will curl up and fall off if water is allowed to collect on them. Use a separate cloth to clean the black keys, in case any black stain comes off. Never use chemical solvents, furniture polish, or cleaning fluids on the keys.

Cleaning the interior of the piano. Dust inevitably collects inside a piano no matter how good a housekeeper you are. When the technician removes the outer case parts during regular servicing it's a good time to dust some of their less accessible spots. In a vertical, you can also vacuum behind the lower panel, where the pedals and trapwork are. In a grand, the area around the tuning pins and the inside perimeter of the case can be vacuumed out. The tops of the dampers in a grand can be cleaned very gently with a clean, dry cloth (no water here, please).

The big question is how to clean the grand piano soundboard under the strings. Piano technicians clean this area with a cloth attached to a thin, flexible piece of steel, called a "soundboard steel," which is inserted between the strings. Thoroughly cleaning the soundboard in this manner can take a long time. A simpler way that will suffice for most piano owners is to attach the vacuum cleaner hose to the exhaust end of the appliance (you can't do this with all vacuum cleaners, however) and to blow the dust toward the tail end and straight side of the piano, where it can then be vacuumed up. An air compressor will do the job even better. This method won't get the soundboard spanking clean, but it will put off the day when the more thorough cleaning will be necessary. Cleaning the piano action and under the keys on both verticals and grands should be left to a piano technician. In most cases, once every few years will be often enough.

Mothproofing. Moths love the wool cloths and felts in pianos, especially the hammers, dampers, and under the keys. The wool is mothproofed in the factory, but this is only a temporary treatment, good for a few years. In most situations, a periodic, thorough cleaning of the piano action, as described above, will keep the moth problem under control. In more severe cases, the technician can provide mothproofing agents that are safe to put inside the piano.

The Long-Range Outlook

As the piano gets on in years, it will need more extensive service, such as replacement of hammer heads, key bushings, dampers, and occasional broken strings or action parts. Read about some of these items in Chapter 5, "Buying A Used Piano." Ultimately, there will come a time when the piano will either have to be completely rebuilt or (sniffle, sniffle) disposed of. Since pianos do not usually abruptly die, it's hard to say just what their lifetime is, but a figure of forty or fifty years is often given. Strings are said to lose their resiliency and thus their potential for good tone after about twenty-five years, though certainly many pianos and their owners have not yet figured this out and are quite happy with their forty-, sixty-, or eighty-year-old strings. Suffice it to say that if you choose your piano carefully, give it good care, and use the services of a competent piano technician, your piano will enjoy a long life and enrich yours as well.

THE PIANO TECHNICIAN

Throughout this book I've used the term *piano technician* rather than the better-known *piano tuner*. Technically speaking, a tuner is one who only tunes, and perhaps is capable of a few minor repairs, whereas a technician—sometimes called a tuner-technician—both tunes and does most kinds of on-site repair and regulating. It's much better to hire the latter, even if you believe your piano doesn't need any repair at a given time. One very pleasant fellow who tunes in another part of the state confessed to me that he always avoided raising the pitch of pianos that were flat for fear he might break a string—he didn't know how to replace strings. If you hire people like this, they may have to cover up for their ignorance, and you may have to hire someone else to undo the damage. Even an experienced technician, though, may sometimes subcontract out work or refer you elsewhere for certain complicated or specialized jobs, such as key recovering, rebuilding, or refinishing.

The best way to find a piano technician is to ask for a referral from someone whose needs are similar to your own. If you are a piano teacher with a high-quality instrument, ask another teacher or professional musician who seems to take good care of his or her instrument, or inquire as to who tunes for the local symphony. If you own a spinet, the person who tunes for the symphony may decline the job, so you should ask someone else who owns a home piano, or ask your teacher (if you have one) for an appropriate referral. Of course, since very few pianists know much about their instrument, there's no guarantee that the referral will get you someone who will do a good job, but at the very least it will get you the peace of mind that comes with not having to deal with a total stranger.

The worst way to find a technician is through the *Yellow Pages*. One doesn't have to have any certification to hang out a shingle as a piano technician, and all it takes to advertise in the *Yellow Pages* is the money to buy the business phone service. Some of the best technicians don't advertise because they don't want to pay for business service and because they prefer the rapport with customers who were referred to them by word of mouth. They also don't want to be bothered by people who call around just to find the lowest price. The better technicians usually don't charge the least, although they may not charge the most, either.

If in a total quandary about whom to hire, you might check to see if there is a chapter of the Piano Technicians Guild in your area. The Guild is an international organization of piano technicians devoted to promoting a high level of skill and business ethics among its members. To that end it sponsors regular technical meetings and seminars and produces a technical magazine. Extensive testing of tuning and repair skills and theoretical knowledge is required to attain the Guild's "Craftsman" rating. The Guild is not a labor union and does not set rates. To find out if there are Guild members in your area, look in the *Yellow Pages* (here's one way the *Yellow Pages* can be helpful), which may have a list of Guild members, or write to the Piano Technicians Guild at 4510 Belleview, Suite 100, Kansas City, Missouri 64111. The Guild advertises that you should allow someone to service your piano only if he or she can show a current, paid-up Guild membership card at the door. This is, in my opinion, a bit overzealous. For a variety of reasons, only about half the qualified technicians in the country choose to belong to the Guild. It would therefore be foolish to turn away someone who came otherwise well recommended.

Here are some specific pointers to help your piano service go smoothly:

Calling a technician. When you call a piano technician for the first time, be prepared to give the following information: who referred you or where you heard about his or her service; whether your piano is a grand or a vertical, and, if a vertical, whether or not it is a spinet; the brand name and age of the piano, if known; when it was last tuned; if the piano has been moved from a radically different climate since the last tuning; and any special service requirements or needed repairs that you are aware of (be as specific as possible). Having this information will make it easier for the technician to bring along the proper tools and supplies and to budget an adequate amount of time for the job. Although binding price estimates can never be given over the phone because of the many variables involved, having information about the condition of the piano may allow the technician to give you in advance some rough idea of the kind of expense that may be involved.

Making an appointment. Technicians vary in their willingness to work at odd hours to suit their customers' schedules. It may be necessary for you to leave a key with a neighbor or make other arrangements to let the technician in. This is very commonly done, and if you have chosen someone reputable to service your piano, you need have no fear about doing this. I usually prefer that my customers be present at the first appointment so we can meet each other, talk about any special problems the piano may have, and agree on what work is to be done. Thereafter, the presence of the customer is not necessary, although, of course, it is often pleasant. If you won't be there, try to leave a number where you can be reached, in case there is a problem.

Unless the technician specifically agrees otherwise, assume that the time agreed upon for the appointment is very approximate. The pianos being serviced before yours may require extra tuning work or unexpected repairs, and traffic conditions are highly variable.

Payment. So as not to be caught short, find out in advance whether the technician will be sending a bill or wants to be paid at the time the work is done, and whether cash or check is preferred.

Remember that if no work can be performed, through no fault of the technician (such as if the piano turns out to be untunable or unrepairable), you will be expected to pay a minimum service fee, usually a little less than the regular tuning fee. Also, if you live outside the technician's regular area, an additional travel charge may apply.

Cancellations. Without a doubt, the most exasperating situation technicians encounter is when a customer fails to be home at the appointed time or cancels the appointment with less than twenty-four hours' notice. Some people can be incredibly rude, or seem not to realize that we do this for a living, not as a hobby. Once I drove forty miles to do a full day of repair, only to find the customer gone, the door locked, and no note of explanation. My phone calls to him were never returned. It's nearly impossible to fill holes in one's schedule at such short notice, so I spent the day twiddling my thumbs, with no income, and paying for gas besides. You should expect to pay the technician's minimum service fee for appointments missed or cancelled at short notice, even if you had to cancel for a good reason.

Working conditions. Noise and poor lighting are technicians' two biggest enemies on the job, the first much more than the second. Remember that when we tune, we are not just listening to the notes being played, but also to very faint vibrations related to those notes' higher harmonics, sounds which you are probably unaware of. Noises that bother us are those with high-pitched vibrations, such as electric fans, vacuum cleaners, garbage disposals, egg beaters, and running water; sounds that capture our attention, such as talking, music, and television; and general clatter, such as setting up chairs in an auditorium or stage set-up before a concert. Your walking around the room also gets in our way, not because of the noise (tiptoeing doesn't help), but rather because sound waves reflecting off a moving object cause irregularities in the vibrations we listen to.

Poor lighting is more of a problem when doing repair work than when tuning. Clubs and bars are the very worst places for both noise and lighting. If you're the manager of such an establishment, do your very best to minimize these distractions when having your piano serviced.

Be sure the technician has enough time to do a thorough job. Teachers should have their pianos tuned on days when their teaching schedule is less crowded or more flexible. Concert producers should give the technician enough time, when possible, to complete the work before the musicians start to set up, not just before the audience arrives.

If you store the Harvard University library, museum, and arboretum on your piano, please clear them off before the technician arrives. You know best where to put them and how to handle them to avoid break-age, and it only wastes our time to have to deal with them. (You wouldn't believe how much stuff some people pile on their pianos!)

Blind technicians, of whom there are many, should be warned about any potential hazards, such as standing lamps and stage microphones.

Complaints. Complaints should be registered first with the person who can do something about it—this means with the technician, not with friends, relatives, and future technicians. (However, we don't mind an occasional word of praise, which you are welcome to spread everywhere.)

Glossary/Index

Most references to trade names occurring in the brand reviews in Chapter 4 are indexed on page 76, Index to Trade Names. A few references to trade names occurring elsewhere in the book are indexed here.

Accelerated action, 100. *A technical feature in Steinway grand pianos, in which the key balances on a rounded, rather than a flat, surface.*

Acoustics, room, 43, 57, 141

Action, 4, 6. *The mechanical part of the piano that transfers the motion of the fingers on the keys to the motion of the hammers that strike the strings.*
  buying tips concerning, 44–47
  cleaning, 163–164
  compressed or compact, 44–45
  design and manufacturing of, 45–47, 115
  direct-blow, 44–45
  effect of humidity on, 148, 160, 163
  Fandrich, 115
  indirect-blow, 44–45
  grand versus vertical, 13–14, 46
  inspection of, in used piano, 134–135
  operation of, 9–11
  plastic in, 47, 134–135
  pneumatic. *See* Player pianos
  regulating, 162–163
  regulation of: examples of, 140; in new piano, 46, 55, 56, 61; and soft pedal, 54, 138–139; in used piano, 139
  removing, 134
  spinet, 15, 44–45
  Stanwood, 115
  Steinway, 100, 148
  tightening of screws in, 137, 163
  vertical piano, types of, 44–45

Action centers, 137, 148. *The pivot points on which action parts move.*

Aeolian, 146

Age of piano, how to determine, 120, 139, 147

Agraffes, 37. *Small brass fittings, with holes through which the strings pass, screwed into the plate of some pianos to keep the strings perfectly spaced.*

Aliquot, 36. *A small metal bar or plate that divides the back end of a string into two parts, one of which vibrates sympathetically, creating a duplex scale. See also Duplex scale*

American Music Conference, 73

Ampico, 114, 122. *A former manufacturer of piano reproducing mechanisms.*

Antique dealers, purchasing used piano from, 124

Antique pianos, 117–118

Appraisal. *See* Inspection; Prices, of used pianos

Asian pianos. *See names of specific countries*

Attack, 42. *The initial sound of the hammer striking the string, lasting milliseconds.*

Auctions, purchasing used piano at, 124

Baby grand. *A small grand piano, usually less than 5 feet 6 inches long. Piano technicians prefer the term small grand.*

Back, vertical piano, 3. *The wooden structural framework of a vertical piano. See also Structural framework*
  inspection of, in used piano, 132–133
  purpose and construction of, 28–29, 31

Backcheck, 9–11, 140. *The part of the piano action, either grand or vertical, that catches the hammer on the rebound.*

Balance point, 47, 48, 49, 50, 135, 136. *The fulcrum on which a key pivots.*

Baldwin
  actions made by, 45
  bridges, 39
  Hamilton studio piano, opening, 129
  pinblocks, 32

Bass, 7. *The lower-pitched notes, played by keys toward the left end of the keyboard. See also Strings; Scale design*
  tonal quality of, 33–34, 36, 43, 131, 132, 141

Bass sustain pedal, 54–55, 138. *The middle pedal on some vertical pianos; sustains the bass notes only.*

Bearing points, 7, 37, 38, 132. *Points on the piano that delineate a string's vibrating portion, or speaking length.*

Bechstein, 118, 119

Beech
  in grand piano rims, 23
  in pinblocks, 32

Bench, piano, 27, 65

Bent side, 8. *The right side of a grand piano as seen from the keyboard.*

Birch, in piano cabinets, 21

Birdcage action, 118. *An antique action found in many uprights from the late nineteenth century; the dampers are actuated by wires in front of the action.*

Blind technicians and tuners, 166

Bluing, of tuning pins, 31. *A controlled oxidation process that makes tuning pins hold better in the pinblock.*

Blüthner, 118, 119

Braces, lyre. *See* Lyre braces

Braces, rim, 29

Brand names
  made up by dealers and distributors. *See* Stencil pianos
  of new and recently made pianos, index to, 76
  of used pianos, recommended, 118–119

Brand reviews, 77–113
  explanation of survey and review procedures for, 69–72

Bridge cap, 38–39, 132. *A top layer on some bridges, intended to minimize splitting of the bridge by the bridge pins.*

Bridge pins, 38, 132. *Small metal pins driven into the bridge, against which the strings press, that aid in transmission of sound to the bridge.*

Bridges, 3, 6, 7. *Narrow hardwood strips, against which the strings press, that transfer the strings' vibrations to the soundboard.*
  construction of, 38–39
  inspection of, in used piano, 132
  notching of, 38–39. *See also* Notch, bridge
  repair of, 132
  and tonal quality, 38–39, 132
  and tuning stability, 158

Bridle straps, 9. *Cloth tapes with leather or vinyl tips that connect the wippen assembly to the hammer assembly on vertical pianos.*
  inspection of, in used piano, 134–135

See also Index to Trade Names, page 76.

See also Index to Trade Names, page 76.

Discontinued merchandise, purchase of, 63
Discounts, on new pianos, 63–65
Dolly, 149. *A small platform on wheels used in moving pianos.*
Double-striking, of hammers, 46
Double tuning, 159. *A rough tuning followed by a fine tuning, often necessary when the pitch of a piano must be raised or lowered to standard pitch.*
Downbearing, 38, 39, 133–134, 141. *The downward pressure of the strings against the bridges, necessary for good tone.*
Down weight, 48, 49. *The force, measured in grams, required to make a key go down at the front (with the damper system disengaged).*
Drop action. *See* Indirect-blow action
Drop screw, 10–11. *A grand piano action part that prevents the repetition lever from rising too high during and after letoff. See also* Letoff
Duo-Art, 114, 122, 146. *A former manufacturer of piano reproducing mechanisms.*
Duplex scale, 36. *A scale design in which the ends of the strings, normally muted with cloth, are allowed to vibrate sympathetically, adding tonal color.*
Duties, import, 154–155

Ebonized finish, 28. *A black piano finish.*
Ebony, in piano keytops, 51
Elbows, spinet, 135. *Elbow-shaped connectors between the lifter wires (inverted stickers) and the wippens in a spinet. Old plastic elbows frequently break.*
Electronic instruments, 113–115
   as player pianos, 114–115
   effect on sales of new pianos, 73
   interface of, with acoustic pianos, 113–114
Escapement, 9–10, 140. *See also* Letoff
Escapement mechanism, 9–10. *The assembly in a grand or vertical piano action that allows escapement, or letoff, to occur. See also* Letoff; Wippen
Estates, disposition of, as source of used pianos, 124
European pianos, 74–75
   discounts on, 65
   pinblock used in, 32
   tone of, 43, 74–75
Exposed pinblock, 118. *A pinblock, usually in an older piano, that is not covered by the plate.*
Extended direct-blow action, 44–45. *A direct-blow action in a full-size upright, connected to the keys with extensions, or stickers. See also* Direct-blow action

Fallboard, 8. *The part of a piano cabinet that covers the keyboard when the piano is not in use.*
   design and serviceability of, 25, 26
   removing, 127
False beats, 38, 159. *Tonal irregularities which, if excessive, cause tuning problems.*
Fandrich action, 46, 115. *A new type of vertical piano action that functions almost like a grand action.*
Felt. *See* Hammer felt; Underfelt, hammer; Muffler felt
Ferrule, 8. *Decorative brass trim at the bottom of some piano legs.*
Filing, of hammers. *See* Resurfacing, of hammers
Financing, of new pianos, 65
Finish, cabinet, 25–26, 28. *See also* Ebonized finish; High-gloss finish; Satin finish
Flange bushings, 148. *Bushings, usually cloth, in which rotate the center pins on which action parts pivot. See also* Bushing; Flanges; Center pins
   Teflon. *See* Teflon bushings
Flanges, 100, 148, 163. *The hinges on which action parts pivot.*
   jack, unglued, 135
   molded, 100
Flange screws. *The screws that attach the flanges to the action rails.*
   tightening of, 137, 163
Floor space, required for piano, 13, 14, 15
Fortepiano, 117. *The forerunner of the modern piano; also the name used*

for the piano until the late 1800s or early 1900s.
Frame. *See* Structural framework; Plate
Frame, cast-iron. *See* Plate
Freight forwarder, 154. *A firm that consolidates goods from a number of customers or movers and makes arrangements with steamship lines for shipping the goods.*
Freight-Maritime Commission, 154
Full-size action, 44–45. *A vertical piano action with full-size parts; used in studio and full-size upright pianos.*
Full-size upright, 14, 44–45. *A vertical piano, usually 48 or more inches tall, with a full-size direct-blow action.*
Fundamental, 42. *The first, or lowest, partial or harmonic.*
Furniture
   as purchase consideration, 13
   restyling of, 125
   styles, 25–28; comparative cost of different, 64
Furniture stores, purchasing pianos from, 63, 124

Gifts, of pianos, 124–125
General average clause, 155. *A moving contract clause that insures against extra costs an overseas shipper might incur and pass on to the customers if damage is sustained en route and the cargo is impounded.*
Grain, of wood. *See* Wood, grain of
Grand-length keys, 48. *Keys whose playing surfaces are of a length normally found on grand pianos, and slightly longer than normally found on verticals.*
Grand-style lid, 25, 26, 128. *A vertical piano lid hinged on the left side in imitation of a grand piano lid.*
Grand piano. *A piano whose strings are stretched horizontally, parallel to the floor. See also* names of specific parts
   action, operation of, 10–11. *See also* Action
   case or cabinet parts of, 6, 7, 8. *See also* Cabinetry
   construction described, 6–7
   cost of, 13, 14, 141–142
   cross-sectional view of, 6
   defined, 1
   dimensions of, 13, 14–15, 151
   exploded view of, 6
   as investment, 14
   moving, 150, 151
   opening, for inspection, 126–128
   versus vertical, 13–14, 46, 115
   weight of, 149

Half pedaling, 55. *Using the sustain pedal so that it is not quite "on" and not quite "off" for greater control and expression.*
Hamilton, opening the Baldwin, studio piano, 129
Hammer butt, 9, 135, 140. *The lower part of the hammer assembly in a vertical piano.*
   buckskin versus cloth on, 45
Hammer felt, 43, 51–52, 163. *The dense felt used on piano hammers.*
Hammer head, 51. *The main part of a hammer, consisting of a wooden molding surrounded by dense felt, mounted on a dowel, or hammer shank.*
   loose, 137, 138
Hammer molding, 51. *The wooden part of a hammer head, around which the hammer felt is glued.*
Hammer rail, 9, 10–11, 54, 140. *A felt-covered wooden rail against which the hammer shanks rest (in a vertical piano) or above which they are suspended (in a grand).*
Hammers, 1, 4, 9–11. *Felt-covered wooden mallets that strike the strings to produce musical sounds.*
   double-striking of, 46
   inspection of, in used piano, 136–137
   quality and construction of, 51–52
   regulation of, 140. *See also* Regulating
   reinforcing of, 52–53
   repair and replacement of, 135, 136–137
   resurfacing of, 136–137, 163

See also Index to Trade Names, page 76.

See also Index to Trade Names, page 76.

Keyslip, 8. *The decorative wooden strip that runs the width of the piano, right in front of the keys.*
    removing, 128
Key stop rail, 156. *A thin wooden strip, above the keys and behind the fallboard in a grand piano, to prevent the keys from falling off the key frame when the piano is put on its side for moving.*
Keytops. *The plastic, ivory, or wooden coverings on the playing surfaces of the keys.*
    cleaning, 163
    length of, 48, 50
    material used for, 51
    missing or broken, inspection of, in a used piano, 135–136
Kilns, wood drying, 23
Knuckle, 10–11. *A small cylinder of wood, cloth, and leather attached to a grand hammer shank, against which the jack pushes.*
Korean pianos, 75

Lacquer finish, 26, 28
Laminated soundboard, 39–40, 57, 58–59. *A soundboard made of three layers of wood glued together with grain running at right angles, like plywood.*
Langer action, 45. *A Schwander-type action made by Herrburger Brooks. See also* Schwander *and* Herrburger Brooks
Lauan, 105. *A soft, cheap wood used in the piano cabinets of many Asian pianos; also known as Philippine mahogany.*
Leg plates, 133. *Metal plates used to fasten grand piano legs to the bottom of the piano.*
Legs, piano, 8
    breakage of, in moving, 151–152
    inspection of, on used piano, for cracks, 133
    styles of, in vertical piano, 25–26, 28
Letoff, 9–10, 140. *Disengagement of the force pushing on the hammer, just before the hammer strikes the strings. Also known as escapement.*
Letoff button, 9–10. *An action part that causes the jack to escape from under the hammer assembly at letoff. See* Letoff.
Licensing, of movers, 152, 153
Lid, 8. *The cabinet part that covers the top of the piano.*
    grand piano, 27; inspection of, on used piano, 133; opening, 126; particle board in, 21; removal of, for moving, 150; and tonal quality, 43
    grand-style vertical, 25–26, 128
    vertical piano, opening, 128
Lid hinges, 8
    loose or missing, 126, 133
    removal of, for moving, 150
Lid prop. *See* Propstick
Lifetime of piano, 164
Liner, soundboard, 41. *A simple wooden frame attached to the front of a vertical piano back, to which the soundboard is glued.*
Locks, for school pianos, 68
Loop stringing, 7. *A system of stringing, found on most pianos, in which a single length of wire serves as two strings.*
Loss leader, 18, 64. *See also* Promotional pianos
Lost motion, 140, 163. *Slack in the action or trapwork, resulting in part of the motion of keys or pedals being wasted in taking up this slack.*
Lost motion compensator, 138–139. *A mechanism in some old uprights that compensated for the lost motion created when the soft pedal was used. See also* Lost motion
Lower panel, 8. *The large rectangular cabinet part on a vertical piano located above the pedals, near the player's legs.*
    removing, 129
Lumber, 23–24. *Wood that has been cut into boards. See also* Wood; Plain-sawn lumber; Quarter-sawn lumber
Lumber-banding, 22. *The framing of a particle-board panel with solid lumber or plywood to increase its strength and to camouflage it.*
Lyre, 8. *The grand piano part that descends from the case bottom and holds the pedals.*
    attachment of, 27
    inspection of, in used piano, 27, 138
Lyre braces, 8, 27, 138, 156. *Diagonal braces of wood or metal that help*

prevent the pedal lyre from being pushed backward under the pressure of the feet on the pedals.
Magnuson-Moss Warranty Act, 58. *A law that set federal standards for warranties on consumer purchases.*
Mahogany
    finish, 28
    in grand piano rims, 23
Maintenance. *See also* Tuning; Regulating; Voicing; Servicing
    cost of, 13
    of school and institutional pianos, 13, 67–68
Maple
    in action parts, 47
    in action rails, 100
    in grand piano rims, 23
    in hammer shanks, 53
    in pinblocks, 32
Marketing, of new pianos, 17–19
Mason & Hamlin
    removal of keyslip from, 128
    reproducers installed in, 122
    used, 118, 119
Materials, synthetic versus traditional, 19
Merchandising, of new pianos, 63–64
MIDI (Musical Instrument Digital Interface), 113–114. *An electronics standard that allows instruments made by different manufacturers to be compatible with each other and with computers and acoustic instruments equipped with it.*
Mirrors, restyling a piano with, 125
Moisture. *See* Humidity
Moisture barrier, 31
Molded flanges, 100. *Steinway action flanges molded in a special shape that matches the shape of their action rails.*
Molding, hammer. *See* Hammer molding
Money. *See also* Prices; Cost
    as purchase consideration, 13
    saving, on new piano, 64–65
Moth damage and mothproofing, 134, 156, 164
Movers, licensing and insurance required for, 152, 153
Moving
    damage to pianos in, 153, 155
    effect on pianos of, 132–133, 156
    industry, deregulation of, 152, 153
    international, 154–155
    interstate, 153–154
    local, 152–153
    methods, 149–151
    of new pianos, 65
    piano dimensions for, 151
    pianos around a room, 151–152
    used piano after purchase, 143
Moving and storage companies, purchasing used piano from, 124
Muffler felt, 54–55, 115. *A strip of felt that muffles the sound of a vertical piano equipped with a practice pedal when that pedal is pressed. See also* Practice pedal
Multi-laminated pinblock, 32. *A pinblock composed of many thin layers, as opposed to a few thick ones.*
Music desk, 8. *The cabinet part that holds the printed music upright for reading.*
    design and construction of, 25, 27
    removing, 127
Music rolls. *See* Piano rolls
Music shelf, 8. *The horizontal case or cabinet part on which printed music stands.*
    removing, 129

Naturals, 48, 51. *The white keys.*
Negotiating
    with dealer of new piano, 60, 63–65
    with seller of used piano, 141

See also Index to Trade Names, page 76.

See also Index to Trade Names, page 76.

See also Index to Trade Names, page 76.

inspection of used piano by, 15, 16, 116, 141
  as piano dealer, 62, 65
  and player pianos, 67, 121
  relations with dealer, 66
  servicing of Steinways by, 148
  and warranty claims, 60
Teflon bushings, 148. *Plastic flange bushings used in Steinway pianos from about 1962 to 1981; the cause of many servicing problems. See also Flange bushings*
Temperature
  effect on pianos of, 13, 155–156, 160, 161
Tenor, 7, 33–34. *The lower portion of the treble string section, just above the bass.*
Tension resonator, 93. *A set of turnbuckles in Mason & Hamlin grands that allegedly preserves the crown of the soundboard by preventing expansion of the rim.*
Three-quarter plate piano, 118. *An older piano in which the plate ends just short of the pinblock.*
Toe constuction, 8, 26. *A vertical piano construction in which the front legs are supported by two "toes" that project forward from the cabinet.*
Tonal quality, 41–43, 131, 163
  and agraffes, 37
  of bass, 33–34, 36, 43, 131–132, 141
  and bridges, 38–39, 132
  and duplex scale, 36
  of European pianos, 43, 74–75
  of grand versus vertical, 14
  and hammers, 43, 52, 56–57, 137, 163
  harmonic content of, 42
  inspection of, in new piano, 41–43
  inspection of, in used piano, 131, 132, 141
  of Japanese pianos, 43, 74
  and piano size, 14, 33–34, 42–43
  and room acoustics, 43, 57, 141
  and scale design, 33–34, 42–43
  and soundboard, 39–41; area, 14; crown, 133–134
  of spinets, 45
  of Steinways, 43
  and string length, 14, 33–34
  and structural framework, 23, 29
  and tuning, 41, 43, 141, 163
  and voicing, 43, 52, 56–57, 67, 141, 163
Tone, quality of. *See Tonal quality*
Tone regulating. *See Voicing*
Tools, for inspection of used piano, 125
Touch weight, 49, 115. *The forces required to maintain key movement, including down weight and up weight. See also down weight and up weight*
Trade-ins, 65. *Old pianos given to piano dealers in return for discounts on new ones.*
Trade names, index to, 76
Tradition, as buzzword, 19
Transshipping, 59. *An unethical transaction in which a dealer unauthorized to sell a particular brand will obtain it from an authorized dealer in order to resell it.*
Trapwork, 5, 55. *The assemblage of levers, dowels, and springs that connects the pedals to the action.*
  inspection of, in used piano, 138
Treble, 7. *The higher-pitched notes, sounded by the keys toward the right end of the keyboard.*
Truck, piano, 26, 152
Trucking companies, purchasing pianos from, 63, 124
Tubular metallic action frame, 100. *The action frame in a Steinway piano, made of maple dowels surrounded by seamless brass tubing.*
Tuner, piano, 164. *See also Technician, piano*
Tuning, 157–159, 164–166. *Adjusting the tension of the strings so they sound in harmony with each other according to certain laws and customs.*
  after delivery of new piano, 56, 61, 65, 66–67, 159

after moving, 156
  before selling your piano, 143
  checking, on used piano, 130
  by dealer, 56, 61, 65
  effect on tonal quality of, 41, 43, 141, 163
  in factory, 56
  and placement of piano, 160
  of player pianos, 67, 121
  problems related to scale design, 34–35
  stability: and humidity, 157–162; and pinblock, 30–33; and soundboard, 40, 158; and structural framework, 28–30, 158
  of used piano after sale, 143
Tuning fork, 125, 130. *A piece of metal designed to vibrate at a specified frequency and pitch when struck; used for testing the pitch of a piano.*
Tuning hammer, 2, 30, 35, 157. *A special wrench used to turn the tuning pins and thus to tune the piano.*
Tuning pin bushings. *See Plate bushings*
Tuning pins, 2, 6, 30–33, 35, 37. *Metal pins around which are coiled one end of each string. Turning a tuning pin adjusts the tension at which a string is stretched.*
  inspection of, for looseness in used piano, 130–131
Twisting, of bass strings, 131. *Tightening the windings on old bass strings to improve the tone by unhitching, twisting, and then rehitching the strings.*

Una corda pedal, 54–55. *The left-hand pedal on most grand pianos; shifts the action slightly so the treble hammers hit only two strings each, softening the sound.*
Underfelt, hammer, 51. *A thinner piece of colored felt between the hammer molding and the hammer felt on some hammers.*
Underlever. *See Damper underlever*
Unison, 7, 131. *A set of one, two, or three strings, all tuned to exactly the same pitch so as to sound as one note when struck by a hammer.*
United States, piano industry in, 73–74
Upper panel, 8. *A vertical piano cabinet part.*
  removing, 128
Upright, full-size, 14, 44–45
"Upright grand," 14. *A misleading term for an upright piano, used in the nineteenth and early twentieth centuries.*
Up weight, 49. *The force, measured in grams at the front of the key (with the damper system disengaged), with which a depressed key pushes up against the finger after being played.*
Used pianos
  dealer of, 123–124
  effect of, on sales of new pianos, 73
  finding, 122–125
  and humidity, 116–117
  inspection of, by buyer, 125–139. *See also names of specific piano parts*
  inspection of, by technician, 15–16, 116, 141
  moving of, after purchase, 143
  prices of, 13, 15, 141–142
  reasons for buying, 15
  recommended brands of, 118–119
  Steinway, 144–148
  tuning of, after sale, 143
  versus new pianos, 15
  warranty on, 143

Vacuum process, 30. *A new plate-casting process using vacuum pressure that produces plates more consistent and with finer detail than the traditional process.*
Value, of used pianos, 141–143
Veneer. *A thin sheet of wood cut from the circumference of a log, like a sheet of paper towel off a roll.*
  loose, 125
  in pinblocks, 32
  in plywood, 21
  and sophistication of cabinet, 25
  in soundboards, 39

See also Index to Trade Names, page 76.

Verdigris, 148. *A green-colored substance produced by a reaction between metal center pins and chemicals in cloth flange bushings. Often found in older Steinways, causing sluggish action.*
Vertical piano. *A piano whose strings are stretched vertically, perpendicular to the floor.* See also *names of specific parts*
   action, operation of, 9. See also Action
   back, 3. See also Back, vertical piano
   cabinet: parts of, 5, 8; styles, 25–28, 64. See also Cabinetry
   construction described, 2–5
   cost of, 13–14, 141–143
   defined, 1
   dimensions of, 13, 14–15, 48, 151
   opening for inspection, 128–129
   types of, 14, 44–45
   versus grand: in action design, 46; in purchase decision, 13–14
   weight of, 149
Vestal Press, 122
Voicing, 43, 52, 56–57, 67, 141, 163. *Tone regulating, usually by softening or hardening the hammer felt.*

Want ads, purchasing used piano through, 124
Warping
   of case, cabinet, and structural parts, 21–24, 26
   of hammer shanks, 53
   of keys, 50
   of trapwork, 55
Warranty
   full, 58

   implied, 143
   limited, 58
   on new piano, 40, 57–60, 61
   on used, reconditioned, or rebuilt piano, 143
Water damage, 125
Weight, of hammer, 52
Weight, of piano, 149
Weight, touch. See Touch weight
Welte, 122, 146. *A former manufacturer of piano reproducing mechanisms.*
Wippen, 9–10, 135, 140. *The action part that serves as the escapement mechanism in both grand and vertical pianos.*
Wood. See also Lumber; *names of wood species; names of piano parts*
   dry and brittle in old piano, 134
   grain of, 21, 22, 23–24; in hammer shanks, 53; in keys, 49–50; in soundboard, 39
   and humidity, 160
   in piano cabinets, 21–25
   quality of, 23–24
   seasoning of, 23
   and tonal quality, 23, 29
   warping of. See Warping
Woodworking, quality in, 23–25
World War II, 119
Wound strings, 33–37, 131, 141. *Music wire wound with copper or other material to slow its rate of vibration without reducing its flexibility; used as bass strings.* See also Strings; Scale design
Wrestplank. See Pinblock

See also Index to Trade Names, page 76.

ADDENDUM TO *THE PIANO BOOK (SECOND EDITION)*

Readers of *The Piano Book (Second Edition)* will notice that product reviews of three companies -- Baldwin, Wurlitzer, and Sojin -- have been omitted, with a note on page 72 giving only a brief, sketchy picture of the reasons for doing so. After the book went to press, I decided that my readers deserved a little more information about what happened and at least some minimal guidance concerning the purchase of these companies' products.

Each manufacturer (or its U.S. distributor) was sent a copy of the proposed review of its products prior to publication, with an invitation to correct factual errors, suggest changes, and if necessary, to submit a rebuttal that would be printed following the review. Most manufacturers were gracious in accepting criticism and made helpful suggestions. Some, however, were very displeased, among them Baldwin, which also owns Wurlitzer. I spent hours on the phone with Baldwin and Wurlitzer technical staff going over their reviews and making changes that I hoped would make the reviews acceptable to both of us. In the end, though, Baldwin sent a letter saying that if I published the reviews the company might file a lawsuit against me. Since even lawsuits that have no merit can be prohibitively expensive and time-consuming to defend oneself against, I decided instead to delete the Baldwin and Wurlitzer reviews from the book.

Sojin, a Korean company, responded to the fairly negative review of their pianos by pointing out that the pianos examined for the review may not have included the "improved" models they introduced in 1989. But Sojin never responded to my fax and phone messages requesting more information about their new models. Again, to be safe, I decided to omit the review from the book.

The following are my own personal opinions and recommendations concerning the purchase of these companies' pianos. Although I know that my opinions are shared by many technicians, I speak here only for myself:

Baldwin. Most Baldwin vertical pianos are acceptable if properly serviced by the dealer. It is my feeling, however, that compared to other brands, Baldwin verticals are not as well made nor as good a value as they once were, and that their reputation among the general public exceeds their quality by a fair margin. In most cases, they would not be my first choice. If you decide to purchase a Baldwin vertical, I would suggest looking only at the 42-1/2" size or larger. Baldwin grands, on the other hand, despite some shortcomings, are still fairly well made, especially the seven- and nine-foot models. I would avoid the 4'10" grand, however, which is too small and not of the same calibre as the other grands. I would also avoid Baldwin's Korean-made pianos, sold under other names such as Howard, Kranich & Bach, and D.H. Baldwin. (The D.H. Baldwin used to be made in Japan and was a good piano; now it is made in Korea.)

Wurlitzer. Wurlitzer pianos come in two varieties -- U.S.-made and Korean-made. When the U.S.-made Wurlitzers were made in their Mississippi factory, the actions were good but the tone was not, especially on the smaller models. The studio verticals often were not bad. Baldwin recently purchased Wurlitzer and moved production to the Baldwin factories. Reports on these new Wurlitzers are few in number but mixed. The studios may be okay if properly serviced by the dealer, but conservatively I would recommend being very cautious about purchasing a U.S.-made Wurlitzer at this time. Korean-made Wurlitzers are made by Young Chang and identical to Young Chang pianos, and may be better than the U.S.-made Wurlitzers. See the review of Young Chang pianos for more information.

Sojin. I recommend not buying a Sojin piano at this time.